南京大学"985"三期建设　　联合资助
江苏高校优势学科建设工程

南京大学人文地理丛书

中国区域管治的演变

——以长江三角洲地区为例

●李　禕　著

南京大学出版社

图书在版编目(CIP)数据

中国区域管治的演变:以长江三角洲地区为例/李禕著. —南京:南京大学
出版社,2013.12
(南京大学人文地理丛书/黄贤金,张捷,张京祥主编)
ISBN 978-7-305-12580-5

Ⅰ.①中… Ⅱ.①李… Ⅲ.①长江三角洲—区域管理—研究 Ⅳ.①F127.5

中国版本图书馆CIP数据核字(2013)第300349号

出版发行　南京大学出版社
社　　　址　南京市汉口路22号　邮　编　210093
网　　　址　http://www.NjupCo.com
出 版 人　左　健

丛 书 名　南京大学人文地理丛书
书　　　名　中国区域管治的演变——以长江三角洲地区为例
著　　　者　李　禕
责任编辑　陈　露　刁晓静　编辑热线　025-83592409

照　　　排　南京紫藤制版印务中心
印　　　刷　江苏凤凰通达印刷有限公司
开　　　本　787×960　1/16　印张27.5　字数524千
版　　　次　2013年12月第1版　2013年12月第1次印刷
ISBN　978-7-305-12580-5
定　　　价　60.00元

发行热线　025-83594756　83686452
电子邮件　Press@NjupCo.com
　　　　　　Sales@NjupCo.com(市场部)

南京大学人文地理丛书

编 委 会

总　序[1]

曾尊固　崔功豪　黄贤金　张　捷　张京祥

自1921年竺可桢先生创立地学系以来,南京大学地理学已走过了九十一年发展路程;若追溯到南京高等师范学校1919年设立的文史地部,南京大学地理学科的历史则已有九十三年之久。九十多年的历史见证了南京大学人文地理学科发展的历程与辉煌,彰显了南京大学人文地理学科对中国当代人文地理学发展的突出贡献。

南京大学是近代中国人文地理学科发展的奠基者。从最初设立的文史地部,到后来的地学系,再到1930年建立地理系,一直引领着中国近代地理学科建设与发展;介绍"新地学",讲授欧美的"人地学原理"、"人生地理",以及区域地理、世界地理、政治地理、历史地理、边疆地理和建设地理等,创建了中国近代人文地理学学科体系;南京大学的人文地理一贯重视田野调查,1931年九一八事变前组织的东北地理考察团,随后又开展的云南、两淮盐垦区考察以及内蒙古、青藏高原等地理考察,还有西北五省铁路旅游、京滇公路六省周览等考察,均开近代中国地理考察风气之先;1934年,竺可桢、胡焕庸、张其昀、黄国璋等先生发起成立中国地理学会的活动,创办了《地理学报》,以弘扬地理科学、普及地理知识为宗旨,使南京大学成为当时全国地理学术活动的组织核心。人文地理学先驱和奠基人胡焕庸、张其昀、李旭旦、任美锷、吴传钧、宋家泰、张同铸等先生都先后在南京大学人文地理学科学习或教学、研究。早在1935

[1] 感谢任美锷、吴传钧、张同铸、宋家泰等先生在《南京大学地理学系建系八十周年纪念》的文章以及胡焕庸、李旭旦先生为南京大学地理系建系65周年作的纪念文章,为本序内容提供了宝贵的借鉴和难得的资料。感谢南京大学地理与海洋科学学院院长、长江学者特聘教授高抒教授对于丛书出版的关心与支持。感谢南京大学地理与海洋科学学院党委书记、长江学者特聘教授鹿化煜教授,为完善序言内容提出了修改意见。

年,任美锷先生、李旭旦先生就翻译、出版了《人地学原理》一书,介绍了法国人地学派;1940年设立中央大学研究院地理学部培养硕士研究生,开展城市地理与土地利用研究;20世纪40年代,任美锷先生在国内首先引介了韦伯工业区位论,并撰写了《建设地理学》,产生了巨大影响;胡焕庸先生提出了划分我国东南半壁和西北半壁地理环境的"胡焕庸线"——瑷珲—腾冲的人口分布线,至今仍然为各界公认。张其昀、沙学浚先生分别著有《人生地理学》、《中国区域志》及《中国历史地理》、《城市与似城聚落》等著作,推进了台湾人文地理学科研究和教育的发展。竺可桢先生倡导的"求是"学风、胡焕庸先生倡导的"学业并重"学风,一直引领着南京大学人文地理学科的建设与发展。

南京大学积极推进当代中国人文地理教育,于1954年在全国最早设立了经济地理专业;1977年招收城市规划方向,1979年吴友仁发表《关于中国社会主义城市化问题》,引起了学界对于中国城市化问题的关注,也推动了城市规划专业教育事业发展;1983年兴办了经济地理与城乡区域规划专业(后为城市规划专业),成为综合性高校最早培养理科背景的城市规划人才的单位之一;1982年与国家计划委员会、中国科学院自然资源综合考察委员会合作创办了自然资源专业(后为自然资源管理专业、资源环境与城乡规划管理专业);1991年又设立了旅游规划与管理专业(现为旅游管理专业)。这不仅为培养我国人文地理学人才提供了多元、多领域的支撑,而且也为南京大学城市地理、区域地理、旅游地理、土地利用、区域规划等人文地理学科的建设与发展提供了有力的支撑。

南京大学不仅在人文地理专业教育与人才培养方面起引导作用,而且在人文地理学科建设方面也走在全国前列,当代人文地理学教学与研究中名家辈出。张同铸先生的非洲地理研究、宋家泰先生的城市地理研究、曾尊固先生的农业地理研究、崔功豪先生的区域规划研究、雍万里先生的旅游地理研究、包浩生先生的自然资源与国土整治研究、彭补拙先生的土地利用研究、林炳耀先生的计量地理研究等,都对我国人文地理学科建设与发展产生了深远的影响,在全国人文地理学科发展历程中占据着重要的地位。同时,南京大学人文地理学科瞄准国际学科发展前沿和国家发展需求,积极探索农户行为地理、社会地理、信息地理、企业地理、文化地理、女性地理、交通地理等新的研究领域,保持着人文地理学学科前沿研究和教学创新的活力。

南京大学当代人文地理学科建设与发展,以经济地理、城市地理、非洲地理、旅游地理、区域土地利用为主流学科,理论人文地理学和应用人文地理学并重发展,人文地理学的学科渗透力和服务社会能力得到持续增强,研究机构建设也得到了积极推进。充分利用南京大学综合性院校多学科的优势,突出人文地理学研究国际化合作,整合学科资源,成立了一系列重要的人文地理研究机构,主要有:南京大学非洲研究所、区域发展研究所、旅游研究所、城市科学院等;同时,还与法国巴黎第十二大学建立了中法城市·区域·规划科学研究中心。按照服务国家战略、服务区域发展以及协同创新的目标,与江苏省土地勘测规划院共建国土资源部海岸带国土开发与重建重点实验室,与江苏省国土资源厅合建了南京大学—江苏省国土资源厅国土资源研究中心。此外,还积极推进人文地理学科实验室以及工程中心建设,业已建立了南京大学—澳大利亚西悉尼大学虚拟城市与区域开发实验室,以及南京大学城市与区域公共安全实验室、旅游景观环境评价实验室、江苏省土地开发整理技术工程中心等。

南京大学当代人文地理教育培养了大量优秀人才,在国内外人文地理教学、研究及区域管理中发挥了中坚作用。如,中国农业区划理论主要奠基人——中国科学院地理与资源研究所邓静中研究员;组建了中国第一个国家级旅游地理研究科学组织,曾任中国区域科学协会副会长,中国科学院地理与资源科学研究所的郭来喜研究员;中国科学院南京分院原院长、中国科学院东南资源环境综合研究中心主任、著名农业地理学家佘之祥研究员;中国区域科学协会副会长、中国科学院地理与资源科学研究所著名区域地理学家毛汉英研究员;我国人文地理学培养的第一位博士和第一位人文地理学国家杰出青年基金获得者——中国地理学会原副理事长、清华大学建筑学院顾朝林教授;教育部人文社会科学重点研究基地、河南大学黄河文明与可持续发展研究中心主任、黄河学者苗长虹教授;中国城市规划学会副理事长石楠教授级高级城市规划师;中国城市规划设计研究院副院长杨保军教授级高级城市规划师;英国伦敦大学学院城市地理学家吴缚龙教授等,都曾在南京大学学习过。曾任南京大学思源教授的美国马里兰大学沈清教授、南京大学国家杰出青年基金(海外)获得者、美国犹他大学魏也华教授也都在人文地理学科工作过,对推进该学科国际合作起到了积极作用。

南京大学当代人文地理学科建设与发展之所以有如此成就,是遵循了任美锷先生提出的"大人文地理学"学科发展思想的结果,现今业已形成了以地理学、城乡规划学为基础学科,以建筑学、经济学、历史学、社会学、公共管理等学科为交融的新"大人文地理科学"学科体系。南京大学正以此为基础,在弘扬人文地理学科传统优势的同时,通过"融入前沿、综合交叉、服务应用"的大人文地理学科发展理念,积极建设和发展"南京大学人文地理研究中心"(www.hugeo.nju.edu.cn)。

新人文地理学科体系建设,更加体现了时代背景,更加体现了学科融合的特点,更加体现了人文地理学方法的探索性,更加体现了新兴学科发展以及国家战略实施的要求。为此,南京大学人文地理学科组织出版了《南京大学人文地理丛书》,这不仅是南京大学人文地理学科发展脉络的延续,更体现了学科前沿、交叉、融合、方法创新等,同时,也是对我国人文地理学科建设与发展新要求、新趋势的体现。

《南京大学人文地理丛书》将秉承南京大学人文地理学科建设与发展的"求是"学风,"学业并重",积极探索人文地理学科新兴领域,不断深化发展人文地理学理论,努力发展应用人文地理学研究,从而为我国人文地理学科建设添砖加瓦,为国内外人文地理学科人才培养提供支持。

我们衷心希望《南京大学人文地理丛书》能更加体现地理学科的包容性理念,不仅反映南京大学在职教师、研究生的研究成果,还反映南京大学校友的优秀研究成果,形成体现南大精神、反映南大文化、传承南大事业的新人文地理学科体系。衷心希望《南京大学人文地理丛书》的出版,不仅能展现南京大学人文地理学的最新研究成果,而且能够成为南京大学人文地理学科发展新的里程碑。

序　一

　　自20世纪90年代从海外引进了"管治"这一术语起,"管治"作为政府管理的新模式和地方提高整体竞争力的重要手段,在学界、规划界和政府部门引起了广泛关注。城市管治、区域管治、空间管治以及"管制"、"善治"、"治理"等相关术语见之于学术文献、规划文本、政府文件,各类研究、学术研讨也纷纷涌现。应当说,这是转型期政府管理制度改革的反映和必然需求。但正如住房和城乡建设部仇保兴副部长所言:"管治"既是"从上到下和从下到上的结合",又"着眼于调动各方面的积极性"。因此,管治是一个复杂而有难度的系统工程,需要不断探索和实践。

　　李禕博士选择了"区域管治"作为博士论文的主题,以探讨中国区域管治的演变为主线,以长江三角洲为案例进行了从概念到理论、过程到特点、区域到国家、数据到解析、案例到阐发的关于区域管治的较为全面系统的探讨,不仅提供了区域管治研究的生动实例,也是区域研究的深化和革新,是具有学术价值和应用价值的。

　　本书有几个特点是值得肯定的。第一,重视理论概念和新理论的引用。作为区域空间范畴的研究,作者梳理了旧区域和新区域主义的核心概念,突出了空间尺度这个中心,开展不同空间尺度层次的研究,尤其是针对中国国家空间尺度的变化,并参照西方关于国家空间尺度、国家尺度调整和尺度政治的理论,构建了研究框架,运用国家理论和战略关联方法作为对区域管治变化的理论解释。这些均为本书奠定了坚实的科学基础。第二,研究中央和地方关系的变化,以及从城市经营、城市管治和区域管治的发展过程,探究了中国自1949年以来权力结构的调整和区域政策的转变,以及区域管治的变化,尤其重点关注这时期区域尺度的政策,这不仅提供了一种区域管治研究的新视角,厘清了中国区域管治演变的脉络,并从中认识到"管治"在区域中的意义和价值及其构建过程。第三,以大量的数据、实例、访谈为基础,分析和对比不同时期、不同区域(尤其是长江三角洲)管治的影响因素,并从国内外宏观背景、体制变化中评析、探讨其演变过程及其动因。由此,提高了本书的说理性、可信性、可读性,也为相似区域研究和有关地方政府提供有益的参考、借鉴。总之,这是一份主题鲜明、重点突出、结构清晰、内容丰富的区域管治论著,也是一本区域研究的新作。

"区域管治"是一个新课题,涉及内容广,影响因素多,主体层次复杂,且与经济基础和社会改革过程相关。因此,需要进行持续研究和探讨。本书只是作为海外归来的年轻学子对区域管治研究的初始作品,且书中也有尚待深入探讨之处。但"千里之行,始于足下",有了这坚实的一步,未来的成就是可以期待的。是为序。

2013年9月

序 二

城市区域研究是人文地理学和城市研究的重要领域。近来在西方涌现了大量关于城市区域研究的文献,其中特别是用政治经济学的视角来分析区域管制的尺度变动,城市区域研究是近来城市学界的重要研究动向。在中国国内,区域研究有着悠久的传统,但大多基于传统的区域地理分析,比如关注区域发展差异和不平衡。近年来关于长三角和珠三角,也出现了丰富的研究成果。但是有关研究往往缺乏政治经济学视角,往往注重描述,缺乏理论分析。海外对中国的研究往往集中在城市层面,而对中国的区域研究,因为体制的差异和认识的偏差,存在着重大的障碍。与城市层面的大量研究相比,中国城市区域的研究显得不足。近来在英文文献中,出现了一些崭新的关于城市之间竞争与合作、城市区域的管制、区域管制的尺度变化等研究成果。这些研究基于城市区域研究的理论框架,用丰富的中国实证材料,既充分展示了中国的独特性,又体现了区域研究的可比性,为中西对比开创了道路。

李禕博士选取该城市区域研究的难点,研读大量西方文献,并针对长三角的案例,展开实证研究,取得了突破性的研究进展,完成了博士论文,并在英文期刊发表多篇研究论文。在整理博士论文的基础上,完成了这本书。我非常高兴看到本书的出版,填补了相关的研究空白,将是今后数年中被引用的重要文献,欣然作序。

吴缚龙

巴特雷特规划教授,于伦敦

目录
Contents

第一章

CHAPTER ONE

Introduction

1.1 Research background

China used to be a socialist country trying to achieve regional egalitarianism. The pattern and the cause of regional inequalities at national, inter‐and‐intra‐provincial levels constituted the key concerns of regional studies of China until the late 1990s (Cannon, 1990; Fan, 1992; Wei, 1996; Wei and Ma, 1996; Wei, 1999; Wei and Fan, 2000). However, economic reform marked the failure of the centrally‐planned economy and regional policies, and the downscaling of state policies and governance towards the urban level (Wu and Zhang, 2010: 60). As a result of economic decentralisation, localities have become substantial decision‐making bodies which depend on their own revenue. Substantial fiscal decentralisation has thus triggered the rise of urban entrepreneurialism. Subsequently, urban studies have enjoyed a boom in China, with a particular focus on the extraordinary urban (re‐) development and changing urban governance (He et al., 2006; He and Wu, 2005; Ma, 2002; Wu, 2002; Wu et al., 2007). It is well documented that, on the one hand, prevailing urban entrepreneurialism has turned out to be a strong driving force for the local economy; on the other hand, entrepreneurialism has also exacerbated interlocality competition and regional inequality (Chien, 2007; Chien and Gordon, 2008).

Since the mid‐2000s, regional studies have re‐proliferated within China, with a volume of monographs and literature calling for inter‐city cooperation and coordinated regional development, especially within the YRD (Hong, 2009; Ji et al., 2006; Tao, 2007; Wang, 2008; Wang, 2009; Zhang et al., 2007; Zong, 2008). Moreover, inter‐locality cooperation has even become popular discourse for government leadership.For instance, the promotion of coordinated regional development is considered to be one of the indispensable aspects of the new keynote concept of 'harmonious development' (Fan, 2006). The heated discussion within governments on regional cooperation and regional coordinated development has demonstrated, to some extent, the trend of changing scale of governance in current China. However, the existing regional governance research in China is eager to learn the purported appropriate institutional design from Western experiences in order to promote inter‐city cooperation in China. It is simply believed that a proper institutional and policy design would just reverse the path to entrepreneurialism or alleviate the downsides of entrepreneurial governance. It is commented that the understanding of regional governance in China as a problem caused by a lack of inter‐governmental communication and coordination is just too simplistic (Wu and Zhang, 2010: 60).

第一章　引言

第一节　研究背景

作为一个社会主义国家,中国曾经致力于实现各区域的均衡发展。全国各区域之间、各省之间以及省内的不均衡发展及其模式和成因,直至上世纪90年代末期仍是中国区域研究的主要研究课题之一(Cannon,1990;Fan,1992;Wei,1996;Wei 和 Ma,1996;Wei,1999;Wei 和 Fan,2000)。然而,改革开放标志着过去中央计划经济和区域政策的失败,国家的政策与管治开始向城市一级下调(Wu 和 Zhang,2010:60)。经济权力下放之后,地方成为决策的基本单位,依靠本地的财政收入办事。于是,分税制刺激了城市管治的转型和城市经营主义的兴起。在这样的背景下,城市研究开始在中国兴起,而且特别关注城市(再)开发和城市管治变化等领域(He 等,2006;He 和 Wu,2005;Ma,2002;Wu,2002;Wu 等,2007)。大量研究资料表明,当前盛行的城市经营主义一方面成为了推动地方经济发展的强劲动力,而另一方面也加剧了地方之间的恶性竞争和各区域的不平衡发展(Chien,2007;Chien 和 Gordon,2008)。

2005年前后,区域研究在国内再度兴起,特别是在长三角区域出现了大批专著和文献呼吁区域合作和区域协调发展(洪世健,2009;纪晓岚等,2006;陶希东,2007;王川兰,2008;王枫云,2009;杨保军,2004;张颢瀚等,2007;宗家峰,2008)。此外,区域合作甚至已成为政府领导人的常用语,例如"促进区域协调发展"被视为"和谐发展"这一新的核心概念中必不可缺的内容(Fan,2006)。各级政府对区域合作与区域协调发展的热切关注在一定程度上反映出当前中国政府管治尺度的变化趋势。然而,目前国内对于区域管治的研究主要集中在借鉴西方的经验上,学习所谓的合理体制设计来促进国内城市间的合作。这些研究存在一定的片面性,简单地认为仅凭一个好的体制或政策设计就可以扭转城市经营主义的发展路径,或可减少经营主义的管治所带来的负面影响。有评论指出,把中国的区域管治问题理解成只是由于缺乏政府间的交流或协调,未免过于简单了(Wu 和 Zhang,2010:60)。

The new phenomenon of changing regional governance has also recently begun to catch the attention of overseas researchers. Ma (2005) investigated the changing urban and regional governance through the adjustment of administrative boundaries and hierarchies. Jiang Xu and Anthony G. O. Yeh conducted a major study based on the experience of the Pearl River Delta area (Xu, 2008; Xu and Yeh, 2010, 2011; Yeh and Xu, 2008, 2011). Although Xu and Yeh's work has provided a profound view of the nature of emerging regional governance practices in China, the nascent trend in regional governance has not yet been fully researched, especially in terms of the dynamics and politics around the development. This research, therefore, attempts to investigate the different agents in the building of regional governance, and their respective motivation. The examination is conducted with special reference to the Yangtze River Delta (YRD). The selection of the YRD region as an empirical study area is based on the following considerations. First of all, the recent emergence of a large number of Chinese - language studies on the governance of the YRD has demonstrated the discursive development of regional governance in the area. However, few studies have been conducted in the area in the English language. Secondly, the development of regional governance in the YRD can be dated back to before economic reform, which is much longer than the history of development in the PRD. Furthermore, regional governance in the YRD involves different provincial actors; thus, it is more complex than that of the PRD. Moreover, the experience of the PRD is not as typical as that of the YRD, since the PRD region is administered under one provincial jurisdiction. Finally, great importance has been attached to the governance of the region by the central government, which is represented by the issue of the YRD regional plan and policies by the central state. In contrast, the attitude of the central government to the PRD regional governance attempt is not very clear (Wu and Zhang, 2010: 63). In other words, central intervention in the PRD development has barely been witnessed so far. Therefore, the case of the YRD offers a good opportunity to explore the trajectory of regional governance development, the diverse agents throughout the process and their inter-relationship.

1.2 Aims of this research

The first aim of this research is to highlight the direction of China's changing governance beyond the well - known and well - documented downscaling of governance towards urban entrepreneurialism. This study aims to call attention to the re - emergence of regional scale in contemporary governance operations and policy delivery in China. Secondly, it attempts to explain the recent transformation through state theory and the strategic - relational approach.

区域管治的变化这一新的现象近期也开始引起了国外的中国学者的广泛关注。Ma(2005)从国内行政区划和层级的调整入手,研究了中国城市与区域管治的变化情况。徐江(Jiang Xu)和叶嘉安(Anthony G. O. Yeh)针对珠江三角洲地区的区域管治经验做了大量的研究工作(Xu,2008;Xu 和 Yeh,2010,2011;Yeh 和 Xu,2008,2011)。虽然 Xu 和 Yeh 深刻地揭示了中国正在兴起的区域管治实践的本质,但并没有对区域管治的新趋势展开充分论证,尤其是区域管治发展变化的动态过程及政治因素。因而本研究以长江三角洲地区(长三角)为例,通过分析区域管治背后不同的影响因子及其动机,试图对这一问题进行解答。选择长三角作为实证研究的区域是基于以下方面的考虑。首先,国外对于中国区域管治的研究主要集中在珠三角,对长三角的研究则相对较少。而国内近年来关于长三角的研究逐渐兴起,长三角区域管治的现有发展和重要性已开始引起学术界的关注。其次,与珠三角相比,长三角区域的管治历史更长,可以追溯到改革开放之前,能够更好地展现区域管治的变化与改革开放前后国家管治政策变化的关系。再次,长三角案例更具有普遍代表性。区域管治在珠三角只是广东省内的城市合作问题,具有一定的特殊性,如果扩大至大珠三角或泛珠三角区域,又涉及香港、澳门两个特别行政区,牵涉到跨境问题,情况更为特殊。而长三角地区跨江苏、浙江、上海三个省级行政单位,更能体现一般性特征。最后,中央政府对长三角的区域管治非常重视。2008年8月,国务院常务会议通过了《关于进一步推进长江三角洲地区改革开放和经济社会发展的指导意见》,标志着"长三角一体化"区域发展战略正式跃至国家层面,这是国务院首次对国内的区域发展提出规划性要求。因此,长三角可以作为一个典型的案例来分析区域管治的发展轨迹,以及整个发展过程中的各种影响因子及其相互关系。

第二节　研究目标

首先,本研究试图指出,中国的管治已发生了新的变化。改革开放后管治下移引发的城市经营主义已为人们所熟知,也出现了大量相关的研究工作。但当前区域尺度在中国的管治和政策活动中重现,有待引起关注。其次,本研究试图运用国家理论(state theory)和战略关系方法(the strategic-relational

Moreover, it aims to understand the links between changing state strategy, the transformation of urban and regional governance, and the major outcome of urban and regional development. The political economy approach is crucial to provide a comprehensive and critical account of regional re – ascendance in contemporary China. Thirdly, the research focuses on an examination of the on-the – ground development of regional governance in China. The focus on the 'existing regional governance' shows the researcher's interest in the process of governance building, which resonates with the call for a process – based and contextualised approach to compensate for abstract regulation theory and the general 'paradigm shift' hypothesis (MacLeod, 2001a, b).

1.3 Organisation of the thesis

The thesis consists of eight chapters, which are structured into three parts. Part I includes Chapters one, two and three; Chapters one and two introduce the research background, research aims and literature review; chapter three made an historical overview on the transformation of urban and regional governance in China since 1949, with an focus on the various regional strategies and projects in China in recent years; characteristics of existing regional governance is china are hence summarised. The following four chapters, i.e. part II, are the main body of the study comprising empirical work. Chapter four develops methodology for this particular research. Then, the Yangtze River Delta region is chosen as the study area and a two-case-study approach is employed to explore the development process and investigate the dynamics and conflicts through the course of evolution. Finally, Chapter eight constitutes the last part of the thesis, Part III, which summarises the major research findings and theoretical implications.

After the introductory chapter, Chapter two attempts to understand the political economies of regions and regional development through reviewing the recent research debate on the rise of 'new regionalism'. Firstly, the key conceptual debate on city – regions and new regionalism is reviewed. Then, a debate on political regionalism in particular is reviewed, covering a range of topics from the relational or territorial approach to regional mapping, the role of the state to regional development and state restructuring. These existing discussions are indispensable if a well – informed theoretical stance for this research project is to be developed. The chapter then reviews the key theoretical perspective adopted by this research, i.e. the existing literature on 'new state spaces'. Finally, contemporary Chinese and international regional literature is reviewed to suggest the current gap between China and the West in terms of theoretical conceptions and empirical studies. The final part also establishes the significance and originality of this research.

approach），为新近发生的变化提供理论解释。研究特别关注了国家战略变化与城市和区域管治变化以及城市和区域发展重大成果之间的关系。在此方面，政治经济学视角对于全面恰当地理解当前中国的区域复兴至关重要。第三，本研究着重探讨了中国区域管治的实际发展状况，特别是管治构建的过程。这也响应了西方对抽象的管制理论（regulation theory）和粗线条的"范式转变"假设的批评，即研究必须重视对过程和当地实际情况的分析。

第三节　研究结构

本书由八个章节组成，主要分为三大部分。第一部分包括第一、二、三章。第一和第二章介绍了本书的研究背景、研究目标和相关文献综述，在此基础上，第三章对中国自1949年以来的城市与区域管治变化做了历史性的回顾，重点总结了中国近期的区域战略和项目以及当前区域管治的特征。随后四章是第二部分，也是主体部分，包含了主要实证研究工作。第四章提出了本研究的实证研究方法，随后以长三角作为研究区域，采用双案例研究的方法，分析当前出现的区域管治的演变过程和其中的各种冲突。最后，第八章是第三部分，总结了研究的主要发现和理论意义。

第一章引言部分结束后，第二章文献综述以近期学术界围绕"新区域主义"的争论为切入点，试图厘清区域政治经济和区域发展的涵义。本章首先对城市区域和新区域主义等核心概念进行了梳理。随后重点回顾了目前关于政治区域主义的讨论，内容包括从地域的视角还是关联的视角来解读区域划分、国家对区域发展的作用以及国家重构。上述关于区域理论的讨论为本研究提供了充分的立论依据。本章还进一步回顾了研究所选取的核心理论视角，即"新国家空间"理论。最后，本章回顾了关于中国区域管治的现有国内外研究文献，指出了国内与国际研究在理论构想和实证研究上的差距，也就说明了本研究的重要意义和原创性。

Chapter three examines the transformation of regional governance in China by looking at the changing state of the central-local relationship, which reflects the evolving power structure and shifting regional policies in China since 1949 to the present day. The chapter then highlights the recent resurgence of policies and programmes articulated at the regional scale; the variety of projects is described in detail. It is summarised that the current emerging regional governance in China is steered by both central and local government and the fact that these regional programmes are very flexible in institutional organisation is confirmed. There is no devolution from the national government to the regional scale to insert a formal regional agency in the existing administrative structure, nor rescaling of authority from the localities towards the regional level. Meanwhile, the conceptual perspective of 'new state spatiality' is deployed here to provide an understanding of the mechanism of China's changing regional governance and statehood.

Chapter four develops the research framework and methodology for the empirical project. First of all, the research questions and hypotheses are raised. Then, a research design is put forward based on the purpose of the research and the theoretical hypothesis. Subsequently, the methods of data collection and data analysis are introduced in detail in the latter part of the chapter. First-hand data, especially in the form of interviews, are collected in addition to a large quantity of secondary data including statistics, reports, monographs, planning and policy documents, etc. Qualitative analysis is the main research technique of the study, although methods of quantitative analysis are also applied when necessary.

Chapter five sets the background for the study area of the research, i.e. the historical development of the Yangtze River Delta in the coastal region, the leading economy in China, is introduced. The chapter is divided into three stages, according to the changing inter-city economic relationship.Broadly speaking, the chapter is also an indispensable part of the thesis which demonstrates that the regional territory is a social construct. Admittedly, it is dependent on economic and technological factors, but it is not limited to these. The actual development of regions is contextualised in its social and political context, and is riddled with conflicts and contradictions. The process is fully illustrated in the following two case study chapters.

Chapter six aims to explore local forces with regard to the development of governance at the regional scale. For this purpose, the chapter examines the changing inter-government relationship between Jiangsu and Shanghai. Firstly, an investigation is conducted on the rivalry competition between the two jurisdictions, which can be perfectly illustrated by the well-known story of '173 project fighting Kunshan'. Interviews from both governments, as well as media reports and government documents, are quoted to illustrate the contents and motivation of the 173 project launched by Shanghai, and the counter-measures

　　第三章试图通过中央和地方关系的变迁,探究中国自1949年至今的权力结构调整和区域政策转变,从而研究国内区域管治的变化。本章重点关注了近期区域尺度政策和项目的再度兴起。研究总结发现,当前新兴的区域管治同时受中央和地方政府的调控,事实证明这些区域项目在体制安排上非常灵活。在现有行政结构中,中央政府并没有向区域尺度下放权力设立正式的区域机构,地方一级也没有向区域一级转移权力。同时,本章还运用"新国家空间"的概念阐释了中国区域管治与国家空间变化的机制假设。

　　第四章构建了整个实证研究的研究框架和方法体系。本章首先提出了研究问题和假设,之后根据研究目的和理论假设提出了研究设计,并接着介绍了收集和分析数据的方法。除统计年鉴、报告、专著、规划和政策文件等大量二手数据外,本研究还通过访谈等形式收集了一手数据。研究主要运用了定性分析,但在必要情况下也进行了定量分析。

　　第五章提供了本书实证研究的案例背景,介绍了中国第一经济体——长三角地区的发展历程。本章按照城市经济关系的变化分为三节。就整体而言,这一章是本书不可或缺的一部分,因为它指出了区域不仅仅是由经济构成的,也是由社会构成的。诚然,区域的实际发展依赖于经济和技术因素,但除此之外还受到社会、政治背景的影响,发展过程充满了冲突和矛盾。区域形成的具体过程将在之后两章的案例研究中进一步展开说明。

　　第六章旨在研究区域尺度管治发展背后的地方动力。为此,本章分析了江苏省与上海市政府间关系的变化。研究首先通过"173打昆山"这一众所周知的案例,生动地诠释了两个辖区间的对抗性竞争关系。研究就此案例采访了两地政府的相关部门,并引用了媒体报道和政府文件,说明上海启动"173工程"的用意和"173工程"的内容,以及昆山政府采取的反击措施。本章随后研

taken by the Kunshan government. Secondly, an examination of the nascent local cooperation practices at the border of the two jurisdictions is carried out. Again, interviews with relevant officials and planners from both sides of the governments are quoted to discover why cooperation is now preferred by the governments rather than hostile competition, the nature of the cooperative projects and the form of the progress and barriers. Finally, the chapter evaluates the degree to which cooperation is pursued by local governments in policy and practice, and reaches the conclusion that the current inter-locality cooperation between Shanghai and Kunshan is actually driven by economic mutual benefit. The economic principle triggers local interest in collaborative development, but it also limits the scope of collaboration since it is dominated by the economic sphere rather than being led by other urgent regional issues such as environment problems. Due to the same reason, the cooperation is merely a partnership based on a particular project. Governments would rather not put too much effort into institutionalisation, which would entail legitimacy and binding power.

Chapter seven attempts to investigate the top-down forces in the development of regional governance; this part is conducted through examining the resurgence of regional plans in the YRD region, which is currently a major instrument for the central government to deliver regional governance. The formation of a regional plan for the YRD can be dated back to the early years after economic reform, but it soon faded away with the rise of localism. Therefore, the new YRD regional plan, the first since the decades after economic reform, can be read as the reassertion of central intervention in local development. Interviews with officials, academics and planners who are involved in or are informed by the plan-making process are quoted in order to illustrate the intention of the plan, and more importantly, to reveal the conflicts throughout the formation of the plan and the problems that could be confronted in the plan's implementation. The chapter draws the conclusion that the top-down regional plan initiated by the central government plays an important role in the process of transforming governance, both as a result of the changing scale of governance and as a driver for transforming the scale of governance. Nevertheless, the re-building of state power is full of contention and conflict between different levels and divisions of government.

Chapter eight summarises and discusses the major research findings. It synthesises the general changing trajectory and the findings from the two case studies and provides an overall picture of the changing regional governance in China. Based on the results of the research, theoretical implications are proposed for the Western theory of 'new state spaces' and for the study of regional ascendance. Meanwhile, the limitations of the research are summarised and suggestions for future study regarding the relevant topics are put forward.

究了近期两个城市交界地区正在萌芽的地方合作实践。研究也就此采访了两个城市的相关官员和规划专家，探寻了两地政府间关系从对抗性竞争转向合作的原因，以及合作项目的性质、进展和障碍。最后，本章评价了上海和昆山目前在政策和实践方面的合作力度，指出当前两地的合作实际上是基于经济上的互利互惠。经济利益触发了地方政府对合作发展的兴趣，但同时也限制了合作范围，主要集中在经济领域，反而忽略了其他更加迫切的区域问题，如环境问题等。出于这一原因，这种合作只能沦为围绕某个特定项目的伙伴关系。两地政府并不愿意花费精力来推动合作的制度化，使合作具备合法性和约束力。

第七章试图通过分析长三角区域规划的复兴，研究自上而下的作用力对区域管治形成的影响。区域规划是目前中央政府实施区域管治的一个主要工具，长三角的区域规划可以追溯到改革开放之初，但很快就因为地方主义的兴起而衰落了。因此，新的长三角区域规划是改革开放几十年以来的第一个区域规划，可以看作中央政府对地方发展干预的回归。研究采访了参与编制规划的官员、学者和规划专家，试图了解规划的意图，但更重要的目的是为了了解规划编制过程中存在的矛盾，以及规划实施过程中可能遇到的困难。本章最后指出，中央政府自上而下的区域规划对管治的转变起到了重要作用，区域规划不仅是管治尺度变化的结果，也是驱动管治尺度变化的工具。但在重塑国家权力的过程中，充满了各级政府间和各个政府部门间的竞争与冲突。

第八章总结并讨论了研究的主要发现。本章综述了管治变化的主要轨迹以及两个案例研究的发现，概括了国内区域管治模式的变化情况。基于研究结果，本章提出了本研究对于西方"新国家空间"理论和区域复兴研究的理论意义，同时阐述了本研究的局限性，并提出了对未来相关研究的建议。

第二章

CHAPTER TWO

Literature Review

2.1 Introduction

The review chapter lays the foundation for the theoretical perspective and research framework that is adopted in this PhD study. The chapter is structured as follows: section 2.2 reviews the different origins of the 'new regionalism' argument. Then, a political economic approach is deployed in section 2.3 and a debate of the perspective is reviewed. Subsequently, section 2.4 reviews the influential work of the political economic approach on state spatiality and new state spaces (NSS) by Brenner (2004b) and other contemporary scholars. By fusing the recent debate on the NSS framework, the author deploys a process-based regulation approach to studying the rescaling of the state, which is combined with the perspective of agency, politics and scale. The relevance of the Western theoretical perspective and the theoretical stance adopted by the research is further specified in section 2.5. Section 2.6 reviews traditional Chinese regional studies, which focus on economic geography, regional development and regional inequality. The theoretical and empirical gap between regional studies and the changing urban and regional governance is identified; nevertheless, a recently emerging group of literature which specifies regional renaissance in China is witnessed. Building upon the existing research, this study intends to use the NSS framework to argue that current regional transformation is part of the process of the restructuring of state spatiality. The research project further aims to extend the well-developed urban governance study to the understanding of the recent regional initiatives. The implication for the analysis framework of this PhD research is drawn in the conclusion section.

2.2 Unpacking the 'new regionalism'

2.2.1 The regional resurgence and the city-region concept

Under the general context of global production and new economic agglomeration, world cities and global city-regions have been recognised to hold prominence in organising future global and national economies (Ohmae, 2004; Scott, 2001). With the main city continuing as the node of the economy, the dispersal of urban functions from the city to the wider city-region is also witnessed. Henceforth, the concept of the city-region is employed to refer to the economic markets or the relational space beyond an urban jurisdiction on a scale ranging from metropolitan to a cluster of cities (Etherington and Jones,

第二章 文献综述

第一节 引言

本章的文献综述为本研究的理论视角和研究框架奠定了基础。本章结构如下:第二节回顾了"新区域主义"理论的不同起源。之后,第三节主要回顾了政治经济学方法及围绕该方法的争论。第四节回顾了Brenner(2004b)从政治经济学视角提出的影响广泛的"国家空间尺度"和"新国家空间"理论。本书还借鉴了其他当代学者的观点,采用基于过程的管治研究方法,结合动力因子、政治和尺度的视角,研究国家的空间尺度重组。西方理论视角的适用性和本研究的理论立场在第五节中做了讨论。第六节回顾了国内的传统区域研究,这些研究通常集中在经济地理、区域经济发展和区域不均衡发展等方面。本书认为,传统区域研究与城市区域管治变化研究在理论与实证上都存在差距,不过近期涌现出了一批研究文献,专门研究中国的区域复兴问题。在已有研究的基础上,本研究试图运用"新国家空间"的框架,提出当前的区域转变属于国家空间尺度重组过程的一部分。本研究还希望将已经发展成熟的城市管治理论延伸应用到对最近国内区域复兴的理解上。结论部分总结了现有国内外研究对本研究分析框架的启示。

第二节 解读"新区域主义"

一、区域复兴与城市区域概念

在全球生产和新经济集聚的大背景下,全球城市和全球城市区域被认为是组织未来全球和国家经济的重要单元(Ohmae,2004;Scott,2001)。原有主要城市继续作为经济节点,城市功能从城市向辐射面更广的城市区域扩散。因此,城市区域的概念常用来表示尺度范围从都市区到城市群的这种突破单一城市辖区的经济市场或关联空间(Etherington和Jones,2009:261,注1;

2009: 261, note 1; Hall, 2009). It is conceived that the city-regions will be the locus of various kinds of activities and 'the integrators of the spaces of flows' (Neuman and Hull, 2009: 779). Compared to the traditional urbanisation and suburbanisation, the urban expansion is stretched out and decentralised to a wider region; moreover, compared to the megalopolis analysis established by Gottmann (1961), the contemporary city-region is filled with functional connectivity, in addition to geographical proximities. Parr (2005) has analysed the typical interactions within the city-region, such as the flow of trade, labour forces, commuting, and capital movement between the city core and the hinterland surrounding it. Hall and his colleagues have made great efforts to examine the polycentric structure and connectivity of the city-region (Hall and Pain, 2006).

On the other hand, the regional reifications based on the global city-region thesis (Scott, 2001) are challenged by alternative ways of defining and delimiting regions. It is argued that, in addition to the material change of regional economics, there is also a plethora of representations of the city-region structure in terms of technological, infrastructure, ecological, political, social, institutional, governance and territorial policies (MacLeod and Jones, 2001). In these circumstances, the term of 'city-region' particularly refers to 'a strategic and political level of administration and policy making, extending beyond the administrative boundaries of single urban local government authorities to include urban and/or semi-urban hinterlands' (Tewdwr-Jones and McNeil, 2000: 131, note 1). In contrast to the presumably objective and hard boundaries of economic city-regions, these forms of city-regions are mostly represented by policies and institutions, narratives and initiatives, with ambiguous, fuzzy or artificial apparatus (Harding, 2007: 451). In other words, the geographical notions of 'region' are not only built upon pure spatial economy, but are also invented and reinvented by state institutions and social and cultural forces. It is hence argued that 'regions are anything but natural entities: they are, at the same time, institutional, political and socio-cultural spaces' (Gualini, 2004: 330).

2.2.2 The different origins of the 'new regionalism'

One consequence of the intensifying interest in the contemporary city-regions is the urban-regional renaissance in all research fields ranging from geography and planning to political science (MacLeod, 2001a: 805). It is suggested that the key schools of thought can generally be categorised under the banners of 'economic' and 'political' new regionalism (Harrison, 2006: 23). Firstly, the 'new regionalism' literature derives from a group of economic geography literature with a shift towards institutional aspects (MacLeod, 2001a: 807). It

Hall,2009)。城市区域被认为是各种活动的集聚地和"各种流空间的汇聚"(Neuman 和 Hull,2009:779)。与传统的城市化和郊区化相比,城市扩张的延伸和分散范围更广,而与 Gottmann(1961)提出的大都市带分析相比,现代的城市区域除了地域上的连绵,还存在紧密的功能联系。Parr(2005)分析了城市区域内的典型关联,如中心城市与腹地城市间的商贸流、劳动力流、通勤流和资金流。Hall 及其同事对城市区域的多中心结构和关联特征做了大量研究(Hall 和 Pain,2006)。

另一方面,基于全球城市区域理论的区域阐释(Scott,2001)也受到了其他定义和划分区域方法的挑战。这些方法认为区域除了物质经济变化以外,还有许多其他体现城市区域结构的方面,包括技术、基础设施、生态、政治、社会、制度、管治和地域政策等(MacLeod 和 Jones,2001)。在这些语境中,"城市区域"所指的是"突破了单一城市地方政府管辖范围的、纳入了城市和/或半城市腹地的行政管理和政策制定的战略和政治尺度"(Tewdwr-Jones 和 McNeil,2000:131,注1)。相比经济城市区域的客观而严格的边界特征,这种城市区域的形式往往表现在政策和机构、语言和行动上,边界也较为模糊,依靠人为界定(Harding,2007:451)。也就是说,"区域"的地理概念不只是建立在单纯的空间经济上,同时也由政府机构和社会文化力量进行创造和再创造。因此,可以说"区域绝不是一个自然的实体,而是集制度、政治和社会文化为一体的空间"(Gualini,2004:330)。

二、"新区域主义"的不同起源

当代城市区域研究不断升温的一个结果就是从地理、规划到政治科学各领域都出现了城市区域研究的复兴(MacLeod,2001a:805)。通常认为主要有两种思想流派,一种是"经济"新区域主义,另一种是"政治"新区域主义(Harrison,2006:23)。首先,"新区域主义"源自一批采用制度学研究角度的经济地理学文献(MacLeod,2001a:807)。它将区域的复兴作为研究的对象,并从制度

takes the resurgence of a region as an object of investigation and uses the institutional perspective to understand the dynamics of regional economic development (Harrison, 2006: 21). The thrust of the research is the role of non-economic factors in the resurgent regional economies of paradigmatic regions such as Third Italy, South Wales, and many more, i.e. the investigation of social and cultural capital (Hadjimichalis, 2006: 691-92). Some of the new regionalists even use the argument to clamour for a more progressive and democratic sub-national political environment (Hadjimichalis, 2006: 691; Harrison, 2006: 22). It is argued that devolution and regionalism is a form of 'good governance', based on the actual or perceived 'economic dividends' that would be brought about by the decentralisation and cooperation (Jones et al., 2005: 398; Pike and Tomaney, 2009: 16). Although opening a brand new perspective for economic geography, the new regionalism thesis is criticised for a lack of precise empirical studies, the failure of theorisation of social capital, depoliticising politics, and narrow territorial studies without scalar analysis (Hadjimichalis, 2006; Harrison, 2008: 5-6; MacLeod, 2001a).

A new generation of research from the perspective of political and policy regionalism studies the 'new regionalism' of the rise of regional institutions since the 1990s in the Western context (Brenner, 2003a; Deas and Ward, 2000; Jones, 2001; Keating, 1998). It is argued that 'new regionalism' is particularly characterised by the powerful economic arguments revolving around 'economic competitiveness' (Norris, 2001: 557-558). It is further argued that although the contemporary regional agendas are also concerned about region-wide problems such as urban sprawl, fiscal disparities, air and water pollution and large-scale regional infrastructure, somehow these purposes are pursued because they are viewed as essential to achieving regional economic competitiveness (Norris, 2001: 558). That is, the primary objective for contemporary regional projects has shifted from efficiency and equity to competitiveness (Keating, 1998; Norris, 2001: 558), which is qualitatively different from former regional projects (Valler et al., 2002: 187). Therefore, supply-side policy options are selected, since the environment for technological innovation, the quality of education, knowledge and skills, and the convenience of infrastructures are believed to be the driving forces behind regional development (Valler et al., 2002: 187; Lovering, 1999). Moreover, instead of covering the whole territory, regional intervention privileges specific territories such as individual urban regions which are central to national economies (Wheeler, 2002: 270). As a consequence, the normatively good governance projects are actually played out by the agents to pursue 'a neo-liberally oriented "competitiveness" agenda' (Lovering, 1999; cited in Lagendijk, 2007: 1195). Nevertheless, studies move forward to argue that the actual existing

学视角来理解区域经济发展的动力机制(Harrison,2006:21)。这类研究关注的是非经济因素,即社会和文化资本在典型的复兴区域经济体中的作用,例如在第三意大利、南威尔士以及其他许多地区(Hadjimichalis,2006:691-92)。一些新区域主义者甚至用这一理论来呼吁更进步更民主的次国家政治环境(Hadjimichalis,2006:691;Harrison,2006:22)。鉴于分权与合作可能带来实际的或期望的"经济利益",权力下放和区域主义被认为是一种"好的管治"(Jones等,2005:398;Pike和Tomaney,2009:16)。尽管为经济地理学开辟了一个全新的视角,但新区域主义理论也被批评缺少严谨的实证研究,未能将社会资本理论化,淡化了政治因素,以及地域研究的范围过窄而没有涉及尺度分析。

　　而另有一些新的研究则是从政治和政策区域主义的角度来研究20世纪90年代开始的以西方国家区域组织的兴起为特征的"新区域主义"(如Brenner,2003a;Deas和Ward,2000;Jones,2001;Keating,1998)。这些研究认为"新区域主义"的显著特征是其强有力的有关"经济竞争力"的经济学论点 (如Norris,2001:557-558)。这些研究还认为,尽管当今的区域议程也关注区域性问题,例如城市的无计划扩张、区域财税差异、空气与水污染和大规模区域基础设施等,但这是因为这些问题被认为是对获得区域的经济竞争力至关重要的(Norris,2001:558)。也就是说,当今区域项目的首要目的已从追求效率和公平转向追求竞争力(Keating,1998;Norris,2001:558),这与之前的区域项目有着本质的不同(Valler等,2002:187)。因此,以供应为导向的政策方案被频频选用,因为技术创新的环境、教育及知识和技能掌握的质量、基础设施的便利被看作区域经济发展的主要推动力(Valler等,2002:187;Lovering,1999)。此外,与以往全面覆盖整个地域的做法不同,当前的区域干预注重的是一些特定的地域,例如对国家经济至关重要的一些城市区域(Wheeler,2002:270)。因此,这些所谓的"好的管治"项目实际上成为了相关利益者追求"新自由导向的'竞争力'"的工具(Lovering,1999;引自Lagendijk,2007:1195)。然而还有研究进一步认为,目前实际存在的区域战略、政策和管治并不只是由围绕"经济竞争力"的政治因素决定的,同时也受到制度资产、社会力量和政治选择等因

regional strategies, policies and governance are not only defined by the politics around 'economic competitiveness', but are also subject to institutional assets, social determination and political choices (Jonas and Ward, 2002; Norris, 2001; Ward and Jonas, 2004). A variety of case studies have demonstrated that the initial regional designation, in accordance with 'ideological perceptions of changing nature of space economy' (Deas and Lord, 2006: 1865; original emphasis), is to be constrained and reproduced by the political, administrative, democratic and cultural assets of the place (Boudreau, 2003; Deas and Ward, 2000; Deas and Lord, 2006; Harrison, 2010; Jones and MacLeod, 2004). That is, the trajectory of regional territorial development is contingent and open to uncertainties (MacLeod and Jones, 2001). It is 'political, institutional, and discursive constructs of which the development is structurally conditioned and enabled, but not fully determined, by external conditions' (Lagendijk, 2007: 1195; original emphasis).

2.2.3 The regional concept and (city-) regionalism in political economy

As reviewed by Harrison (2007, 2008), the new regionalism thesis within the political economy (Keating, 1999) is now being superseded by the new term of 'new city‐regionalism' developed within economic geography. The resurgence of the concept of 'city-region' causes further confusion in the area, where region and city-region do not enjoy a common analytical definition in various academic and policy communities. For example, in the research oriented for policy design and application, the use of terms such as 'regions', 'city‐regions' and 'sub‐regions' should be careful and subject to strict analytical methodologies. This is because each of the term may indicate particular policy recommendations at different administrative units. Therefore, it is important to clarify the meaning and nature of these terms in different purposes of research.

What is of particular note is that the 'city‐region' concept in political economy terms does not necessarily indicate a scalar feature of a specific kind of region, such as an metropolitan area around a city core. 'City-region' here is a concept with its emphasis to a distinct territorial feature, that is, ① urban focused; ② functional connectivity and relational spatiality; ③ soft and porous, and not necessarily constrained by administrative boundaries. This is discussed by Harrison (2008: 932) who writes,

> ... city‐regions in political economy have strong relational undertones. Where regions were presented to be by and large territorially bounded political–administrative units in the new regionalism, the literature on the new city-regionalism has been quick to emphasise how 'the geographic structure of these networks tends more and

素的制约(Jonas 和 Ward,2002;Norris,2001;Ward 和 Jonas,2004)。许多案例研究表明,即使最初的区域划分是根据"所认为的变化的空间经济本质来进行的"(Deas 和 Lord,2006:1865;原文强调),但它的实际形成过程受到本地政治、行政、民主和文化特征的制约(Boudreau,2003;Deas 和 Ward,2000;Deas 和 Lord,2006;Harrison,2010;Jones 和 MacLeod,2004)。也就是说,区域地域的形成轨迹是具有偶然性的,充满了不确定性(MacLeod 和 Jones,2001)。它的本质是由"政治、制度和表述构成的,其形成过程受到外部条件的制约和促成,但并不完全由外部条件决定"(Lagendijk,2007:1195;原文强调)。

三、政治经济学中的区域概念和(城市)区域主义

正如 Harrison(2007,2008)所述,政治经济学范畴的新区域主义理论(Keating,1999)正被经济地理学范畴的"新城市区域主义"的概念所取代。"城市区域"概念的兴起给这个领域带来了更多混乱,因为"区域"和"城市区域"在学术界与政策界都没有统一的分析界定。例如,在以政策设计和运用为导向的研究领域,"区域"、"城市区域"和"次区域"等术语应当谨慎使用,并遵从严格的分析方法。因为每个词都可能指向针对不同行政单位的特定政策建议。因此,在不同目的的研究中阐明这些术语的含义和性质是很重要的。

特别值得注意的是,政治经济学术语中的"城市区域"概念并不一定是指一个特定区域的尺度特征,例如可能是指一个围绕城市中心的都市地区。这里的"城市区域"概念强调的是某些独特的地域特征:①以城市为中心;②功能性联系和空间关联;③具有灵活性和可渗透性,并不一定受到行政边界的制约。正如 Harrison(2008:932)所写:

……在政治经济学中,城市区域有很强的关联含义。虽然在新区域主义的概念中'区域'大多是指按地域划分的政治行政单元,但是关于新城市区域主义的文献急于强调"这些网络的地理结构越来

more to override purely political boundaries' such that city-regions are open, porous spaces, easily permeated by flows of capital, knowledge and finance, and increasingly free from regulatory control on the part of national states.(Scott, 2001: 4)

Therefore, the scalar boundaries of the city-region in the political economy can range from being relatively small scale metropolitan areas to grand and large scale regions as indicated by the term such as 'mega-city region' (Hall and Pain, 2006) and 'global city-region' (Scott, 2001). Overall, the regional resurgence indicated by 'new (city-) regionalism' does not indicate a particular scalar institution of region or a certain regional territorial form. A further example is that, the study on the emergence of the new regionalism in North America tends to be focused on the metropolitan-scale, while studies in Europe are generally orientated towards larger geographical entities, 'extending beyond functional metropolitan areas and encompass other cities and their hinterlands, freestanding towns, and rural areas' (Jonas and Ward, 2002; Deas and Giordano, 2003: 226). Therefore, the regional resurgence is only indicative of the general sub-national governance changes, or the emergence of multi-level governance at the sub-national level beyond the dominant localisation and urban governance at the earlier state neo-liberalism stage. As remarked by Jonas (2006: 402), '[T]he "region" can be seen to operate both as a between space and a mesolevel concept, which is amenable to thinking about a spatial combination of flows, connections, processes, structures, networks, sites, places, settings, agencies and institutions'.

Furthermore, the new 'city-regionalism' used in the political economy holds that the research subject is not an existing scale of regional territory but a developing process in formation and transformation. The process reflects the latest transition in the regulation and governance landscape, associated with a restless de-territorialisation of various forces at different scales and their re-territorialisation on a variety of regions. The (city-) regionalism in political economy is hence concentrated on the conflict-ridden forming process of the sub-national governance, and to examine the degree to which the struggles have shaped or constrained the development of different forms of regionalism (Deas and Giordano, 2003). It aims to explain why regional state spaces (be they trans-national, trans-regional, pan-regional, regional, sub-regional, or city-regional) are produced as a particular scale in economic and social life, and how a certain regional territorial configuration is subsequently constructed and reconstructed. Overall, the city-regionalism in political economy is understood as an ongoing struggle for control of space (Ward and Jonas, 2004: 2135). The research subject is not an established object specific in scale or configuration, and the examining process may involve a flux of regional practices at the same time and various origins of

越倾向于超越纯粹的政治边界",以至于城市区域作为开放的、可渗透的空间,很容易被资金流、知识流和金融流所渗透,而且越来越不受到来自国家政府的管治控制。(Scott,2001:4)

因此,政治经济学中城市区域的尺度边界可以小至尺度相对较小的都市地区,也可以大至像"巨型城市区域"(Hall 和 Pain,2006)和"全球性城市区域"(Scott,2001)那样的大尺度地区。总之,"新(城市)区域主义"所指的区域复兴并不代表一个具体的区域尺度制度或一种特定的区域地域形式。进一步举例来说,北美的新区域主义研究关注的往往是都市区尺度,而欧洲的研究则通常面向更大的地理实体,"超越了功能性的都市地区,同时还包含其他的一些城市及其腹地、独立的城镇及乡村地区"(Jonas 和 Ward,2002;Deas 和 Giordano,2003:226)。因此,区域复兴只是说明一种总体的次国家管治空间的变化,或一种在次国家空间尺度上的超越国家新自由主义早期阶段盛行的地方化和城市管治的多层级管治。正如 Jonas(2006:402)所说,"区域既可以看作一个中间地带性质的空间,也可以看作一个中观层次的概念,我们完全可以认为那就是一个由各种流、相互联系、过程、结构、网络、地点、场所、背景、动因和制度组成的空间集合"。

再者,政治经济学的新"城市区域主义"认为研究对象并不是当前存在的区域地域的尺度,而是一个形成和改变的发展过程。这个过程反映出管制和管治局面的最新变化,关系到各种力量在不同尺度上的不断去地域化和在不同区域里的再地域化。因此政治经济学的新"(城市)区域主义"关注的是次国家管治空间形成的充满冲突的过程,并研究这些冲突在多大程度上塑造或限制了不同形式的区域主义的发展(Deas 和 Giordano,2003)。这个概念是为了解释为什么区域性的国家空间(无论是跨国家的、跨区域的、泛区域的、区域的、次区域的还是城市区域的)会作为经济和社会生活中一个特定的尺度而出现,以及某个区域地域空间是如何构建和重新构建的。总之,政治经济学中的城市区域主义被理解为不断争夺控制空间的过程(Ward 和 Jonas,2004:2135)。其研究对象不是一个既定的尺度或形态,整个研究过程也可能涉及同一时期的一系列区域实践,以及历史上区域的不同起源。下一节将综述现有

regions during history. In terms of how to conceptualise the process, examine the dynamics and conceive the agency, the following sections are going to review the existing approaches and debate.

2.3 The debate within the political economic perspective

2.3.1 The role of the state in the 'new regionalism'

As reviewed above, the recent resurgence of regionalism has fundamentally shifted in its rationale from administrative efficiency to economic efficiency. Additionally, the new regionalism differs from the old regionalism in that voluntary and flexible cooperation instead of formal government structural change is called for by new regionalists (Norris, 2001: 558 – 559). The new approach, linked with public actions, partnership and negotiations rather than an authoritarian, top-down and rigid approach, overcomes the deficiencies of earlier regional reform projects in terms of legitimacy, local particularities, and implementation (Lefevre, 1998). In the new experiments, different localities and institutions may be grouped and involved in particular cases instead of building a fully-fledged supra-municipality or inter-municipality government structure to substitute or re-divide power divisions at the local level (ibid). However, it is contended that, albeit as a main characteristic, over-emphasis on the merits of local institutions might lead to 'soft institutionalism' (MacLeod, 2001b). The specific agents underlying the regional governance advocated by the new regionalists are not clarified, which seems to infer that the region is an automatic agent itself. In contrast, the new regionalist practitioners have particularly downplayed the role of the state. In order to illuminate the actual mechanism of new regionalism, it is argued that an exploration of the agent underlying these specific projects is significant.

The mechanism of regional territorial development in the UK is mainly orchestrated by the national state. Throughout the 1970s and 1980s, localities emerged into the main territory to deliver government economic development policies in the UK (Valler et al., 2002: 186), as well as a number of Western European states (Brenner, 2004a: 465). This big transformation from traditional Keynesian macroeconomic policies to local devolution and national urban policy has been expressed as 'central government localism' (Valler et al., 2002: 186) or 'new localism' (Deas and Ward, 2000). That is, central government intervention was downscaled around urban and intra-urban areas (Deas and Ward, 2000: 275). Regional planning, as well as other regional policies, was marginalised as the tool of redistribution and inequality management; instead, economic regeneration of central cities was highlighted. In other words, the

的研究方法和争议,讨论如何将这个过程概念化,并研究这个过程的形成机制及其动力因子。

第三节 政治经济学视角下的讨论

一、"新区域主义"中的国家作用

综上所述,最近兴起的区域主义在逻辑上发生了从行政效率向经济效率的根本转变。不仅如此,新区域主义与旧区域主义的不同之处还在于,新区域主义者主张自愿灵活的合作,而不是正式的政府结构变化(Norris,2001:558-559)。这种新方法结合的是公共行为、合作和谈判,而不是自上而下的、死板的权力做法,克服了早期区域改革项目在合法性、地方特色和执行方面的缺陷(Lefevre,1998)。在新的区域改革尝试中,不同的地方和机构可能因参与特定的项目而组合或联系在一起,而不是建立一个完全成熟的、凌驾于城市之上或介于城市之间的政府结构来取代或重新划分地方政府的权力(同上)。但是也有学者认为,尽管这是一个重要特征,但是过度强调地方制度的优越性可能会导致"软制度主义"(MacLeod,2001b)。现有解释并没有澄清新区域主义者所推崇的区域管治背后的具体动因,似乎是想说区域本身就是个自主的个体。相比之下,新区域主义的实践者尤其弱化了国家的作用。为了说明新区域主义的实际机制,分析具体项目背后的动力和作用者是非常重要的。

英国区域地域的形成机制主要是由国家政府精心策划的。在上世纪70到80年代,地方成为英国(Valler等,2002:186)和其他一些西欧国家(Brenner,2004a:465)推行政府经济发展政策的主要地域。这种从传统凯恩斯宏观经济政策到地方分权和国家城市政策的巨大转变被称作"中央政府引导的地方主义"(Valler等,2002:186)或"新地方主义"(Deas和Ward,2000)。具体来说,中央政府的干预指令被下达到城市及城市内部的地区(Deas和Ward,2000:275)。区域规划以及其他区域政策被边缘化,沦为再分配和不平等管理的工具;而中心城市的经济复兴则受到了重视。也就是说,城市内部的社会经济问

socioeconomic problems of inner cities were assumed to be the priority to achieve national territorial equalisation and remove deprivation (Webb and Collis, 2000: 860). However, since the early 1990s, there has been a salient refocusing from the urban level to the regional level. The Government Offices for the English regions, Regional Development Agencies in England and Regional Assemblies in Scotland, Wales and Northern Ireland have marked a partial switch from previously urban‐based regeneration to regionally‐based intervention (Deas and Ward, 2000: 275). Nevertheless, it is noted that the national state still plays a crucial role in 'delimiting the spatial boundaries, operational parameters and key actors out of which the new regionalism is being forged' (Jones and MacLeod, 1999: 308; Jones, 2001). It is further established that centrally orchestrated regionalism again centralises power at the regional level and disempowers sub‐regions in England (Harrison, 2008). Hence, it is argued that regionalism and regionalisation in the UK does not represent real decentralisation, but retains a high level of centralisation (Morgan, 2007; Musson et al., 2005; Pearce and Ayres, 2009).

In contrast, some other studies have highlighted the bottom‐up mechanism in building region‐wide governance. For instance, Jonas and Pincetl (2006) explored the 'new civic regionalism' in California, which is mainly backed by business interests in partnership with non‐profit and private foundations and grassroots organisations. The project is part of the long‐standing social movement to address localised conflicts around land use and environment, affordable housing, infrastructure, property tax and so forth (ibid: 482). The new regionalist discourse has been embraced, since it circumvented formal administrative reform, idealised regional economic spaces, and empowered the regional public (ibid: 501). Similarly, McCann (2007) highlighted the bottom‐up regional initiatives by local state, neighbourhood and activist groups. Institutions are envisioned and policies are articulated at a scale beyond the local jurisdictional boundaries to achieve 'smart growth' and pursue urban liveability (ibid: 189). Overall, the different top‐down and bottom‐up phenomena have broadened the perspective of studying what 'city-regionalism' really is (Harding, 2007: 444-445).

2.3.2 Regionalisation, regionalism and the restructuring of the state

Scholars who recognise the role of the state in developing regionalism argue 'the extent to which some new initiatives in the emerging regionalism are in reality rescaled governmental and quasi‐governmental intervention' (Jones and MacLeod, 1999: 307; original emphasis). For example, Jones (2001) has argued that, rather than a bottom‐up social capital approach to networked governance,

题被认为是促进国家各地域均衡发展和消除贫困的当务之急（Webb 和 Collis，2000：860）。然而，从上世纪90年代初开始，就有大量的项目和政策从城市层面重新转向区域层面。英格兰区域政府办公室、英格兰区域发展办公署及苏格兰、威尔士和北爱尔兰的区域议会已在一定程度上将城市层面的经济复兴项目转变为区域层面的干预（Deas 和 Ward，2000：275）。然而，国家政府对"如何划定新区域项目的空间范围、制度框架和主导者"仍起着关键作用（Jones 和 MacLeod，1999：308；Jones，2001）。有学者进一步认为，这种中央主导的区域主义只是将英格兰的权力从次区域层面再次集中到了区域层面（Harrison，2008）。因此，也有学者认为英国的区域主义和区域化并没有真正做到权力下放，而是依然保留着高度的中央集权（Morgan，2007；Musson 等，2005；Pearce 和 Ayres，2009）。

相反，其他一些研究则凸显了自下而上建立区域管治尺度的机制。例如，Jonas 和 Pincetl（2006）研究了美国加利福尼亚的"新公民区域主义"，这项区域活动主要是由商业公司与非盈利的私营基金会和普通民众组织支持的。这个项目是为解决土地利用和环境问题、保障性住房、基础设施、房产税等地方冲突的长期社会运动的一部分（同上：482）。此项研究之所以采纳新区域主义者的观点，是因为它规避了正式的行政改革，理想化了区域经济空间，赋予了区域公众权利（同上：501）。同样，McCann（2007）的研究也强调了地方政府、社区民众和维权团体自下而上的区域举措。这些举措在超越地方管辖范围的区域尺度上设想区域制度和政策，以便实现"精明增长"和提高城市宜居性（同上：189）。总之，这些不同的自上而下和自下而上的区域形成现象拓宽了关于"城市区域主义"本质的研究视野（Harding，2007：444-445）。

二、区域化、区域主义和国家的重组

认识到国家对区域主义形成的重要作用之后，有学者认为"新区域主义的一些举措实际上是重新尺度化后的政府和准政府干预"（Jones 和 MacLeod，1999：307；原文强调）。例如，Jones 认为英格兰的区域发展办公署就不是一种自下而上的社会资本途径的网络化管治，而实际上是"国家权力的一种新的

the Regional Development Agencies (RDAs) for regions of England are actually 'a new (regionalised) scale of state power' (p.1188). Later studies have echoed the view that the state orchestrated the regional institutions to 'reassert its functional importance and deliver its policies more effectively' (Goodwin et al., 2006; Jones et al., 2005). It is further contended that the regional institution is actually an additional hierarchy rather than a substantial restructuring of the traditional administrative system (Harrison, 2007; Deas and Lord, 2006; Goodwin et al., 2005; Goodwin et al., 2006; Jones et al., 2005; Pearce and Ayres, 2009). The institutional system of regional-level governance 'affords direct channels of influence to central government departments' (Musson et al., 2005: 1397).

The resurgence of regions results in the restructuring of governance between and across different levels of territories. Along with the significant number of devolution projects undertaken in Western Europe, the concept of multi-level governance (MLG) has been invented to indicate the dispersed distribution of state power at various levels of governance (Marks et al., 1996, cited in Yang, 2005: 2147). However, the MLG approach is found to be deficient in two main respects. Multi-level governance, nevertheless,

> ...overplays the vertical nesting of discrete policy competencies, at the expense of analyzing the dense network of 'tangled hierarchies' (Jessop, 2001) which mesh together to produce and implement policy horizontally across any one scale or over any one territory. Multi-level governance also tends to reify the different scales within these hierarchies, when in practice scales of governance are relative and are actively produced (not least by the national state). (Goodwin et al., 2005: 423)

That is to say, the state restructuring process is far from straightforward and pre-established, but is open to conflict and contests. Moreover, the complex restructuring of governance is not only represented by vertical rescaling between scales, but also by horizontal relationships between institutions in the same territory (Goodwin et al., 2005: 432; Allmendinger and Haughton, 2007). More importantly, the MLG only gives a descriptive outline of the contemporary governance landscape, and does not offer any perspective to examine the actual mechanism through which state rescaling processes take place. Analogously, the 'hollowing out' metaphor simply describes 'the delegation of powers away from the national level, and makes no explicit claims about the organizational or institutional forms that may result from this' (Goodwin et al., 2005: 424). It is thus argued that the state rescaling process should be conceptualised as the twin process of the 'hollowing out' of powers at the national scale, as well as the transfer, or 'filling in', of powers to other scales (ibid: 425). That is, the state

（区域化）尺度"（Jones，2001：1188）。后来的研究都同意这个观点，认为国家建立这些区域机构就是"为了更有效地强化其功能重要性并推行其政策"（Goodwin等，2006；Jones等，2005）。有学者进一步认为，区域机构实际上是一个新的政府层级，而不是传统行政体系的实质性重组（Harrison，2007；Deas和Lord，2006；Goodwin等，2005；Goodwin等，2006；Jones等，2005；Pearce和Ayres，2009）。这种区域层面管治的机构体系"为中央政府部门提供了直接的影响渠道"（Musson等，2005：1397）。

区域的复兴引发了不同地域之间管治的重组。随着西欧大量放权项目的开展，出现了一个新的概念——多层级管治，用来说明国家权力在不同尺度的管治层级上的分配（Marks等，1996，引自Yang，2005：2147）。然而，多层级管治概念被认为具有两方面的缺陷。多层级管治

> ……只强调了纵向的政策关系，而忽略了可能"交错多个尺度"的政策体系（Jessop，2001）。政策体系往往交织在一起影响多个尺度或某一地域的横向空间。多层级管治还试图显化这些层级内部的不同尺度——而在实践中管治的尺度实际是相对的，是不断被生产的（不只是由国家政府所创造）。（Goodwin等，2005：423）

也就是说，国家重组的过程是非常曲折的，完全不是预先设定的，而是充满了矛盾和冲突的。而且，复杂的管治重组不仅表现为纵向尺度上的重组，同时还涉及相同地域内各机构间的横向关系（Goodwin等，2005：432；Allmendinger和Haughton，2007）。更重要的是，多层级管治概念只是为当代管治现象提供了一个描述性框架，而没有提供任何视角来研究国家重组过程中实际发生的机制。同样，有关"国家空心化"的比喻也只是描述了"中央层级的权力被下放至其他尺度，而没有明确指出这样可能形成的组织和制度形式"（Goodwin等，2005：424）。因此，有学者认为国家重组的过程应该既是国家尺度权力的"空心化"过程，也是权力向其他尺度转移或"植入"的过程（同上：425）。也

rescaling process is 'a complex " qualitative process of state restructuring" rather than a simple " quantitative process of state erosion or diminution" ' (Peck, 2001: 447; cited in ibid: 424). As such, any investigation should not centre on the extent to which the national state has become less powerful, but rather how its power has been differently articulated (Musson et al., 2005; Peck, 2001: 447).

2.3.3 Territorial or relational approach to conceptualising spatiality

Although consensus is reached that regional geography is not pre-given or pre-established, but is an ongoing and contested process, theoretical disputes remain in terms of how to frame the spatial relations of the region. It is argued that the re-territorialisation argument has largely become entangled in a 'territorial trap' (Agnew, 1994, cited in Gualini, 2004: 331), or in other words, has gone too far in the direction of the state to 'state centrism' (Brenner, 1999b). That is, the re-territorialisation analysis is premised upon pre-defined multi-level governance and the macro-phenomenon of political economy and territorialisation of the state (Gualini, 2004: 331). Instead, it is argued that interested actors should be perceived from a micro- and aspatial dimension in order to reflect the network and relational aspects of the agents (ibid). That is, the non-scalar perspectives focus on the spatiality of socio-economic practices in terms of flow and connectivity (Lagendijk, 2007: 1202). Allen and Cochrane (2007) argue that the regional conception should be freed from the articulation of the hierarchical territorial jurisdictions, and the contemporary fuzzy and discontinuous region should be viewed as produced through a diffuse and fragmented engagement of both public and private political actors lodged at the regional assemblage. Yet, Harrison (2010: 22) contends that the investigated area of southeast England, on which the research of Allen and Cochrane (2007) is based, is a specific region in the UK territory. The boundaries in this region have less effect and appear to be more open and porous since southeast England is considered to be a polycentric global mega-city region with long-established economic links with the global city of London and political ties with Westminster and Whitehall (Pain, 2008; cited in Harrison, 2010: 22).

The relational approach does have certain merits in framing the agents in the territorial governance building process. However, MacKinnon and Shaw (2010) have argued that the territorial approach 'retains value over relational approaches' in that 'the relational approaches tend to view spaces as essentially unstructured and empty prior to its constitution by actor networks, reflecting an element of ontological 'levelling' derived from actor-network theory and other poststructuralist philosophies' (Mackinnon and Shaw, 2010: 1246). Similarly, Pike and Tomaney (2009) have also mentioned 'relational accounts ... risk

就是说,国家重组的过程是"一个复杂的'国家权力重组的质变过程',而不是一个简单的'国家权力消失或减弱的量变过程'"(Peck,2001:447;引自同上:424)。因此,任何研究的关注点都不应该是国家权力的弱化程度,而应该是国家权力的实施与以往有何不同(Musson等,2005;Peck,2001:447)。

三、从地域角度还是关联角度解读空间尺度

尽管理论界已经达成共识,同意区域地理不是一成不变或预先设定的,而是一个持续不断、充满矛盾和竞争的过程,但是在如何界定区域的空间关系上理论界仍存在争议。有学者认为再地域化的观点很大程度上落入了"地域陷阱"的圈套(Agnew,1994,引自Gualini,2004:331),或者说,在强调国家能动性上走偏了,变成了"国家中心主义"(Brenner,1999b)。总之,再地域化分析的前提是基于事先确定的多层级管治以及国家政治经济和再地域化的宏观环境(Gualini,2004:331)。相反,另一些学者认为需要从微观或非空间的角度来分析相关能动者,以便反映能动者之间相互关联的网络关系(ibid)。也就是说,这种非尺度的视角关注的是社会经济实践在流动性和关联联系方面的空间尺度(Lagendijk,2007:1202)。Allen和Cochrane(2007)认为区域概念应当摆脱层级制地域辖区的束缚;当今概念模糊、形式不连续的区域对象的产生,应当被看作一些代表公共及私人利益的政治能动者零星地、部分地参与区域事务的结果。但是,Harrison(2010:22)认为Allen和Cochrane(2007)所研究的东南英格兰是英国的一个特殊区域。这个区域的行政边界效力不大,而且更具开放性和可渗透性,因为东南英格兰是多中心的全球巨型城市区域,与全球城市伦敦和英国政治有着紧密的联系(Pain,2008;引自Harrison,2010:22)。

关联视角的研究方法对研究地域管治形成过程中的能动性的确有一定的帮助。但是,MacKinnon和Shaw(2010)认为地域视角"相比关联视角依然更有价值",因为"关联视角往往认为在能动者网络构筑空间之前,空间是无结构的、空白的,这反映了能动者网络理论和其他后结构主义理论的'扁平的'本体论观点"(Mackinnon和Shaw,2010:1246)。与之相似,Pike和Tomaney(2009)也提到"关联主义……可能给出的解释并不充分,它低估或忽视了制度和疆界

providing a partial explanation that can underplay or disregard the continued import of the territorialities of institutions and boundaries in governing economic development' (Pike and Tomaney, 2009: 29). In contrast, the territorially – and hierarchically – addressed state rescaling framework stresses the 'historically embedded and path-dependent nature of [the] restructuring process' (MacKinnon and Shaw, 2010: 1227). In other words, rather than a 'flattening ontology', it is admitted that the development of city-regions is embedded and is also influenced by the existing structure of political-administrative units.

With regard to the binary divisions of the territorial and relational approaches, it is deemed valuable not to set the territorial and relational views against each other. It is argued that bounded territory is not necessarily exclusively porous in its boundaries; thus, the territorial view of regions does not opt out of the concept of horizontal interaction from civil society, social institutions and business sectors (Morgan, 2007). It is further argued that the relational approach definitely has value in comprehending the contemporary economic space of flows; however, as for perceiving the politics of regions, 'the degree to which one interprets cities or regions as territorial and scalar or topological and networked "remains an open question: a matter to be resolved ex post and empirically rather than a priori and theoretically"' (MacLeod and Jones, 2007: 1186, cited in Harrison, 2010: 19). Based on England's southwest region, Jones and MacLeod found that the empirical case has 'realized both a political – economy of scale and a cultural construction of scale' (2004: 448). Alternatively, Harrison (2010) has demonstrated the production of a city-region is tangled with both 'the outcome of both relational economic processes and political claims to territory' (Harrison, 2010: 19) through exploring the initiatives and implications of The Northern Way Project of England. Overall, it is widely acknowledged that scale and territory is not withering away and that the state retains a pivotal regulatory role in city-region development, although this includes the considerable participation of social institutions and individuals. City-regions are therefore unable to escape territorially oriented designations; nevertheless, when appropriate, non – territorial and/or relational socio – economic and political strategies should be conjoined (Jones and MacLeod, 2004: 448).

2.4 Regions and new state spatiality

2.4.1 Regional scale, state spatial selectivity and new state spaces

Acknowledgment of the persistent role of the state, the rising importance of regional scale in contemporary policy and territorial governance is conceptualised to manifest a new form of 'spatial selectivity' by the state

在管治经济发展中的作用"(Pike 和 Tomaney,2009:29)。相反,地域视角则强调了"国家重组过程中的历史根植性和路径依赖"(MacKinnon 和 Shaw,2010:1227)。也就是说,相比关联主义"扁平的本体论",地域视角认为城市区域的形成是根植于历史的,并受现有政治行政单元结构的影响。

关于地域和关联视角这两种不同的取向,有学者认为二者不应该被视作是对立的。有学者提出封闭的地域并不一定是在边界上完全不可渗透的;也就是说,从地域角度理解的区域并非不接受存在来自民间、社会组织或商业部门等横向因素的影响的观点(Morgan,2007)。有人进一步提出,关联角度对于理解当今由各种流形成的经济空间显然很有意义;然而,就理解区域的政治因素影响来说,"到底在何种程度上可以把城市或区域解释成地域的、等级的,或拓扑关联的、网络的,'是个开放的问题:应该在实证研究后得出结论,而不是预先作出理论假设'"(MacLeod 和 Jones,2007:1186,引自 Harrison 2010:19)。基于英格兰西南区域的案例,Jones 和 MacLeod 发现,这个案例"同时体现了空间尺度的政治经济性和空间尺度的文化社会性"(2004:448)。另外,Harrison(2010)通过研究英格兰 Northern Way 区域政策提案及其影响,也证明了城市区域的形成是与"关联的经济过程和政治对地域的诉求"(Harrison,2010:19)交织在一起的。总之,学者普遍认为现实中空间尺度和地域并没有消亡,国家对城市区域的形成依然起着重要的监管作用,尽管这个形成过程中也包含大量社会机构和个人的参与。因此城市区域的理论解释不能脱离地域视角;然而,在符合现状的条件下,地域视角可以酌情添加非地域性的关联视角以给出理论框架(Jones 和 MacLeod,2004:448)。

第四节　区域与新国家空间尺度

一、区域尺度、国家空间尺度选择和新国家空间

在认识到了国家对区域形成的持久作用之后,区域尺度在当今政策和地域管治中日益重要的作用被认为是体现了一种新的国家"空间选择"(Jones,

(Jones, 1997, 2001; Goodwin et al., 2005; MacLeod and Goodwin, 1999b; MacLeod and Jones, 1999). In this sense, Jessop's strategic relational approach (SRA) to conceptualising the state and state power is highly relevant here (Jessop, 1990). It is perceived that the state 'has no power—it is merely an institutional ensemble; it has only a set of institutional capacities and liabilities which mediate that power; the power of the state is the power of the forces acting in and through the state. These forces include state managers as well as class forces, gender groups as well as regional interests, and so forth' (Jessop, 1990: 269-270: cited in Goodwin et al., 2006: 981). Drawing on the SRA, the concept of state spatiality, i.e. the multi-scalar organisation of state power (Brenner, 2004a: 452-53), is created to spatialise the form of the state. Built on the conceptualisation that state spatiality is more a dynamic, transformative and contested process than a fixed, pre-given and permanent thing, Brenner (2004a) perceives the development of statehood as a spatial process. Moreover, it is deemed that territoriality is only one dimension 'within the multi-layered geographical architectures of modern state spatiality' (Brenner, 2004b: 77). The state space not only refers to the institutional apparatus of the state organisation, but also to the strategies and policies that state institutions are mobilised to undertake (ibid: 80). Henceforth, each scale of state power can be analysed 'with reference to its internal organization form, institutional structure, and geographical boundaries,' as well as with reference to state activities and state interventions (ibid: 82). Thus, the process of change within states to different territorial parameters and structural configurations is defined as the unfolding of the rescaling of statehood (ibid: 105).

According to Jessop's strategic-relational state theory, the state is, in actuality, a system of strategic selectivity, through which state intervention is enacted (MacKinnon and Shaw, 2010: 1228). Brenner (2004b: 89 - 94) extended the concept of strategic selectivity and defined state spatial selectivity as comprising state spatial projects and state spatial strategies. This corresponds with Brenner's view of state space. The concept of state spatial projects refers to the specific programmes and initiatives that attempt to differentiate between or integrate state institutions and policy regimes across geographical scales and among different locations within the state's territory, whereas state spatial strategies relate to a range of policy instruments beyond the state apparatus (ibid: 92-93). Brenner (2004b: 97 - 100) then summarises the four axes of the evolution of state spatial selectivity, comprising the scalar and territorial dimensions of state spatial projects and state spatial strategies. The grid is thus divided into the centralising state spatial projects and singular state spatial strategies, the uniform administrative state spatial projects and equalising state spatial strategies, the decentralising state spatial projects and multiple scalar of state spatial strategies,

1997，2001；Goodwin 等，2005；MacLeod 和 Goodwin，1999b；MacLeod 和 Jones，1999）。从这个意义上说，Jessop 的战略关联方法（SRA）对理解国家和国家权力特别有益（Jessop，1990）。该理论认为国家本身"并不具有权力——它不过是一个制度体系而已；国家只是通过一系列的制度能力和责任来调解国家权力；国家的权力是国家背后的执政力量通过国家制度实施产生的权力。这些执政力量包括国家的管理者以及阶级力量、性别群体和区域利益集团，等等"（Jessop，1990：269-270：引自 Goodwin 等，2006：981）。为了使国家形态具有空间特征，有学者借鉴战略关联方法的观点提出了国家空间尺度的概念，亦即国家权力在多种空间尺度上的组织（Brenner，2004a：452-53）。Brenner（2004a）认为国家空间尺度是一个动态的、可变的、充满竞争的过程，而不是固定的、预设的、一成不变的。正是基于这一概念，Brenner 将国家权力的形成看作是一个空间过程。而且，他认为地域性只是"现代国家空间尺度的多层地理结构中"的一个维度（Brenner，2004b：77）。国家空间不仅指国家组织的制度框架，同时也包括国家机构所采取的战略和政策（同上：80）。因此，国家权力的各个尺度都可以"参照其内部组织形式、制度结构和地理边界"以及国家行为和国家干预来加以分析（同上：82）。国家内部不同地域边界和结构形态的变化过程可以定义为国家权力的尺度重组过程（同上：105）。

根据 Jessop 的战略关联国家理论，国家机器实际上是由一系列战略选择构成的，进而形成了国家干预（MacKinnon 和 Shaw，2010：1228）。Brenner（2004b：89-94）扩展了战略选择的概念，将国家空间选择定义为包含国家空间项目和国家空间战略。这与 Brenner 对国家空间的理解相吻合。国家空间项目是指用于区分或整合任何区域尺度或地域空间上的国家制度或政策机制的项目或措施；而国家空间战略则是指超越国家制度框架的一系列政策实施机制（同上：92-93）。Brenner（2004b：97-100）总结了国家空间选择演变的四个方向，包括国家空间项目和国家空间战略的尺度与地域维度。也就是说，这个网格可以分为集权的国家空间项目和单一的国家空间战略，统一的行政国家空间项目和均衡的国家空间战略，分权的国家空间项目和多尺度的国家空间战

and customised state spatial projects and differentiating state spatial strategies (Brenner, 2004b: 102). Subsequently, the evolution of state spaces can be decoded as the 'complex amalgamations' of state spatial selectivity with a particular historical formation of state spatiality. It is hence argued that the new state spaces of the changing statehood: '···should be viewed as the outcomes of multiple tendencies of state spatial restructuring whose precise institutional and geographical contours remain deeply contested and thus highly unstable ...' 'The restructuring of state spatiality rarely entails the complete dissolution of entrenched political geographies ...' (Brenner, 2004b: 107).

> ...New territorial and scalar geographies of state power are forged through a contested open – ended interaction of historically inherited configurations of state spatial organization with newly emergent state spatial projects and state spatial strategies at various geographical scales.
> (Brenner, 2004b: 111)

Although the above abstract concept introduced by Brenner has demonstrated his recognition of the contingency and social construction of state spaces, it is argued that the conceptual framework only shows concern for economic and political logic by the tool of state spatial projects and state spatial strategies, thus neglecting the factors of social power and the process of social reproduction (Varro, 2010: 1257–1258, 1273; Ward and Jonas, 2004). In other words, the abstract logic of structural contradictions between state regulation and economic accumulation tend to be privileged over civil society as the driver of hegemonic projects when analysing the state (Oosterlynck, 2010: 1156). It is generalised by Brenner (2004b) that the state apparatus has been downscaled from the national state to urban localities in response to post–Fordist crises such as fiscal deficit and urban degradation resulting from post – Fordist industrial restructuring; recently, statehood has again been upscaled from the urban to the meso – level region to counterbalance severe inter – locality competition and to prevent enlarging uneven development. Overall, it is perceived that the changing state spatiality, i.e. the process of state rescaling, represents the restless search of the state for 'spatio – temporal fixes' to the ever – changing wider political economy. It is hence contended that the approach is more effective in identifying the general trend and driving forces such as competition – oriented local politics than in decoding the particularities of the politics (Varro, 2010: 1254).

In short, while the social and political construct of the state is a fundamental concept in strategic–relational state theory and new state spaces, the current analysis tends to be structurally rather than contextually charged. It is contended that the strategic projects and strategies, or the process of rescaling, can be adapted and utilised for a multitude of purposes by different groups. As

略,以及定制化的国家空间项目和差异化的国家空间战略(Brenner,2004b:102)。由此,国家空间的演变可以理解为国家空间选择与特定国家空间尺度历史结构的"复杂融合"。因此,在国家权力变化中产生的新的国家空间"……应该被看作多重国家空间重组趋势的结果,而最终的制度和地理轮廓则依然受到不同力量的挑战,非常不稳定……""国家空间尺度的重组很少会引发长久形成的政治地理的瓦解……"(Brenner,2004b:107)

> ……国家权力的新地域和尺度地理是通过历史形成的国家空间结构与新出现的各种地理尺度上的国家空间项目和国家空间战略之间不断发生相互竞争作用而形成的,最终什么可能性都有。(Brenner,2004b:111)

从Brenner提出的上述抽象概念中可以看出他对国家空间形成的偶然性和社会建构性的认同,但是有些学者认为这个概念框架只关注了国家空间项目和国家空间战略及其经济和政治逻辑,忽略了社会力量的因素和社会再生产过程(Varro,2010:1257-1258,1273;Ward 和 Jonas,2004)。也就是说,在对国家能动性进行分析时,总会倾向认为是抽象的国家管制和经济积累的结构性矛盾导致了国家重组,而忽略了民间社会推动重要项目的力量(Oosterlynck,2010:1156)。就如Brenner(2004b)总结的那样,国家制度框架从国家尺度下移至地方城市尺度,是为了应对财政赤字和城市衰败等后福特工业时代的危机,而最近国家尺度又从城市尺度上移至中间一级的区域尺度,则是为了减少地方之间的激烈竞争,并防止日益加剧的发展不均衡问题。总之,他认为不断变化的国家空间尺度,亦即国家尺度重组的过程,反映了国家在不断寻找"时空解决策略"来应对时刻变化着的政治经济状况。因此有学者认为这种理论视角更适用于厘清一般性的演变趋势和驱动力,例如竞争导向的地方政治,而不适合用来解释特殊的政治因素(Varro,2010:1254)。

简言之,尽管国家的社会和政治构成性是战略关联国家理论和新国家空间理论的基础概念之一,但目前的分析仍是着眼于结构性的问题,而不是基于地方情况的具体分析。有学者认为,事实上这些战略项目和策略,或者说国家

such, the research should focus on understanding the divergent sub-national politics where regionalism is situated, rather than summarising what is convergent around the new regionalism.

2.4.2 Process-based approach to scale and the politics of re-scaling: the building process of regional scale

As put forward by Jonas and Ward (2007: 176), 'the emergence of city-regions [is]... the product of a particular set of economic, cultural, environmental and political projects, each with their own logics'. With regard to the attempt to understand the place-specific and actual-existing process involved in the production of regions, Jonas and Ward (2002: 396-397) propose that three fundamental questions need to be addressed, namely, the roles played by different levels of government, the different logic underpinning urban and regional programmes, and the local development contexts within these city-regions, rather than merely focus on global context. That is, there are not only different context-sensible regionalisms across territories, but also different actors from multiple scales to manipulate at the same scale for different interests. The introduction of the lens of political agencies to the state relational approach is of crucial importance, since it shows that it is actually the actors that are 'acting through the state' rather than '...the state itself that is pursuing glocalisation strategies' (Oosterlynck, 2010: 1158). That is to say, 'place-sensitive (or locally dependent) agents may act in the name of certain regionally based and imagined community places and localities' (ibid).

While some of Brenner's work (2004a, b) is criticised for seeming to imply that state rescaling is 'pre-formed from abstract processes that operate "behind the backs" of individual actors' (MacKinnon and Shaw, 2010: 1231), Brenner (2002) has demonstrated his recognition that the regional building process is not consolidated, with a singular, unified and internally coherent agenda. He argues that, under the general conditions of post-Fordist state restructuring, the urban and regional transforming project is, in the meantime, permeated by internal conflict and contradictions. These place-specific internal processes make various regional projects heterogeneous from each other, both institutionally and politically. Brenner identified the movement towards a 'new politics of scales', in which 'local, state-level and federal institutions and actors, as well as local social movements, are struggling to adjust to diverse restructuring processes that are unsettling inherited patterns of territorial and scalar organization within major US city-regions' (Brenner, 2002: 3). That is, various interactions exist between state and non-state actors, and various forms of political actions at the root of rescaling processes (Boudreau, 2007: 2608).

空间重组的过程,可以被不同团体根据各种目的进行调整和利用。因此,研究不应只是总结新区域主义共性的地方,而是发现和解释造成区域主义产生的不同的国内政治因素。

二、基于过程分析尺度和尺度重组的政治因素:区域尺度的形成过程

正如 Jonas 和 Ward(2007:176)所提出的那样,"城市区域的出现(是)……一系列特定的经济、文化、环境和政治项目的产物,这些项目都各有自己的逻辑"。为了理解各地不同而又实际存在的区域产生过程,Jonas 和 Ward(2002:396-97)提出不能仅仅关注国际环境,还应该关注三个基本研究问题,即不同层级政府发挥的作用,不同城市和区域项目背后的逻辑,以及这些城市或区域内的地方发展背景。也就是说,区域主义不仅因地域背景不同而不同,还因不同尺度的不同作用者的不同利益而不同。因此,在国家关联视角中引入政治动因的研究至关重要,因为它表明实际上是能动者"在透过国家制度发挥作用",而不是"……国家本身在推行全球地方化战略"(Oosterlynck,2010:1158)。也就是说,"地方性的(或地方依赖的)能动者可以以某种想象的区域性的地方社区的名义来发挥作用"(同上)。

尽管有人批评 Brenner 的一些研究(2004a,b)似乎意味着国家重组"是由个体作用者'背后'的抽象经济力量所主导"(MacKinnon 和 Shaw,2010:1231),但 Brenner(2002)表明他已认识到区域的建构过程并不稳固稳定,没有统一的议程。他认为在后福特主义时代国家重塑的大背景下,城市和区域转型项目同时也充斥着内部冲突和矛盾。这些地方性的内部过程使各种区域项目不论在体制形式上还是政治目的上都各不相同。Brenner 将这种过程称为"新的尺度政治",即"地方、国家和联邦机构及能动者,以及地方社会运动,都在极力适应各种打破美国既有主要城市区域地域尺度结构的重组过程"(Brenner,2002:3)。这就是说,在重组的根源上存在着国家与非国家能动者,以及各种形式的政治行动之间的相互作用(Boudreau,2007:2608)。根据这个推论,新的国家

Following the line of reasoning, the new state spaces are actually 'the subject of political conflict and struggle between actors and interests operating in and across different spatial scales' (MacKinnon and Shaw, 2010: 1231). Overall, 'political agencies' and 'politics of scale' are the crucial concepts through which to examine the actual existing state rescaling process. Furthermore, the rise of new state spaces is something that should be investigated than assumed or generalised.

2.4.3 Planning and governance: the production of 'new state spaces' by means of planning

Since the 1990s, Western European countries have witnessed the revival of strategic spatial planning, especially at the national and regional scale (Albrechts, 2004, 2006; Albrechts et al., 2003). The changing trajectory is well represented by the fall and rise of regional planning in the UK. British regional planning culminated in the 1950s and 1960s: plans were not only imposed on large cities and metropolitan areas to enhance amenities and direct overspill (Cullingworth and Nadin, 2006: 23), but were also accompanied by a role of social redistribution through a strategic approach to land use control and investment (Healey et al., 1997: 3). However, regional planning was devalued and shifted to urban policies and projects (Hall, 1999), and was narrowed down to land use regulation in the 1980s (Thornley, 1993). In the late 1990s, regional planning was reinvigorated, which was marked by the 1997 Blair government, which re-established the regional government bodies and reintroduced regional planning. Further reform was undertaken in 2004, when the spatial planning approach was widely adopted within the UK planning system.

In comparison to regional planning in the 1960s, strategic planning since the 1980s has been re-modified, both in terms of its planning objectives and policy priorities. Whilst traditional British planning is labelled as regulative and allocative, the more recent version is found to be more strategic, proactive and developmental (Faludi, 2000; Healey et al., 1997: 241; Healey, 2006). Policy priorities are reoriented from reorganising physical space to broader scopes including economic development and environmental sustainability, in particular (Healey et al., 1997: 241). Land use regulations have been simplified to speed decision - making and ensure the growth of projects (Allmendinger and Haughton, 2009; Nadin, 2007). Moreover, the new spatial planning approach in the 2000s has further seen the reworking of the scale of policy making, as well as an expansion of the scope of the policy parameters (Allmendinger and Haughton, 2007). First of all, spatial planning is privileged to the sub-national level of planning, away from urban regeneration projects. Particularly in the

空间实际上是"在不同空间尺度上运作的各种能动者和利益体政治冲突与争夺的对象"(MacKinnon和Shaw,2010:1231)。总之,"政治能动性"和"尺度政治"是研究现实中发生的国家尺度重组过程的核心概念。而新国家空间的出现是一个必须进行实证研究的问题,并不是可以简单推测或概括的。

三、规划和管治:通过规划产生的"新国家空间"

上世纪90年代以来,西欧国家见证了战略空间规划的复兴,特别是在国家和区域尺度(Albrechts,2004;2006;Albrechts等,2003)。英国区域规划的起落恰好说明了这个变化的轨迹。英国区域规划在20世纪50至60年代达到顶峰:不仅对大城市和都市地区进行规划以改善其生活设施和疏散过剩人口(Cullingworth和Nadin,2006:23),同时也采取土地利用管制和投资等战略手段产生了社会再分配的作用(Healey等,1997:3)。然而,到了80年代,区域规划不再受到重视,开始转向城市政策和城市项目(Hall,1999),规划内容缩小到了土地利用监管(Thornley,1993)。到90年代后期,区域规划重新兴起,其标志性事件就是1997年布莱尔政府重新设立了区域政府机构并重新推行区域规划。2004年实行了进一步改革,整个英国规划体系自此广泛采用空间规划方法。

与60年代的区域规划相比,80年代开始的战略规划在规划目标和政策重点上都发生了改变。传统的英国规划是以管制和分配为主,而近年来的规划却更具战略性和前瞻性,更重视发展(Faludi,2000;Healey等,1997:241;Healey,2006)。政策重点从重新组织物质空间转向更宽泛的方面,特别是包括经济发展和环境可持续发展(Healey等,1997:241)。土地利用管制的程序被简化以加速决策和保证项目的开发(Allmendinger和Haughton,2009;Nadin,2007)。此外,进入21世纪以后,实施的新空间规划方法更体现了政策制定尺度的变化,以及政策范围的扩展(Allmendinger和Haughton,2007)。首先,空间规划侧重于次国家层级的规划,不再以城市复兴项目为主。特别是英国,次区

case of British planning, the Structure Plan at the sub-regional level has been abolished, while the Regional Spatial Strategies (RSS) steered by the central government has been empowered with statutory status (Bianconi et al., 2006). As a result, although new spatial planning is embedded in community engagement and closer communication between hierarchies of government, the power of strategy making is rescaled from the local to the central and regional level. Secondly, the renewed positive view for planning is shaped by the ambition that new spatial planning will bring all involved policy sectors and stakeholders within and outside government to work together for the far-reaching development vision. In this way, the content of planning is not limited to land use planning, but to a broadened agenda such as environmental issues and economic development. As a consequence, the ownership of spatial planning is not only restricted to planners, but is open to all departments of government and partnerships that have a spatial concern or effect (Nadin, 2007). Apart from the existing levels of sub-national and sub-regional planning, many new plans are initiated by actors outside the public sector and do not correspond with the boundaries of administrative divisions. The emergence of soft planning spaces aims to break down bureaucratic barriers and directly point to the real boundaries of problems (Allmendinger and Haughton, 2009). In other words, the spatial and policy boundaries of new spatial planning are becoming soft and fuzzy (Allmendinger and Haughton, 2007). To sum up, the broadened thematic focus, the privilege of the city-regional realm transcending beyond administrative boundaries to functional geographies, and the transition from hierarchical and bureaucratic government to horizontal and associative governance in the new planning practice have been noted as the trend towards 'new regionalism' (Wheeler, 2002).

The notion of 'new state spaces' is helpful in understanding the changing nature of the current regional plan. With reference to the state theory, new spatial planning is considered to be part of the state's 'restless search' for governance (Allmendinger and Haughton, 2009: 631). It suggests that the new planning spaces are strategically 'filled in' by the state to create or privilege new scales of governance (Haughton et al., 2009: 234). The re-working of the scale and the scope of planning are argued to be two indispensable elements of the current state restructuring process (Allmendinger and Haughton, 2007). The shifted scale of planning represents the renewed policy terrain for state intervention in response to the changing context: '...spatial planning is a contributor to and a reflection of a more fundamental reform of territorial management...' (Allmendinger and Haughton, 2009: 620). For example, the networked feature of new economies leads to the privilege of the city-region scale in new spatial planning (Nadin, 2007). However, on the other hand, and

域层级的结构规划被取消了,而由中央政府主导的区域空间战略规划(RSS)则被赋予了法律地位(Bianconi 等,2006)。因此,尽管新空间规划也有社区的参与和各层级政府的交流,但制定战略规划的大权实际是由地方上移到了中央和区域层面。其次,之所以重新重视新空间规划,是因为政府希望新空间规划可以使所有政府内外的政策部门和利益相关者共同合作,达成广泛的发展共识。于是,规划的内容不再限于土地利用规划,而是扩展至更宽泛的议题,如环境问题和经济发展。因此,空间规划的所有权不再只属于规划编制者,而同时属于所有对空间有关注或影响的政府部门和合作团体(Nadin,2007)。除了现有的次国家和次区域尺度的规划以外,非公共部门的行动者也发起了许多新的规划,而且这些规划往往与行政区划的边界并不完全吻合。这种软规划空间的出现是为了打破行政壁垒,直接针对实际存在问题的边界(Allmendinger 和 Haughton,2009)。换言之,新空间规划的空间和政策边界变得软化而模糊了(Allmendinger 和 Haughton,2007)。总之,新规划中主题的拓宽、对超越行政边界的城市区域和功能性地理范围的重视,以及从等级制和行政制政府运作到横向的联合管治的转变,被认为是"新区域主义"的发展趋势(Wheeler,2002)。

"新国家空间"的概念对理解当前区域规划变化的本质非常有益。根据国家理论,新空间规划是国家"不断寻找"管治方法的一部分(Allmendinger 和 Haughton,2009:631)。该理论认为,新规划空间是国家战略性的"植入",目的是创建或强调新的管治尺度(Haughton 等,2009:234)。规划尺度和内容的重组被认为是当前国家重组过程中不可或缺的两个要素(Allmendinger 和 Haughton,2007)。规划尺度的变化体现了国家干预为应对环境变化而开拓的新政策领域:"……空间规划促进并反映了更根本性的地域管制改革……"(Allmendinger 和 Haughton,2009:620)。例如,新经济体的网络化特征导致新空间规划更加强调城市区域的尺度(如 Nadin,2007)。然而,另一方面,作为一

as a more fundamental mechanism, the re-introduction of regional-level governance is a new 'fix' to the crisis produced by urban entrepreneurialism in the 1980s (Brenner, 2004a, b). For example, the aim of collaboration between regional spatial planning in England and different levels of government and disparate policymakers is the main improvement that is sought after: fragmented government and partnerships is just like 'a bowl of spaghetti' and leads to confusion over lines of accountability (Nadin, 2007: 45-47). Overall, even though the new strategic spatial planning process is more democratic and less exclusive, it is found that governments still play a significant role in plan-making (Albrechts, 2006). These regional planning efforts have represented revived 'government-led strategic interventions at the urban and regional level' (Albrechts et al., 2003: 114).

2.5 Summary: theoretical perspectives on city-region governance

The above literature, from the political economic perspective, has presented city-region development in a reflective way. The approach sees the designation of the city-region as politically constructed, historically embedded and culturally contested, and emphasises the role of the state in the formation process. The NSS framework (Brenner, 2004b) further explores the ongoing transformation of regional governance with regard to the restructuring of state power. The political economic perspective and the NSS framework are useful in addressing Chinese regional manifestations because they do not treat the emergence of regions as a neutral occurrence, which seems to be naturally-developed and pre-given; rather, it is a result of political-economic struggles. Therefore, the perspective is particularly useful to unravel the actual processes by which such regional territories have been constructed and reconstructed throughout history.

The territorial/scale approach, rather than the relational approach, is assumed to be more appropriate in the Chinese context, since democracy has not improved much in China over the past decades. Therefore, 'state-centred political economy perspectives incorporating the imperative of sustaining control by the Party-state', which are applicable to China in the last half century from 1949 to 2000 (Ma, 2002: 1546), may still account for many of the Chinese transformations in the present day. Therefore, the NSS framework developed by Brenner (2004b) is followed by the study as a key framework to conceptualise the restructuring of state and the development of regional scale. The notions of 'state spatiality' and 'state spatial selectivity' are helpful, since they incorporate all the state activities ranging from strategies and policies to administrative institutions. By these means, all of the state actions can be examined through the insights of state theory, which can help to understand the nature of the

个更具根本性的机制,区域层面管治的重新引入是为了"解决"上世纪80年代以来城市经营主义导致的危机(Brenner,2004a,b)。例如,英格兰区域空间规划与不同层级政府和不同政策制定者之间的合作目的就是为了解决像"一碗意大利面一样"纠缠不清的分割的政府管治和公共合作关系,厘清混乱的公私部门职责界限(Nadin,2007:45-47)。总之,尽管新战略空间规划的过程更加民主、更具包容性,但是政府在规划制定中仍然发挥着重要作用(Albrechts,2006)。这些区域规划的尝试代表了"政府在城市和区域层面所主导的战略干预"(Albrechts等,2003:114)。

第五节　小结:城市区域管治的理论视角

上述文献从政治经济学角度反映了对城市区域形成的辩证认识。这种研究方法认为城市区域的形成受到政治因素、历史沿袭、文化冲突的影响,同时强调了国家在这一形成过程中的作用。新国家空间理论框架(Brenner,2004b)进一步将区域管治的变化与国家权力的重塑联系在一起。政治经济学视角和新国家空间理论框架对研究中国的区域形成非常有用,因为它们并未将区域的出现看作一种自然形成的、约定俗成的孤立的现象,而是政治经济矛盾的结果。因此,这个视角对揭示历史上区域地域的形成和重塑的过程特别有帮助。

地域/尺度方法或许要比关联方法更适用于中国的背景,因为中国的民主发展在过去几十年间的进步并不大。因此,1949年到2000年这半个世纪以来"以国家为中心的政治经济学视角及一贯的党政控制"(Ma,2002:1546)依然可以用来解释当前中国的许多变化。本研究采纳了Brenner(2004b)的新国家空间理论框架作为本研究的主要框架来阐述国家的重塑和区域尺度的形成。"国家空间尺度"和"国家空间尺度选择"的概念对本研究非常有帮助,因为它们包含了各种国家行动,包括国家战略、政策和行政体制等。借助这些概念,所有的国家行动都可以从国家理论的视角来进行研究,从而帮助理解这些变化的

changes, for example, in terms of planning. All in all, even though Brenner's work predominantly aims to theorise the transformation of regional governance from the capitalist state and economy in general, the concept tools in his framework are still relevant and can be borrowed for the analysis of the state, even in a totally different context.

Although the NSS framework fundamentally accepts that the state spaces are politically charged, socially constructed and culturally contested, the framework does not offer effective tools to examine the causal relationships and dynamic processes of the changing statehood. Brenner's theory (2004a, b) is criticised for its predisposition to conceptualise the new regionalism as a process of state rescaling in response to the broader context of political economy under globalisation and crisis management of capitalism (Jonas and Pincetl, 2006; Oosterlynck, 2010; Varro, 2010; Ward and Jonas, 2004). This also runs contrary to the central discussion from the political economic perspective that regionalism is not pre - established or consolidated. Therefore, building upon the NSS framework on state spatiality, the study has also introduced the lens of 'political agency' and 'politics of scale' for use as research tools to examine Chinese specific processes and politics of the development of city-region governance.

Meanwhile, although the theoretical stance adopted by the research is generally based on the political economic approach, the awareness of the debate on the economics in the political economy of city-regions (Harding, 2007) also reminds the researcher to be aware of the role of economic development and economic logic in the process of city-regional development. In the next section, the existing regional studies in China will be reviewed and the theoretical and empirical gap will be highlighted.

2.6 A literature review of contemporary regional studies in China

2.6.1 Regional development, model transition and the implication for regional inequalities

Since the first decade after economic reform, the rapid development and transformation of the Pearl River Delta (PRD) in Guangdong Province has caught the attention of scholars. The southern region, which is the first area opened to the outside, has become a laboratory in which to examine China's changing regional development and governance in the 1980s.

Lo (1989) examined the impact of rural reform and the open-door policy on the urbanisation and economic development of the PRD. One significant

实质,例如规划变化的本质。总之,尽管 Brenner 的理论主要是针对资本主义国家的区域管治变化,但我们依然可以借鉴他的理论框架中的这些概念工具来分析国家的变化,即使是在一个完全不同的背景下。

尽管新国家空间理论框架本质上认为国家空间受到政治、社会和文化因素的影响,但是该框架本身并未提供有效的工具来研究国家空间尺度变化的驱动力量及动态过程。有学者对 Brenner 的理论(2004a,b)提出批评,认为他的主要观点是将新区域主义看作全球化和资本主义危机治理的政治经济大背景下产生的国家尺度变化过程(Jonas 和 Pincetl,2006;Oosterlynck,2010;Varro,2010;Ward 和 Jonas,2004)。这也与政治经济学视角的观点相悖,政治经济学理论认为区域主义既不是预先设定的,也不成熟稳定。因此,本研究以新国家空间理论框架的国家空间尺度概念为基础,同时还以"政治能动性"和"尺度政治"的视角为工具来研究中国城市区域管治形成的具体过程和政治因素。

同时,尽管本研究采用的主要理论观点是基于政治经济学视角的,但研究者也注意到了有关城市区域政治经济中经济因素的作用的讨论(Harding,2007),因此也对城市区域形成过程中经济发展和经济逻辑的作用予以了相应重视。下一节中将回顾中国现有的区域研究,并指出这些研究在理论和实证上的不足。

第六节 中国当代区域研究的文献综述

一、区域发展、模式转变和对区域不平衡发展的影响

中国经济改革十年后,广东省珠三角地区的快速发展和变化吸引了众多学者的关注。这个位于中国南部的区域是第一个对外开放的地区,现在已经成为研究中国自上世纪80年代以来区域发展和管治变化的实验样板。

Lo(1989)研究了农村改革以及改革开放政策对珠三角地区城市化和经济

change is the industrialisation of the rural economy in the villages and towns (Lo, 1989: 299). With the advantage of cultural affinity, county level officials (ibid) scrambled for foreign investment, mainly from Hong Kong. The economic restructuring subsequently brought along urbanisation and population change (ibid: 301). The changes are uneven in the delta, since the cities of Foshan, Shunde, Panyu, Dongguan and Jiangmen, which are close to the provincial capital Guangzhou, received the most benefit from the development and become the core of the growth in the region (ibid: 302). Correspondently, clusters of town settlements were stimulated in the area (ibid: 304). During the early stage of development, migration in the delta was short - distanced: industrial workers were formerly the surplus agricultural work forces from the same county/city or from the same village (ibid: 305). Moreover, because urban reform lagged behind rural reform in the 1980s, the overall industrial development in the surrounding rural area even surpassed that of Guangzhou and, hence, there was no overwhelming migration into the large cities (ibid).

The general features of PRD development revealed by Lo (1989) were intensively studied in the following decade. Sit and Yang (1997) identified the peculiar urbanisation pattern in the post - reform period, which was predominantly induced by external forces of foreign investment. Therefore, the economic momentum was contingent upon the distribution of foreign direct investment (FDI). Shen et al. (2000) found that, initially, areas with a geographical proximity to Hong Kong tended to receive more FDI. Although the distance factor gradually faded after the 1980s, the attractiveness of these cities was reinforced over development (Shen et al., 2000: 320). This is because industrial know - how, infrastructures and business environments were developing in the area (ibid: 321).

The metropolitan development of PRD in the first decade is characterised by rural industrialisation and the enormous transformation at the periphery of existing urban centres (Lin, 2001a, b). In other words, the urbanisation did not result in magnificent rural-urban migration and the increase of the primary city (Xu and Li, 1990). Conversely, urbanisation was accelerated by the relaxed control on town designations; hence, the increased number of designated towns, as well as the growth of towns in terms of both economy and population (Ma and Lin, 1993). Henceforth, the development of peri-urban zones produced a high mixture of agricultural and industrial activities in towns and villages (Lin, 2001a: 67), and the distinct spatial phenomenon of desa kota found in other developing Asian countries (Lin, 2001b). This is in stark contrast to the situation during the Maoist period, when the delineation between city and countryside was strictly constrained. Compared to the rapid development of some selective rural areas, the growth of major cities was relatively slow during

发展的影响。其中一个重要的变化就是乡镇农村经济的工业化(Lo,1989：299)。县级官员纷纷利用文化亲缘优势争夺外资,主要是港资(同上)。经济结构的重组随即带来了城市化和人口构成的变化(同上：301)。这种变化在珠三角地区的分布并不是均匀的,靠近省会广州的城市,如佛山、顺德、番禺、东莞和江门从经济发展中获益最多,成为了该区域经济增长的核心(同上：302)。这种经济发展相应地刺激了该区域城镇的集聚(同上：304)。在发展早期,珠三角地区内的人口迁徙都是短距离的:产业工人都是来自本市、本县乃至本村的剩余农业劳动力(同上：305)。而且,由于80年代城市改革落后于农村改革,周边农村地区的整体工业发展水平甚至超过了广州,因而并没有出现大量人口向大城市迁徙的情况(Lo,1989：305)。

在随后的十年里有不少学者对Lo(1989)所揭示的珠三角发展的一般特征进行了研究。Sit和Yang(1997)探讨了改革开放后这个地区特有的城市化模式,认为这种变化主要是由外资等外力因素驱动的。因此,经济发展的势头依赖于外商直接投资的分布。Shen等(2000)发现,起初邻近香港的地区往往因地理优势而获得更多外商直接投资。尽管20世纪80年代后这种距离效应逐渐减弱,但是这些靠近香港的城市也在发展的过程中增强了自身的吸引力(Shen等,2000：320)。这是因为这些地区的工业技术、基础设施和商务环境都在不断发展(同上：321)。

改革开放头十年珠三角地区都市发展的主要特征是现有城市中心周边地区的农村工业化和巨大转型(Lin,2001a,b)。也就是说,城市化并没有导致农村人口向城市的大规模迁徙和首位城市的增长(Xu和Li,1990)。相反,城市化的进程还因城镇建制的放松而有所加快,建制镇的数量增加了,城镇的经济和人口也有了增长(Ma和Lin,1993)。由此,半城市化地区的发展使得乡镇出现了农业与工业活动的高度混合(Lin,2001a：67),同时也出现了亚洲其他发展中国家所见到的那种"desa kota"(乡村城市)的特殊空间形态(Lin,2001b)。这与改革开放前的状况是完全不同的,当时城市与乡村之间有着严格的界限。

the period of time (Lin, 2001b). This is because of the state policy to control the development of large cities and the persistent control of population movement to large cities.

As a result, even the regional discrepancy in Guangdong Province was weakened to some extent (Weng, 1998: 440), particularly between Guangzhou and the nearby countryside (Lo, 1989: 305). However, since the development of rural towns was intensively concentrated in the delta area around Shenzhen, Dongguan, Zhongshan, Shunde, and Panyu, there was still a remarkable gap between the delta core and the periphery area of Guangdong Province (Lo, 1989: 306–307; Fan, 1995: 443; Gu et al., 2001). It appears this tendency has been reinforced since the 1990s, with further globalisation and marketisation, maybe even more so due to the current economic restructuring from manufacturing to a knowledge and service economy (Lu and Wei, 2007).

The flourishing of towns in PRD is termed by scholars as 'urbanization from below' (Ma and Lin, 1993: 603) or 'spontaneous urbanization' (Shen et al, 2002) in comparison with city-based urbanisation in the period prior to reform. Before economic reform, the development of urbanisation was reliant on the top-down allocation of resources according to a central plan. Large cities were the major recipients of resources because they were located with large state enterprises, which was more efficient in terms of production (Ma and Lin, 1993: 583). Even the satellite towns of Shanghai and Beijing were mostly engaged in agricultural production with sluggish growth (ibid: 603). The massive transformation of the rural economy after economic reform resulted from the state's 'tacit laissez faire' policy towards rural areas rather than the central government's active support (ibid: 602). Lin (1997) affirmed that market forces and local developmental initiatives were the main contributors to the rural economy in the post-reform PRD region. More recently, Shen et al. (2002, 2006) and Wong et al. (2003) have conducted further investigations into the urbanisation pattern in the PRD region during the 1980s and 1990s. It is argued that both city-based urbanisation and town-based rural urbanisation exist in the post-reform urbanisation process. Furthermore, since the late 1990s, more concentrated urbanisation has appeared to take place in large cities such as Shenzhen (Shen et al., 2006).

Through examination of regional development, the changing governance and rising role of the local state have been detected and documented by many scholars. Eng (1997: 555) described officials of local governments and foreign investors as the most important players in Guangdong's market-oriented economic development processes. The structural changes that came with economic reform and decentralisation have reoriented local governments from being agents of central government to implementing administrative commands to

与某些农村地区的快速发展相比,大城市的发展在这段时期相对缓慢(Lin,2001b)。这是因为国家实行了控制大城市发展的政策,并且一直在控制向大城市的人口迁移。

因此,即使在广东省内,区域差异也在一定程度上有所降低(Weng,1998:440),特别是广州与周边农村地区之间的差异(Lo,1989:305)。然而,由于农村乡镇的发展主要集中在珠三角的深圳、东莞、中山、顺德和番禺地区,因此实际上三角洲中心与边缘地域的差距仍然很大(Lo,1989:306-307;Fan,1995:443;Gu等,2001)。这种趋势似乎在20世纪90年代后随着全球化和市场化的进一步发展而有所强化,而近期从制造业向知识经济和服务经济的转型甚至可能使这种趋势更为突出(Lu和Wei,2007)。

珠三角地区城镇的迅猛发展被学者称为"自下而上的城市化"(Ma和Lin,1993:603)或"自发的城市化"(Shen等,2002),这种农村城市化显示出了与改革开放前以城市为基础的城市化的区别。在经济改革之前,城市化的发展依赖于中央计划自上而下的资源分配。大城市是主要的资源接受者,因为生产效率较高的大型国家企业一般都在大城市(Ma和Lin,1993:583)。在这个时期,即使是上海和北京的卫星城市发展也相当慢,主要从事农业生产(参见同上:603)。改革开放后农村经济巨大转变的主要原因在于中央对农村地区的"自由发展"政策,而不是中央政府的积极支持(同上:602)。Lin(1997)的研究也证明市场力量和地方发展的积极性是改革开放后珠三角地区农村经济发展的主要促进因素。其后,Shen等(2002,2006)和Wong等(2003)对珠三角地区20世纪80至90年代的城市化发展模式做了跟进研究。他们认为改革开放后珠三角的城市化进程中同时存在基于城市的城市化和基于乡镇的农村工业化现象。此外,从90年代末期开始,在深圳等大城市似乎出现了更为集中的城市化发展(Shen等,2006)。

基于对区域发展的研究,许多学者发现并论述了政府管治的相应变化以及地方政府日益重要的作用。Eng(1997:555)认为地方政府官员和投资外商是广东市场经济发展中最重要的角色。经济改革和权力下放所带来的结构性变化使地方政府从中央政府行政指令的执行机构转变为地方经济发展中的主

actors of the development of local economies, which has realigned the interests of local officials with those of foreign investors (Eng, 1997: 555 – 556). The local governments gained development capital, local taxes, administrative fees and land revenue from foreign investors (ibid: 558), while foreign investors have benefited from a large pool of cheap labour, sufficient supply of land, efficient and friendly government service, and relaxed and flexible governance (ibid: 555). However, the alliance between local governments and investors would skew the priority of urban development from the provision of public goods to production – related services such as infrastructure, and this type of development poses ecological tensions and human resources problems for future economic growth and urbanisation (ibid: 565-566).

In the meantime, revitalised towns and countryside were seen in the Yangtze River Delta (YRD) in the 1980s (Ma and Fan, 1994). In contrast to PRD, this progress was mainly driven by the growth of collectively – owned town and village enterprises (TVEs) (Oi, 1995; Walder, 1995) rather than FDI. However, since the mid-1990s, there has been a gradual transformation of TVEs in YRD in terms of both organisation and ownership (Shen and Ma, 2005: 761 – 762). This is because the Sunan model, the regional development driven by TVEs (ibid: 764), has met with bottlenecks since the early 1990s (ibid: 763). Because the Wenzhou model in Zhejiang Province, which was developed through private enterprises (Liu, 1992; Parris, 1993), remained vibrant and competitive, the privatisation of collective ownership was encouraged (Shen and Ma, 2005: 763).

The pervasive privatisation of property rights since the second half of the 1990s (Han and Pannell, 1999; Li and Rozelle, 2000; Wei, 2002: 1740) has changed the nature of the Sunan model. Subsequently, the model's transition has implied the changing role of local state in YRD. Before privatisation, the local government was intimately involved in enterprise activities (Huang, 1990; Oi, 1995; Walder, 1995) with the benefits of direct administrative interventions in the market, bank loans and other resources. After the reform of property rights, the government was expected to refrain from running businesses. The transition was accompanied by Deng Xiaoping's 1992 southern tour and China's decision to open up Pudong and develop Shanghai as a global city in 1990 (e.g. She et al., 1997). In consequence, all local governments turned to preparing land for the construction of industrial parks in order to attract investors and enable industrialisation (Shen and Ma, 2005: 770). As a result, there appeared to be increasing enthusiasm for setting up industrial zones and increasing the volume of foreign investment across the nation, particularly in the YRD region. The transformation of local states away from bureaucratic entrepreneurs (Sunan model) has laid the foundation for the area to embrace

要干预者,这使地方官员的利益与投资外商的利益变得一致(Eng,1997:555-556)。地方政府从投资外商手中获得了发展资本、地方税收、行政管理费用和土地租金(同上:558),而外商则获得了大量廉价劳动力、充足的土地使用、高效而友好的政府服务,以及宽松灵活的政府管治(同上:555)。然而,这种投资商与地方政府之间的利益结合也使城市发展的重心从提供公共服务转向为生产服务,如提供基础设施。这种发展模式使得未来的经济发展和城市化面临生态资源紧张和人力资源问题(同上:565-566)。

与此同时,长江三角洲地区在20世纪80年代也出现了乡镇和农村经济的复兴(Ma和Fan,1994)。与珠三角地区不同,长三角的发展主要是受到乡镇集体企业发展的带动(Oi,1995;Walder,1995),而不是外商直接投资的推动。然而,自90年代中期以来,长三角的乡镇企业也逐渐改制转型(Shen和Ma,2005:761-62)。这是因为原苏南模式,即乡镇企业推动的区域发展(同上:764)从90年代初期开始遇到了发展瓶颈(同上:763)。而由于浙江依赖私营企业发展起来的温州模式(Liu,1992;Parris,1993)依然充满活力和竞争力,大量乡镇企业也由集体所有制走向了私有化的道路(Shen和Ma,2005:763)。

90年代后半期开始的大规模产权私有化(Han和Pannell,1999;Li和Rozelle,2000;Wei,2002:1740)完全改变了苏南模式的实质。同时,模式的改变也隐含着长三角地区地方政府作用的变化。在私有化以前,地方政府密切参与企业运作(如Huang,1990;Oi,1995;Walder,1995),可以对市场直接进行行政干预,并为企业提供银行贷款和其他资源。而在产权改革之后,政府则开始退出企业管理的舞台。这个转变与邓小平1992年南巡以及1990年中国决定开放浦东,把上海建成国际大都市发生在同一时期(如She等,1997)。因此,为了吸引投资和推动工业化发展,所有地方政府都开始规划土地建设工业园区(Shen和Ma,2005:770)。结果在全国掀起了建设工业园区和吸引外资的热潮,长三角地区尤其如此。地方政府不再充当行政企业人(苏南模式),这个转

FDI (Wang and Lee, 2007: 1874).

Therefore, since the late 1990s, there seems to have been convergence between the dynamics of regional development in the YRD and PRD in the sense that their rapid economic growth is driven by foreign investment and exports (Chen, 2007). It is suggested that the traditional Sunan and Kunshan models in the YRD have had to integrate nationally and globally in order to maintain competitiveness (Wei et al., 2007, 2009). However, implicit differences exist between the two regions in terms of state governance and local initiatives. According to Yang's (2009) research on Taiwanese IT redistribution from the PRD to the YRD, the desktop cluster in Dongguan in the PRD has mainly been fostered by 'bottom-up dynamics of Taiwanese third-tier firms without proactive local initiatives' (ibid: 403); whereas the laptop cluster in Suzhou in the YRD has been initiated top-down by local governments and explicitly fostered with intentional direction by those local governments (ibid: 404). This directive and entrepreneurial role of local governments is labelled as the Kunshan model, which has gradually diffused and replaced the prior Sunan model in YRD (Chien, 2007; Chien and Zhao, 2008; Wei, 2002; Wang and Lee, 2007). Kunshan is one of the county-level cities under the administrative purview of Suzhou. In the 1980s, Kunshan commenced industrialisation by following the fashion of setting up TVEs; however, it was not competitive at the time (Chien and Zhao, 2008: 431). Since the 1990s, Kunshan has witnessed a tremendous increase in FDI, coupled with the opening up of Pudong, Shanghai (Chien and Zhao, 2008: 432; Wei, 2002: 1739). In 1997, its volume of FDI even surpassed that of Wuxi and Suzhou (Wei, 2002: 1740). The dramatic success of Kunshan's economic development is contingent upon two conditions. The first is the transfer of a large amount of capital and production activities from overseas to the YRD (Wang and Lee, 2007: 1880; Yang, 2009). The second is greatly attributed to the active and facilitating role of local government - the key tasks of Kunshan's leaders are to engage in attracting external projects and satisfying external investors with the most friendly and efficient services (Wang and Lee, 2007: 1883; Wei, 2002: 1741-1742). The institution building and entrepreneurial skills of Kunshan's government have been learned and adopted through working alongside external investors (Chien and Zhao, 2008; Wang and Lee, 2007: 1883).

The endorsement of Kunshan practices by central government greatly impelled the diffusion of the Kunshan model (Chien, 2007). Even Wenzhou, which is well-known for its prosperous private economy, started to copy the Kunshan model (Lu and Shi, 2008: 218); that is, all levels of governments were encouraged to attract foreign investment. This was in part forced by the embarrassing situation that Wenzhou, although ahead of others in terms of the

变为整个地区吸引外商直接投资奠定了基础(Wang和Lee,2007:1874)。

因此,自90年代末以来,长三角和珠三角的区域发展动力似乎变得一致,即都是依靠外资和出口拉动经济的快速发展(Chen,2007)。学者认为长三角地区传统的苏南模式和昆山模式必须与全国乃至全世界的经济发展相融合才能保持竞争力(Wei等,2007,2009)。然而,这两个区域在国家管治和地方主动性方面还是存在着一定差异。根据Yang(2009)对台湾IT产业从珠三角向长三角地区转移的研究发现,集中在珠三角地区东莞的台式电脑产业集群主要是由"台湾三流企业自下而上的自然发展而不是地方政府的积极举措"所推动的(同上:403);而集中在长三角地区苏州的笔记本电脑生产基地却是由地方政府自上而下推动的,明显是在这些地方政府有意识的引导下发展起来的(同上:404)。这种地方政府的主导经营角色称为昆山模式,并逐渐得到了推广,取代了长三角地区先前的苏南模式(Chien,2007;Chien和Zhao,2008;Wei,2002;Wang和Lee,2007)。昆山是苏州行政辖区内的一个县级市。在上世纪80年代,昆山通过开办乡镇企业踏上了工业化道路;然而当时昆山的乡镇企业并没有太大的竞争力(Chien和Zhao,2008:431)。90年代以来,随着上海浦东的开放,昆山的外商直接投资开始大幅增长(Chien和Zhao,2008:432;Wei,2002:1739)。1997年,当地吸引的外商直接投资总额甚至超过了无锡和苏州(Wei,2002:1740)。昆山经济发展的巨大成功主要得益于两个条件。首先是大量资本和生产活动从海外转入长三角地区(Wang和Lee,2007:1880;Yang,2009)。其次是地方政府积极的推动作用——昆山政府官员的主要任务就是吸引外来项目并为外商提供最友好高效的服务(Wang和Lee,2007:1883;Wei,2002:1741-42)。昆山政府的体制建设和经营技巧是在与外来投资商的合作中逐渐学习并付诸应用的(Chien和Zhao,2008;Wang和Lee,2007:1883)。

中央政府对昆山做法的赞许大大推动了昆山模式在全国的推广(Chien,2007)。甚至以私营经济繁荣而著称的温州也开始学习昆山模式(Lu和Shi,2008:218),鼓励各级政府去开展招商引资。温州这样做的部分原因是受迫于

development of market institutionalisation, is relatively backward compared with Hangzhou and Ningbo in terms of economic growth and fiscal revenue (ibid: 219).

　　With entry into the World Trade Organisation (WTO) at the end of 2001, China, especially its coastal regions, has effectively become the world's workshop.However, regional problems such as land encroachment, environmental pollution, rising inequalities and competition also intensified from this point. The widespread imitation and implementation of GDP and FDI evaluation for local cadres has produced vicious competition between localities for mobile capital in the regions and across the nation. Policy isomorphism, which refers to the formulation and implementation of very similar or even identical economic development policies, according to Chien (2008), caused cut-throat competition based on aggressively reducing development costs by, for example, tax concessions and land price reductions (Chien and Gordon, 2008; Wang and Lee, 2007: 1886). As a result of crude competition, the locales occupied a weakened bargaining position in negotiation with foreign investors (Wang and Lee, 2007: 1886). Moreover, fierce competition made cross-boundary policy coordination difficult and regional production networks lacked agents and motivation (ibid), which is detrimental to long-term local development. The production network and economic zone are virtually detached from the local community, and are not an organic part of the local economic base (ibid). They contributed to the growth of current GDP, tax, land price, and property speculation, but not the real development of the local state-owned, private or collective economy. It seems the great success of the region is as a result of benefiting from the institutional innovation of local governments, but now it is also the earlier innovation that impedes the upgrade of the local economy (ibid: 1887).

　　With the paradigm shift of economic development, the dispersed town development of the 1980s is gradually being transcended by new 'city-based' 'urbanization' (Lin, 2007). The spectacular expansion of cities is the visible result of the rampant development of economic zones, industrialisation, and urban and rural settlements, but also the ironic outcome of institutional innovation: the adoption of 'place promotion' strategy and the land lease policy (ibid: 1832). The prior-reform city-based urbanisation is dependant on centrally planned and controlled investment, whereas the current post-reform city-based urbanisation is reliant on heavy investment from local governments (Xu and Yeh, 2005). Using the 1990 and 2000 census data by county, Zheng et al., (2009) found that, by 2000, there was a regional scale of urban growth and net migration gains in the YRD, PRD and Bohai-Sea-Rim (Jing-Jin-Tang) regions, whereas, elsewhere, economic development and concentration still focused on major cities and their peripheral zones. These three mega-city

自己尴尬的发展处境,因为尽管温州在市场机制发展上独占鳌头,但在经济发展和财政税收方面则比同省的杭州和宁波相对落后(同上:219)。

在2001年年底中国加入世界贸易组织之后,中国,特别是其沿海地区,成为了名副其实的世界工厂。然而,诸如侵占耕地、环境污染、日益严重的不平等发展和恶性竞争等区域问题也从这个时期开始愈演愈烈。各地争相效仿和采用以GDP和外商直接投资作为对地方官员的考核指标的做法,导致各地对区域内及全国范围的流动资本展开了恶性竞争。政策的效仿,即制定和实施非常相似甚至完全相同的经济发展政策(Chien,2008),导致了为大幅降低发展成本而进行的残酷竞争,如减免税收或降低土地出让价格等(Chien和 Gordon,2008;Wang和Lee,2007:1886)。恶性竞争的格局使地方在与投资外商谈判时常常处于劣势地位(Wang和Lee,2007:1886)。不仅如此,激烈的竞争亦使得跨境政策协调非常困难,缺少形成区域生产网络的动因和动力(同上),不利于地方的长期发展。生产网络和经济开发区与地方社区完全隔离,并没有成为地方经济体的有机组成部分(同上)。它们虽然为地方贡献了GDP和税收、抬高了土地价格并促进了房产投机,但并没有推动地方国有、私营或集体经济的实质发展。虽然长三角区域的巨大成功得益于地方政府的制度创新,但是,也正是这种创新阻碍了地方经济的升级发展 (同上:1887)。

随着经济发展模式的转变,20世纪80年代分散的乡镇发展模式逐渐被新的"基于城市的""城市化"所取代(Lin,2007)。城市的大规模扩张不仅明显是经济开发区、工业化和城市农村聚集地的迅猛发展导致的结果,同时也是采取"地方营销"战略和土地租赁政策这一体制创新举措所带来的负面后果(同上:1832)。改革开放前基于城市的城市化发展依靠的是由中央计划和控制的投资,而目前改革开放后基于城市的城市化则是依靠地方政府的巨额投资来推动的(Xu和Yeh,2005)。根据1990年和2000年县级以上的普查数据,Zheng等(2009)发现,截至2000年,城市化发展和净人口迁徙率增长集中发生在长三角、珠三角和环渤海(京津唐)地区,而其他地区的经济发展重心则依然集聚在主要城市及其周边地区。这三个巨型城市区域吸引了最多的外商直接投资和

regions represent the greatest absorption of FDI and a huge concentration of cross - border economic activities (Zhao and Zhang, 2007). The reinforced economic clustering and agglomeration in the three city regions demonstrate a spatial polarisation of national development (ibid: 991). Meanwhile, a sharp contrast also exists within these mega–city regions, as development is not evenly dispersed within the regions (Wei and Fan, 2000; Ye and Wei, 2005). Although regional inequality declined earlier in the 1980s as a consequence of rural industrialisation and town development outside the large cities, uneven development has tended to intensify due to the new city - based development (Lin, 2007, 2009) and the dominance of large cities (Zhao et al., 2003).

2.6.2 Current literature on emerging regional governance

With the liberalisation of trade and investment after economic reform, China's regional economy witnessed increasing economic interplay, as well as conflict. With the development of economic regionalisation, economic interaction within the private sector and civil society would develop spontaneously according to economic returns, even though at the time inter-governmental communication was still very weak. The development of the relationship between Hong Kong and the Pearl River Delta (PRD) is a case in point. In the 1980s, the economic cooperation between Hong Kong and PRD started from the traditional area of investment and trade. The link with export - oriented processed industries led to an increase in the movement of people and vehicles between the regions after the mid-1990s (Yang, 2004: 10-15). During this long time period, inter-region economic interactions were spontaneously initiated by the manufacturing businesses of Hong Kong and local governments in the PRD (ibid: 24), based on the conditions of cultural connections and geographical proximity. In 1998, informal inter-governmental communication was established in the form of the 'Annual Hong Kong - Guangdong Cooperation Joint Conference' (ibid: 16). Afterwards, in 2002, a new mechanism in the form of the 'Mainland and Hong Kong Large - Scale Infrastructure Coordination Meeting' was instituted to cope with keen competition in container ports and the coordination of airports in the region (ibid: 18). As positive as the progress was, there was no organisation to provide a coordinated vision for the regional groupings (ibid: 19). However, since mid - 2003, a significant transition has occurred towards institutional regionalism with the agreement of CEPA. The central government has played a key role in the marked progress in cross–border economic integration. However, it is more important to recognise the context leading the interests of each side towards institution - based integration. Hong Kong was not interested in integration during the economic boom years. Only

高度集中的跨境经济活动(Zhao 和 Zhang,2007)。这三个城市区域日益增强的经济集聚发展说明了中国国家发展在空间上的极化(同上:991)。同时,在这些巨型城市区域内也存在巨大差异,各区域的发展并不平衡(Wei 和 Fan,2000;Ye 和 Wei,2005)。尽管80年代区域发展的不均衡因大城市周边的农村工业化和乡镇的发展而有所缩小,但这种不均衡发展将因新的基于城市的发展(Lin,2007,2009)和大城市的主导作用(Zhao 等,2003)而进一步加剧。

二、新兴区域管治研究综述

随着改革开放后贸易和投资的自由化,中国的区域经济互动日益频繁,矛盾也逐渐增加。随着经济的区域化发展,私营部门和民间团体内的经济互动会依据经济回报而自然发展,即便当时政府间的互动联系可能还非常少。香港与珠三角地区的关系发展就是一个最好的例子。在20世纪80年代,香港与珠三角开始在投资和贸易等传统领域合作。外贸加工业上的联系使得区域间的人员和车辆往来自90年代中期开始增多(Yang,2004:10-15)。在这个相当长的时期内,区域之间的经济互动都是由香港制造业与珠三角地方政府基于文化和地缘联系自发产生的(同上:24)。1998年,两地开始建立非正式的政府间联系,即"粤港合作联席会议"(同上:16)。随后在2002年,两地建立了一个新的机制"内地与香港大型基础设施协调会议",以解决区域内集装箱码头和机场协调的竞争问题(同上:18)。尽管有着积极的进步,但是区域内依然没有一个机构为区域成员制定统一的区域远景(同上:19)。不过,自2003年年中开始,香港与广东合作的制度建设随着 CEPA 协议的签订而发生了重要变化。中央政府在这次跨境经济合作中扮演了重要角色。但是,更重要的是要认识到导致双方有兴趣建立制度性合作的背景。香港在其经济繁荣的时候对经济

after the 1997/1998 Asian Financial Crisis did the Hong Kong government show more enthusiasm for the initiative. Therefore, for both Hong Kong and the PRD, it was in the context of anticipation of increasing competition from Shanghai and the YRD that strategic cooperation was agreed (ibid: 20, 25).

A similar trajectory of changing inter-city relationships is also found in the YRD (Zhang, 2006). During the 1980s, the cities in the region were more partners with Shanghai to gain technology assistance and industrial transfer. However, since the 1990s, they have turned into competitors to Shanghai, as every city can be accessed by FDI after the introduction of China's open policy. With aggressive development, many cities such as Suzhou and Nanjing have become the economic peers of Shanghai in terms of FDI and GDP competition. However, since 2000, the region has been faced with the reorientation of central policy and external competition from Bohai Sea Rim centred on Beijing, as well as rising regions in the neighbouring countries of Asia. Under the circumstances, collaboration dialogue is intensified within the region. From the experience of both the PRD and YRD regions, it seems that the tendency of urban governance towards regionalisation and regional cooperation are fostered by potential external competition. However, it is still a long way from this point to the achievement of a regional alliance, a unified regional governance structure or regional collaborative planning.

In order to strengthen urban competitiveness in the climate of inter-city and inter-region competition, the city government is found to be actively involved in the formulation of 'repositioning strategies' for local development (Wu and Zhang, 2007; Xu and Yeh, 2005). For example, Guangzhou repositioned itself as a regional centre by restructuring its spatial resources and expanding its development boundary from a congested city proper to a city-region incorporating suburban counties and county-level cities (Xu and Yeh, 2005: 295-298). It is anticipated that the renewed metropolis city image will conform to Guangzhou's economic status in the region, and boost the city's publicity and competitiveness for FDI. In order to better coordinate the development of the suburban region with the central city, the Guangzhou municipal government and Guangdong provincial government even managed to redraw the administrative boundary by adjusting adjacent county-level cities, Panyu and Huadu, into the city districts of Guangzhou (Xu and Yeh, 2005: 298).

For a short period of time following Guangzhou's practice, regional repositioning and administrative annexation occurred across the country with the aim of pursuing collaboration and coordination in order to enhance competitiveness (Wu and Zhang, 2007). Coordination was particularly necessary between the central city and the outskirts because the economy and civil life had already been regionalised in the area, but the facilities and transport system

合作并不感兴趣。直到1997/1998年亚洲金融危机爆发后,香港政府才开始对合作倡议表现出更多热情。因此,对于香港和珠三角地区来说,正是由于预计到来自上海和长三角地区的竞争会日益激烈才达成了这项战略合作(同上:20,25)。

在长三角地区也发生了类似的城市关系变化(Zhang,2006)。在整个80年代,区域内的城市大多是上海的合作伙伴,从上海获得技术援助并接受产业转移。但是从90年代开始,它们变成了上海的竞争者,因为中国改革开放后每个城市都能够获得外商直接投资。苏州和南京等许多城市都经历了迅猛发展,在外商直接投资和GDP方面都成为上海的有力竞争者。然而,自2000年以来,该区域经历了中央政策的转变和来自京津唐区域及亚洲邻国的竞争。在这种情况下,区域内部的合作对话开始加强。因此,从珠三角和长三角地区的经历来看,城市管治向区域化和区域合作的变化趋势源于潜在的外部竞争。然而,要从当前的状况发展到实现区域联盟,建立统一的区域管治框架或区域合作规划,还有很长的路要走。

为了在城市和区域竞争的背景下加强城市竞争力,城市政府积极为地方发展制定"转型战略"(Wu和Zhang,2007;Xu和Yeh,2005)。例如,广州通过重组空间资源,将其发展范围从拥挤的城区扩大至包括郊县和县级市的城市区域,将自己重新定位为区域中心(Xu和Yeh,2005:295-298)。广州期望这个新的大都市形象能够与其在该区域内的经济地位相符,提升城市的知名度和吸引外商直接投资的竞争力。为了更好地协调中心城市和郊区的发展,广州市政府和广东省政府甚至重新调整了城市的行政边界,将邻近的县级市番禺和花都改为广州市辖区(Xu和Yeh,2005:298)。

在广州采取此项做法后不久,全国许多城市都纷纷重新调整了区域定位并进行了行政兼并,以增强合作与协调,提升竞争力(Wu和Zhang,2007)。区域协调在中心城市及其周边地区尤其必要,因为这种地区的经济和城市生

could not be unified because of the separation of administrative systems. Zhang and Wu (2006) documented the wave of administrative annexations in YRD. In addition, they found the downside of administrative annexations: mandatory coordination with coercion by top-down administrative power (Zhang and Wu, 2006: 17), which was in favour of prefecture-level government and undermined the interests of county-level jurisdictions. Furthermore, this powerful and direct measure was not an absolute resolution to coordination, since it could not handle the problems between prefecture - level cities and between provinces (ibid: 15).

Though still not prevalent, inter-governmental negotiation and inter-city partnership are seen on some occasions. The cross-border development zone between Jingjiang and Jiangyin in Jiangsu Province is a case in point. The need for cooperation originated with the opening of the Jiangyin Bridge of the Yangtze River in 1999, which links and facilitates the interaction between Jiangyin and Jingjiang. However, friction has also arisen due to 'regionalisation' (Luo and Shen, 2006: 7). For example, the enterprises registered in Jiangyin, but operated in Jingjiang, still submit administration fees to the Jiangyin government according to the rules, although they are actually using land and infrastructure services offered by the Jingjiang government. Due to the conflict, a 'forum for the enhancement of Jiangyin-Jingjiang river-side area development' has been established between the local leadership since 2001 (ibid: 9). Moreover, the positive involvement of provincial government at this point has played an important role in facilitating inter-city cooperation. Subsequently, cross-boundary projects were launched in the area with the cooperation of Jiangyin and Jingjiang ports and the cooperative development of the JZJ economic zone (ibid: 9-13). For the purpose, not only were working groups and an administration committee, consisting of local officials from the two sides, formed to liaise and coordinate, a coordination unit at the provincial level was also formed with members from provincial government and prefecture-level government (ibid: 13). The indispensable role of provincial government in the inter-city coalition reflects the persisting hierarchical power structure in China (ibid: 1).

In fact, these cross-boundary infrastructure projects have become a main vehicle to impel the formation of regional integration and regional governance in China (Liu et al., 2010: 31). These projects represent an occasion to bring governments and departments together, and to promote inter-governmental communication and ease administrative hurdles. However, at the same time, the decision-making process of these regional projects is filled with bargaining and power struggles between levels of governments. According to Liu et al. (2010), this process entails re-territorialisation for governments, particularly for hierarchical governments. Currently, their cooperative attitude depends on their conception

活实际上已经区域化,只是基础设施和交通系统却因为行政体制的分隔而不能实现一体化。Zhang 和 Wu(2006)研究了长三角地区的行政兼并浪潮。同时,他们也发现了行政兼并存在的问题:即这种协调是通过自上而下的行政权力强制实现的(Zhang 和 Wu,2006:17),这个做法对地级市政府更为有利,却损害了县级辖区的利益。而且,这种直接通过权力实施的方法并不能根本解决协调问题,因为它不能解决地级市之间和省级之间的合作问题(同上:15)。

在某些地区,政府之间的谈判和城市之间的合作关系也开始出现,但仍不普遍。江苏省江阴和靖江之间的跨境开发区就是一个典型案例。这种合作需求源自1999年跨越长江的江阴大桥的开通,大桥连接了江阴和靖江,促进了两个城市之间的交流。但是,"区域化"也带来了一些矛盾(Luo 和 Shen,2006:7)。例如,在江阴注册的企业即使在靖江运营,根据规定也依然需要向江阴市政府缴纳行政管理费,然而他们实际使用的是靖江市政府提供的土地和基础设施服务。为了解决这个矛盾,2001年起两地领导建立起了"促进江阴和靖江两岸区域发展的论坛"(Luo 和 Shen,2006:9)。而省政府在此时的积极参与对促进两地合作发挥了重要作用。随后,该地区启动了一系列跨境项目,如江阴—靖江港口合作和联合投资开发的省级开发区江阴—靖江工业园区(同上:9-13)。为此,不仅建立了由两地政府官员组成的工作小组和管理委员会来负责联络和协调工作,还建立了一个由省级和地级政府官员组成的省级协调单位(同上:13)。省政府在城市间的联盟中发挥着不可或缺的作用,这反映出中国的等级权力结构依然存在(同上:1)。

事实上,这种跨境的基础设施项目已经成为促进中国区域合作和区域管治的一个主要手段(刘超群等,2010:31)。这些项目为各地政府和相关部门开展合作、推动政府间交流和扫清行政障碍提供了机会。但同时,这些区域项目的决策过程也充满了各级政府之间的讨价还价和权力斗争。根据刘超群等(2010)的研究,这个过程带来了政府的再地域化,特别是等级较高的政府。目前,他们的合作态度取决于他们对利益和权力的判断;但是在这一过程中各级

of interests and power; gradually, however, a new division of labour between levels of governments on regional issues will be formed through the process.

Therefore, at the current stage, with neither regional level authority able to resolve delicate cross–boundary issues, nor any power division between levels of governments on regional issues in evidence, the role of higher-level government is significant in terms of acting as a coordinator and facilitator among various government actors. For example, in the proposal for the construction of the Hong Kong – Zhuhai – Macao Bridge, seven relevant parties are involved in negotiations. These are: the central government, Guangdong provincial government, Zhuhai municipal government, Macao Special Administration Region government (Macao SAR government), Hong Kong Special Administration Region government (HKSAR government), Shenzhen municipal government, and Hong Kong businesses and NGOs (Yang, 2006: 829). Each party articulated local interests in the regional infrastructure proposal negotiations. The HKSAR government wanted the landing point at Zhuhai rather than Shenzhen to circumvent future direct competition with Shenzhen in terms of deep – water container ports; whereas the Shenzhen government conceived the proposal as a kind of threat to its position which thus represented marginalisation in the region; hence, the Shenzhen government initiated an alternative proposal to collaborate with Zhongshan, another city in Guangdong Province, to build an inter – city bridge (ibid: 830 – 832). Finally, central government intervened and enforced the consensus on HKSAR government's scheme. In other words, the central government played an important backstage role to step in and mediate between multiple and disparate jurisdictions and actors in the region (Yang, 2005).

In addition to the negotiation process involving multi – scalar actors to coordinate regional development, efforts have been initiated by some governments to establish types of inter – governmental coordinating mechanisms, for example, via regional plans or regional organisation. For example, YRD established its Economic Coordination Joint Conference in 1992, although at the time it only consisted of 14 cities; for a long time, the organisation had only nominal power with no concrete agenda (Luo and Shen, 2009: 55). It was not until 2003 that the member cities of the forum progressed into actual cooperative agenda negotiations involving issues such as the tourism market, human resources, regional transport, market institutions, administrative coordination and so forth (ibid: 56).

The PRD has also operated a regional cooperation scheme since 2003, which has a tremendous territorial coverage of eleven provincial level jurisdictions. The Pan-Pearl River Delta regional cooperation project is intended to dismantle administrative barriers and shape coordinated development by

政府之间将逐渐形成在区域问题上的重新分工。

　　因此,在现阶段,由于既没有可以解决跨境敏感问题的区域级政府,各级政府也没有就区域问题形成明确的权力分配,上级政府对跨境问题仍起着非常重要的作用,是不同政府行动者之间的协调者和促成者。例如,关于建造港珠澳大桥方案的谈判就涉及了七个相关方,即中央政府、广东省政府、珠海市政府、澳门特别行政区政府、香港特别行政区政府、深圳市政府及香港的企业和非政府组织(Yang,2006:829)。各方都希望在这个区域基础设施的谈判中实现自己的地方利益。香港特别行政区政府希望跨境大桥对岸连接点落在珠海而不是深圳,以避免未来与深圳在深水集装箱码头上的直接竞争;而深圳市政府则认为香港提出的方案是对其地位的威胁,将导致其边缘化。因此,深圳市政府提出了另一个方案,即与广东省的另一个城市中山联合建一座城际大桥(同上:830-832)。最终,中央政府从中斡旋,推动达成了香港特别行政区政府提出的方案。也就是说,在该区域多方不同行政单位和行动者的谈判中,中央政府仍起着重要的后台介入与斡旋作用(Yang,2005)。

　　除了开展多方谈判以协调区域发展外,一些政府也试图通过区域规划或区域组织等建立各类政府间的协调机制。例如,长三角就在1992年建立了经济合作联席会议,尽管当时仅有14个城市参与,而且在很长一段时间内,这个组织都只有形式上的权力而没有具体的议程(Luo和Shen,2009:55)。直至2003年,该论坛的成员城市才真正迈入实质性的合作议程谈判,谈判内容涉及旅游市场、人力资源、区域交通、市场体制建设、行政合作,等等(同上:56)。

　　自2003年起,珠三角也实施了这样的区域合作方案,覆盖地域多达11个省级辖区。这个泛珠三角合作项目旨在打破行政壁垒,并依托各省之间的互

drawing on the complementary advantages of different provinces. Partnership was established with the operation of the Pan - Pearl River Delta regional cooperation and development forum. However, according to Yeh and Xu (2008), currently the project may be not integrative enough to be conceived as a single region. The regional scheme is contested by individual intentions to maximise local benefit from the project, and a lack of support from the central government for the mega-cooperative project (ibid).

The other major form of regional cooperation mechanism is manifest by the proliferation of regional plans in China (Wong et al., 2008). It is observed that the regional plan is being used as an instrument to juxtapose policy and spatial integration, regional infrastructure provision, as well as environment conservation (ibid). However, it is still a challenge for it to perform as an effective form of regional governance. There are actually different actors and motives behind these plans and the destiny of each plan is subject to local political processes (ibid: 165). Meanwhile, coordination is undermined by a lack of consistency between different plans (ibid: 167, 170, 172).

The argument can be demonstrated by the failure of city-region planning for Suzhou–Wuxi–Changzhou, initiated by the Jiangsu provincial government in 2001. Anticipated to be a solution to excessive competition between these three prefecture - level cities, the plan resulted in a new competition by individual prefecture - level cities to define their own city - region centred on themselves, rather than a goal to compromise and coordinate with one another (Luo and Shen, 2008: 214). On the one hand, the reason this occurred is because the plan-making is more of a top-down commanded administrative task, which did not pay due respect to local stakeholders' interests; however, more importantly, it is also due to decentralisation and the weakened role of provincial government (ibid: 215).

A more recent case is the formulation of a regional plan for the PRD region in 2004. Xu (2008) examined the various rationales of individual actors. The central and provincial governments attempted to use the region-level plan to reassert central regulation on local territorial development after decentralisation; however, for the provincial and municipal governments, it is alternatively an institutional fix to build regional competitiveness in order to cope with fierce inter-city competition and keen competition from outside cities and regions. Thus, the provincial government is involved in both top-down and bottom - up initiatives due to the diverse roles of its different departments. Therefore, if not properly represented, regional planning may be caught up in local interpretation based on present political capacity (ibid: 33) and, hence, cause even greater regional disparities (Xu and Yeh, 2010: 21). In addition to the conflicts between tiers of governments, it is found there are even tensions

补优势实现协调发展。通过泛珠三角区域合作与发展论坛,合作关系已经初步建立起来。但是,根据 Yeh 和 Xu(2008)的研究,目前该项目缺乏整体性,还不能将该区域视为一个整体。各地都试图通过该项目最大化自身利益,同时由于缺少中央政府对这一巨型合作项目的支持,该区域方案遇到了很多挑战(同上)。

在中国,另一种主要的区域合作机制形式就是名目繁多的区域规划(Wong 等,2008)。研究发现,区域规划被用作政策和空间协调、区域基础设施建设和环境保护的工具(同上)。但是,区域规划要成为有效的区域管治形式依然面临巨大挑战。这些规划背后的行动者和动机各不相同,而这些规划的命运则取决于地方的政治流程(同上:165)。同时,合作协调也因不同规划之间缺乏一致性而受到影响(同上:167,170,172)。

2001年江苏省政府制定的苏锡常都市圈规划的失败证实了这一论断。虽然当时期望这个规划可以作为这三个地级市之间过度竞争的解决方法,但实际上规划却导致各市之间出现了新的竞争——各地级市不但没有相互商榷和妥协协调,还纷纷以自己为中心划定自己的都市圈范围(Luo 和 Shen,2008:214)。另一方面,导致这个局面的另一原因是规划的制定过程还是自上而下的命令式行政任务,而对各地方相关者的利益不够尊重;但更重要的是,这也是分权后省级政府权力减弱所带来的后果(同上:215)。

还有一个最近的例子就是2004年珠三角区域规划的制定。Xu(2008)研究了规划所涉及各行动者的不同意图。中央和省政府试图通过区域一级的规划来重新加强地方分权后中央对地方地域发展的管理;但是对省政府和市政府来说,这也是一种增强区域竞争力的制度手段,旨在应对区域内城市之间的竞争以及来自其他城市和区域的竞争。可见,由于各部门的作用不尽相同,省政府可能同时涉及自上而下和自下而上的区域项目或动机。因此,如果界定不清,区域规划往往会被政治势力更强大的地方所主导(同上:33),从而导致更大的区域差异(Xu 和 Yeh,2010:21)。除了不同层级政府间的冲突之外,不同政府部门之间甚至也会出现紧张关系,例如住建部与发改委之间为争夺区

between different government departments, for example, between central ministries of UCCDP and NDRC to compete to be top authority on the issue (ibid), and those brought about by the mixed role of provincial government in initiating regional governance attempts.

2.6.3 Regional studies in China

This section mainly reviewed the contemporary Chinese regional literature focusing on the period after the economic reform. Regions in Chinese studies have changed dramatically in its division and spatial scales over time. This is associated with the big transformation of the usage and meanings of region in Chinese context. Regional studies in the pre-reform period were focused on regional inequalities between six large regions or three regional belts, owing to the official division of regions in the national five-year plan at that time (see Goodman, 1989). However, due to the diminishment of regional policies after the economic reform, regions become loosely defined and refer to all sorts of spatial configurations bigger than cities. For instance, a large number of regional studies after the economic reform are addressed to the regions of PRD and YRD, the two most dynamic regional economies in China. While the PRD region constitutes an assemblage of cities under Guangdong Province, the YRD consists of cities which are administered under different provinces.

Regional studies after the economic reform are at first largely concerned with the strong regional development in China and the implications to spatial transformation and regional inequalities. Only recently has regional governance begun to catch the attention of researchers. At first, intensive studies have been conducted on PRD and YRD regions in terms of development dynamics, urbanisation pattern, the role of the state, and regional inequalities and so forth. The development trajectories of the two regions in the 1980s were slightly different in that the economy of the PRD was largely influenced by the Hong Kong-based FDI, while that of the YRD was led by the development of TVEs. Yet, both of the developments demonstrated the pattern of bottom-up urbanisation, which was manifested by the rapid development of small towns (Ma and Lin, 1993; Ma and Fan, 1994). However, the development mode of the two regions seems to have converged since the 1990s. The YRD region also began to embrace FDI with the opening up of Pudong, Shanghai. A great number of researchers made the effort to posit the regional growth in these regions using various threads of theories, ranging from the micro-lens of cultural connections and interpersonal trust (guanxi) (Hsing, 1996) and the Marshallian Industrial District concept (Wei et al., 2007, 2009) to the macro-angle of globalisation, for example, strategic coupling (Yang, 2009) and the global

域规划的最高权力而产生了矛盾(同上),而省政府在开展区域管治工作时承担的多重角色也引起了一些矛盾。

三、中国的区域研究

本节主要回顾了针对改革开放后的当代中国区域研究文献。随着时间的推移,中国的区域研究在地域划分和空间尺度上经历了巨大变化。这与区域在中国的作用和意义发生了巨大改变有关。在改革开放前,区域研究主要针对的是当时五年计划中正式划分的六大区或三大带(见 Goodman,1989)之间的发展不平衡。然而,由于改革开放后区域政策作用的减弱,区域的定义变得非常宽泛,可以指所有大于城市的空间形态。例如,许多改革开放后的区域研究主要针对的是长三角和珠三角这两个中国最活跃的区域经济体。相比之下,珠三角地区包括的城市都位于广东省内,而长三角地区涵盖的城市则由不同的省管辖。

改革开放后的区域研究最初主要关注的是中国强劲的区域发展趋势及其对空间变化和区域不平衡发展的影响。直到最近,研究者才将目光转向区域管治。起初,学者从发展机制、城市化模式、政府角色和区域发展不平衡等方面对珠三角和长三角区域进行了大量深入研究。这两个区域在上世纪80年代的发展轨迹稍有不同,原因是珠三角经济受香港直接投资的影响很大,而长三角依靠的则是乡镇企业的发展。然而,两个区域的发展都显现出了自下而上城市化的模式,其主要表现为小城镇的快速发展(Ma 和 Lin,1993;Ma 和 Fan,1994)。但是,自90年代以来,这两个区域的发展模式越来越接近。随着上海浦东的开放,长三角也开始大量吸引外商直接投资。许多研究者都试图用各种理论来解释这些区域的发展,包括文化联系和人际关系等微观角度(如 Hsing,1996)、马歇尔工业区理论(Wei 等,2007,2009)以及更宏观的全球化视角,如战略耦合(Yang,2009)和全球生产网络(Wang 和 Lee,2007;Yang 和 Hsia, production network (Wang and Lee, 2007; Yang and Hsia, 2007). Recently, it has been argued that both the localisation factors and the globalisation elements should be taken into account in explaining regional development (Wei, 2010).

Changing urban governance in the regions has also been witnessed through economic development. The local state has been transformed from being a passive implementation agent of the central state to becoming assertive and aligned with capital and economic investors (Chien, 2007; Eng, 1997; Wei, 2002). An outstanding feature of China's regional progression is the fact that the local governments play a strong interventionist role in economic development by using their administrative monopoly. However, it is argued that there are minor differences between the YRD and PRD in terms of the local state. It is suggested that the government of the YRD is stronger and has even more proactive initiatives than that of the PRD (Yang, 2009). Although the active local government has played a crucial role in local economic progression, the interventionist local state has also caused problems in regional development. For example, many local governments are racing to reduce overheads such as tax rebate and land fees in order to attract foreign investment, which results in adverse competition between cities and regions (Chien and Gordon, 2008). Furthermore, unbridled inter-city competition tends to hinder the fostering of local clusters, which is crucial to innovation and industrial upgrading (Wang and Lee, 2007: 1886 - 1887). According to Chen (2007), the regional economies of both YRD and PRD feature low-tech industrialisation. Industrial upgrading is moving slowly in these regions and they are in danger of 'being "locked into" a "low-road" (labour-intensive and wage-squeezing) to economic development', although the YRD is enjoying a slightly more favourable manufacturing and knowledge environment with better timing than the PRD (ibid: 193). Moreover, the active intervention of local state also exacerbates regional inequality and focuses economic concentration on certain city-regions (Lin, 2009; Zhao et al., 2003; Zheng et al., 2009).

Compared to the intensive research on regional development, studies on regional governance in China are just emerging. It is found that, although the 'traditional administrative barriers tend to keep cities in the region somewhat isolated in a vertical administrative system with relatively few horizontal ties' (Chen, 2007: 196), and cities are competing with each other for manufacturing investment and squeezing profit margins for local economic growth (Chien and Gordon, 2008), regional cooperation is just emerging in the regions (Yeh and Xu, 2008; Zhang, 2006). The research has documented the historical development of regional cooperation and planning in China and discerned the intrinsic transformation of the priority of the regional agenda from administrative communication to partnership building (Luo and Shen, 2009; Yeh and Xu,

2007)。最近,有学者提出在解释这种区域发展过程时,应同时考虑地方因素和全球化因素。

在经济发展过程中,这些区域的城市管治也出现了变化。地方政府从服从中央政府的被动执行者变成了主动的政策决断者,并与资本和经济投资者达成了共同利益(Chien,2007;Eng,1997;Wei,2002)。中国区域发展的一个显著特征就是地方政府通过利用其行政专权,在经济发展中发挥了很强的干预作用。但是,研究认为长三角和珠三角的地方政府略有不同。长三角的地方政府作用强于珠三角,并且其采取的举措更加积极(Yang,2009)。虽然积极的地方政府对地方经济发展起到了关键性作用,但地方政府的干预也导致了区域发展中的一些问题。例如,为吸引外资,许多地方政府竞相降低税费和土地费用等开支,这导致城市和区域之间形成了恶性竞争(Chien 和 Gordon,2008)。此外,城市间的激烈竞争往往会阻碍地方产业集群的形成,而产业集群其实对创新和工业升级至关重要(Wang 和 Lee,2007:1886-1887)。根据Chen(2007)的研究,长三角和珠三角的区域经济都是以技术含量较低的工业化为特征的。这些区域的工业升级进展缓慢,经济发展存在"被锁定在低端发展的道路上"(劳动密集型和压榨工资)的风险,尽管与珠三角相比,长三角的制造业和知识产业环境更为有利(同上:193)。除此之外,地方政府的积极干预也加剧了区域的不平衡发展,使经济发展集中在某些城市区域(Lin,2009;Zhao 等,2003;Zheng 等,2009)。

与区域发展的深入研究相比,中国区域管治的研究才刚刚兴起。研究发现,尽管"传统的行政壁垒使区域内的城市更多地是在纵向的行政体系内相联系而较少有横向联系"(Chen,2007:196),并且各城市为了获得制造业投资而相互竞争并压缩地方经济发展的利润空间(Chien 和 Gordon,2008),但区域合作的局面正在这些区域形成(Yeh 和 Xu,2008;Zhang,2006)。本研究阐述了中国区域合作和规划的发展过程,并发现区域议程的重点发生着从行政交流到建立合作关系的内在转变(Luo 和 Shen,2009;Yeh 和 Xu,2008)。地方政府对

2008). It is suggested that the changing attitude of local governments towards cooperative development is fostered by potential external regional competition at home and overseas (Xu and Yeh, 2005; Zhang, 2006). However, it is argued that this attitude is far from eliminating all the hierarchical and horizontal inter-city conflicts (Chen, 2007: 195). In contrast, some major cities take advantage of the cooperative measures or administrative annexations (Luo and Shen, 2006; Yeh and Xu, 2008; Zhang and Wu, 2006). The politics within the local cooperative strategies are very well documented in both the PRD and YRD regions (Luo and Shen, 2006; Yang, 2005; Yeh and Xu, 2008). In addition to the spontaneous cooperative measures taken by the local governments, the two regions have also witnessed the preparation of a regional plan with the involvement of the higher-level government. It is suggested that this marked the rescaling of the central government to intervene in local excessive competition and manufacturing development (Wong et al., 2008; Xu, 2008).

The existing body of literature does well in analysing a particular event and unravelling the complicated and contextually specific power struggles and politics within the region-building process. However, there have been not enough attempts to examine and theorise the mechanism for state rescaling and the emergence of regional governance. Initially, it is explained that economic cooperation is the result of the development of economic regionalisation (Zhang, 2006). However, this assumption is criticised and it is argued that the development of economic regionalisation does not mean a firm consensus is formed between governments regarding the political agenda of economic cooperation (Yeh and Xu, 2008: 409). A hypothesis is then proposed through the lens of the changing economic accumulation regime and the crisis of the entrepreneurial city (Xu, 2008; Xu and Yeh, 2009, 2011), yet the proposition is still problematic in two respects. First of all, it seems to suggest that the transformation of state governance is naturally part of the process of a changing economic regime. Secondly, the literature does not specify the agent underlying the process, or tends to frame the agency vaguely with a single whole state. Therefore, the theoretical concepts developed from the Western context such as new state spaces, agency and politics of scale are helpful to improve understanding on China's emerging regional governance.

2.7 Conclusion

This chapter reviewed relevant debate and sought to understand regional re-ascendance in Western countries through a theoretical lens. A discussion on new regionalism was firstly initiated in the realm of economic geography in the turn towards 'new institutionalism'. It is suggested that recent regional success

合作发展态度的转变源自国内外潜在的区域竞争(Xu和Yeh,2005;Zhang,2006)。但是,这种态度转变远不足以消除上下级政府和平级政府之间的矛盾(Chen,2007:195)。相反,一些大城市乘机对这种合作手段或行政兼并加以利用(Luo和Shen,2006;Yeh和Xu,2008;Zhang和Wu,2006)。这种地方合作战略中所蕴藏的政治机制在长三角和珠三角的研究中都有很好的体现(如Luo和Shen,2006;Yang,2005;Yeh和Xu,2008)。除了地方政府所采取的自发的合作措施,这两个区域也出现了由上级政府参与编制的区域规划。研究认为,这说明了中央政府正在重组尺度,以干预地方的过度竞争和制造业发展(Wong等,2008;Xu,2008)。

大部分现有文献都是基于个别事件的分析从而揭示区域形成过程中复杂而又具有独特背景的权力斗争和政治活动的。然而,目前对国家尺度重组和区域管治兴起的分析与理论研究还不够。这种经济合作的现象最初被解释为经济区域化发展的结果(Zhang,2006)。然而,这种假设遭到了批评,有学者认为经济区域化的发展不代表政府就经济合作的政治议程达成了牢固的共识(Yeh和Xu,2008:409),于是从经济积累机制的变化和经营城市的危机角度提出了一种假设(Xu,2008;Xu和Yeh,2009,2011),但是这种假设也存在两方面的问题。首先,这种假设似乎认为国家管治的转变本质上是经济积累机制变化过程的一部分。其次,这些文献并没有指出这个过程背后的动因,或者倾向于用单一的、笼统的国家概念来模糊界定这种动因。因此,借用西方背景下形成的理论概念如新国家空间、动因和尺度政治等,非常有助于提高对中国新出现的区域管治的认识。

第七节　结论

本章回顾了相关讨论,试图从理论角度解读西方国家的区域复兴。对新区域主义的讨论最早出现在经济地理学转向"新制度主义"的研究中。它认为

stories such as 'the Silicon Valley' resulted from the 'bottom-up', or civil society-based forms of regional governance. Such a governance approach is assumed to be 'good' as it is well suited to enhancing regional competitiveness with regard to its 'reflexivity' and 'institutional learning', which is highly compatible with a neoliberal view (Hadjimichalis, 2006: 696). However, such theorisation is fiercely challenged, particularly from a political economic perspective (MacLeod, 2001a, b). Although acknowledging the general shift from 'government' to 'governance', it is believed that the role of the state is still indispensable because it is the state which orchestrates grassroots empowerment and the process of democratisation. It is thus argued that the transformation does not represent the diminishing role of the state, but rather the rescaling of state power. Henceforth, it is considered that studies focusing on the institutional settings within the regions tend to be based on value judgements rather than logical accuracy or data evidence (Bristow, 2010: 27), or what is called 'soft institutionalism' (MacLeod, 2001b). It is argued that regional transformation cannot be substantially interpreted if the political economy and the changing state are not taken into account (MacLeod and Goodwin, 1999a, b).

This critical regional approach is recognised as highly relevant to regional studies conducted in China, which remain largely influenced by neo-classical analysis. Even though the regulation approach is firstly developed from an abstract theory of capitalism accumulation and economic production, the efforts of spatialising regulation theory oriented it to the changing geographies of governance (Brenner, 1999a). The 'new state space' is hence established to inform the geographical accounts of state restructuring (MacKinnon and Shaw, 2010: 1227). It emphasises that state space is socially produced and fluid; it is historically embedded and path-dependent (Brenner, 2004b). These conceptions allow the NSS framework to be focused on the process and the place-specific politics associated with state restructuring instead of the abstract accumulation process that is perceived to generate state reconfiguration. It is also the context-sensitive approach that makes the NSS framework appropriate to China's experience, which is a transitional society remarkably different from the features of Western capitalism. Following the clues in the review, the study not only aims to examine the rescaling of Chinese statehood, but also to consider the 'agency', e.g. the role of central and local state, or other groups, in the process of changes and development. The study views city-region governance as a scale-building process open to the agenda of economic, political, environment, social and other problems, which needs to be examined carefully in empirical studies rather than presumed theoretically. The analysis framework of the research is hence organised as follows. The study firstly examines the regional

最近如"硅谷"等区域的成功案例源于"自下而上"的或以民间社会为基础的区域管治的成功。这种管治方法被认为是"好的"形式,因为它在"反思反省"和"制度学习"方面很适合提高区域竞争力,也与新自由主义的观点不谋而合(Hadjimichalis,2006:696)。然而,这样的理论解释遭到了强烈质疑,特别是政治经济学角度的质疑(MacLeod,2001a,b)。尽管承认从"政府"到"管治"的大体转变,政治经济学角度的研究认为国家的作用仍然不容忽视,因为正是国家制度催生了这种对基层的赋权和民主化过程,因而提出这种转型并不代表国家作用的减小,而是国家权力的尺度重组。因此,有学者认为有关区域内制度设置的研究往往是基于价值判断而不是基于准确的逻辑或数据证据(Bristow,2010:27),也就是所谓的"软制度主义"(MacLeod,2001b)。他们认为如果不考虑政治经济学和政府角色的转变,就不可能充分解读区域转型(MacLeod 和Goodwin,1999a,b)。

　　本研究认为这种批判性的区域视角对中国开展区域研究非常重要。中国的区域研究仍深受新古典经济学分析的影响。尽管管治研究方法最初是源于资本主义积累和经济生产的抽象理论,但是将管治理论空间化的研究使得管治研究转向了管治的地理空间变化研究(Brenner,1999a)。"新国家空间"正是建立在此基础之上,为国家重组过程提供了地理学解释(MacKinnon 和 Shaw,2010:1227)。该理论强调国家空间是社会产物,是不固定的,是根植于历史和路径依赖的(Brenner,2004b)。这些概念使得新国家空间理论关注的是与国家重组相关的过程和地方政治,而不是促成国家重组的抽象积累过程。尽管中国是处于转型中的社会主义国家,有着与西方资本主义显著不同的特点,但这种依据特定背景的研究方法使得新国家空间理论依然适合中国的区域研究。沿着文献综述的线索,本研究不仅要分析中国国家尺度的重组,同时还要揭示这个过程中的动因,例如地方和中央政府或其他组织在变化发展过程中的作用。本研究将城市区域管治视作一个尺度形成的过程,其诱因有多种可能性,可能包含经济、政治、环境、社会和其他问题,需要通过实证研究仔细分析,而不是从理论上作出假设。因此,本书的分析框架是这样组织的。首先,本书分

renaissance in contemporary China. As informed by Brenner (2002), all regional strategies and projects 'to establish institutions, policies or governance mechanisms at a geographical scale [...] within an urban agglomeration' (p.4-5) are included in the analysis. Afterwards, case studies are conducted to explore the mechanism and rationale behind the changing statehood and the building of regional scale. The examination is conducted from two aspects: the economics and the politics of regional development. The former is focused on the changing geography of the Chinese regional economy over the last half-a-century plus of economic reform and market-oriented development; the latter is concentrated on the agency and logic in the state rescaling in order to uncover the nature of the changing process. Finally, the 'new politics of scale' is revealed through the investigation.

析了当代中国的区域复兴。根据Brenner(2002)的研究,所有"试图在一个城市群的地理尺度内[……]建立制度、政策或管治机制"(第4–5页)的区域战略和项目都属于本书的分析范围。然后,本书通过案例研究对国家空间尺度变迁和区域尺度形成背后的机制与基本原理进行了探索。这个分析主要从两方面展开:即区域发展的经济学和政治学。经济学关注的是中国的区域经济在之前半个多世纪经历了经济改革和市场化发展后的地理变化;而政治学则主要研究国家尺度重组过程中的动因和逻辑,从而揭示这个变化过程的本质。最后,本书通过案例调查揭示了"新尺度政治学"的内涵。

第三章

CHAPTER THREE

Transformation of Regional Governance in China: The Rescaling of Statehood

3.1 Introduction

Regions of various types during the history are reviewed in the chapter to offer a general overview of the changes in territorial governance in China from 1949 to the present day. Through describing the evolution of the central-local relationship and regional governance, it is suggested that although decentralisation from the central government and ministries to localities is a salient feature of China's changing territorial governance after 1978, it is not the entire picture. Throughout the process, regionalisation efforts from both central and local governments also occurred for their own purposes.

In the first section, the evolution of urban and regional governance in China since 1949 is illustrated in detail. The changing administrative apparatus at the urban and regional scale is examined with reference to existing studies on China's economic decentralisation and urban entrepreneurialism. Then, the chapter investigates the changing regional concepts and regional policies in China. After an overview of the consequences of the downscaling of state regulations and state strategy, the recent practices beyond the downscaling of governance are highlighted. In the following sections, a variety of initiatives of governance up-scaling, administrative regionalisation and regional strategies are collected and examined. Particular concern is given to the initiator and the performance of the exercises. Subsequently, features of the recent regional renaissance are summarised. In the final part, the trajectory of the changing territorial governance is generalised and it is argued that the changing governance is dominated by state forces. Henceforth, the theoretical concepts of 'state spaces' and 'state spatial selectivity' (Brenner 2004b) are highly relevant in theorising the transformation of governance in China.

3.2 The development of regional policy and governance in China from 1949 to present

China's territorial governance has undergone dramatic transformations since the launch of economic reforms. One salient change is the extensively documented decentralisation and the resultant changing urban governance. Specific forms of governance, such as pro-growth machine (Zhu, 1999; Zhang, 2002a), place promotion and entrepreneurial governance (Wu, 2000a, 2000b,

第三章　中国区域管治的转型：国家尺度空间的变化

第一节　引言

　　本章回顾了历史上的各种区域类型，以揭示中国自1949年到现在的地域管治变化的概况。通过描述中央与地方的关系和区域管治的演变，本研究认为虽然中央政府和部委的放权是中国改革开放以来地域管治变化的一大特征，但并非是全部特征。在放权过程中，中央和地方政府也根据各自的目的开展了区域化的尝试。

　　第一节详细阐述了中国自1949年以来的城市与区域管治的变化。本书参考了关于中国经济放权和城市经营主义的现有研究，分析了城市和区域尺度的行政框架的相应变化。之后，本章分析了中国区域概念和区域政策的变化。在总结了国家体制和国家战略尺度下移的后果之后，本研究重点分析了除管治尺度下移以外的其他近期动态。随后几节收集和分析了各种管治尺度上移、行政区域化和区域化战略的举措，并特别关注了这些举措的发起者和实施成效。紧接着研究总结了近期区域复兴的特征。最后一节概括了地域管治的变化轨迹，并指出这种管治变化是由国家力量主导的。因此，"国家空间"和"国家空间尺度选择"的理论概念（Brenner 2004b）完全可用于中国管治转型的理论研究。

第二节　1949年至今中国区域政策和管治的演变

　　中国的地域管治自改革开放以来经历了巨大的转变。一个显著变化就是经济放权及其所导致的城市管治变化。大量文献都记载了这一变化。一些管治形式，如促增长机器（Zhu, 1999; Zhang, 2002a）、地方营销和经营型管治（Wu, 2000a, 2000b, 2003）等，主要以案例研究的形式被广泛论证。然而，这种

2003), are widely documented, mainly based on case studies. However, the conventional notion of 'decentralisation' is just too general and simplistic. This section will examine the evolution of both state apparatus and spatial strategies. China used to be a country with a socialist tradition of strong regional policies and the issue of regional inequalities was of significant concern to both academia and national governors. Yet, the dimension of changing spatial strategies has kept being overlooked by previous studies. To fill the gap, this section is going to examine the demise and re-emergence of regions during the last few decades. Moreover, it will also reflect upon how governance was facilitating the implementation of the regional policies, and how the regional policies were drifting away with the shift in governance.

3.2.1 State centralism and redistributive policies in the socialist period (1949—1978)

Prior to 1978, China operated a centrally - planned economic system dominated by vertical administration. It was characterised by constraints of resources; all production materials were nationalised and the national state held the monopoly to make final decisions. The State Planning Commission (guojia jihua weiyuan hui) was the backbone of the planned economy, deciding on input allocation and resource distribution across the country. The Five-Year Social and Economic Development Plan was the important government tool in managing investment projects and allocating production materials. The plan was manipulated in accordance with different sectors of economy. Under the State Planning Commission, subordinate ministries of different sectors were responsible for preparing individual plans for the investment, production, distribution and reproduction of their industries; afterwards, the command and quota was sent down from central ministries to local work - units (Unger, 1987: 16). The multiple levels of local states mirrored those of central government (Figure 3.1). The identical institutional design between central and local governments facilitated top - down administration through layers of government bureaucracy. Overall, except for some short-term decentralisation during the Great Leap-forward and Cultural Revolution (Donnithorne, 1972), power was highly centralised and rested with the central government during the period. Even during the Maoist administrative decentralisation period, central control continued and attempts were made to harness local initiatives to improve the implementation of national goals, rather than real devolution (Lardy, 1975; Wong, 1991b). In a word, local development did not take place without a central decision regarding financial investment and resource allocation (Naughton, 1995: 74; Ng and Tang, 1999: 593).

传统的"分权"概念过于简单笼统。本节将系统分析国家体制和空间战略的演变。中国过去是一个有着社会主义传统和强有力的区域政策的国家,区域不平等的问题曾引起了学术界和政府官员的高度重视。但是,空间战略的变化特点却一直被前人的研究所忽视。为了填补这一空白,本节主要分析过去几十年来中国区域衰落和复兴的过程。同时还将思考管治如何促进了区域政策的实施,以及区域政策如何随着管治的变化而变化。

一、社会主义计划经济时期国家集权主义和再分配政策(1949—1978)

1978年前,中国实行的是中央集权的计划经济。这个时期的特征是物资紧缺;所有生产资料都是国有化的,中央政府制定所有决策。国家计划委员会是计划经济的核心部门,决定着国家的投入和资源分配。国民经济和社会发展五年计划是政府管理投资项目和分配生产资料的重要工具。五年计划是针对不同的经济部门编制的。在国家计划委员会的领导下,不同产业部门的下属部委负责编制本产业的投资、生产、分配和再生产计划;之后,这些指令和配额从中央部委传达至地方单位(如Unger,1987:16)。地方政府也是多层级的,就和中央政府一样(图3.1)。这种中央和地方一致的机构设计有利于通过各层级政府实行自上而下的行政管理。总之,除了"大跃进"和"文化大革命"时期的短暂放权(Donnithorne,1972)之外,权力一直高度集中于中央政府。即便是在那样的放权时期,中央的控制也是非常强的,当时的放权只是想刺激地方的积极性,使其更好地完成国家分配的目标,并不是真正意义上的权力下放(Lardy,1975;Wong,1991b)。总之,在社会主义计划经济时期,如果没有中央的财政投入和资源分配,地方经济是不可能发展起来的(Naughton,1995:74;Ng和Tang,1999:593)。

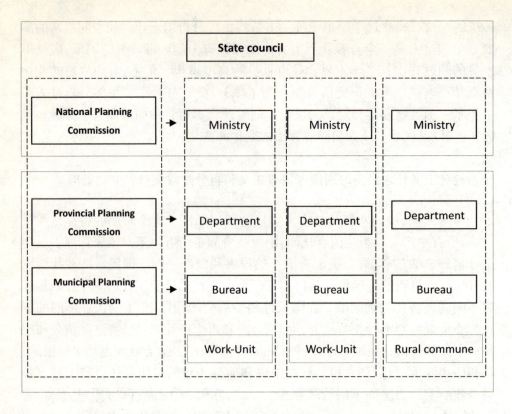

Figure 3.1 Sectoral dominance and administrative hierarchy

Source: compiled from Yeh and Wu, 1998: 216.

Under state centralism, regional institutions above provinces were developed by the state to consolidate central control and intra-regional coordination. Table 3.1 shows the regional units established from 1949 until the 1970s. The regions of the early 1950s housed the military, the Party and a full set of governmental departments; the 'economic coordination regions' in the late 1950s were equipped with coordinating commissions and regional economic planning offices without Party - State organisations; whilst in the 1960s, Party Bureaus were reinserted into these regions to reinforce the regional authority (Solinger, 1978: 630).

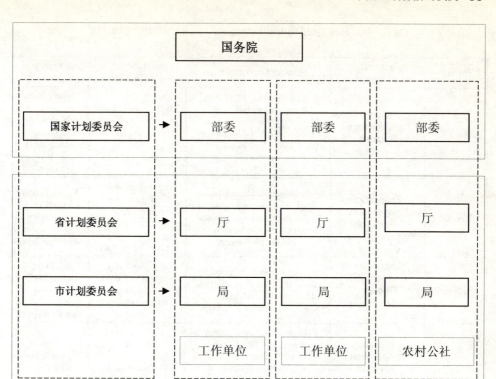

图3.1 部门管理与行政等级

来源:编自Yeh和Wu,1998:216。

　　在国家集中计划经济时期,国家设立了省级以上的区域机构来加强中央管理和区域内合作。表3.1显示了我国从1949年到70年代设立的区域单位。50年代初的区域包含了党政机构和全套政府部门;而50年代末的"经济协作区"只包含协调委员会和区域经济计划办公室,而没有党政部门;到60年代,党委又被重新加入区域政府以加强区域权力(Solinger,1978:630)。

Table 3.1 Regional administrations from 1949 to 1978

Period	Regional administrations	Regional constitution	Institutional settings	Intention and task
1949-1954	Great Administrative Regions (*da xingzheng qu*)	Six regions, including the Northeast, the North China, the Northwest, the Southeast, the Central South, and the Southwest	The regions housed the military, Party and complete governmental departments	To strengthen central regulation, and facilitate sending down mandatory orders
1958-1961	Economic Cooperation Regions (*jingji xiezuo qu*)	Seven regions, including North China, the Northeast, the East China, the Central China, the South China, the Southwest and the Northwest	The regions were equipped with coordinating commissions and regional economic planning offices	To function as self-reliant economic regions under central guidance
1961-1966	Economic Cooperation Regions (*jingji xiezuo qu*)	Six regions, including North China, the Northeast, the East China, the Central-South, the Southwest and the Northwest	The regions were equipped with Party Bureaus and regional economic planning offices	To function as self-reliant economic regions under central guidance
1970	Economic Cooperation Regions (*jingji xiezuo qu*)	Ten regions including the Southwest, the Northwest, the Central China, the South China, the North China, the Northeast, the East China, the Min-Gan region, the Shandong region and the Xinjiang region	Not materialized	To function as self-reliant economic regions under central guidance

Source: compiled from Liu and Feng, 2008: 34-35.

The institutional settings of these regions were slightly different, yet they all served a similar rationale. During each period of region building, politics and the economy at the local level were conceived to be in chaos; hence, regions that spanned provinces were used in the service of the central state to enforce the implementation of central plans, to build rationally designed regional economic systems and to oversee the discretion of local agents (Solinger, 1978). Take the East China Economic Coordination Region (1958—1966) for example. It comprised Shanghai municipality and other six provinces, namely, Jiangsu, Zhejiang, Anhui, Jiangxi, Shandong, and Fujian. It was intended to establish a comprehensive industrial system within the region in accordance with centrally-planned orders. The region was equipped with a regional bureau and a regional economic planning office, which were directly led by the State Planning Commission and State Economic and Trade Commission of that time. The regional institutions worked as the agents of the central government to implement and coordinate targets (Chen X. Y., 2007: 6). For instance, the

表3.1　1949至1978年的区域行政部门

时期	区域部门	区域构成	机构设置	目的任务
1949-1954	大行政区	六个区域,包括东北、华北、西北、东南、中南和西南	各区设置党政机构和全套政府部门	加强中央监管,便于下达强制性命令
1958-1961	经济协作区	七个区域,包括华北、东北、华东、华中、华南、西南和西北	各区设置协调委员会和区域经济计划办公室	作为中央指导下的独立经济区域
1961-1966	经济协作区	六个区域,包括华北、东北、华东、中南、西南和西北	各区设置党委和区域经济计划办公室	作为中央指导下的独立经济区域
1970	经济协作区	十个区域,包括西南、西北、华中、华南、华北、东北、华东、闽赣区、山东区和新疆区	未形成建制	作为中央指导下的独立经济区域

来源:编自刘玉和冯健,2008: 34-35。

　　虽然这些区域的机构设置稍有不同,但是它们的建立都是出于一个相似的认识。在每个区域形成时期,中央都认为地方的政治和经济状况是混乱的;因此,中央政府用跨省的区域来推行中央计划,以建立理想的区域经济体系并监督地方政府的自主行为(Solinger,1978)。以华东经济协作区(1958—1966)为例,它包括上海市及其他六省,即江苏、浙江、安徽、江西、山东和福建,目的是根据中央计划指令在区域内建立一个全面的工业体系。该区域设置了区域委员会和区域经济计划办公室,直接受当时国家计划委员会和国家经济贸易委员会的领导。这些区域机构是中央政府的代理机构,负责实施和协调中央目标(陈晓云,2007:6)。例如,区域内省市制定的经济计划必须提交给区域办公

economic plans prepared by the provinces and municipalities within the region had to be submitted to the regional office. Then, a regional balance would be made to ensure a coordinated distribution of industries in the region. This was intended to optimise the use of production resources and the division of labour. In 1961, a Party Bureau was added to help to enforce the decisions made by the regional office. In short, the region did not represent a central concession to provincial autonomy, but acted as a path to centralisation. It was expected that these regions, smaller in size and closer to the central government, would share the burden of central management and meanwhile facilitate regional coordination under the dominance of ministerial planning.

Meanwhile, a salient characteristic of China's post-1949 development strategy was the commitment to 'redistributive' goals. Equipped with the powerful centralised control of national economic planning and central-provincial revenue sharing, the state was enabled to redistribute material and financial resources both inter-sectorally and inter-regionally (Donnithorne and Lardy, 1976: 340-341). The integrated strategy was made, as the old Chinese saying goes, 'to take all regions into account like in playing chess (quanguo yipanqi)'. During the period of the First Social and Economic Five-Year Plan (1953-1958), industrial and infrastructure investment was channelled to interior areas in order to reverse the disproportionate distribution of industries between coastal and inner areas (Yang, 1990: 234-235). For instance, among the proposed 156 large-scale industrial projects, 42 were located in the western area and 58 were placed in the northeast, with only 5 along the eastern coast; as to the 694 middle-scale projects, 472 out of the 694 were sited away from the coast (Wang et al., 1997: 23). This inland investment focus is illustrated in Figure 3.2.

室,然后由区域办公室协调平衡,以保证区域内工业的合理分布。这是为了优化生产资源的利用和合理分工。1961年,该区域增设党委来帮助实施区域办公室制定的决策。总之,这样的区域并不代表中央对省级自主权的让步,反而是加强中央集权的途径。中央期望,这些规模较小、更接近中央政府的区域建制能分担中央的管理负担,同时促进部委领导下的区域经济协调发展。

　　与此同时,中国在1949年后的发展战略的一大显著特征是致力于"反哺"目标。仰赖于中央牢牢控制的国家经济规划以及中央与省级的税收共享制度,国家可以跨部门跨区域地反馈物资和财政资源(Donnithorne 和 Lardy,1976:340-341)。这个统一的战略是根据"全国一盘棋"的思想制定的。在第一个五年计划时期(1953—1958),大量工业和基础设施投资被转移至内地以逆转沿海和内陆地区工业的不均衡分布(Yang,1990:234-35)。例如,在156个大型工业项目中,有42个被安排在了西部地区,而58个落在东北地区,只有5个在东部沿海地区;而在694个中型项目中,有472个项目被安排在内陆地区(Wang等,1997:23)。图3.2显示了这种以内陆地区为重点的投资情况。

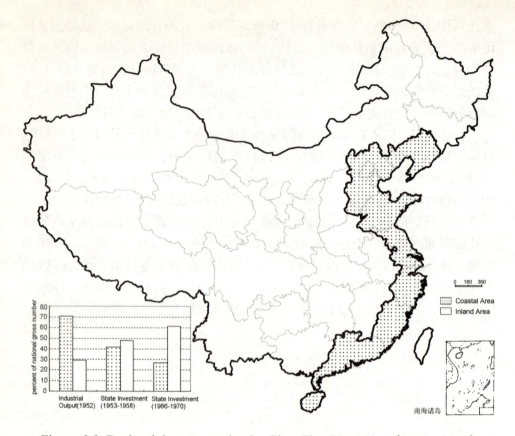

Figure 3.2 Regional investment in the First Five-Year Plan (1953—1958)
Source: data is compiled from Liu and Feng, 2008: 34, 61.

During the periods of the second and third Five-Year Plan (1966—1975), the country was divided into 'First-Front', 'Second-Front' and 'Third-Front' regions (Figure 3.3). Furthermore, 'Third-Front Construction' (sanxian jianshe) was prompted by the central authorities through the decade. Under the strategy, military and manufacturing industries were allocated or transferred to the Third-Front Area, which was mountainous, inland and remote from the coastal area. The strategic decision was made under the circumstances of the Cold War and deteriorating relationships with the Soviet Union, and hence was mainly out of consideration for national defence (Naughton, 1988). Just in the years of 1964 and 1965, 174 plants were moved from industrial cities such as Shanghai, Beijing, Tianjin and Shenyang to the Third - Front region (State Council Development and Research Institute, 2008: 3). It is claimed that 20 billion *yuan* were devoted to Third-front development during the period (Kirkby and Cannon, 1989: 9). The capital assets of SOEs in the region accounted for 35

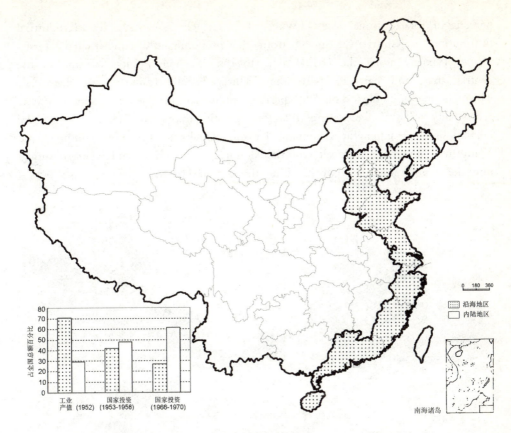

图3.2 第一个五年计划的区域投资（1953—1958）

来源：根据刘玉和冯健，2008：34，61所提供数据绘制。

　　在第二个和第三个五年计划时期（1966—1975），中国被划分为"一线""二线"和"三线"地区（图3.3）。在这十年期间，中央政府提出了"三线建设"战略。根据这个战略，军工和制造业被部署或转移至多山、内陆、远离沿海的三线地区。这个战略决策是在冷战环境和与苏联关系恶化的情况下做出的，因此更多的是出于国防的考虑（Naughton，1988）。仅在1964年和1965年，就有174个工厂从上海、北京、天津、沈阳等工业城市迁至三线地区（国务院发展研究中心，2008：3）。据称，这个时期国家在三线建设上投入了200亿元人民币（Kirkby和Cannon，1989：9）。三线地区的国有企业资产占全国总资产的35%

percent of total national assets (Wang et al., 1997: 27). As a result, industrial distribution in China was spread from the predominantly concentrated 'First - Front' (yixian) along the coastal area, to the 'Second - Front' (erxian) in the central area, and particularly to the 'Third - Front' (sanxian) in the west. Throughout the course of the period, industrial productivity and transport accessibility in the west were therefore greatly improved (Figure 3.4). The railway lines of Chengdu - Kunming, Jiaozuo - Zhicheng, Zhuzhou - Guiding, and Xiangfan - Chongqing were all constructed during the period, and were subsumed into the main transport network within the region (Chen, 2006).

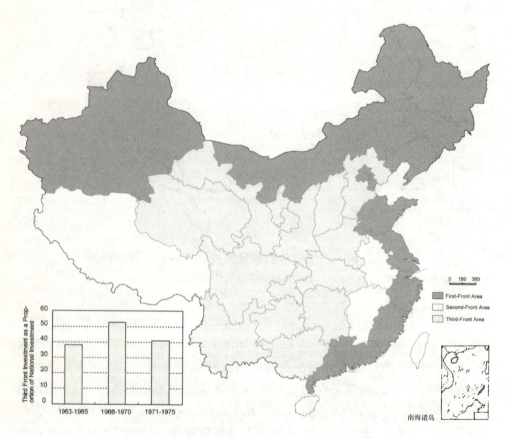

Figure 3.3 Regional division and investment
in the Third and Fourt Five-Year Plans (1966—1975)

Source: compiled from Kirkby and Cannon, 1989: 5, 6, 8 - 9; Naughton, 1988: 365; Wang et al., 1997: 23-28.

（Wang 等,1997:27）。结果,中国的工业分布从原先集中的"一线"沿海地区转移到"二线"中部地区和"三线"西部地区,特别是"三线"西部地区。在这个时期,西部的工业产能和交通便利程度大大提高(图3.4)。成昆、焦枝、湘黔和襄渝铁路线相继建成,并被纳入了该区域的主要交通网络中(陈东林,2006)。

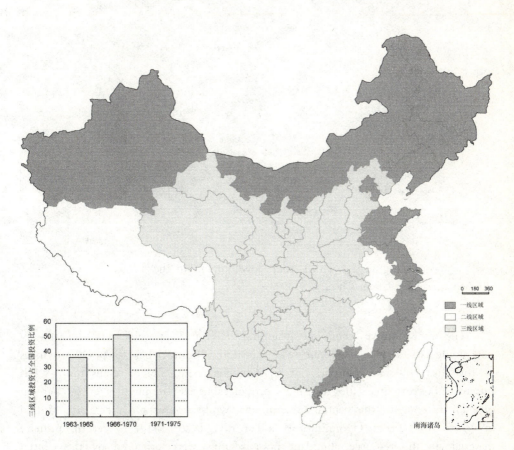

图 3.3 第三和第四个五年计划的区域划分和投资(1966—1975)

来源:编自Kirkby和Cannon, 1989: 5, 6, 8-9; Naughton, 1988: 365; Wang 等, 1997: 23-28.

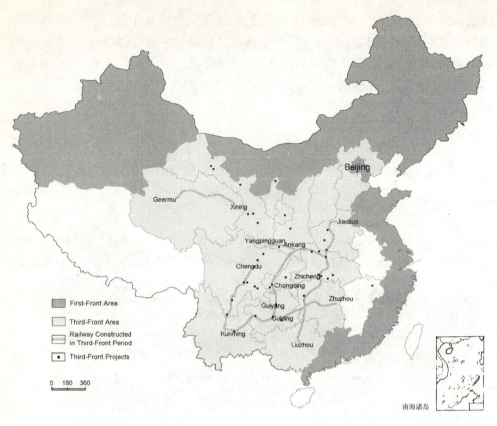

Figure 3.4 Third-front development in the 1960s
Source: compiled from Chen, 2006: 99.

The redistributive economic planning was made possible via the unitary state budgetary system. Revenue was transferred from richer to poor provinces in the form of state subsidies, or in Chinese terms, 'blood transfusions' (da shuxue). For example, the wealthiest provinces usually remitted over 60 percent of their revenue to the central government, whilst poorer provinces only turned in 10 to 40 percent (Donnithorne and Lardy, 1976: 341). In return, primary materials in the resource‑abundant poor regions were procured by the central state at low prices to support manufacturing in the richer production provinces (Wu and Zhang, 2010: 60). When compared with the compensatory regional policies in the UK, the two practices were fundamentally divergent. Whereas regional institutions and regional policy in the UK at the time was trying to equalise the distribution of population, industry, infrastructure and public services across the nation, the redistributive efforts made in China in the form of channelling industrial projects to the interior were much more limited in scale.

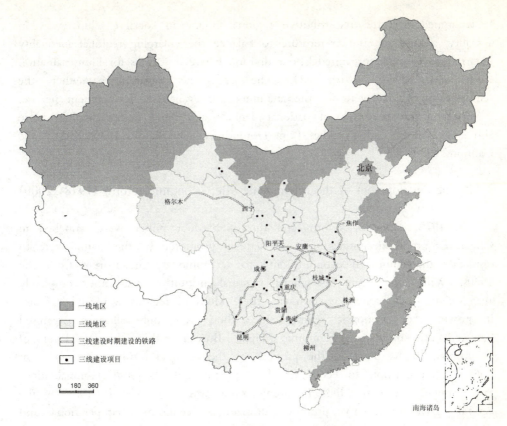

图3.4 20世纪60年代的三线建设

来源:编自陈东林, 2006: 99。

区域平衡的计划经济通过统一的国家财政预算体系而成为可能。财政收入通过政府补助从较富有的地区转向较贫穷的省份,也就是"大输血"。例如,最富裕的省份通常要上缴60%的税收给中央政府,而贫困省份只需上缴10%至40%(Donnithorne 和 Lardy, 1976: 341)。相应地,中央政府以低价从资源丰富的贫困地区采购原材料,用以支持富裕省份的工业生产(Wu 和 Zhang, 2010: 60)。这种政策与英国的补偿性区域政策存在巨大差异。英国当时的区域机构和区域政策是为了在整个国家尺度上平衡人口、工业、基础设施和公共服务的分布,而中国将大量工业项目转移至内陆地区的反哺政策在尺度上存在明

It is argued that the redistributive regional policy in socialist China was, in actuality, a kind of counter-measure to balance the enlarging regional inequality incurred by centrally-organised labour division between regions for industrialisation (Wu and Zhang, 2010: 62). The arguments regarding whether the redistribution efforts were for the attainment of egalitarian development per se, or primarily for the ends of national defence and rapid industrialisation, were also examined by earlier studies (e.g. Donnithorne and Lardy, 1976; Kirkby and Cannon, 1989: 5).

3.2.2 The development of the urban scale after economic reform (1978—2000)

In 1978, economic reform and the open - door policy were launched in China. Economic decentralisation was actively promoted by the central state to dismantle the command economy and to accommodate the market from the 1980s. While the supra - provincial regional institution was not completely abandoned by the central government, these kinds of regions were much frailer in power after economic reform, since they were only alliances organised between the municipal Economic Trade Bureau rather than a level of government body. That is, the purpose of the regional settings changed from political consolidation to economic development and economic regionalisation. For example, the East China Economic Zone was announced in 1981 by the central government to promote horizontal economic cooperation and coordination. The founding of the economic regions rose to a peak in 1986 when the State Council published an official document on promoting horizontal economic alliances. Prior to the end of 1987, more than 100 economic zones had been established under the proposal of the central state (Xu, 2008: 14). Although these regions were centrally mandated, they were essentially loosely organised and informally institutionalised (Xu and Yeh, 2011: 106). These organisations were actually coalitions on a voluntary basis, conferred with no central power or any funding resources.

In contrast to the weakened role of regions, profound administrative adjustments were introduced after economic reform, which contributed to the sharp increase in the number of cities in China (Chung, 2007; Ma and Cui, 1987). 'City administering counties (shi dai xian or shi guan xian)' and 'converting entire counties to county-level cities (xian gai shi)' are the two measures that transformed the territorial management of cities in the 1980s. The 'city administering counties' was the new administrative system in which prefecture - level cities were authorised to administer their surrounding counties. The new system was carried out in three ways: 'merge prefecture - level cities with prefectures', 'abolish prefectures and establish prefecture - level cities', and

显的局限性。有学者认为,社会主义计划经济时期中国的反哺区域政策实际
上是一种反制措施,为了调整日益严重的区域不平等状况,而这种不平等正是
由于中央为实现工业化而对不同区域进行劳动分工所导致的(Wu 和 Zhang,
2010:62)。早期研究对这种反哺到底是为了实现均衡发展,还是主要为了国
防和快速工业化也存在争议(Donnithorne 和 Lardy,1976;Kirkby 和 Cannon,
1989:5)。

二、改革开放后城市尺度的形成（1978—2000）

1978年中国实行了改革开放。自80年代以来,中央政府积极推动经济分
权以瓦解命令经济,并期望引入市场机制。尽管省级以上的区域设置没有被
中央政府完全取消,但是这些区域的权力在改革开放后削弱了很多,在形式上
它们只是市经贸委组织的联席会议而不是一级政府机构。也就是说,区域设
置的目的不再是为了巩固政治,而是为了经济发展和经济区域化发展。例如,
1981年中央政府宣布成立华东经济区来促进横向的经济合作和协调。这种经
济区域的设置在1986年国务院发布文件促进横向经济联系的发展后达到顶
峰。到1987年年底,在中央政府的提议下,全国共设了超过100个经济区(Xu,
2008:14)。虽然这些经济区是由中央指定的,但其实它们的组织非常松散,属
于非正式机构。这些组织其实是自愿形成的联盟,并没有中央授予的权力或
任何资金来源。

与弱化的区域角色形成对比的是,中国在经济改革开放之后进行了大幅
度的行政调整,导致中国城市的数量急速增多(Chung,2007;Ma 和 Cui,
1987)。"市带县"或"市管县"和"县改市"是20世纪80年代采取的地域管理转
型的两个举措。"市管县"是当时出现的一种新的行政管理体制,授权地级市管
理其周边的县。此新体制通过三种方式实施:"将地级市与地区合并","取消

'promote some counties directly to prefecture - level cities' (Ma, 2005: 487). The three means contributed to a decrease in prefectures and an increase in prefecture - level cities. Figure 3.5 shows that the number of prefectures decreased from 173 in 1978 to 58 in 1999, and that prefecture - level cities increased from 98 in 1978 to 236 in 1999. 'Converting entire counties to county - level cities' was the administrative means to turn counties, which by definition are rural areas, into cities (Ma, 2005: 490). This was considered to be the main way to establish 'cities' in the 1980s and 1990s (ibid: 491). Figure 3.5 demonstrates that the number of counties decreased from 2,009 in 1978 to 1,510 in 1999, whereas county - level cities increased from 92 to 427 during the same period. As a result, the total number of cities increased considerably from 190 to 668 between 1978 and 1998.

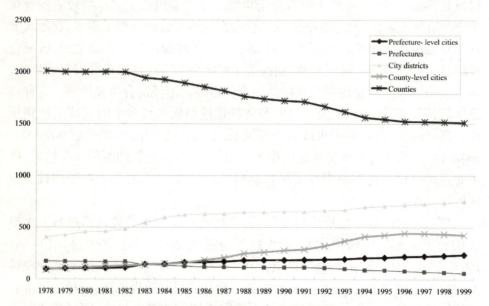

Figure 3.5 Urban administrative changes from 1978 to 1999

Source: compiled from Ministry of Civil Affairs, 1998a, b, 1999, 2000.

It is suggested that the administrative changes at the urban level were '... associated with a localization process' (Chung, 2007: 793). This is because political - economic power rapidly devolved from the central government to provinces and localities since the economic reform, and a dominant degree of administrative power was delegated to city governments. The reformed fiscal system is widely cited as the beginning of decentralisation in China. From the late 1970s, the responsibility for collecting fiscal revenue was decentralised, along with the right of disposal. It is argued that this reform caused China's fiscal

地区设立地级市","将一些县直接升格为地级市"(Ma,2005：487)。采用这三种方式减少了地区的数量,而地级市的数量有所增多。图3.5显示地区的数量从1978年的173个下降到了1999年的58个,而地级市的数量从1978年的98个增长到了1999年的236个。按定义来理解,"县改市"就是通过行政区划手段将属于农村地区的县变成市(Ma,2005：490)。"县改市"被认为是20世纪80年代和90年代设"市"的主要方式(同上：491)。从图3.5可以看出,县的数量从1978年的2009个下降到了1999年的1510个,而同期县级市的数量从92个增加到了427个。因此,市的总数量大幅增加,在1978年到1998年期间从190个增加到了668个。

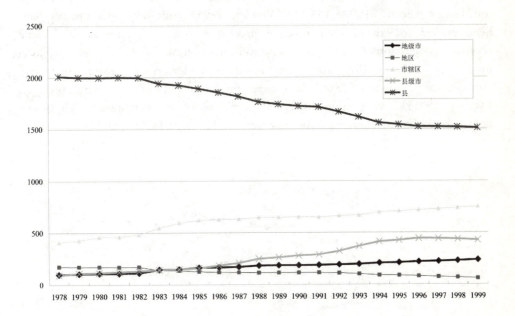

图3.5　1978至1999年城市行政区划变化

来源：根据民政部1998a, b, 1999, 2000数据编制。

　　有学者认为城市层面的行政变革是"……与地方化的政治经济进程相联系的"(Chung,2007：793),这是因为在经济改革之后,政治经济权力迅速从中央政府转移到了各省和地方政府,而行政权则在很大程度上下放至城市政府。财政体制改革被广泛认为是中国地方分权的开端。从70年代末开始,财政征收的责任也与财政使用权一起逐渐下放到了地方。有人认为这场改革导致中国的财政和金融体系经历了巨变,从一元财政体系走向了"联邦"财政体

and financial system to go through a dramatic transformation from a unitary system to a 'federal' one (Montinola et al., 1995; Qian and Weignast, 1997). After the fiscal contracting reform, local government expenditures accounted for around half of total government expenditure; the proportion increased from 1985 and stabilised at around 70 percent in 1989 for ten years. Furthermore, the percentage has kept rising since 2004, after a slight drop in 2000 (Figure 3.6). Figure 3.6 shows that the central government maintained a decentralised pattern of government expenditure, even after the 1994 tax sharing reform, when fiscal distribution became more favourable to the central government and better methods of taxation were put into the central government's pocket (Tao et al., 2010: 2222). Faced with the mounting spending obligation, local revenue was starved to a great extent. Fiscal decentralisation has effectively hardened the soft budget (Smart, 1998: 435,439; Walder, 1995) and local governments have been pushed to expand their revenue making capacity. As long as the central revenue is guaranteed, the central government turns a blind eye to local discretions such as diverting resources from budgetary to extra - budgetary channels or expanding extra - budgetary funds instead of budgetary revenues (Wong, 1991a). As a consequence, the volume of extra - budgetary funds was drastically expanded after the economic reform (Zhang, 1999: 123-127).

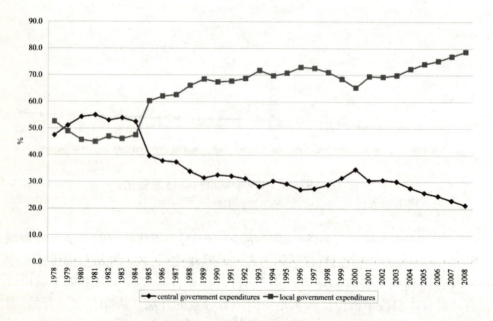

Figure 3.6 Percentage of central and local
government expenditures between 1978 and 2008

Source: National Statistical Bureau, 2009.

系(如 Montinola 等,1995;Qian 和 Weignast,1997)。实行财政包干制改革之后,地方政府支出大约占政府总支出的一半;这一比例从1985年开始上升,1989年升至约70%,此后十年内保持稳定;到2000年这一比例稍有下降,此后自2004年起持续攀升(图3.6)。图3.6显示,即使在1994年实施更有利于中央政府税收的分税制改革之后(Tao等,2010:2222),政府支出依然以地方为主。面对日益巨大的支出负担,地方财政严重吃紧。财政权力下放有效地强化了软预算(Smart,1998:435,439;Walder,1995),推动了地方政府拓展财政增收能力。只要中央财政收入能够保证,中央政府对于地方政府的自主行为也是睁一只眼闭一只眼,例如地方政府可以把资源从预算渠道转移到预算外渠道,或者扩大预算外资金而不是预算内收入(Wong,1991a)。这样做的后果就是预算外资金在经济改革之后急剧增长(Zhang,1999:123-127)。

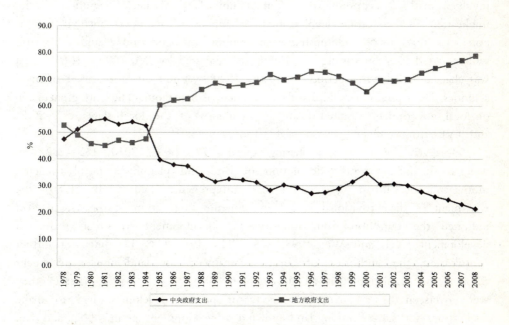

图3.6 1978年到2008年中央政府支出和地方政府支出的比例

来源:国家统计局,2009年。

The fiscal restraint and expenditure obligations triggered provinces to put forward further fiscal contracts and devolve power towards localities. Local fiscal and administrative autonomy was conceived as the means to promote local initiatives in economic development. Some administrative decision powers were downscaled and finally dissolved, due to the gradual domination of the market mechanism, for example, in the sphere of commodity trade and foreign trade. However, some devolved administrative powers, such as investment approval for big projects, urban planning control, and land use management, transferred fundamental state power from provinces to cities. In respect of investment regulation, since 2001, local governments have been empowered to make decisions on overseas - invested projects with a value below 50 million US dollars, and have full authority on infrastructure construction projects as long as they are not funded by local revenue (Zhang and Zhang, 2005: 17). As a result, 70 percent of social investment is actually approved by the local government (ibid: 43). That is to say, central government is generally not involved in local economic development nowadays. While of significance, the implication of economic devolution to changing urban governance is not as potent as that of the administrative devolution on land and planning control, which started later on during the 1990s. As suggested by Wu (2003: 1678), what was characterised by this period before the 1990s was just random market-oriented activities, i.e. a preliminary form of entrepreneurial behaviour. The entrepreneurship of local government resulted from the symbiosis of the local state with SOEs and TVEs from a revenue perspective (Tao et al., 2010: 2221).

However, the 1994 fiscal sharing reform (Tao et al., 2010: 2220-2222) as well as the administrative devolution of land and planning control triggered more strategic urban governance of entrepreneurial cities. In 1980, the enactment of the Provisional Regulation for the Preparation of the Urban Plan indicated the transition from ministry - led development to urban plan - led development (Yeh and Wu, 1998: 178). The 1989 City Planning Act further consolidated the authority of local governments in land use management through the regulation that all development projects, no matter whether they were overseen by a government body or private developers, had to make applications for site-selection, land use and a development permit (Ng and Xu, 2000: 412). More importantly, the preparation of the local plan was implemented by the same authority and the plan making proceeded without much guidance from upper-level government. In other words, local plan making was generally a kind of local issue, without much involvement by upper-level government. Although plan documents and revisions were required to be approved by the higher-level or even central government, local strategies were predominantly formulated by localities under the will of local government (Wu

财政紧缩和支出负担促使省级政府进一步推动向地方政府的财政包干和权力下放。地方财政和行政自主被认为是一种提高地方经济发展积极性的方式。由于市场经济体制在中国逐渐占据主导地位,一些行政决策权被逐渐削减并最终取消,例如在大宗商品贸易和对外贸易领域。但是,一些基本的国家行政权由省下放到城市,比如大项目的投资审批权、城市规划管理权和土地使用管理权。在投资监管方面,从2001年起,地方政府有权对5000万美元以下的海外投资项目作出决策,并对基础设施建设项目拥有完全的决策权,只要这些项目不是由地方财政提供资金(Zhang 和 Zhang,2005:17)。结果,70%的社会投资实际上都是由地方政府批准的(同上:43)。也就是说,中央政府现在一般不介入地方上的经济发展。值得关注的是,改变城市管治的经济权力下放带来的影响不如在土地和城市规划管理上的行政权力下放带来的影响大,后者是20世纪90年代逐渐开始的。Wu(2003:1678)认为,20世纪90年代之前的那个时期所表现的特征就是一种随意的市场导向行为,亦即一种初级形式的经营行为。从财政收入角度看,地方政府的这种经营行为来源于地方与国有企业和乡镇企业的共生发展(Tao 等,2010:2221)。

但是,1994年的分税制改革(Tao 等,2010:2220-2222)以及土地和城市规划管理上的行政权力下放使得经营型城市的管治更加具有战略性。1980年实施的《城市规划编制审批暂行办法》表明了部委主导的发展开始向以城市自主规划引导的发展模式转变(Yeh 和 Wu,1998:178)。1989年颁布的《城市规划法》规定,所有的开发项目,不论是由政府机构还是私营开发商监管的项目,都需要申请选址、土地使用和开发许可证(Ng 和 Xu,2000:412),这进一步增强了地方政府在土地使用管理方面的权力。更为重要的是,地方规划的编制是由同一个权力机关执行的,而在制定的过程中也没有上级政府的具体指导。也就是说,地方规划的制定基本上成为了地方性的事务,上级政府很少介入。尽管规划文件和修订文件必须得到上一级政府乃至中央政府的批准,但是地方发展战略绝大多数还是由地方政府按照自己的意愿拟定的(Wu 和 Zhang, and Zhang, 2007). Additionally, the enactment of the Land Administration Law in 1986 also transformed the land administration from central allocation to urban authorities (Wu, 2000b: 1362). Subsequently, local land administration bureaus at or above the county level were established to grant land use rights and land leasing (Chen and Wills, 1999: 37). Furthermore, the amended Constitution Article in 1988 legitimised land as a commodity. The land conveyance fees were, in practice, pocketed by local governments as local extra-budgetary incomes, although by law 30 percent of the revenues should have belonged to the central government (Tao et al., 2010: 2225). In a word, the local governments virtually became the managers, as well as the main beneficiary parties, of local land development. As land revenue became a significant source for local revenue, the local governments were turned into entrepreneurial agents in land development (Zhu, 1999; Zhang, 2002a).

Henceforth, particularly since the 1990s, cities gained unprecedented autonomy in local development, and possessed privileged administration resources such as making comprehensive economic plans, formulating local strategies, setting local taxation rates, leasing urban land and granting urban land use. In contrast to the socialist hierarchical control, urban government became the major actor in the local economy. The changing role of the local state was firstly documented by, for example, Oi (1992, 1995), Walder (1995) and Unger and Chan (1999). Impelled by the growth imperative from fiscal strain and cadre tenure evaluation by an overriding criterion of economic growth, urban government formed an alliance with the capital and, hence, city-based entrepreneurial governance was established (Wu, 2000a). Through place-marketing to sell cities as production sites, urban government achieved not only enormous GDP growth, but also huge amounts of land-leasing income through land commodification.

Moreover, urban governance also witnessed consistent down-scaling towards urban districts, towns and townships within the municipality. For example, in 1992, Shanghai devolved an array of key administrative powers such as fiscal revenues, construction fees, urban planning, financial management, state asset management, regulation of foreign trade and investment, and land leasing to district governments (Wu, 2002). Furthermore, power was decentralised to residential offices and communities to help the municipal and district governments to manage fluid population and community service (Zhang, 2002b: 312; Wu et al., 2007: 127-130). On the one hand, it is observed that the devolution and reconfiguration of the local state strengthened and consolidated state governance at the local level (Shue, 1995: 97; Chung, 2007: 793; Wu et al., 2007: 132-133). The state fostered urban communities and extended government functions into base-level organisations to re-fill the governance vacuum caused by

2007）。此外，1986年实施的《土地管理法》也将土地管理权从中央调配转移到了城市相关部门（Wu，2000b：1362）。因此，县或县级以上的地方政府设立了地方土地管理局来管理土地使用权和土地租赁（Chen和Wills，1999：37）。同时，1988年的《宪法修正案》以立法形式规定了土地是一种商品。虽然按照法律土地转让收入的30%应当上缴中央政府，但在实际操作中这些土地出让金还是作为预算外收入进入了地方政府的腰包（Tao等，2010：2225）。总之，地方政府实际上成了地方土地开发的经理人，也是主要的受益方。随着土地收入成为地方财政的一个重要的收入来源，地方政府逐渐变成了土地开发的经营代理人（Zhu，1999；Zhang，2002a）。

因此，特别是从20世纪90年代开始，中国的各个城市获得了前所未有的本地发展自主权，拥有了掌控多种行政资源的特权，例如制定总体经济规划和地方发展战略、确定地方税率、租赁城市土地、审批城市土地使用等。与社会主义计划经济时期的逐级控制形成对比，地方政府在当地经济发展中扮演了主要的角色。Oi（1992，1995）、Walder（1995）、Unger和Chan（1999）等人最早记载了地方政府的角色演变。地方政府在财政紧缩的前提下仍需完成经济增长的任务，而且经济增长成了干部任期的首要评价标准，地方政府势必与资本结成联盟，由此建立了以城市为基础的经营型政府管治（Wu，2000a）。通过地方营销将城市作为生产基地，地方政府不仅实现了国内生产总值的快速增长，而且通过土地商品化获得了巨额的土地租赁收入。

不仅如此，城市管治也经历了相应的权力下放，从市政府逐级下放到市辖区和本市的乡镇一级。例如，上海在1992年将一系列重要的行政权力下放到区政府，如财政收入、建设费、城市规划、金融管理、国有资产管理、对外贸易和投资管理以及土地租赁等权力（Wu，2002）。除此之外，有些权力还下放到了居委会和社区，以帮助市政府和区政府管理流动人口和社区服务（Zhang，2002b：312；Wu等，2007：127-130）。一方面，我们可以看到政府权力的下放和重组的确加强和巩固了地方一级的政府管治（Shue，1995：97；Chung，2007：793；Wu等，2007：132-133）。国家促进城市社区的兴起，并将政府职能赋予基层组织，以此来填补市场化带来的流动性增加所导致的管治真空（Wu等，

increasing mobility after marketisation (Wu et al., 2007: 132-133). However, on the other hand, decentralisation also empowered grassroots organisations and fostered entrepreneurial governance (Wu, 2002: 1084-1087). As shown by the studies of He and Wu (2005) and Yang and Chang (2007), district governments have become the major actors engaged in current urban redevelopment. In part, this is due to the fact that the devolution of power accompanies responsibility for self-finance, which pushes district governments to scramble for fiscal resources (Zhang, 2002b: 311). As a result, the devolved regulatory power is utilised instrumentally by local authorities for local revenue creation.

Fiscal burdens at a higher level of government led to the radical solution of self-financing for almost all the localities, which also laid down the premises for fiscal autonomy, economic and administrative devolution. Pushed by financial responsibility and driven by growth first mentality, even towns and villages entered the race for inward investment alongside city and county government (Wei, 2002). In order to stimulate local economic development, Zhejiang Province began testing power devolution from municipal governments (prefecture -level cities) to county-level governments (county-level cities, counties, and city districts) as early as 1992. By 2006, four rounds of power devolution had been carried out to expand the power of economically strong counties (kuoquan qiangxian). Twelve main categories of administrative power have been devolved, including economic planning, commodity and trade, foreign trade, land and resources, transport and construction (Z.B. Zhang, 2009: 61). The broad range of new competencies in the county-level government has improved the business environment of county-level jurisdictions, and even freed county-level governments from control by prefecture-level governments (Chien, 2010: 144). Throughout the process, these county-level units have almost possessed equivalent administrative power to municipal governments. However, although power devolution has greatly helped to flatten hierarchical control and fix administrative procedures, it also decentralised the decision-making structure in the local territories and caused it to be scattered in discrete territorial administrations.

The simultaneous downward shift to the urban scale was also taking place in state spatial strategies. After 1978, the ideology of egalitarianism was abandoned due to the practical problems of production efficiency and fiscal deficit (Luo and Pannell, 1991: 29; Yang, 1990: 240). The national policy framework was sharply reoriented from the pursuit of equality to efficiency (Prime, 1991: 9; Fan, 1995: 424). An uneven economic strategy was introduced by the central state to emphasise comparative advantages and efficiency. It was stated that uneven development was an inevitable stage and

2007:132-133)。但是,另一方面,地方分权也增加了基层组织的权力并促使经营型管治模式应运而生(Wu,2002:1084-1087)。正如 He 与 Wu(2005)和 Yang 与 Chang(2007)的研究表明,区级政府在当前的城市再发展进程中扮演了主要角色。在某种程度上,这是由于分权带来了地方财政独立的责任,进而促使地方政府纷纷争夺财政资源(Zhang,2002b:311)。结果,下放的管治权力演变成了地方权力机构用来创造财政收入的工具。

上级政府的财政负担导致几乎所有的地方政府都采取激进的做法来解决财政独立的问题,这也为地方财政自主权及经济和行政上的分权创造了条件。在财政责任和增长第一的心态驱动下,镇政府和村政府也与市政府和县政府一起加入了对内投资的竞赛(Wei,2002)。为了刺激地方经济发展,浙江省早在 1992 年就开始试验将市级政府(地级市)的权力下放到县级政府(县级市、县和市下辖的各区政府)。截至 2006 年,浙江省已进行了四轮权力下放以扩大经济强县的权力(扩权强县),下放的行政权有十二大类,覆盖经济规划、商品贸易、对外贸易、土地和资源、交通和建设等领域(张占斌,2009:61)。县级政府因此获得了大量新的优势,提升了县级政府辖区的商业环境,甚至使县级政府摆脱了地级市政府的控制(Chien,2010:144)。在整个权力下放过程中,这些县级政府机构几乎获得了与市级政府同等的行政权。但是,尽管权力下放大大有助于弱化层级控制、提高行政程序的效率,然而这同时也导致了地方决策结构的权力松散,使得地方行政管理各行其是,头绪不清。

国家空间发展战略同时也在向城市尺度下移。由于存在生产低效和财政赤字这些实际问题(如 Luo 和 Pannell,1991:29;Yang,1990:240),1978 年后平均主义的思想遭到摈弃。国家政策框架明显由追求平等转向追求效率(Prime,1991:9;Fan,1995:424)。中央政府通过推行不均衡的经济战略来强调比较优势和效率。有学者认为,不均衡发展是一个必经阶段,最终会通过渗滴效应走向共同富裕(Fan,1997)。因此,更有竞争力的沿海地区取代了内陆地

would eventually lead to uniform wealth via a trickle-down effect (Fan, 1997). As a result, the more competitive coastal area, in place of the interior, was prioritised in national policies. Since the late 1970s, the coastal share of central government investment increased from 40 percent to about half (Yang, 1990: 246). In contrast, a redistributive policy to poorer regions was addressed to more pragmatic objectives – poverty alleviation rather than regional disparity alleviation (ibid: 255). It is argued that active programmes on local initiatives and endogenous development would have been more effective and efficient than prior passive ones relying on subsidies (Wang et al., 1997).

In contrast to the fading regional policies, many urban programmes were launched during the period, with an explicit regional bias towards the coast. For example, various open zones were designated to attract foreign investment, all in the coastal area. After the announcement of four Special Economic Zones in 1980, another fourteen open coastal cities were assigned in 1984. These urban programmes entailed a package of preferential policies and power decentralisation, ranging from investment, through foreign – exchange retention, revenue remittance and price, to finance (Fan, 1995: 426). As a result of the preferential policies for foreign investors locating projects in the coastal area, of the total of 41,998 foreign projects approved by the governments from 1979 to 1991, 37, 665 (89.7%) were located on the coast whilst 3,973 (9.5%) were based inland (Liu, 2007: 222). Apart from the economic zones and the opening of cities for trade, the state was also determined to build some global cities to introduce China to the global stage. One striking example is the phenomenal development of Shanghai. Rather than being the 'pump of blood transfusion' to the whole country, it is documented that Shanghai received a massive central tax return and reduction in the 1990s, which significantly helped its initial infrastructure investment (Wu, 2003: 1688). Moreover, the Pudong New area was conferred with a sub-municipality administrative rank, which is higher than ordinary urban districts (Wu, 2000b: 352). Overall, the socialist regional redistributive policies have been largely substituted by urban programmes, in which growth poles are expected to lead the regional development and spontaneously remove the uneven pattern of growth distribution.

3.2.3 Consequences of the downscaling of governance

Under the centrally-planned economy, continuous efforts were made to build a regional economy by a ministry-led economy, where horizontal links were inherently highly insufficient (Donnithorne, 1972: 610; Wong, 1991b; Fan, 1995: 423). In the market economy, however, economic regionalisation was developing spontaneously, but was nevertheless under artificial barriers. This

区,优先享受到国家政策。从20世纪70年代末开始,沿海地区享受的中央政府投资份额从40%上升到大约50%(Yang,1990:246)。对比而言,对较贫穷地区实行的再分配政策目标变得更加务实,主要是为了减贫而不是缩小地区差距(同上:255)。有学者认为,这种依靠地方主动性和内生式发展的积极经济发展方案应当会比以往依赖补贴的被动经济方案更有成效和效率(Wang等,1997)。

与逐渐淡出的区域政策相比,在这一时期启动了很多城市项目,重心明显偏向沿海地区。例如,用来吸引外资的各种开发区都设立在沿海地区。在1980年宣布成立4个经济特区后,1984年又指定了14个沿海开放城市。这些城市项目引发了一系列优惠政策和权力下放,涉及投资、外汇留成、上缴利税和价格到金融等诸多方面(Fan,1995:426)。由于外国投资者将项目设在沿海地区可以享受优惠政策,因此在1979到1991年政府批准的41 998个外资项目中有37 665个(89.7%)都设在沿海地区,而仅有3 973个(9.5%)项目设在内陆地区(刘玉,2007:222)。除了建立经济特区和开放城市贸易,国家还决定建设一些全球性城市,让中国走向世界舞台。一个明显的例子就是上海的惊人发展。上海并不是要发展成全国的"输血泵",据记载,上海在90年代享受到了中央政府大量的返税和减税优惠,极大地推动了其初期的基础设施投资(Wu,2003:1688)。此外,浦东新区也获得了比直辖市略低,却比一般市辖区高的行政级别(Wu,2000b:352)。总体而言,社会主义区域再分配政策已在很大程度上由城市项目所取代,国家期望通过城市经济增长点带动整个地区发展,从而自发地消除经济增长分布不均衡的模式。

三、管治权力下移的后果

在中央计划经济的体制下,国家不断努力,建立一种以部委主导的区域经济,这种机制势必存在横向联系严重不足的内在问题(Donnithorne,1972:610;Wong,1991b;Fan,1995:423)。然而,在市场经济中,经济区域化自发发展,却又遭遇人为障碍。这是因为经济权力下放和竞争导致经济地方主义开始出

was because economic localism was beginning to emerge due to economic decentralisation and competition. 'Dukedom economies' (zhuhoujingji) were particularly common in the second half of the 1980s (for more materials and documentary sources, please see e.g. Breslin, 1995: 68-70; Breslin, 2000: 224, note 27-28; Zhao and Zhang, 1999: 272), when economic trade and outflow was blockaded by China's provincial and local governments (Lee, 1998: 281). Local protectionism and impediments to economic integration were so common between provinces that economists think the domestic market was even less developed than openness to foreign trade (Poncet, 2003). Although regional blockading of the market gradually subsided due to substantial progress in price reform, the 1994 tax assignment reform and the increasing share of non-state economic sectors, fierce inter-city competition did not reduce in the least (Chien and Gordon, 2008; Wu and Zhang, 2007; Xu and Yeh, 2005; Zhang and Wu, 2006). Inter-locality competition was then particularly manifested in the implicit realms of policies and strategies, as well as in project competition and road disconnection. For example, Shanghai used local funds to construct its own sea port, despite the fact that Ningbo port is just nearby. Such policy emulation and repetitive construction worsened the zero-sum competition (Chien, 2008).Furthermore, it is observed that the border area was often marginalised and deficiently invested by local jurisdictions (Zhou, 2008: 242). That is, local government would make no investment outside its own jurisdiction, or make any investment that was expected to benefit others more than itself. Overall, the economic contour was still dominantly confined by administrative boundaries. It is suggested that local governments showed little interest in cross-border cooperation (Wang et al., 1997: 39). This is conceptualised by Chinese scholars as a phenomenon unique to China, and is termed as 'economy based on administrative divisions' (xingzhengqujingji) (Liu, 2001). That is, market activities and economic development were divided by invisible walls established by administrative boundaries.

On the other hand, the downscaling of governance power also challenged the authority of higher-level regulation. One typical example was in the sphere of land use and planning control. In order to tackle the environmental problems caused by rapid and widespread economic development, the State Planning Commission launched territorial planning (guotuguihua), a kind of trans-administrative regional plan, in the late 1980s and the 1990s across the country. However, since planning power had been decentralised from the central government, the requirements for rational land use and spatial labour division from the central government were nearly impossible to carry out in provinces, cities and counties. As a result, these formulated plans eventually failed to be applied (Hu, 2006: 586). This kind of local discretion was not

现。在20世纪80年代后半期,"诸侯经济"尤其普遍(更多资料和文件出处可参阅如Breslin,1995:68-70;Breslin,2000:224,注27-28;Zhao和Zhang,1999:272),当时经济贸易和资金外流被中国省级政府和地方政府封锁(Lee,1998:281)。地方保护主义和经济一体化的阻碍在各省之间极为普遍,以至有经济学家认为国内市场的发育程度甚至不如对外贸易的开放程度(Poncet,2003)。虽然随着价格改革、分税制改革以及经济改革的实质性进展,区域市场封锁的程度也在逐渐消退,但是城市间的激烈竞争却丝毫没有减弱(Chien和Gordon,2008;Wu和Zhang,2007;Xu和Yeh,2005;Zhang和Wu,2006)。随后的地区间竞争特别体现在政策和战略这些隐性领域,还体现在项目竞争和切断道路联系上。比如,虽然宁波港就在上海附近,但上海还是利用本地资金建设了自己的海港。这种政策模仿和重复建设加剧了零和竞争(Chien,2008)。此外,也有学者认为边界区域常常被边缘化,缺乏地方政府的投资(周黎安,2008:242)。也就是说,地方政府不会在自己的辖区之外进行投资,也不会进行有可能惠及他人而影响自己收益的投资。总体而言,经济格局仍然主要受到行政边界的限制。有资料表明,地方政府对跨界合作兴趣不大(Wang等,1997:39)。中国学者将此看作中国特有的现象,称之为"行政区经济"(刘君德,2001)。也就是说,市场活动和经济发展被行政边界造成的无形屏障割裂了。

另一方面,下放管治权也挑战了高层监管部门的权威。一个典型的例子出现在土地使用和规划控制上。为了解决经济快速发展所带来的环境问题,国家计委开始推行国土规划,也就是20世纪80年代末和90年代在全国范围推行的一种跨行政区的区域规划。然而,由于中央政府规划的权力已经下放,中央政府提出的合理使用土地和实行劳动空间分工的要求在各省、市、县几乎不可能得到贯彻。结果,这些拟定的规划最终未能实施(胡序威,2006:586)。这

only present between the central government and localities, but within localities as well. Provinces and municipalities all met with difficulties in remedying rampant land encroachment and uncoordinated development in their jurisdiction, owing to the devolution of planning control towards cities and counties (Ng and Tang, 1999).Take urban planning as another example. As administrative power had been devolved from the municipality to districts and towns, the municipal urban planning turned out to be merely responsible for central city land management. Even the statutory urban system plan at the municipal level couldn't regulate town and village development under its jurisdiction, since they had been empowered with local decisions (Xu, 2006: 40). In other words, the governance downscaling towards localities at the mean time produced governance fragmentation and in – coordination. Due to insufficient coordination at the urban and regional level, duplicate development across administrative boundaries became pervasive. It is concerning that production over –capacity built up in some industries. In 2004, the nationwide over–investment in steel, cement, and the electrolytic aluminium industry was so severe that austere economic programmes were applied by the central state (Zhang and Zhang, 2005: 12). Another example is from the YRD region. It is calculated that the average industrial similarity coefficient[1] between Jiangsu and Zhejiang was 0.954 from 1993 to 2002, the coefficient between Shanghai and Jiangsu was 0.843, while that between Zhejiang and Shanghai was 0.747 (Zhang et al., 2007: 309). The same conclusion can be made from similar manufacturing products produced by each economic development zone within the region (ibid: 311).

In terms of uneven development, it is widely recognised that the disparities between rich and poor areas had been enlarging, especially after the economic reform. During the 1950s and 1960s, it is shown that productive capacity underwent some relative shifts from the coast to inland, particularly to the Third –Front area (Wang et al., 1997: 29). However, in terms of industrial output and per capita income, the pattern is inconclusive (Fan, 1995: 423–424, 427; Wang et al., 1997: 29). Although a large amount of state capital did go to the interior provinces by means of a centralised fiscal and investment system (Wei and Ma, 1996), it was far from enough to effect fundamental change in regional inequality (Wei, 1996). The persistence of inequality is primarily attributable to the legacy of an uneven spatial economy, urban – centred

---

[1] The similarity coefficient calculation formula is $S_{ij} = \sum (X_{in} \cdot X_{jn}) / \sqrt{(\sum X^2_{in}) \cdot (\sum X^2_{jn})}$. X_{in} represents the concentration of industrial sector n in the area i, and X_{jn} represents the concentration of industrial sector n in the area j. The S_{ij} index is the similarity coefficient. A higher S_{ij} index suggests a higher similarity of industrial structure between two areas.

种地方自行其是的情况不仅存在于中央与地方政府之间,还存在于地方内部。由于规划控制权下放到市和县,导致各省、市在解决辖区内严重的土地侵占和不协调发展问题上都遇到了重重困难(Ng 和 Tang,1999)。以城市规划作为另一个例子。由于行政权力由市下放到区和镇,市政府的城市规划最终变成了只负责中心城区的土地管理。甚至市一级的法定城市体系规划也无法监管辖区内的城镇和乡村的发展,因为这些乡镇已经有权自己制定地方决策(徐海贤,2006:40)。换言之,管治权下放到地方的同时也造成了管治的分散和不协调。由于城市和区域层面的协调不够,跨行政边界的重复建设相当普遍。值得注意的是,许多行业还出现了产能过剩。2004 年在全国范围内出现了极为严重的钢铁、水泥和电解铝行业过度投资,迫使中央政府采取严厉的经济政策来作出调节(张汉亚和张欣宁,2005:12)。另一个例子发生在长三角地区。据计算,1993 年至 2002 年江苏与浙江之间的平均产业结构相似系数❶为 0.954,上海与江苏之间是 0.843,而浙江与上海之间为 0.747(张颢瀚等,2007:309)。从同一区域各经济开发区生产类似的制造业产品这一事实中也可得出相同的结论(同上:311)。

从发展不平衡的角度来看,人们普遍认识到贫富地区之间的差距在不断扩大,特别是在经济改革之后。在 20 世纪 50 年代和 60 年代,国内生产能力发生了相对转移,从沿海地区陆续转向内陆地区,特别是转向三线地区(Wang 等,1997:29)。然而,这个转移模式并没有在工业产值和人均收入上产生决定性的影响(Fan,1995:423-424,427;Wang 等,1997:29)。虽然的确有大量的国家资本通过中央财政和投资体系流向了内陆省份(Wei 和 Ma,1996),却还是远不足以从根本上改变区域不平等的状况(Wei,1996)。造成不平等长期存在的主要原因是空间经济不均衡,工业化以城市为中心,内部投资的回报低(Wei,

---

❶ 相似系数计算公式为 $S_{ij} = \sum (X_{in} \cdot X_{jn}) / \sqrt{(\sum X_{in}^2) \cdot (\sum X_{jn}^2)}$。$X_{in}$ 表示在地区 i 中工业部门 n 的集中程度,X_{jn} 表示在地区 j 中工业部门 n 的集中程度。S_{ij} 指数为相似系数。S_{ij} 指数越大表明两个地区之间的工业结构相似度越高。

industrialisation, and poor returns of interior investment (Wei, 1999: 51). In particular, the subsidised energy and raw material supplies to urban sectors under a distorted price structure contributed to the problem of urban-rural and inter-sectoral dualism in the Socialist economy (Naughton, 1995: 71-73). In the 1980s, interprovincial inequality declined, especially in the eastern regions due to the slow growth of old industrial cores such as Shanghai, Beijing and Tianjin and the rapid development of other growth cores in previously less developed provinces (Wei and Ma, 1996). Nevertheless, interregional inequality persisted and economic growth did not spread from the initially developed areas to the central and western region, as previously justified. In the 1990s, inequality even surged and the rate stabilised from the late 1990s (Fan and Sun, 2008). It is recognised that regionally-biased fiscal, investment, FDI and decentralisation policies launched after economic reform were the main determinants of regional inequality (Fan, 1992; Ma and Wei, 1997; Wei, 1996, 2000; Wei and Fan, 2000; Zhao and Tong, 2000; Long and Ng, 2001). Although the openness policy was actually extended to the whole country in the 1990s, foreign direct investment kept concentrating on the coastal area. Furthermore, the development gap not only existed between regions and within regions, but also within provinces and cities (Wei and Fan, 2000; Wei and Ye, 2004;Wei, 2007). According to a case study set in Zhejiang (Ye and Wei, 2005), it is found that the historical inequality between the coast and southern interior within the province widened, and the emergence of rapidly growing cores tended to concentrate in three clusters, that is, Hangzhou - Shaoxing - Ningbo, the coastal Wenzhou-Taizhou, and the central Jinhua-Quzhou. In other words, the spatial pattern of inequality is now not simply between cities and counties, but between certain city-regions and the remaining area.

Fiscal decentralisation contributed to and exacerbated the growing gap between rich and poor regions. Firstly, it is argued that the revenue contract scheme influenced the proportion of central revenue and, hence, impacted on the capability of central transfer. However, the situation did not improve after tax sharing reform in 1994 (Yep, 2008). Secondly, it is revealed that after inter-regional transfer was reduced in the post-reform period, the replacement scheme had not yet been well addressed (Ma, 1995: 230; Wong, 1991a: 712; Zhang, 1999: 140). The substituted national poverty alleviation plan was limited to certain extremely deprived areas and although programmes of inter-provincial assistance, joint development and technological transfer were firmly encouraged by the central government, they were voluntary and based on a principle of mutual benefit. It is reported that the cooperation dialogue was effectively more favourable to the coast than to the interior (Prime, 1991: 21; Yang, 1990: 253). Thirdly, it is suggested that the limited amount of transferred money was

1999：51）。特别是以扭曲的价格结构为城市部门供应能源补贴和原材料，造成了社会主义经济中城乡之间和部门之间的双重标准问题（Naughton，1995：71-73）。在20世纪80年代，省与省之间的不平等程度有所降低，特别是在东部地区，原因在于上海、北京和天津等老工业核心的经济增长放缓，而以前发展程度较低省份的其他经济增长核心发展较快（Wei和Ma，1996）。尽管如此，区域不平等依然存在，经济增长并没有如以前推断的那样由最初的发达地区向中西部蔓延。到了90年代，不平等程度甚至一度飙升，直到90年代后期开始稳定下来（Fan和Sun，2008）。有学者认为，经济改革后所采取的有区域偏向的财政、投资、外商直接投资和中央权力下放等政策，是导致区域不平等的主要决定因素（Fan，1992；Ma和Wei，1997；Wei，1996，2000；Wei和Fan，2000）。虽然在90年代，开放政策实际上已扩大到全国范围，但是外商直接投资仍一直集中在沿海区域。此外，发展差距不仅存在于各区域之间和区域内部，也存在于各省、市内部（Wei和Fan，2000；Wei和Ye，2004；Wei，2007）。在浙江进行的一个案例研究（Ye和Wei，2005）发现，省内沿海地区和南方内陆地区之间在历史上就存在的不平等进一步加大，新出现的快速增长核心主要集中在三大区域：杭州—绍兴—宁波、沿海的温州—台州、中部的金华—衢州。换句话说，在空间格局上现在不只是城市与县之间存在不平等，某些城市区域与其他地区之间也存在不平等现象。

财政权下放导致贫富区域之间出现差距并使这种差距不断扩大。首先，有观点认为财税包干制影响了中央财政收入的比例，因而也影响了中央的转移支付能力。然而，经历了1994年的分税制改革后，这种情况依然没有得到改善（Yep，2008）。其次，有研究表明，改革开放区域间资金转移减少后并没有实施相应的替代方案（Ma，1995：230；Wong，1991a：712；Zhang，1999：140）。国家减贫计划作为替代方案只局限于某些极度贫困地区，虽然中央政府坚持鼓励跨省援助计划、共同发展计划和技术转移计划，但这些计划都是自愿性质并且以互利互惠的原则为基础。有报道指出，沿海地区与内陆地区之间的合作对话往往对前者更为有利（Prime，1991：21；Yang，1990：253）。再次，也有人认为，出于政治方面的考虑，政府往往将有限的援助资金更多地投入到少数民族

oriented more to minority regions for political concerns rather than all the poor regions (Liu, 2007: 214-217). Finally, the inter-governmental transfer functioned poorly and could even be manipulated by provincial or municipal governments in the midway. The countryside, particularly in the backward areas, therefore experienced extreme difficulties (ibid: 218 - 219). Overall, local discretions, fragmented governance, adverse inter - locality competition and the enlargement of uneven development have come to be conceived as the urgent issues that caused the governance capacity crises in China.

3.2.4 The re-emergence of the regional scale in China (2000—present)

After decades of marginalisation of regional institutions and policies, new regional concepts have reappeared in China since 2000. Not only regional policies have been resumed, but also regional plans and alliances have been rejuvenated. The emergence of regional governance is being heatedly discussed in the Chinese literature, especially from the perspectives of planning, administration and institutions (Hong, 2009; Ji et al., 2006; Tao, 2007; Wang, 2008; Wang, 2009; B. J. Yang, 2004; Zhang et al., 2007; Zong, 2008). The following sections will elaborate the changes and practices of various aspects. They include the new western, middle and coastal regional polices, and the main functional area plan, which represents the return of regional policies; the recentralisation of land management, and province - leading - county administrative reform, which manifests an upward scaling of governance towards the regional scale; and various regionalisation exercises undertaken by both central and local governments, which consist of urban administrative annexation and mergers, the building of regional alliances and partnerships, and the formulation of regional plans.

3.3 The re-emergence of coordinated regional policies since 2000

Regional policies in China have been characterised by preferential treatment for coastal and urban areas (especially large cities) since economic reform. However, the central state has launched a series of new regional policies since 2000 in order to cope with the regional issue of enlarging economic disparities. Following the proposal of Developing the Western Region in late 1999, the central government successively proposed the strategy of Reviving North - East Industrial Base and Boosting the Midland Economic Growth in 2003 and in 2004 (See Figure 3.7). The proposal of the three regional policies marks the revival of balanced regional policies after a long absence since the economic reform.

地区,而不是所有的贫困地区(刘玉,2007:214-17)。最后,政府间的资金转移并未发挥较好的作用,甚至在转移过程中还会受到省政府或市政府的操控。农村,尤其是落后地区的农村,因此陷入了极大的困境(同上:218-19)。总的来说,地方的自行其是、管治的分散、地方之间的恶性竞争以及发展水平差距的扩大,都被认为是导致中国政府管治能力危机的问题,亟待解决。

四、区域尺度在中国的重现(2000年至今)

在中国,区域制度和区域政策经历了长达几十年的边缘化之后,从2000年开始新的区域概念再次出现。不仅区域政策重新实施,区域规划和区域联盟也再现活力。许多中文文献对区域管治的兴起展开了大量讨论,尤其是从规划、行政管理和机构设置的角度进行了探讨(洪世健,2009;纪晓岚等,2006;陶希东,2007;王川兰,2008;王枫云,2009;杨保军,2004;张颢瀚等,2007;踪家峰,2008)。以下各节将会详述区域管治在多个方面的变化与做法。西部、中部和沿海地区实施的新的区域政策以及主体功能区规划,都标志着区域政策的回归;土地资源的重新集中管理和省管县行政改革,体现了政府管治尺度向区域层面的上移;新增和合并城市行政辖区,建立区域联盟和区域合作伙伴关系,以及制定区域规划等,代表了中央和地方政府所实行的各项区域化举措。

第三节　2000年起区域协调发展政策的重现

中国在改革开放后实施的区域政策的特征是为沿海地区和城市地区(尤其是大城市)提供优惠待遇。但是从2000年开始,中央政府推出了一系列新的区域政策,来应对区域间经济差距不断扩大的问题。中央政府在1999年年底提出了西部大开发的方案之后,又分别在2003年和2004年提出振兴东北老工业基地和中部地区崛起的战略(见图3.7)。这三个区域政策的提出,标志着改革开放后较长时间内不再实施的区域平衡发展政策的重现。

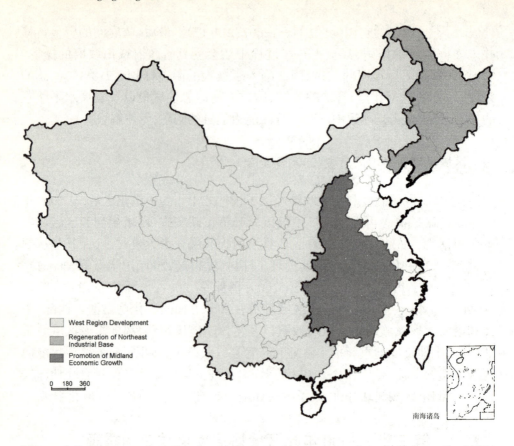

Figure 3.7 Strategy of regional coordinated development launched in early 2000s
Source: compiled by the author.

These programmes contain a package of discrete policies. The current policy packages and institutional apparatus in the western, middle and northeast regional programmes have been compiled from various sources and are listed in Table 3.2. Take the west development for instance; the programme involves massive state investment and strong political support. As early as 1997, the central government elevated Chongqing, a major city within the region, to be directly administered under the State Council in order to use its conspicuous administrative status to build a growth pole in the western region. In January of 2000, the Leading Group Office for Western Region Development was set up under the State Council. Moreover, a specific Five-Year Plan was prepared for the region in both Tenth and Eleventh Five-Year Plan periods. In addition to increasing central fiscal expenditure, a favourable bank credit scheme and tax policies have also been designed for western provinces (Naughton, 2004: 267).

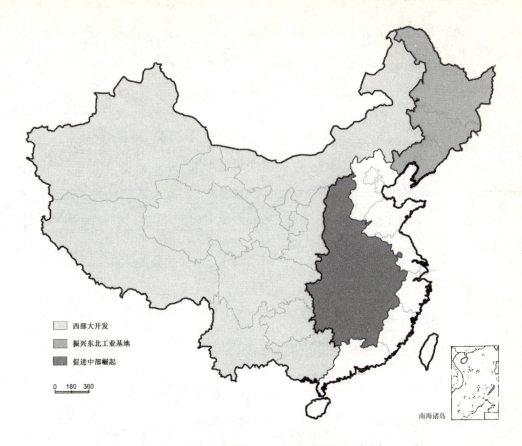

图3.7 21世纪初推行的区域协调发展战略

来源：作者编制。

这些区域发展方案包括了一揽子不同的政策。根据不同资料来源编制的表3.2列出了西部、中部和东北地区发展方案中的各项现行政策和机构设置。以西部大开发为例：该方案涉及大规模的国家投资和强有力的政治支持。早在1997年，中央政府就将该区域的主要城市重庆升格为直辖市，以用其突出的行政地位在西部地区建立一个增长点。2000年1月，国务院下设西部大开发领导小组办公室。此外，"十五"和"十一五"规划都为西部地区制订了专门的五年计划。除了增加中央财政支出之外，国家还为西部省份出台了优惠的银行信贷方案和税收政策（Naughton，2004：267）。

Table 3.2 National policies for western, central and northeast regions from 1999 to 2009

	Western	Northeast	Central
Institutional setting	West Development Leading Group Office set up under the State Council in 2000	Northeast Regeneration Leading Group Office set up under the State Council in 2004	Reviving Mid-land Region Office set up under the National Development and Reform Commission in 2007
Policy focus	To make development strategy, planning and policies; To ensure environmental protection; To encourage investment	To make industrial planning and policies; To assist the restructuring of state-owned heavy manufacturing enterprises	To make development strategy and planning; To coordinate development policies; To encourage investment
Published central documents	Circular on implementing West Development Policies by the State Council in 2000; Implementation of a Directive on Western Development Policies by the State Council in 2001; West Region Development Master Plan in the Tenth Five-Year Plan period in 2002; The formulation of laws on the promotion of western development is taken into procedural consideration in 2003; Further Implementing Advice on Western Development Policies issued by State Council in 2004; West Region Development Master Plan in the Eleventh Five-Year Plan period issued in 2005	Directive on Implementing Old Industrial Base Regeneration Policies by State Council in 2003; Implementation of a Directive on Promoting the further Opening of Northeast Old Industrial Base by State Council in 2005	Directive on Implementing Middle Region Revival Policies by State Council in 2006
Preferential policies	Tax reduction from 2001 to 2010 for both domestic and foreign investors who invest in the west in preferred industries; Exemption from tax on land occupation if invested in highway construction; Exemption from tariffs on imported equipment of encouraged industries; Relaxed restrictions on the foreign investment field mean telecom, insurance, retailing business and so on will be opened to foreign investors	VAT tax rebate for eight industries, including equipment manufacture, petrochemical industry, metallurgy, marine manufacturing, motor industry, military manufacturing, high-technology industry, and agricultural processing	To be materialised

Source: compiled from http://www.chinawest.gov.cn/web/Column.asp?ColumnId=16; http://xbkfs.ndrc.gov.cn/jgsz/default.htm; http://chinaneast.xinhuanet.com/jianjie.htm; http://dbzxs.ndrc.gov.cn/.

表3.2 1999至2009年在西部、中部和东北地区实施的国家政策

	西部地区	东北地区	中部地区
机构设置	2000年国务院下设西部大开发领导小组办公室	2004年国务院下设振兴东北地区等老工业基地领导小组办公室	2007年国家发改委下设促进中部地区崛起工作办公室
政策重点	制定西部大开发的战略、规划和政策；提出及协调实施环境保护的政策措施；鼓励投资	组织拟订振兴东北等老工业基地的规划和重大政策；协助国有重工业企业改革重组	制定中部崛起的发展战略和规划；协调实施发展政策；鼓励投资
中央发文	《国务院关于实施西部大开发若干政策措施的通知》(2000年)；国务院发布《关于西部大开发若干政策措施的实施意见》(2001年)；"十五"西部开发总体规划(2002年)；促进西部开发的法规制定于2003年被列入立法程序；《国务院关于进一步推进西部大开发的若干意见》(2004年)；"十一五"规划中的西部大开发计划(2005年)	国务院发布《关于实施东北地区等老工业基地振兴战略的若干意见》(2003年)；《国务院办公厅关于促进东北老工业基地进一步扩大对外开放的实施意见》(2005年)	《中共中央国务院关于促进中部地区崛起的若干意见》(2006年)
优惠政策	对设在西部地区的投资国家鼓励类产业的内资企业和外商投资企业，在2001年至2010年期间，减少征收企业所得税；对投资公路建设的企业免征耕地占用税；对鼓励类产业的进口设备免征关税；放宽外商投资领域，电信、保险、零售等业务将对外国投资者开放	在八大行业施行增值税退税，包括装备制造业、石油化工业、冶金工业、船舶制造业、汽车制造业、军品工业、高新技术产业和农产品加工业	有待出台

来源：编自 http://www.chinawest.gov.cn/web/Column.asp?ColumnId=16; http://xbkfs.ndrc.gov.cn/jgsz/default.htm; http://chinaeast.xinhuanet.com/jianjie. htm; http://dbzxs.ndrc.gov.cn/。

In addition to the mega-regional policies, the state council initiated a new socialist countryside project in 2002 in order to tackle the entrenched inequalities between urban and rural areas. Before then, the countryside had been suffering from fiscal deficits and poorer infrastructure, since the city-leading-county system and the post-reform economic policies had been biased toward the urban area (Chung, 2007). Nevertheless, the central government prioritised rural problems from 2004. The First State Council Document has been dedicated to rural development for eight successive years (Table 3.3). The document is also dubbed as 'No.1 central document'. This is the first document released by the CPC Central Committee and the State Council at the beginning of every year. The document is of great significance, since it represents the government's priorities for that year. Due to the importance of the document, all relevant ministries and departments of the government will subsequently present their working programmes in order to implement the central policy. Therefore, the eight consecutive documents targeted at issues of agriculture and peasants have demonstrated the efforts and determination of the central government to improve rural conditions. These policies comprise five main aspects: subsidies and price support as a commitment to rural income, the abolition of agricultural tax and fees, the protection of rural collective land rights, the gradual elimination of restrictions of hukou and rural-urban migration, and increasing central government spending on rural health, technology, education, physical and social infrastructures in rural areas. It is estimated that the appropriation and subsidies from the state budget since 2004 have amounted to 30 billion *yuan* (Liu, 2007: 173). The initiatives manifest a remarkable reorientation of national development priority from urban areas to the vast rural regions.

Table 3.3 The series of No.1 State Council Documents from 2004 to 2011

Issued date	Name of the document	Key issues
February 8, 2004	Instructions on increasing peasant income by Chinese Communist Party Central Committee and State Council	To solve the problem that the rural income per capita was increasing very slowly
January 30, 2005	Instructions on broadening government work on rural development and improving rural comprehensive productivity by Chinese Communist Party Central Committee and State Council	To consolidate existing agricultural policies; To improve agricultural productivity; To adjust the agricultural and rural economic structure

除了这些涉及多个省市的大区域政策之外,国务院还在2002年推行社会主义新农村建设项目,以解决长久存在的城乡发展不平等的问题。在此之前,农村地区在财政上一直入不敷出,基础设施落后,就因为市管县体制和改革开放后的经济政策一直偏向于城市地区(Chung,2007)。不过从2004年起中央政府开始着力解决农村问题。国务院一号文件已连续八年专门关注农村地区的发展问题(表3.3)。该文件也被称作"中央一号文件"。它是党中央、国务院在每年年初发布的第一份文件。这份文件具有重大意义,内容涉及政府在该年度的首要任务。正是由于这份文件的重要性,有关部委和政府部门随后都会出台各自的工作方案来贯彻落实中央的政策。因此,这八个连续发布的针对农业和农民问题的文件体现了中央政府改善农村条件的努力和决心。这些政策包括五个主要方面:发放补贴和保护农产品价格以增加农民收入;取消农业税费;保护农村集体土地权;逐步消除户籍制度的约束和农村向城市迁移的限制;增加中央政府在农村地区卫生、科技、教育、体育和社会基础设施的投入。据估计,自2004年以来,出自国家预算的拨款和补贴就达到300亿元(刘玉,2007:173)。这些举措体现了国家发展重心由城市地区向广大农村地区转变的显著趋势。

表3.3 2004至2011年国务院发布的一号文件

发布日期	文件名称	关注焦点
2004年2月8日	《中共中央国务院关于促进农民增加收入若干政策的意见》	解决农村人均收入增长缓慢的问题
2005年1月30日	《中共中央国务院关于进一步加强农村工作提高农业综合生产能力若干政策的意见》	巩固现有的农业政策; 提高农业生产力; 调整农业和农村经济结构

continued

Issued date	Name of the document	Key issues
February 21, 2006	Instructions on promoting the construction of a new socialist countryside by Chinese Communist Party Central Committee and State Council	To consolidate existing agricultural policies; To improve rural infrastructure; To promote the development of human services in rural areas
January 29, 2007	Instructions on advocating modern agriculture and steadily promoting the construction of anew socialist countryside by Chinese Communist Party Central Committee and State Council	To modernise agricultural development by means of modern engineering, modern technology, a modern industrial system and a modern management style
January 30, 2008	Instructions on intensifying rural infrastructure construction and promoting rural development and improving rural income by Chinese Communist Party Central Committee and State Council	To promote the urban–rural coordinated development; To industrialise agricultural industry; To urbanise rural areas
February 1, 2009	Instructions on promoting steady agricultural growth and improving rural income by Chinese Communist Party Central Committee and State Council	To keep supporting agricultural development; To stabilise agricultural production; To improve modern engineering and service systems in rural areas; To promote urban–rural coordinated development
January 31, 2010	Instructions on consolidating urban and rural coordinated development and rural growth by Chinese Communist Party Central Committee and State Council	To stabilise rice production; To modernise agricultural industry; To increase rural income; To promote the development of human services in rural areas; To reform rural land management systems and financial systems
January 29, 2011	Decision on accelerating water conservancy reform and development by Chinese Communist Party Central Committee and State Council	To accelerate the development of water conservation; To tackle flood and drought issues and promote the sustainable use of resources

Source: compiled from http://politics.people.com.cn/GB/1026/10893986.html, and http://europe.chinadaily.com.cn/china/2011-01/31/content_11945533.htm, accessed on 7 Feb, 2011.

续表

发布日期	文件名称	关注焦点
2006年2月21日	《中共中央国务院关于推进社会主义新农村建设的若干意见》	巩固现有的农业政策； 改善农村基础设施； 促进农村地区公共服务的发展
2007年1月29日	《中共中央国务院关于积极发展现代农业扎实推进社会主义新农村建设的若干意见》	通过现代工程、现代技术、现代产业体系和现代化管理模式实现农业发展现代化
2008年1月30日	《中共中央国务院关于切实加强农业基础建设进一步促进农业发展农民增收的若干意见》	统筹城乡发展； 实现农业产业化； 推动农村地区城市化
2009年2月1日	《中共中央国务院关于2009年促进农业稳定发展农民持续增收的若干意见》	继续支持农业发展； 稳定农业生产； 完善农村地区现代工程和服务体系； 统筹城乡发展
2010年1月31日	《中共中央国务院关于加大统筹城乡发展力度进一步夯实农业农村发展基础的若干意见》	稳定粮食生产； 农业产业现代化； 增加农民收入； 促进农村地区公共服务的发展； 改革农村土地管理制度和农村金融体系
2011年1月29日	《中共中央国务院关于加快水利改革发展的决定》	加快水利发展； 解决洪水和干旱问题,促进水资源可持续利用

来源：编自 http://politics.people.com.cn/GB/1026/10893986.html；http://europe.chinadaily.com.cn/china/2011-01/31/content_11945533.htm（网站访问日期：2011年2月7日）。

Overall, it seems the national regional policy has entered a new stage since 2000. In place of the ideology of growth being of overriding importance, the concept of coordinated development was put forward during the Third Plenary Sessions of the Sixteenth Central Committee (11/10/2003 – 14/10/2003). This represents that a balanced, coordinated and sustainable development mode is advocated by the central state to replace decades of uneven development and growth-first mentality (Fan, 2006). New emphases are now laid on balanced urban-rural and regional development, social harmony, environmental protection and energy conservation. In 2007, the Scientific Development (kexuefazhan guan) was written into the Party Law and the strategy of coordinated development was reaffirmed by the Seventeenth Communist Party Committee National Congress (15/10/2007 - 21/10/2007). It is put forward that the forthcoming core issue for all the governments is to narrow the regional development gap, optimise the pattern of territorial development, and equalise public services between different regions. Nevertheless, it is still too early to examine the real effect of these discursive policies on redressing inequality.

3.4 Launch of the main functional area policy in 2005

After economic reform, the territory plan (guotuguihua) was imported from Japan and Western Europe, and the State Council prepared to enforce it in the early 1980s. At that time, various tiers of local planning commissions above the county-level were instructed to prepare their levels of territory plan, and a national-level plan and nineteen key trans-boundary plans were formulated by the National Planning Commission (NPC) (Wang and Hague, 1993: 567). The plan was anticipated to justify national leaders in constraining the downsides of market-oriented development and to preserve natural resources through land use regulation (Hu, 2006). In other words, the territory plan was intended to be used to guide local development in place of top-down economic planning and economic command. However, the making of the territorial plan came to a halt in 1996 (Hu, 2006) due to many reasons. For example, the formulation of the plan and its document lacked legitimate status; moreover, the plan was only a blueprint document without any concern for the implementation mechanism and public policies. As a result, the effect of the plan was increasingly challenged by decentralisation and market reform, where the governance context was much more complicated than purely top-down instructions and administrative obedience. Furthermore, the territory plan was criticised for being actually grounded upon economic growth and was, in essence, a productivity distribution plan like that in the socialist period, since the plan mainly placed locations of growth centres (Wang and Hague, 1993:

总体来看,国家区域政策自2000年以来进入了一个新阶段。党的十六届三中全会(2003年10月11日—2003年10月14日)提出了科学发展观,取代了之前的发展才是硬道理的指导思想。这表示中央政府开始提倡均衡、协调、可持续的发展模式,摈弃沿用了数十年的不均衡发展和发展第一的理念(Fan,2006)。现在发展的重点放在了城乡和区域均衡发展、社会和谐、环境保护和能源节约上。2007年,科学发展观被写入党章,中国共产党第十七次全国代表大会(2007年10月15日—2007年10月21日)重申了协调发展战略。会上提出各级政府部门面临的核心问题是如何缩小区域发展差异、优化区域发展格局和促使各地区公共服务均衡发展。然而,各级各地政府解决发展失衡问题的政策比较散乱,要检验其实际效果仍为时过早。

第四节　2005年主体功能区政策的出台

经济改革之后,国务院计划在20世纪80年代初开始实施从日本和西欧引入的国土规划。当时,中央指示各县级以上的地方规划委员会制定与其各级相应的国土规划,国家计划委员会也出台了一个国家级规划和十九个重点跨界计划(Wang和Hague,1993:567)。实行国土规划的预期目的是证明国家领导人抑制市场化发展负面影响的举措是正确的,并通过监管土地利用来保护自然资源(胡序威,2006)。换言之,国土规划的目的是用来指导地区的发展,取代自上而下的经济规划和经济指令。然而,国土规划的制定在1996年突然停止(胡序威,2006),其中的原因有很多。例如国土规划的制定及其文件缺乏合法地位;此外,国土规划仅仅是蓝图文件,并没有关注实施机制和公共政策。结果,国土规划的效力受到的地方分权和市场改革的挑战日益显著,因为地方和市场的管治背景要比纯粹自上而下的行政指令复杂得多。而且,国土规划还被指责实际上是以经济增长为基础的规划,其实质就是社会主义计划经济时期的生产力分配计划,因为规划主要还是在安排经济增长中心的发展(Wang和Hague,1993:571;毛汉英和方创琳,2002:270;殷为华等,2007:14)。

571; Mao and Fang, 2002: 270; Yin et al., 2007: 14).

In October 2006, the National Development and Reform Commission (NDRC) took the initiative to prepare The Main Functional Area Plan for the whole national territory. The initiative gained strong support from the State Council. Compared with the previous territory plan, the new plan divided the national territory into four types of development units: a ' prioritised development area, optimised development area, constrained development area and forbidden development area'. This was intended to plan the intensity of territorial development and population distribution in order to achieve the 'scientific development' advocated by the central government, i.e. coordinated and sustainable development. In addition, each type of unit was to be incorporated with a corresponding investment policy, industrial policy, migration policy, land policy, environment policy, fiscal redistribution mechanism and differentiated economic growth target and political achievement rating policy (see Table 3.4). For the prioritised area, the package of policies revolved around encouraging advanced industries and controlling resource – consuming manufacturing; for the optimised development zone, the set of policies concentrated on building new growth poles and the development of labour – intensive industries; in the constrained and forbidden development areas, policies were otherwise focused on the environment. Therefore, the development of the so – called main functional area plan represented national policies in different types of regions. Compared with the macro-regional policies aimed at uneven development, these procedures were designed to prevent all jurisdictions matching their economic growth under GDP evaluation and fiscal pressure disregarding their comparative advantages and environmental conditions. That is, a dominant feature of the plan, which distinguishes itself from earlier territorial plans or regional policies, was its focus on control rather than development. This represented a transformation of national policies from universal growth incentive to differentiated regional policies to advocate the rational distribution of labour based on comparative advantage. Furthermore, and for the first time, compensatory policies were proposed to equalise public service and living conditions between different regions. Overall, the plan demonstrated an attempt by the central government to intervene in local discretionary development. The basic planning unit of the central main functional area was county – level jurisdiction, except that the forbidden development area was based on the boundaries of natural reserves. By delegating the main functional area with the county – level units, the plan also related the duty of controlling the intensity of development and setting an environment threshold to each level of local government.

2006年10月,国家发展和改革委员会倡议在全国范围内制定《主体功能区规划》。该倡议得到了国务院的大力支持。和之前的国土规划不同,新的《主体功能区规划》把全国地域分成四类开发区域:"重点开发区域、优化开发区域、限制开发区域和禁止开发区域"。这是为了规划国土开发力度和人口分布,以实现中央政府提出的"科学发展观",即协调和可持续的发展。此外,每个主体功能区都有相应的投资政策、产业政策、人口户籍迁移管理政策、土地政策、环境保护政策、财政再分配机制、差异化经济增长目标和政绩考核政策(表3.4)。对于重点开发区域,制定的一揽子政策主要围绕鼓励先进产业和控制资源高消耗制造业;对于优化开发区域,政策主要集中于打造新的增长点和发展劳动密集型产业;对于限制开发区域和禁止开发区域,政策则集中于环境保护方面。因此,所谓的主体功能区规划代表了国家在不同类型区域上的政策。和针对发展不平衡的宏观区域政策相比,这些规划就是为了防止地方政府在GDP指标和财政压力下,不顾自身的比较优势和环境条件,一味地攀比经济增长。也就是说,主体功能区规划和之前的国土规划或区域政策的一个显著不同特征是该规划注重调控,而不是发展。这表明国家政策从普遍的增长激励措施转向差异化的区域政策,提倡根据比较优势合理分配劳动力。而且,国家首次提出补偿政策,以促使各地区公共服务和生活条件得到均衡发展。总体来说,该规划体现了中央政府试图对地方的自主开发决定权进行干预。除了禁止开发区域的规划是以自然保护区为基本规划单元之外,国家主体功能区都是以县级行政区为基本规划单元的。通过将主体功能区区划单元设为县级政府,也就将调控开发力度和设置环境准入门槛的责任与地方各级政府关联在了一起。

Table 3.4 Definition of the main functional areas and corresponding policies

	Prioritised development area	Optimised development area	Constrained development area	Forbidden development area
Concept	Area with high development density which is going to or has threaten(ed) the environment	Area with high environment carrying capability and a favourable economic location	Area with low environment carrying capability and poor economic location, Or an area with concern for ecological security	All types of natural areas established by law
Fiscal policy	To advocate the development of high-tech and high value added industries; To restrict the development of high energy consuming and high pollution industries; To encourage technology advancement in resource conservation and environmental protection	To advance infrastructural conditions; To encourage the development of labour-intensive industries; To encourage the development of supporting industries	To advance infrastructural conditions; Fiscal transfer for public services and environment; To support the development of specialty industries that are suited to the local conditions and environment	Fiscal transfer for public services and the environment
Government investment policy	To control the projects that are incompatible with assigned main functions	Government investment will be directed to support infrastructure development; To create an economic growth pole	Government investment will be directed to support public infrastructure development, ecological construction and environmental protection in the area	Government investment will be directed to support public infrastructure development, ecological construction and environmental protection in the area
Industrial policy	To strengthen innovation capability; To upgrade industrial structure and promote competitiveness	To strengthen supporting industries, to receive an industrial shift, to increase innovation capacity	To develop industries appropriate to the area; To restrict the expansion of inappropriate industries	Prudent industrial development policies
Land policy	Strict control of construction land increase	Increase land supply on a appropriate scale	Strict land use regulation, changes to ecological land use are strictly prohibited	Strict land use regulation, changes to ecological land use are strictly prohibited

表3.4 主体功能区的定义及相应政策

	重点开发区域	优化开发区域	限制开发区域	禁止开发区域
概念	将对或已经对环境造成威胁的高密度开发区域	环境承载能力强和经济区位有利的区域	环境承载能力弱和经济区位不利的区域，或有生态安全顾虑的区域	各种依法设立的自然保护区
财政政策	提倡发展高科技和高附加值产业；限制发展高能耗和高污染产业；鼓励资源保护和环境保护方面的科技进步	完善基础设施条件；鼓励发展劳动密集型产业；鼓励发展支持性产业	完善基础设施条件；财政转向公共服务和环境领域；支持发展符合地方条件和环境的特色产业	财政转向公共服务和环境领域
政府投资政策	控制与所指定主体功能不相符合的项目	政府投资将针对配套基础设施发展；打造经济增长点	政府投资将针对该区域的公共配套基础设施发展、生态建设和环境保护	政府投资将针对该区域的公共配套基础设施发展、生态建设和环境保护
产业政策	加强创新能力；升级产业结构，提升竞争力	加强支持性产业，接受产业转移，提高创新能力	发展适合该区域的产业；限制不合适产业的扩张	稳健的产业发展政策
土地政策	严格控制建设用地增长	适当增加土地供应	严格管制土地使用，严厉禁止改变生态用地	严格管制土地使用，严厉禁止改变生态用地

continued

	Prioritised development area	Optimised development area	Constrained development area	Forbidden development area
Migration policy	In-migration is encouraged; To promote the open labour market	In-migration is encouraged; To promote the open labour market	Out-migration is encouraged on a voluntary basis and in a steady process to reduce environmental tension	Out-migration is encouraged on a voluntary basis and in a steady process to reduce environmental tension
Environmen- tal policy	Strict requirements on pollution discharge and environmental protection; Priority work to reduce pollution discharge	Balance the environmental carrying capacity, Increase production and reduce pollution	Protection is the priority, to ensure environmental restoration and protection	Strict protection by the law
Government achievements rating policy	More emphasis on economic structure, resource consumption and innovation, less emphasis on economic growth	Comprehensive evaluation on economic growth, cost and benefit, industrialisation rate, and urbanisation; The quality of development is encouraged	Evaluation of ecology development and environmental protection will be highlighted, Evaluation of economic growth, industrialisation rates and the urbanisation level will be weakened	Evaluation will be focused on ecology and environmental protection
Planning policy	To strictly control the land use of high energy consuming and high pollution industries; To encourage high-tech and high value added industries	To encourage economic growth poles; To encourage the development of labour-intensive industries	To strictly control development activities that are incompatible with assigned main functions; To encourage the development of some specialty industries	To strictly control development activities that are incompatible with assigned main functions

Source: compiled from Instructions on Preparing National Development Priority Zone Plan Issued by the State Council, 2007 - 07 - 26; State Council Development and Research Institute, 2008: 137-138.

	重点开发区域	优化开发区域	限制开发区域	禁止开发区域
人口户籍迁移管理政策	鼓励迁入；扩大劳动力市场的开放	鼓励迁入；扩大劳动力市场的开放	鼓励自愿平稳迁出，以减轻环境压力	鼓励逐步自愿迁出，以减轻环境压力
环境保护政策	严格的排污要求和环保要求；优先减排工作	平衡环境承载能力，增加生产，降低污染	优先保护环境，确保环境修复和保护	严格依法保护环境
政绩考核政策	更多关注经济结构、资源消耗和创新，较少关注经济增长	对经济增长、成本收益、工业化率和城市化水平进行综合评价；鼓励注重发展质量	重点评价生态发展和环境保护；弱化评价经济增长、工业化率和城市化水平	重点评价生态发展和环境保护
规划政策	严格控制高能耗和高污染产业的土地使用；鼓励高科技和高附加值产业	鼓励打造经济增长点；鼓励发展劳动密集型产业	严格控制与分配主体功能不符的开发活动；鼓励发展某些特色产业	严格控制与分配主体功能不符的开发活动

来源：编自 2007 年 7 月 26 日国务院发布的《关于编制全国主体功能区规划的意见》；国务院发展研究中心，2008：137-138。

The plan was reported to be approved on June 12, 2010 at a meeting of the Standing Committee of the State Council chaired by Premier Wen Jiabao❶. However, the contents of the overall plan and the spatial zoning map have not yet been published, except for some vague and literal clarification on the boundary of the constrained and forbidden development areas. Based on a comprehensive consideration of environmental capacity, current development intensity, future development opportunity and potential, population distribution, industrial distribution and urbanisation level, the plan identified certain agricultural production areas in Northeast Plateau, Yellow Huaihai Plateau and the Yangtze River Basin as the constrained development area, and the Tibet Plateau, Huangtu – Yungui Plateau, Northeast Forest, and rivers and other environmentally vulnerable areas as the forbidden development area. It is realised by the central government that the main functional area plan making and implementation will not be an easy process, but requires a long-term trial and negotiation. Currently, the plan is still at the preliminary stage and the recommended policy packages for different spatial zones are still being researched, not to mention the implementation process.

3.5 Recentralisation of land management since the late 1990s

Since the economic reform, land management has been substantially downscaled. After the economic reform, the 1986 Land Administration Law authorised territorial governments to take power from central ministries and subordinate work units to perform functions in land administration (Wu et al., 2007: 31). Hence a five-tiered system was set up at the central, provincial, municipal, county and township levels. Each tier of bureaus was responsible for land administration under the jurisdiction. Local governments, especially city and county governments, gained substantial power in authorising land expropriation, land supply, rural land conversion and land income disposal (Xu and Yeh, 2009: 575). However, the territorialisation of land management put land administration under threat. For example, the majority of industrial land has been transferred through negotiated trading since the 1990s, the price of which is much lower than the real value of the land. Many local governments have sacrificed enormous rent and land use fees for potential industrial enterprises. In turn, local governments usually grab vast areas of land at the city margin by moving resident farmers away in order to ensure the supply of cheaper land. Consequently, a large amount of land has been encroached upon and a large number of peasants have lost their land and means of subsistence. As a counter

❶ central government website, http://www.gov.cn/ldhd/2010–06/12/content_1626813.htm.

2010年6月12日,时任总理温家宝主持国务院常务会议,会议批准了主体功能区规划❶。然而,总体规划的内容和空间区划图仍未发布,只有一些关于限制发展区域和禁止发展区域边界的模糊字面说明。基于环境容量、当前开发力度、未来发展机遇与潜力、人口分布、工业分布和城市化水平的综合考虑,该规划认为东北平原、黄淮海平原和长江流域的某些农业生产区是限制开发区域,青藏高原、黄土—云贵高原生态屏障、东北森林带以及河流和其他环境脆弱地区是禁止开发区域。中央政府意识到主体功能区规划的制定和实施并非易事,需要经过长期的试验和协商。目前,该规划仍然处在起步阶段,针对不同空间区域的一揽子政策仍在研讨中,具体实施程序更有待提上议事日程。

第五节　20世纪90年代末开始的土地管理收权

自改革开放以来,土地管理权大量下放到地方。改革开放之后,1986年颁布的《土地管理法》授权地方政府从中央部委和下属单位接管权力,履行土地管理职能(Wu等,2007:31)。从中央到省、市、县和乡镇的五级土地管理制度也因此建立起来。每一级相关部门负责各自辖区的土地管理。地方政府,尤其是市级和县级政府,在授权土地征用、土地供应、农村土地流转和土地收入处理方面获得了巨大的权力(Xu和Yeh,2009:575)。然而,土地管理的地方化使土地管理面临威胁。例如,自20世纪90年代开始,工业用地大部分是通过协商交易获得的,价格比土地的实际价值低了很多。许多地方政府为了潜在的工业企业放弃收取巨额租赁费用和土地使用费用。反过来,地方政府会让居住在城市边缘的农民搬走,攫取大片的土地,以确保供应廉价土地。结果,大量的土地被侵占,许多农民失去了土地和生活资料。为了改变这种现状,自

---

❶ 中央政府网站,http://www.gov.cn/ldhd/2010-06/12/content_1626813.htm。

measure, the land system has undergone practices of recentralisation since 1998, not only in terms of administrative structure, but also in law and policy regulation. This represents a reaction exerted by the central state to handle widespread local discretion on land disposal (Xu and Yeh, 2009).

In 1998, along with the reorganisation of central governments, the Ministry of Land and Resources was established to take the place of its predecessor, the State Land Management Bureau. The change from bureau to ministry is of great significance, as ministries and commissions represented the constituent departments of the State Council, while agencies and bureaus were attached to the State Council. That is, land management became one of the major functions of the central government (Xu and Yeh, 2009: 574). More importantly, the Fourth Session of the Ninth National People's Congress held in 1998 revised and approved the new Land Administration Law. The 1998 law commenced new power divisions between levels of government and new procedures of land administration. Before 1999, municipal and district governments had certain powers to authorise land acquisition, land allocation and land use conversion. However, after the 1998 Land Administration Law, the approval power for land conversion and land acquisition was taken over by the central and provincial governments, especially in terms of agricultural land conversion (ibid: 575). The system set up a land quota for each local government. As a result, it became much more difficult to obtain a land quota for urban expansion, and cities and counties could only seek to readjust existing construction land use to accommodate land demand. According to the new rule, the new urban construction land could not be selected beyond the boundary of land use plan. Furthermore, centralised management (chuizhi guanli) was engineered by the central government in 2003. This involved the means of personnel/budgetary allocation, cadre appointment, and revenue collection (Mertha, 2005: 797). For example, the director of land management department was no longer under the direct appointment and management of territorial governments, but answered to its higher-level land department (ibid: 792; 798). At the same time, the new land revenue division, in terms of income from converting rural land, stipulated that 30 percent must be surrendered to the central government rather than the whole amount be retained by local government (Xu et al., 2009: 903). Obviously, the central government hoped to govern local land management by fiscal disincentives and direct regulation of senior land management officials.

In addition, the central government published a number of land administration policies to reassert control over local discretion on land disposal from the late 1990s (see Table 3.5). Firstly, from 1997 to 2002, great efforts were exerted by the central government to protect arable land. Measures were

1998年开始,土地管理制度经历了收权的过程,不仅是在行政结构方面进行了收权,在法律和政策管理上也有体现。这表明中央政府已采取措施来控制土地处理上普遍出现的地方滥用职权(Xu和Yeh,2009)。

1998年,中央进行机构改革,成立了国土资源部取代之前的国家土地管理局。从"局"到"部"的转变意义重大,因为部委是国务院的构成部门,而局只是国务院的下属机构。这表明,土地管理已成为中央政府的一项主要职能(Xu和Yeh,2009:574)。更重要的是,第九届全国人大常委会第四次会议于1998年修订并通过了新的《土地管理法》。新的《土地管理法》对各级政府的权限进行了重新划分,推出了新的土地管理程序。在1999年之前,市级和区级政府对土地征用、土地分配和土地用途转换拥有一定的批准权限。但是,1998年的《土地管理法》实施之后,中央和省级政府收回了土地转换和征用的批准权,尤其是农村土地转换的批准权(同上:575)。在此机制下,各地方政府的土地使用都有一个配额。因此,想要争取城市土地扩张的配额变得格外艰难,县市只能设法调整现有建设用地的使用,以满足土地需求。根据新的规定,新的城市建设用地不可超出土地利用规划的范围。此外,2003年中央政府开始实行土地的垂直管理。这其中包括人员/预算分配、干部任命以及税款征收(Mertha,2005:797)。例如,土地管理部门的负责干部不再由所在地方政府直接任命和管理,而是向上一级土地管理部门负责(同上:792;798)。同时,新的土地收益分配条款规定30%的农村土地转换收入必须上缴中央政府,而不是全部归地方政府所有(Xu等,2009:903)。显而易见的是,中央政府希望通过财政制约和对土地管理部门高级官员的直接监管来控制地方的土地管理。

此外,从20世纪90年代末起,中央政府也颁布了一系列土地管理政策以重塑对地方土地管理自主权的控制(表3.5)。首先,从1997年到2002年,中央政府狠抓耕地保护,采取措施规范土地使用批准程序,强化公务员管理,从而

taken to strengthen land use approval procedures and the management of civil servants, thus constraining arable land conversion to industrial or commercial land use, and retaking leased land which was not developed for a certain period. Then, from 2003, the central government initiated several campaigns to check economic development zones for problems of aggressive industrial land development and land encroachment. In July 2003, the State Council issued the 'Urgent Notice on a Temporary Ban on the Approval of Various Kinds of Development Zones'. The approval was temporarily halted in a measure to check various development zones established by local governments at and below the provincial level, as well as by government ministries. The check was also intended to crack down on unauthorised national industrial park extensions. In August of the same year, the State Council released 'The Notice on the Clean-up and Rectification of Development Zones of Different Types and Tightening-up of the Construction Land Management'. This was reiterated in the document issued by the State Council in November. Shortly afterwards in December, further stipulations on the rectification were released by the Ministry of Land and Resources, together with other relevant ministries such as the Ministry of Construction. In February of the following year, the Ministry of Land and Resources issued another official letter to cancel unqualified development zones or those with poor performance. In August 2005, a document released by the State Council stipulated that some economic zones must be abolished if the zones were populated with only a few enterprises and the development rates were lower than 20 percent after 5 years of operation. In 2008, the Urban and Rural Planning Law also stipulated that industrial zones should not be established outside the area designated by the master plan. The series of land policies demonstrated the determination, as well as the difficulty, to control excessive industrial land development.

In summary, the changes in land management and the great number of land policies launched by the central government have illustrated the re-consolidation of state regulatory power, which is opposite to the main trend of decentralisation and rising localities. It is true that the central campaign is progressing with great difficulties, hampered by local circumvention on central regulations (Yang and Wang, 2008). However, the efforts taken by the central state to more effectively regulate infringements of land management cannot be ignored.

限制耕地被用作工业或商业用途,并且收回在规定时限内未开发的已租出土地。之后,从2003年起,中央政府组织了多次活动,核查经济开发区中工业用地恶性扩张和土地侵占的问题。2003年7月,国务院发布《关于暂停审批各类开发区的紧急通知》。暂停审批的目的是审查省级及省级以下政府,包括中央各部委设立的各类开发区。同时借此整顿未经审批的国家工业园区扩张行为。同年8月,国务院下发《关于清理整顿各类开发区加强建设用地管理的通知》。国务院在11月发布的文件中对此再次进行了强调。时隔不久,国土资源部于12月会同建设部等有关部委下发进一步的整顿细则。2004年2月,国土资源部下发通知,要求纠正不合格或业绩较差的开发区。2005年8月,国务院下发文件,规定只有少数企业进驻或在运营5年后开发速度低于20%的开发区必须予以取缔。2008年,《城乡规划法》也作出规定,不得在总体规划指定区域之外的地区建设工业园区。这一系列的土地政策表明了中央遏制工业用地过分扩张势头的决心,同时也反映了这其中的难度。

　　总而言之,土地管理上的变化及中央政府大量土地政策的出台表明国家在重新巩固对土地的管制权力,这同放权和地区自主性增强的主流趋势恰恰是相反的。可以肯定的是,由于地方会对中央的规定进行规避,中央发起的这项收权运动会遇到重重困难(Yang和Wang,2008)。但是,中央为了更加有效地规范土地管理、惩处违规行为所作出的努力不容忽视。

Table 3.5 Changing national land administration policies

Policy name	Date issued	Issued by	Key issues/effects
The circular on strengthening land administration and protecting arable land	Apr. 1997	Central Party Committee & State Council	To strengthen macro-regulation on land, to implement more stringent construction land approval, to control the construction land area of cities, to strengthen the administration of collective land in rural areas, to strengthen the management of national land assets, to strengthen the supervision and examination of land management enforcement
The circular on freezing the land approval for occupying arable land for non-agricultural constructions	Mar. 1998	Central Party Committee & State Council	No land approval for occupying arable land for non-agricultural constructions, except through examination and approval from State Council
Disposition on vacant land	Apr. 1999	Ministry of Land and Resources	Land owners who postpone development on land sites longer than allowed are subject to the relevant disposition agenda or confiscation to control land speculation
The circular on strengthening land transferral management and prohibiting land speculation	May 1999	State Council	To strengthen land transferral supervision and prohibit the acquisition of rural collective land for large commercial development such as orchards and manor development
Provisional regulation on national investment in land development and arrangement projects	Nov. 2000	Ministry of Land and Resources	Specifies the project application and supervision procedures
The decision to rectify and regulate market economy order & The circular on strengthening administration on national land assets	Jun. 2001	State Council	The Ministry of Land and Resources issued a notice to rectify and regulate land market order and began to check six types of activities against law and discipline
The tenth Five-Year Plan outline on land asset management	Apr. 2002	Ministry of Land and Resources	To strengthen the land supply for construction, to strengthen the implementation of compensated land use, to vigorously promote open bidding or auctions, to strengthen land use transferral management and land price administration, to regulate land use approval

表3.5 国家土地管理政策的变化

政策名称	颁布日期	签发单位	主要事由/作用
关于进一步加强土地管理切实保护耕地的通知	1997年4月	党中央,国务院	加强土地的宏观管理,进一步严格建设用地的审批管理,严格控制城市建设用地规模,加强农村集体土地的管理,加强对国有土地资产的管理,加强土地管理的执法监督检查
关于继续冻结非农业建设项目占用耕地的通知	1998年3月	党中央,国务院	继续冻结非农业建设项目占用耕地,确实需要占用耕地的,报国务院审批
闲置土地处置办法	1999年4月	国土资源部	土地使用者超过规定期限未动工开发建设,必须遵从有关处置方案,或服从政府安排,由政府收回土地以防投机买卖
关于加强土地转让管理严禁炒卖土地的通知	1999年5月	国务院	加强对农民集体土地的转让管理,禁止征用农民集体土地进行"果园"、"庄园"等大规模商业开发
国家投资土地开发整理项目管理暂行办法	2000年11月	国土资源部	明确项目申报和监督程序
关于整顿和规范市场经济秩序的决定、关于加强国有土地资产管理的通知	2001年6月	国务院	国土资源部下发通知,整顿和规范市场经济秩序,并开始查处违反法律法规的六项活动
土地资产管理"十五"计划纲要	2002年4月	国土资源部	增强建设用地供给能力,加大土地有偿使用的实施力度,积极推动土地公开招标或拍卖,加强对土地用途转变和土地价格的管理,规范土地使用的审批

continued

Policy name	Date issued	Issued by	Key issues/effects
The circular on checking and rectifying all kinds of development zones and strengthening construction land administration	Jul. 2003	State Council	Check the real land use area and approval departments of all kinds of development zones, and abolish development zones which are against the law and discipline. The list of approved development zones was published by the central government and provincial government
The urgent notice on further rectifying and regulating land market order	Nov. 2003	State Council	Continue to check development zones; to resolve the livelihood problems of land-loss farmers; to conduct stringent investigations of all kinds of activities against law and discipline
The specific standards and policy boundaries for checking and rectifying all kinds of development zones	Dec. 2003	Ministry of Land and Resources & National Development and Reform Commission & Ministry of Construction & Ministry of Business	To implement the documents issued by the State Council on July and November of 2003; Establishing development zones is stipulated to be approved by the central and provincial-level government; local government are not authorised to establish development zones at its own will; To abolish all the development zones established by the county-level government or below; All development projects in existing development zones must abide by the city or town master plan, urban system plan, and land use plan
The urgent notice on deepening the rectification and regulation programme and strengthening land control	Apr. 2004	State Council	General land approvals have been suspended
The Advancement of Rural Reform and Development	Oct. 2008	The Communist Party of China	To allow farmers to "lease their contracted farmland or transfer their land use right" to boost the scale of operation for farm production and provide funds for them to start new businesses

Source: compiled from documents downloaded from the official website of the State Land and Resources Ministry (http://www.mlr.gov.cn/).

续表

政策名称	颁布日期	签发单位	主要事由/作用
关于清理整顿各类开发区加强建设用地管理的通知	2003年7月	国务院	清查各类开发区真实用地情况及各级审批部门,撤销违反相关法律法纪的开发区。中央政府和各省政府公布已批准的开发区名单
关于加大工作力度进一步治理整顿土地市场秩序的紧急通知	2003年11月	国务院	继续清查开发区;解决失地农民的生活问题;开展针对各类违法违纪活动的调查
关于清理整顿现有各类开发区的具体标准和政策界限的通知	2003年12月	国土资源部、国家发改委、建设部、商务部	落实国务院2003年7月和11月发布的文件; 规定设立开发区必须获得国务院和省级政府的批准;地方政府不得随意设立开发区;撤销县级及以下政府设立的各类开发区;现有开发区的各类开发项目必须遵从城镇总体规划,城镇体系规划及土地利用规划
关于深入开展土地市场治理整顿严格土地管理的紧急通知	2004年4月	国务院	暂停审批一般性用地
关于推进农村改革发展若干重大问题的决定	2008年10月	中共中央	允许农民"以转包、出租等形式流转土地承包经营权",以扩大农业生产规模,提供创业资金

来源:编自国土资源部官方网站（http://www.mlr.gov.cn/）下载文件。

3.6 A new experiment of province-leading-county administrative reform since 2005

China has five levels of administrative system, i.e. the nation state, province, municipality, county, town and township (Figure 3.8). The administrative hierarchy in China results in bureaucratic mandates and subordination, which delivers instructions and management in a top - down fashion. All communications are transmitted upwards or downwards, level by level, through the structure, and the skipping of levels is not the norm. As commented by Ma (2005: 478), China's administrative system has always been hierarchical and it is by this means that state power retains its grip and succeeds in being rearticulated at the local level, even after the substantial economic decentralisation since economic reform. However, conflicts with the five - level hierarchical system are becoming more acute, especially at the local level in recent years.

First of all, since the distribution of fiscal revenue and public investment follows the hierarchical structure, the administrative rank has significantly impacted on the development of cities and counties (c.f. Chung, 2007: 794; Ma, 2005: 481). The lower the administrative rank, the poorer the living conditions and public services; this is especially the case in terms of education, health care, public infrastructure and so forth. Therefore, the counties and townships, which are also the countryside units, are often the poorest areas in China in terms of both economy and infrastructure. This is generally the case even for the economically - developed counties and cities in the developed coastal area. This can be exemplified by the prevalent discourse of 'prefecture - level cities extorting counties (county-level-cities)', which means funding for counties is often diverted by the provincial and municipal governments for their own uses (Yep, 2008; Z. B. Zhang, 2009: 26). Secondly, under the city-leading-county system, the county-level units are not actually independent jurisdictions and are not even granted a whole institutional apparatus. The lack of competencies in project approval, foreign trade, outbound permits, land development and so forth stifle administrative efficiency at the grass - roots level. The administrative procedure is so bureaucratic that many issues have to ask for instructions and wait for approval from the prefecture-level cities. This is especially inconvenient for economically robust counties and cities, especially for those who have constant foreign trade and foreign investment. Thirdly, the five - level administrative structure means the lower level government is at the periphery of central control. A vivid example is documented by Wu and Phelps (2008: 473) with regard to the central control on property and villa development. It

第六节　2005年开始的省管县行政改革试验

中国行政体系共设五个层级，即中央、省、地级市、县、乡镇（图3.8）。在这样的行政等级制度下，上级与下级行政机构之间形成了官僚式的命令与服从关系，自上而下地逐级传达指示并进行管理。所有交流都是在这一结构中向上或向下逐级传递的，按惯例不得越级。正如Ma（2005：478）所指出的，中国的行政体系一直等级分明，而正是通过这种方式，国家才能牢牢掌控权力，使各类指示清楚地传达到地方。即使在改革开放后经济权力大规模下放的时期，这一情况也并未改变。然而，五级行政体系所引发的冲突已日渐尖锐，近几年来地方层面的冲突更是日益突出。

首先，由于财政收入和公共投资的分配要遵守行政等级制度，因此行政层级对市、县的发展具有深刻影响（Chung，2007：794；Ma，2005：481）。行政层级越低，人民生活水平和公共服务质量就越差，其中尤其体现在教育、医疗保健和公共基础设施等领域。因此，作为农村地区政权设置的县和乡镇通常是中国经济和基础设施最落后的地区。即使是在沿海经济发达地区的市和县，情况也大多如此。人们通常所说的"地级市掠夺县（或县级市）"就是一个例子，即省、市政府经常会把发放给县的资金挪作己用（Yep，2008；张占斌2009：26）。其次，在市管县的体系下，县级单位实际上没有独立的行政权力，甚至连完整的机构设置也没有。由于县级单位在项目审批、对外贸易、出境许可、土地开发等方面缺乏权力，因而降低了基层政府的行政效率。行政程序过于官僚化，以至于许多问题不得不请示地级市政府并等候批准。对于经济活动繁荣的一些县和县级市，尤其是能长期吸引对外贸易和国外投资的地方来说，这造成了极大的不便。再次，五级行政结构使得基层政府处在中央控制的边缘。Wu和Phelps（2008：473）列举了一个关于对房地产和别墅开发进行中央调控的生动案例。县级市领导普遍认为，中央对土地和房地产开发的监管只

is believed by the county-level city leaders that the central regulation on land and property development is targeted at a central city such as Shanghai; thus, when the regulation is finally delivered to the county level, the construction of the villa project would have been finished already. Administrative discretion is now even more conspicuous at the grass-roots administrative units in terms of land seizures. A number of forced and violent demolitions have been reported in the media since 2001, the majority of which are located in the rural areas of the rich Eastern region❶. Some experts argue that 'as long as the central government could guarantee local governments financially, local governments can act as the service provider rather than the money maker in land management'❷.

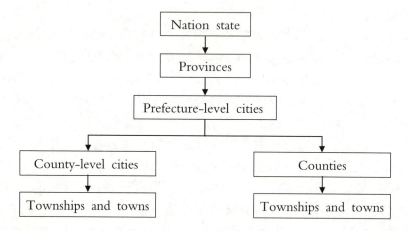

Figure 3.8 Administrative hierarchy under city-leading-county administrative system

In order to ease the fiscal pressure at the grass-roots level, fiscal management system reform under the provincial level by the National 11th Five-Year Plan was suggested in 2005. Instead of the current five-level fiscal system, it was proposed that a province-leading-county administrative system should be carried out in areas where conditions permit. In early July 2009, the Fiscal Ministry released 'the Directive on Promoting the Province-Leading-County Fiscal Reform', which aims to re-establish a separate fiscal system for prefecture-level cities and counties/county-level cities. In other words, counties are to deal directly with provinces instead of via prefecture-level cities in taxation and fiscal distribution, budgetary schemes, fiscal transfer and fiscal rebate, central and

---

❶ for a map that marks these violent demolitions and land disputes, please see http://www.chinadaily.com.cn/china/2010-10/27/content_11462495.htm, accessed on 7 Dec., 2010.

❷ http://www.chinadaily.com.cn/bizchina/2010-11/06/content_11511477.htm, accessed on 7 Dec., 2010.

是针对像上海这样的中心城市,因此当规定最终下达到县级政府的时候,别墅项目的建设早已完工了。在土地征用上,基层行政单位也越来越多地滥用行政权力。从2001年起,媒体上曝光了多起强拆和暴力拆迁事件,其中绝大多数都发生在富裕的东部农村地区❶。有专家认为,"只要中央政府能保证地方政府的财政来源,地方政府就会在土地管理中发挥公共服务职能,而不是设法敛财"❷。

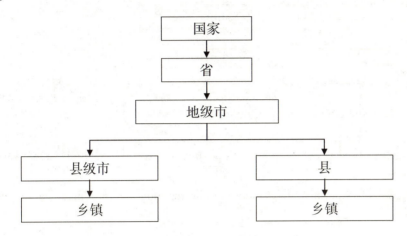

图3.8 市管县体制下的行政等级

　为了缓解地方政府的财政压力,"十一五"规划中提出了财政管理体制改革,在条件允许的地区使用省管县的管理体系来代替原先的五级财政体制。2009年7月上旬,财政部公布了《关于推进省直接管理县财政改革的意见》,目的是在地级市、县和县级市重新建立独立的财政体制。换言之,在税收和财政分配、预算方案、财政转移、财政返还以及中央和省级补助等方面,县政府可以

---

❶ 查看标有暴力拆迁和土地纠纷地区的地图请浏览http://www.chinadaily.com.cn/china/2010-10/27/ content_11462495.htm,网站访问日期2010年12月7日。

❷ http://www.chinadaily.com.cn/china/2010-10/27/ content_11462495.htm,网站访问日期2010年12月7日。

provincial subsidies, and so forth. The reform is likely to be fully adopted across the country as of 2012, which will eventually extend from the fiscal sphere to the whole institutional framework. By this means, the power of the prefecture‑level city over the county‑level would be gradually eliminated and removed. That is, the main cities, secondary cities and the vast number of counties would be equalised at the same administrative rank (Figure 3.9).

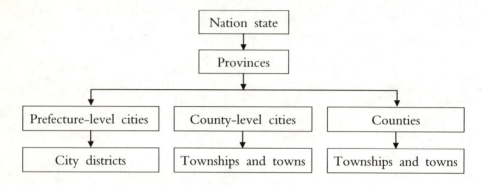

Figure 3.9 Administrative hierarchy in the ongoing province‑leading‑county reform

The new fiscal management measure has triggered an extensive experimentation of the province‑leading‑county administrative system across the country. Hainan, Hubei, Anhui, Guangdong, Henan, Jilin, Jiangxi and other provinces have all initiated their reform agenda (Z. B. Zhang, 2009; Zhou, 2008: 43). Many of them have followed the prototype of Zhejiang, which is generally recognised to be the premier in the country. Zhejiang began experimenting with power devolution from municipal governments (government of prefecture‑level cities) to county‑level governments (including governments of county‑level cities, counties, and city districts) as early as 1992. At that time, this experiment was applied to 13 counties and county‑level cities out of a total of 58 county‑level jurisdictions. The economic administrative power of the 13 jurisdictions was expanded to include approval rights for infrastructure construction, technological innovation projects and foreign investment expansion; furthermore, some approval procedures had also been simplified (Zhang, 2009: 61). In the subsequent years of 1997, 2002 and 2006, Zhejiang Province continued to transfer administrative power which used to be possessed by the prefecture‑level cities to selective county‑level units. In 2006, the county‑level city Yiwu, which is well‑known for producing accessories and home wares for both the domestic and global markets, was chosen as the subject of an experiment which entitled it with the equivalent economic administration rights

越过地级市政府直接与省政府交涉。截至2012年,这项改革有望在全国范围内得到推行,并从财政领域拓展到整个体制框架内。这样一来,地级市对县级市的管辖权会逐渐被削弱,直到完全消除。也就是说,一线城市、二线城市和各县在行政等级上可以平起平坐了(图3.9)。

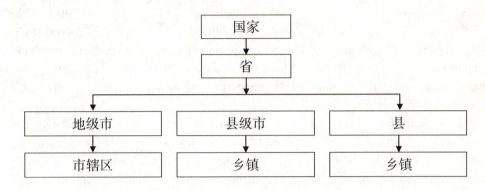

图3.9　现行省管县改革中的行政等级

　　新的财政管理措施引发了省管县行政体系在全国范围内的广泛试验。海南、湖北、安徽、广东、河南、吉林、江西等省份相继推出了改革议程(张占斌,2009;周天勇,2008:43)。这些省份大多采用了浙江的改革模式。浙江被公认为国内的改革先锋省份,早在1992年就开始尝试把部分权力从市政府(即地级市政府)下放到县级政府(包括县级市政府、县政府和区政府),当时共在58个县级辖区中的13个县和县级市进行试点。这13个辖区的经济行政权扩大到对基础设施建设、技术创新项目和增加外商投资等拥有审批权;此外,一些审批程序也得到了简化(张占斌,2009:61)。在接下来的1997年、2002年和2006年,浙江省先后将原本属于地级市政府的权力下放到选定的一些县级单位。2006年,义乌被选为改革试点,使这个以生产配件和家居用品并销往国内和全

of a municipal government. In addition, Yiwu was granted additional functional institutions such as customs, goods inspection and quarantine and foreign exchange management, which used to be led and managed by prefecture-level authorities on behalf of county-level governments (ibid: 62).

In addition to power devolution to the county-level administrations, the cadre management at the county-level has also been reshuffled. The management of county-level cadres, especially the heads of the county Party organisation and government, has been promoted from prefectural to provincial appointments and supervision. Moreover, the county-level cadres have even been summoned to Beijing for training by the Party School of the CCP Central Committee since 2008❶.

To sum up, there are two perspectives associated with the tentative administrative structure reform from the city-leading-county system to the province-leading-county system. On the one hand, this shift represents recognition from the central government of the devolution, legitimacy and accountability of county-level governments. The so-called rural units are no longer affiliated outposts that are peripheral to central cities. The gradual equalisation of different levels of cities may help to redress the unequal development between urban and rural areas. Furthermore, this may facilitate communication and negotiation between cities over the regional issues. On the other hand, the strengthened central training and provincial management of the county-level cadres goes hand in hand with the power devolution. That is, the central government wants to relate its regulation more closely with lower-level local governments by means of direct cadre management. This carries great implications because it means the regional administration system is restructured from a three-tier to a two-tier hierarchy. In the prefecture-leading-county system, the prefecture-level city government was expected to function as 'central administration' in the area to eliminate conflicts between various local authorities. However, with the decentralisation to the county-level jurisdictions over the last decades, the nested administrative hierarchy has, in fact, been dismantled. The urban scale at the prefecture-level is fragmented. The hierarchy restructuring makes the provincial level responsible for replacing the 'dead' prefecture-level governance and coordinating local development. It seems the weakened regional governance can be strengthened by these means.

However, it is found that some prefectural-level governments resent the reform, since they would lose a certain amount of power and authority. For example, it is documented that, in Hubei Province, although over 200 administrative approval rights are said to have been decentralised to the county-level, nearly half of

❶ http://politics.people.com.cn/GB/1025/9788437.html, accessed on 12 Nov., 2010.

球市场闻名的县级市获得了与市政府相当的经济行政权。另外,还在义乌设立了其他职能机制,比如海关、货品检验检疫和外汇管理等。这些职能体制之前都是由地级市机构代表县级政府领导并管理的(同上:62)。

除了把权力下放到县级行政机构之外,国家还对县级干部的管理作出了调整。对县级干部,尤其是县级党组织和政府领导的管理从地一级提高到由省一级任命和监督。而且,从2008年起,县级干部陆续进入北京中央党校接受集训❶。

总的来说,从市管县到省管县的试探性行政结构改革有两个层面。一方面,这样的转变表示中央政府对权力下放的认可,体现了县级政府的合法性和责任。所谓的农村单位不再是中心城市边缘的附属机制。各级城市在行政层级上逐渐趋于均衡,有助于解决城乡之间发展不均衡的问题,并且促进各个城市在区域问题上的交流和协商。另一方面,在权力下放的同时,加强了对县级干部的中央培训和省级管理。这表明,中央政府希望通过对干部进行直接管理的方式,拉近中央与基层政府之间的距离。省管县这样的改革意义深远,因为它意味着区域行政体系将由三级结构变成两级结构。在传统市管县体制中,地级市政府在该地区发挥“中心管理”职能,以消除各个地方机构间的冲突。然而在过去几十年中,随着权力下放到县级行政区,这样一个嵌套式的行政结构实际上已经瓦解。地级市的城市尺度变得碎片化。省管县改革所带来的行政层级结构的重组将使省级政府直接代替不起作用的地级市政府进行管理,并且统筹地方的发展。弱化的区域管治似乎可以通过这些途径得到加强。

但是也不难看出,一些地级市政府对改革抱有抵触情绪,因为这意味着会它们失去一定的权力。例如,有文献表明,河北省曾向县级政府下放了200多

---

❶ http://politics.people.com.cn/GB/1025/9788437.html, 网站访问日期2010年11月12日。

them have either not been implemented or are impractical (Zong, 2008: 203). That is, the real progress of the province-leading-county reform is in doubt in reality. Moreover, the current reform seems to be simply addressed towards promoting the economic development of county-level units; the corresponding reform for the provincial government is much less discussed. Therefore, the implication of province-leading-county reform for regional governance and regional development needs to be closely observed.

3.7 Administrative regionalisation with jurisdictional mergers and annexations since 2000

After economic reform, China relaxed the criteria for city and town designations (e.g. Lee, 1980; Ma and Cui, 1987; Zhang and Zhao, 1998). As a result, the number of cities and towns has considerably increased since 1983. The total number of designated cities increased from 190 to 668 in 1998. Coupled with economic devolution, the number of individual local agents available to participate in economic activities has increased phenomenally. However, 1998 seemed to be a turning point because the number started to decrease from 1999.Figure 3.10 extends the data from Figure 3.5 to 2008. It demonstrates that the number of county-level cities started to decrease for the first time in 1997, which meant the total number of city units declined from the peak total of 668 to 655 in 2008. Simultaneously, the quantity of city districts has undergone an unprecedented increase. This is due to the recent administrative incorporations of suburban counties and county-level cities into prefecture-level cities as city districts (c.f. Ma, 2005; Zhang and Wu, 2006).

个行政审批权,但实际上接近半数没有得到实施或无法实施(踪家峰,2008:203)。这就说明省管县改革的实际进展并非确凿无疑。另外,当前的改革似乎只是为了促进县级单位的经济发展,而省政府相应的改革却很少得到讨论。因此省管县改革对区域管理和发展的影响还有待进一步的密切关注。

第七节 2000年开始的行政区域化和行政辖区合并

经济改革之后,中国放宽了设市和设镇的标准(Lee,1980;Ma和Cui,1987;Zhang和Zhao,1998)。结果是,城市和乡镇的数量在1983年以后大幅增加。设市城市总数从190个增加到1998年的668个。随着经济权力下放,参与经济活动的地方机构数量显著增加。但1998年似乎是一个转折点,从1999年开始,这个数字就逐渐下滑。图3.10将图3.5中的数据范围延伸到2008年。图中显示,县级市的数量在1997年首次开始减少,城市总量从最高峰的668个减少到2008年的655个。与此同时,市辖区的数量经历了空前的激增。这是因为近期一些郊区县和县级市被并入地级市成为市辖区(Ma,2005;Zhang和Wu,2006)。

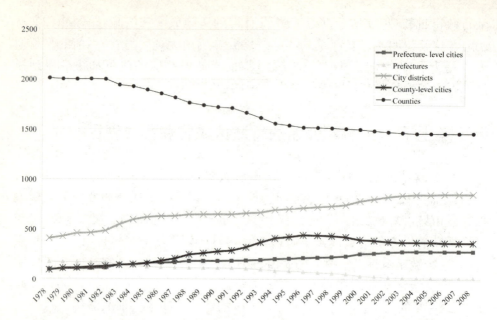

Figure 3.10 Urban administrative changes from 1978 to 2008

Source: compiled from Ministry of Civil Affairs, 1998a, b, 1999, 2000, 2001, 2002, 2003, 2004, 2005, 2006, 2007, 2008, 2009.

For example, 19 new city districts were set up between 2000 and 2004 in the Yangtze River Delta region through the abolition of counties or county-level cities. As a consequence of the administrative adjustment, the jurisdictional area of the 15 prefecture - level cities has expanded massively, before and after administrative readjustment. As shown in Figures 3.11 and 3.12, the areas of some cities, such as Suqian, even multiplied tenfold. In addition to the sharp increase of land area, the merger also means a change in the relationship between prefecture - level cities and the former county - level units. Before the annexation, these county-level units were under the leadership of prefecture-level governments, according to the city-leading-county system. However, the central administration of the prefecture - level government was actually greatly weakened and, to some extent, was retained in name only due to the power decentralisation after economic reform. After the annexation, these previous county - level units were transformed into city districts, which were no longer independent county-level administration centres, but became units directly under the city government. In other words, the central administration of the prefecture-level city governments was strengthened through the means of administrative merger.

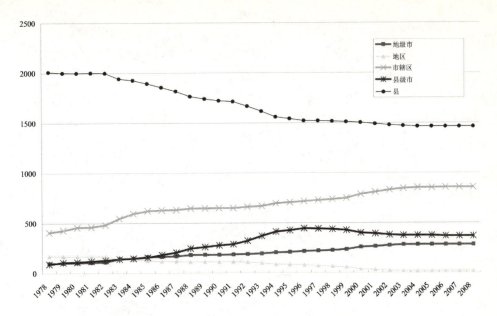

图 3.10 1978 至 2008 年的城市行政体制变化

来源：编自民政部资料，1998a，b，1999，2000，2001，2002，2003，2004，2005，2006，2007，2008，2009。

例如长江三角洲地区19个新的市辖区就是在2000至2004年间通过撤销一些县和县级市设立的。行政区划调整带来的结果是，15个地级市的管辖区域大幅度扩大。正如图3.11和图3.12所示，宿迁等一些城市的辖区范围甚至翻了十倍。除了土地面积的激增，合并也意味着地级市和以前的县级单位之间的关系发生了变化。在合并之前，按照市管县体制，这些县级单位受地级市政府的管辖。但是实际上，由于经济改革后权力下放，地级市政府的中心管理职能被大大地削弱，甚至在某种程度上只是有名无实了。在合并之后，这些原来的县级单位变成市辖区，不再是独立的县级行政中心，而是市政府直接领导下的单位。换言之，地级市政府的中心管理职能在行政合并后得到了加强。

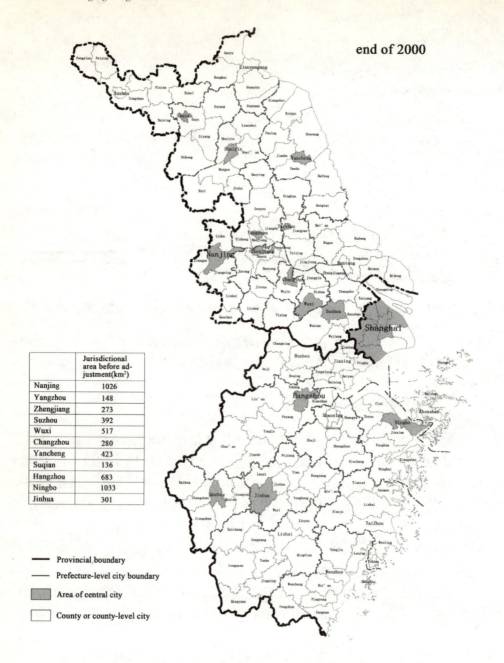

	Jurisdictional area before adjustment(km²)
Nanjing	1026
Yangzhou	148
Zhengjiang	273
Suzhou	392
Wuxi	517
Changzhou	280
Yancheng	423
Suqian	136
Hangzhou	683
Ningbo	1033
Jinhua	301

end of 2000

— Provincial boundary

— Prefecture-level city boundary

▨ Area of central city

☐ County or county-level city

Figure 3.11 Administrative boundary of the city proper
displaying prefecture-level cities before administrative adjustment

Source for area of jurisdictions: National Statistical Bureau, 2000.

Note: data for another four cities are not included in the table due to a lack of information.

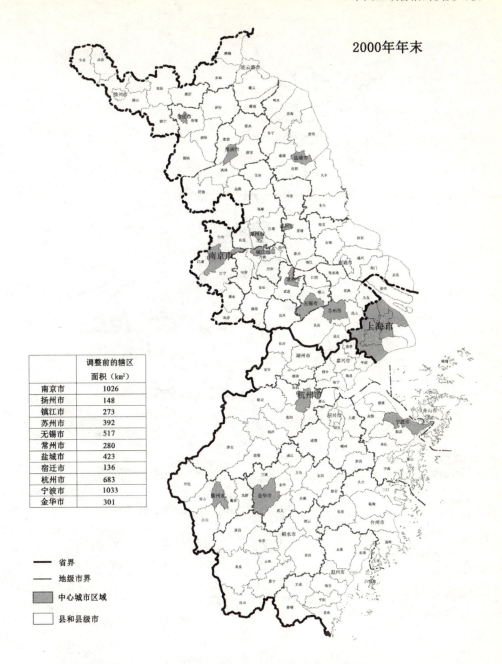

2000年年末

	调整前的辖区面积（km²）
南京市	1026
扬州市	148
镇江市	273
苏州市	392
无锡市	517
常州市	280
盐城市	423
宿迁市	136
杭州市	683
宁波市	1033
金华市	301

省界
地级市界
中心城市区域
县和县级市

图3.11 行政区划调整之前的地级市市区分界图

辖区面积数据来源：国家统计局，2000。

注：由于资料缺乏，有四个城市的数据未在图表中列出。

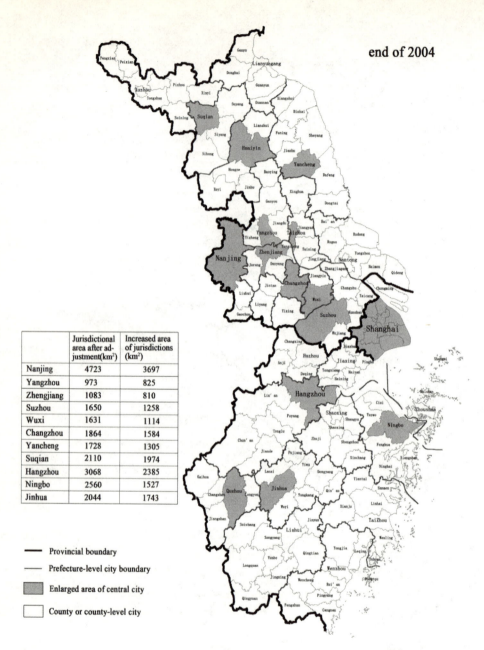

	Jurisdictional area after adjustment(km²)	Increased area of jurisdictions (km²)
Nanjing	4723	3697
Yangzhou	973	825
Zhengjiang	1083	810
Suzhou	1650	1258
Wuxi	1631	1114
Changzhou	1864	1584
Yancheng	1728	1305
Suqian	2110	1974
Hangzhou	3068	2385
Ningbo	2560	1527
Jinhua	2044	1743

Figure 3.12 Administrative boundary of the city proper
displaying prefecture-level cities after administrative adjustment

Source for area of jurisdictions: National Statistical Bureau, 2002, 2004, 2005.

Note: data for another four cities are not included in the table due to a lack of information.

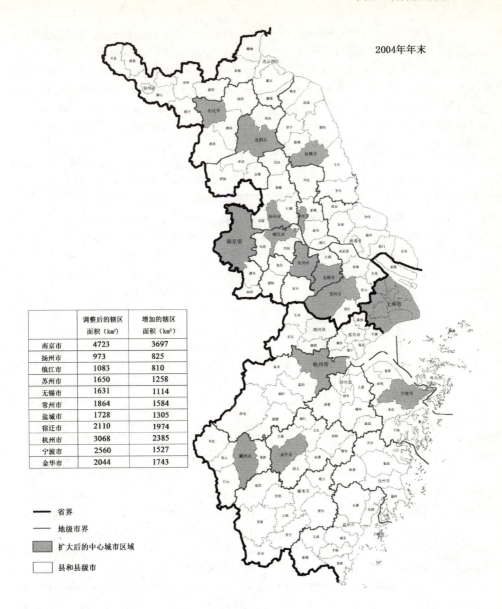

	调整后的辖区 面积（km²）	增加的辖区 面积（km²）
南京市	4723	3697
扬州市	973	825
镇江市	1083	810
苏州市	1650	1258
无锡市	1631	1114
常州市	1864	1584
盐城市	1728	1305
宿迁市	2110	1974
杭州市	3068	2385
宁波市	2560	1527
金华市	2044	1743

—— 省界

—— 地级市界

▨ 扩大后的中心城市区域

☐ 县和县级市

图3.12 行政区划调整之后的地级市市区分界图

辖区面积数据来源：国家统计局，2002,2004,2005。

注：由于资料缺乏，有四个城市的数据未在图表中列出。

The administrative regionalisation has reduced the number of administrative divisions within the region. Coordinated infrastructure development tends to be more easily resolved within a municipality than between central cities and nearby counties. The administrative annexation represents an important attempt by the state to enforce 'big government' strategy in order to handle incoordination and solve zero-sum competition (Yeh and Xu, 2008: 414). However, these administrative realignments have been conceived as short-term oriented and are an unfavourable form of regional governance (Zhang and Wu, 2006). On the one hand, the crude administrative annexations are severely detrimental to the interests of the annexed counties and cities. Due to the discontent of the counties and cities, the municipal governments often had to make significant compromises for these 'new' districts to let them keep their financial independence and ability to make decisions (for example, ibid: 13-14). In this sense, administrative annexation alone is a poor way to implement a unified strategy and a plan to resolve the fundamental problems of inter-city competition and incoordination. On the other hand, annexation is often considered by the municipal government to be an effective instrument to secure its central city position amongst the competition and to exploit the land resources of the countryside (ibid: 15). As a result, annexation has only solidified the process of urbanisation contingent upon huge land consumption and inequality between core municipalities and peripheral areas within the larger regions, and exacerbated the rapid loss of farmland, the livelihood of landless farmers, the informal economy in the city and so forth (Lin, 2009). These unfavourable consequences resulted in the reduced frequency of administrative annexations, which were carried out in a more prudent manner after 2004. Since then, the administrative structure of the whole country has basically remained unchanged except for some small adjustments. Small-scale annexations have occurred at the township and town tier, which is highlighted by a decrease in the number of towns and an increase in street offices (Table 3.6). Overall, the administrative annexation to counties and towns represents the expansion of functional urban areas and the consequent consolidation of the corresponding institutional territory. However, the legitimacy of the administrative measure is challenged due to the authoritarian manner of the agglomeration process. Meanwhile, the impact of annexation on coordinated development is also under suspicion owing to the pragmatic rationale held by the localities. Local governments often make use of the annexation to seek out ample land resources and to enhance economic competitiveness, instead of promoting efficiency and the equalisation of government services.

行政区域化使区域内的行政分区数量减少。中心城市与周边各县合并为地级市后,更便于协调基础设施的发展。行政合并是国家实施"大政府"战略的一项重要尝试,目的在于解决发展不协调问题,消除零和竞争(如 Yeh 和 Xu,2008:414)。然而,有人认为,这种行政重组着眼于短期,且不利于区域管治(Zhang 和 Wu,2006)。一方面,简单粗暴的行政合并会对被兼并县市的利益造成严重损害。为了安抚这些县市的不满情绪,市政府常常不得不作出重大让步,允许这些"新区"保持财政独立并拥有决策权(同上:13-14)。因此,要实现统一发展战略,解决城市竞争与发展不协调等基本问题,单靠行政合并远远不够。另一方面,地级市政府常把行政合并看作稳固中心地位、开发郊区土地资源的一种有效手段(同上:15)。结果,行政合并只是巩固了以土地资源高消耗为推动力、以核心城区与周边地区不均衡发展为特征的城市化进程,同时加剧了农地快速流失、失地农民生计困难、城市非正式经济活跃等问题(Lin,2009)。由于这些不利后果的出现,2004 年后国家开始采取更加谨慎的态度,放缓了行政合并的步伐。之后,全国的行政区划结构基本稳定,只发生过几次微调。例如,在乡镇一级进行过几次小规模的合并,结果是乡镇数目减少,街道办事处的数量增加(表3.6)。总之,对县和镇的行政兼并意味着城市功能区域的扩张以及相应管辖地域的合并。然而,由于合并过程中权力主义突出,行政合并的合理性遭到了质疑。同时,地方政府的功利倾向使行政合并对协调发展的效果也受到了质疑。地方政府不但没能利用行政合并提高政府服务的效率、增进服务公平,反而常常借合并之机开发土地资源,强化自身的经济实力。

Table 3.6 Administrative changes below county-level from 2000 to 2007

Year	2000	2001	2002	2003	2004	2005	2006	2007	2008
Number of Townships	23199	19341	17196	16636	16130	15951	15306	13928	13872
Number of Towns	20312	20374	20600	20226	19892	19522	19369	19249	19234
Number of Street Offices	5902	5510	5516	5751	5829	6152	6355	6434	6524

Source: compiled from Ministry of Civil Affairs, 2001, 2002, 2003, 2004, 2005, 2006, 2007, 2008, 2009.

Note: the number of townships excludes nationality townships and others.

3.8 The rejuvenation of inter - city regional associations since 2000

In order to promote horizontal inter - government relationships under the hierarchical administrative system in China, the central government established institutions such as regional economic cooperative regions at the end of 1980. Following 1981, the North China Economic and Technological Cooperation Region, Middle and South Liaoning Urban Economy Region, Changsha-Zhuzhou-Xiangtan Economic Cooperation Region, Yangtze-Riverside Main City Economic Coordination Association, Nanjing Regional Economic Association and Wuhan Regional Economic Association were subsequently set up.Some associations even spanned several provincial units, which were far ahead of the development of the regional economy. Meanwhile, regional cooperation was residual with central command. This so-called cooperation was, in fact, used by the central state as an alternative means of resource appropriation (Zong, 2008: 193). As a consequence, these regional institutions failed due to a lack of local enthusiasm, as well as the remains of an authoritarian manner. Nevertheless, forms of regional economic associations were rejuvenated after 2000. In contrast to the previous top-down efforts, the new regional activities have been spontaneously built from the bottom. Collaborative initiatives have become prevalent, especially in the regions of Yangtze River Delta, Pearl River Delta and Bohai Sea Rim. For example, the Guangdong province put forward the 'Pan-PRD' concept in 2003. Afterwards, a series of agreements were signed due to Pan - PRD cooperation including transport, human resources, tourism, energy, and trade

表3.6　2000至2007年县级以下基层行政区划的数量变化

年份	2000	2001	2002	2003	2004	2005	2006	2007	2008
乡	23199	19341	17196	16636	16130	15951	15306	13928	13872
镇	20312	20374	20600	20226	19892	19522	19369	19249	19234
街道办事处	5902	5510	5516	5751	5829	6152	6355	6434	6524

来源:编自民政部,2001，2002，2003，2004，2005，2006，2007，2008，2009。
注:乡的数目不包含民族乡及其他乡级行政单位。

第八节　2000年开始的城市间区域联合组织的复兴

为了在行政层级体系内推行政府间的横向关系,中央政府建立了一系列机制,例如在1980年年末设立了经济协作区。1981年起,类似的协作机制相继成立,如:华北地区经济技术协作区、辽中南城市群、长株潭经济协作区、长江沿岸中心城市经济协调会、南京区域经济协调会及武汉经济协作区。有些联合组织甚至覆盖多个省份,远远领先于区域经济的发展速度。然而,区域协作在一定程度上依旧由中央政府主导。这种所谓的协作实际上是中央政府用来进行资源分配的另一种手段(踪家峰,2008:193)。在这种背景下,由于主要是中央操纵,地方积极性不足,这些区域协作机制终告失败。尽管如此,2000年之后,区域经济联合组织又重新焕发活力。与之前自上而下的模式不同,新的区域协作由地方政府自发组建。各地普遍推出协作计划,其中以长江三角洲、珠江三角洲和环渤海地区最为活跃。例如,2003年广东省提出"泛珠三角"的概念,之后,泛珠三角地区在交通、人力资源、旅游、能源及贸易等多方面签署了

(Yeh and Xu, 2008; Zong, 2008: 197). Likewise, the cooperation agenda in the Bohai Sea Rim has also been proceeding rapidly between Beijing, Hebei and Tianjin since 2004 (Zong, 2008: 199).

The evolution of the Yangtze River Delta Economic Region can be taken as a striking example to demonstrate the dynamics of the inter‐municipality regional institutions. The Yangtze River Delta Economic Region was initiated by the Economic and Trade Bureau of fourteen municipal-level governments in 1992, including Shanghai, Suzhou, Wuxi, Changzhou, Nantong, Hangzhou, Jiaxing, Huzhou, Ningbo, Zhoushan, Zhenjiang and Shaoxing. The development of the area‐wide inter-municipality organisation can be divided into four stages: the initial stage from 1992 to 1997; the second stage from 1997 to 2003; the recent stage from 2003 to 2008; and the latest stage since 2008. Initially, the institution was managed by a member system and operated in the form of a forum. The biennial forum was attended by officials from the economic coordination office, usually belonging to the economic and trade bureau in each city. Hence, the forum was at first named the Joint Conference of Directors of Coordination Offices of the Yangtze River Delta Region. The original purpose of the forum was merely information exchange and investment attractions between cities (Luo and Shen, 2009: 55). At the time, the main task was enterprise‐oriented, namely to promote the business connections between local (particularly state‐owned) enterprises. For instance, the Nanjing economic coordination office made efforts to help Nanjing enterprises to set up retail stores in Shanghai, and to facilitate the collaboration between Shanghai Baoshan Steel Enterprise and Nanjing Rolling Mill (The Yangtze River Delta Urban Economic Coordination Office, 2007: 38). This is contextualised in the period of residual planned economy. During the time, SOE was still the dominator in the economy, which was used to following administrative orders and was very weak at horizontal cooperation. However, except for assisting business cooperation, the YRD institution could not make any resolution in terms of general regional development. This is because the institution was only an economic collaboration office under the economic and trade bureau. Many propositions that lay beyond departmental powers had to be submitted to the mayor in charge, which would take a long time (ibid, 39).

In 1997, the joint conference was upgraded to the mayor‐level and was renamed as the Coordination Committee of Urban Economy in the YRD Region. Mayors in charge of economic development, as well as officials of economic coordination offices, were expected to take precedence at the meeting. In addition, another two cities were qualified in 1997 and 2003 respectively, enlarging the membership from 14 to 16 cities. The political upgrade facilitated the communication between city leaders and functional

一系列合作协议(Yeh和Xu,2008;踪家峰,2008:197)。无独有偶,自2004年起,京津冀三地也开始加速推进环渤海地区的合作(踪家峰,2008:199)。

长江三角洲经济区的发展可以被看作体现跨市区域合作机制活力的典型案例。1992年,上海、苏州、无锡、常州、南通、杭州、嘉兴、湖州、宁波、舟山、镇江、绍兴等14个城市的经济贸易委员会共同发起成立长三角经济区。这个覆盖面广的跨市合作机制的发展经历了四个阶段:第一阶段自1992年至1997年;第二阶段自1997年至2003年;第三阶段自2003年至2008年;第四阶段自2008年至今。最初,长三角经济区采取成员制,以论坛形式运作。论坛每两年举办一届,与会人员通常是各个成员市经济贸易委员会(经贸委)下属经济协作办公室(经协办)的负责人。因此,论坛最初的名称是长江三角洲城市协作部门主任联席会议。论坛的最初目的仅仅是为了推动城市间的信息交流和招商引资(Luo和Shen,2009:55)。当时,会议的主要重心放在企业上,意图促进地方企业(尤其是地方国有企业)之间的业务合作。例如,南京经协办曾协助南京企业在上海成立零售商店,并促成上海宝山钢铁公司与南京轧钢厂之间的合作(长江三角洲城市经济协调会办公室,2007:38)。这种以企业为重的做法反映了当时残留的计划经济思想。当时,国家经济仍由国有企业主导,国企向来习惯于服从上级部门的行政命令,缺乏横向合作。然而,当时的长三角经济区机制也只能发挥协助开展业务合作的作用,在总体区域发展问题上并无作为。这是因为该机制只是经贸委下属的一个经济协作办公室,许多超出部门决策权力范围的提议都得交由分管市长决定,而这一过程往往耗时较长(同上:39)。

1997年,联席会议升格为市长级会议,并更名为长江三角洲城市经济协调会。要求出席会议的是各市分管经济发展的市长及协作办(委)的负责人。此外,江苏泰州市和浙江台州市分别于1997年和2003年成为正式成员,成员城市由原来的14个增至16个。政治层面上的升格促进了市领导与各职能部门之间的沟通,这些职能部门包括:经济计划委员会、科技办、国有企业办公室、

departments, including an economic planning committee, a science and technology office, a state-owned enterprises office, a trade bureau, a tourism bureau, and so forth. Even though the political tag of the forum was enhanced, the institution that remained in charge was the department of economic and trade bureau. In other words, no specific institutions were established for the purpose, but remained merely as a liaison under the existing government framework. As shown in Table 3.7, the collaboration agenda during the stage was narrowly confined to specific department issues such as information sharing, common market building, and tourism regionalisation, which are also considered to be mutually beneficial. It was not until 2001 that a unified plan on regional development appeared on the agenda.

To sum up, the committee forum is more like 'an occasional tea party, which is not a priority in government routine work, and no institution or department is afterwards responsible for the agenda put forward by the forum' (interview, professor and expert on YRD regional development, Nanjing University, 19 March 2010). As a consequence, regional governance functions in name only. It largely remains as a working meeting for local departments to exchange information, and represents a dialogue between local governments for symbolic meaning. The agenda and agreements are at a superficial level, seeming to be more of a kind of slogan than concrete actions for cooperation (Luo and Shen, 2009: 55-56). Sensitive topics such as industrial development tend to be skirted around, as no agreements can be reached among the members themselves.

Table 3.7 The agenda of the Urban Economic Coordination Committee of the YRD Region

Year	Place	Agenda
1997	Yangzhou	The joining of Taizhou of Jiangsu province Collaborative development of YRD tourism industry, and active promotion of YRD chain store development
1999	Hangzhou	Regional cooperation in terms of science and technology; promotion of trans-border business annexation; regional information website construction; deepening of tourism, trade and business collaboration
2001	Shaoxing	The deepening of last year's agenda Attempts to strengthen the integration of regional transport network, the collaboration of industries, and the integration of financing
2003	Nanjing	The joining of Taizhou of Zhejiang province Sharing 2010 Shanghai Expo opportunities and expanding the expo's effects; collaboration in investment attraction; deepening of tourism integration, regional transport network, environment, logistics and trade cooperation.

Source: compiled from The Yangtze River Delta Urban Economic Coordination Office, 2007: 48-84.

贸易局和旅游局等。尽管协调会的政治地位得到提升,但该机制中的负责部门仍是经贸委的下属部门。也就是说,协调会没有设立专门的机构来履行自身的职能,而只是在现有政府架构下起到联络作用。如表3.7所示,该阶段的协作议程仅限于讨论解决具体的部门问题,如信息共享、市场开拓、旅游区域化等,而解决这些问题当然也被认为是互利互惠的。直到2001年,议程中才提出区域发展的统一规划。

总体来说,协调会更像是"偶尔举办的茶话会,而不是政府日常工作的重心,会后也没有任何机构或部门对论坛上提出的议程负责"(2010年3月19日对长三角区域发展专家、南京大学某教授的采访)。这样一来,协调会的区域管治功能也只是有名无实。大体说来,协调会主要是各地方部门之间交流信息的工作会议,只是象征性地代表了地方政府之间的对话。议程及达成的协议都只是停留在表面,不过是提出一些口号,而不是具体的合作行动方案(Luo和Shen,2009:55-56)。由于成员市之间无法就工业发展等敏感话题达成一致意见,因此协调会也总是尽量回避这类话题。

表3.7 长江三角洲城市经济协调会议程

年份	举办城市	议程
1997	扬州	江苏省泰州市加入; 长三角地区旅游业协同发展,积极推动长三角地区连锁店的发展
1999	杭州	加强区域科技合作;促进跨境业务合并;筹建区域信息网;深化旅游、贸易及商务合作
2001	绍兴	深化上一年议程; 加强整合区域交通网络、促进产业协作和融资整合
2003	南京	浙江省台州市加入; 分享2010年上海世博会带来的机遇,扩大世博影响;合作开展招商引资;深化旅游一体化,完善区域交通网络,促进环境、物流及贸易合作

来源:根据长三角城市经济协调会办公室资料编制,2007:48-84。

Since the new millennium, inter-municipality communication has become even more active than before. The Urban Economic Coordination Committee of the YRD Region has changed from a biennial to an annual forum since 2003 (Wang, 2009: 120). Furthermore, provinces have also become actively involved in the building of a YRD area-wide institution. For example, a provincial-level forum mechanism was established between Jiangsu, Zhejiang and Shanghai in 2001, namely, the Jiangsu, Zhejiang and Shanghai Forum on Economic Coordination and Development. The annual forum is attended by executive vice-provincial governors and prefecture-level city mayors. The senior-level government meeting demonstrates the positive attitude of the top leaders to regional coordination. Strategic proposals have been made in various fields, such as the sharing of information resources and human resources, and the building of a common market and coordinated infrastructure system. Overall, YRD regional integration has been turned into a catchphrase in the 2000s that various kinds of seminars and communication have been promoting. It is estimated that over 100 seminars were held in 2002 and 2003 on YRD regional development (Lu and Shi, 2008: 157) and around 20 agreements were signed between Jiangsu, Zhejiang and Shanghai in 2003 and 2004 (Ji et al., 2006: 88). Table 3.8 lists the newly emerging events or forums based on the provincial level. Although no assessment has ever been made to evaluate how these agendas have progressed in reality, it is recognised that the involvement of the provincial sector shows a progressive tendency. As commented by a scholar in Shanghai,

> These moves are of significance as provincial governments, who used to be the main barrier of integration, showed the gesture to push cooperative development between cities. In the past, it is always the provinces that made 'red-headed' document to obstruct trade and unified market. (interview, professor and expert in YRD regional development, East China Normal University, 21 April 2010)

　　进入新世纪以来,各市之间的交流日益活跃。2003年开始,长江三角洲城市经济协调会会议由每两年一届变为每年一届(王枫云,2009:120)。此外,长三角地区的各省也积极投入建立覆盖整个地区的机制。例如,江苏、浙江和上海在2001年建立了一个省级座谈会机制,即苏浙沪经济合作与发展座谈会。座谈会每年召开一次,由三省市的常务副省长和市长参加。省级政府座谈会的召开,反映了高层领导对区域协调发展的积极态度。会上对多个领域的发展提出了战略性建议:如分享信息资源和人力资源,以及建设统一市场和整体协调的基础设施系统等。总的来说,长三角地区的区域一体化问题成为进入21世纪以来各类研讨会和交流会上反复热议的话题。据估计,2002年到2003年间,共举办了百余场有关长三角地区区域发展问题的研讨会(陆阳和史文学,2008:157);2003年到2004年间,江苏、浙江和上海三地共签署了20余项合作协议(纪晓岚等,2006:88)。表3.8列出了最近召开的省级活动或会议。尽管这些议程的具体进展尚未得到评估,但是省级部门的参与已经显示出了合作的发展趋势。正如上海一位学者所评价的:

　　　　这些做法意义深远,省级政府曾经是一体化发展的主要障碍,现在却展现出了推进城市合作发展的姿态。过去省级政府总是发布一些"红头文件"来阻碍贸易,使市场变得单一化。(摘自2010年4月21日对长三角区域发展专家、华东师范大学某教授的采访)

Table 3.8 The emergence of provincial‑level cooperation forums in the YRD region

Name	Attendees	Year of commencement and regularity
International Symposium of the Development of YRD Region	Key cadres from the region, governors from central ministries, and even overseas academics	1999 annual forum
Jiangsu, Zhejiang and Shanghai Forum on Economic Coordination and Development (Su‑Zhe‑Hu jingji hezuo yu fazhan zuotan hui)	Executive vice‑provincial governors and prefecture‑level deputy city mayors	2001; annual forum
Jiangsu, Zhejiang and Shanghai Joint Conference on Financial Coordinated development	Provincial governors of Jiangsu, Zhejiang and Shanghai, the Bank of China, and other associated banks	2008; annual forum

Source: compiled from Ji et al., 2006: 87-88; Sun and Zhao, 2009: 435.

In 2008, the various associations within the region were formalised into an integrated three-tiered cooperation channel. At the top is the annual round-table conference attended by provincial top leadership from the YRD region, which is held to discuss common issues and make strategic decisions; the top‑level is followed by a lower‑level joint‑conference between executive vice provincial governors and executive deputy mayors, which is supposed to follow up the agreed agenda and put forward coordinated arrangements. The implementation is the responsibility of the offices of the joint conference convened by the development and reform committee in each jurisdictional city, the working groups for specific cooperation subjects, and the coordination forum between the 16 cities convened by the economic coordination offices (interview, civil servant, Nanjing Economic and Trade Bureau, Feb. 16, 2009).

To sum up, the cooperation agenda has obtained greater support from both local and higher‑level governments since 2000. Since the current cooperation mechanism is spontaneously initiated and the decision power rests with the member authorities, the inter-municipality has gained more recognition from the localities. However, the disadvantages are that the inter‑municipal structure is based on forums and conferences on special occasions, rather than a permanent institution. Moreover, it is not supported by stable financial support granted from anywhere. The omission of a standing agency means the function of coordination remain fragmented throughout different governments and ministries, which is detrimental to its effects and efficiency. As noted by Yang and Chen (2007: 21), the forum or conference form of cooperation channel is

表3.8 长三角区域省级经济合作论坛的出现

会议名称	参会人员	首次召开年份和举办周期
长江三角洲区域发展国际研讨会	长三角区域主要领导干部、中央部委领导和海外学术专家	1999年；一年一次
苏浙沪经济合作与发展座谈会	常务副省长和常务副市长	2001年；一年一次
推进长江三角洲地区金融协调发展工作联席会议	苏浙沪三省市领导,中国人民银行及其他银行	2008年；一年一次

来源:编自纪晓岚等, 2006: 87-88;孙海鸣和赵晓雷, 2009:435。

　　2008年,长三角地区相关机构正式整合为一个三层架构的合作渠道。顶层为一年一次的圆桌会议,由长三角地区各省市高层领导出席参加,旨在讨论共同关心的问题并作出战略决策;第二层是级别稍低的联席会议,由常务副省(市)长参加,旨在就商定的议程开展后续工作并作出协调安排;最后一层是执行层,负责执行工作的部门包括:各市发展和改革委员会联席会议办公室、各具体合作事宜工作组以及由经济协调办公室举办的16市协调论坛(2009年2月16日对南京市经济贸易委员会某公务员的采访)。

　　总之,2000年以来,各地方及上级政府对于合作议程给予了更大的支持。由于当前的合作机制是自发建立的,且决策权在成员城市权威部门的手上,因此,这种城市间的合作获得了地方政府的更多认可。然而,这种城市交流模式的弊端在于它并非固定机制,而只是在某些特定情况下举办论坛或召开会议,并且当前机制也没有获得任何稳定的财政支持。同时,由于缺乏常设机构,各地政府部门和部委之间不能很好地统一协调,大大影响了工作成效和办事效率。正如杨俊宴和陈雯(2007:21)所指出的,依托论坛或会议的合作机制

far too reliant upon senior officials and governors, which is not an efficient dialogue platform, and lacks an implementation and monitoring mechanism. Overall, enthusiasm for inter-city cooperation has increased since 2000 compared to levels in the 1980s and 1990s. However, as observed by Yeh and Xu (2008) in PRD experiences, the current inter-municipality cooperation mechanism in China is largely based on imagination rather than on concrete and consolidated institutions. In other words, the bottom-up regional institution is still 'a collection of loosely assembled local governments' (Wu and Zhang, 2009: 12).

3.9 Formulation of regional spatial plans since 2005

In order to promote regional coordination, planning in China is experiencing its second period of change after the previous 'entrepreneurial city plans'. In the late 1990s, city plans in China underwent some important changes, from a traditional land use blueprint plan to a strategic spatial plan (Wu, 2007). These non-statutory city plans made attempts to reposition urban development on a larger regional scale than by local administrative boundaries. This type of strategic plan has played a positive role in building inter-city highways and regional transport network. Nevertheless, the locally-initiated plans are addressed from a position of local competitiveness and tend to position themselves more favourably in the region, which marginalises other regional issues such as environment protection and coordinated industrial development. In effect, these plans are used as promotional instruments by local governments to attract additional investments, and as justification for entrepreneurial strategies such as expanding existing built-up urban space for GDP growth (Wu and Zhang, 2007).

However, the spatial plan approach has recently been employed by the central and provincial governments for larger regions such as the Pearl River Delta and the Yangtze River Delta (Figure 3.13). As opposed to previously, the current wave of plan-making is not only compiled by the Ministry of Housing and Urban and Rural Development (MHURD) and its subordinates, which are the main plan-making institutions after economic reform, but also by the National Development and Reform Commission (NDRC), the previous overall planning commission during the Socialist period. As a matter of fact, the powerful organisation NDRC, rather than MHURD, leads current regional plan-making. In 2009 alone, over ten regional plans were published by NDRC, with even more under preparation or waiting to be approved. Finally, the rationale and functionality of the current regional plans have undergone a great transformation from development plans towards development control, whether they are undertaken by NDRC or MHURD. For example, NDRC changed

过于依赖政府高层领导,未形成一个有效的对话平台,且缺乏执行和监管机制。总之,与20世纪80、90年代相比,2000年以后城市合作的热情有所增加。但是Yeh和Xu(2008)在观察珠三角地区的发展经验后指出,目前中国的城市合作机制很大程度上只是空想,并未形成切实统一的机制。也就是说,自下而上的区域制度仍然是"松散的地方政府集合"(Wu和Zhang,2009:12)。

第九节　2005年开始形成的区域空间规划

为了促进区域协调,中国的城市规划正在经历继之前的"经营型城市规划"之后的第二阶段的转变。20世纪90年代末,中国的城市规划经历了从传统的土地利用规划到空间战略规划的一系列重大转变(Wu,2007)。这些非法定的城市规划方案试图打破地方行政区域的界限,将城市发展放到一个更大的区域尺度范围内。这种战略规划在建设城际高速公路和区域交通运输网络时发挥了积极的作用。然而,这种地方发起的规划项目为了保护地方竞争力,往往只考虑对自己有利的情况,而忽视了其他区域问题,如环保问题和工业协调发展等问题。事实上,地方政府正是将这些规划项目作为吸引更多投资的宣传工具,并以此为由推广城市经营战略,比如扩大现有城市空间以实现GDP增长的战略(Wu和Zhang,2007)。

然而,近来中央政府和各省政府也针对更大的区域采用了空间规划方法,如珠江三角洲地区和长江三角洲地区(图3.13)。与过去不同的是,在当前这股热潮中,负责计划制定工作的并不仅仅是国家住房和城乡建设部及其下属机构,还有国家发展和改革委员会。前者及其下属机构是经济改革后负责计划制定的主要机构,而后者原为社会主义计划经济时期的国家计划委员会。事实上,目前掌握区域规划实权的部门是发改委,而非住建部。仅2009年一年,发改委就发布了十多个区域规划政策,还有更多规划正在筹备之中或等待

the name of the conventional five-year economic plan to the 'five-year spatial plan' in 2002, which officially announced the new direction of the plan. In the past, the five-year economic plan was prepared by the planning commissions of various government levels to find resources to sustain economic growth. As the government used to be the only investor in the planned economy, each level of the five-year economic plan was hence the virtual government spending plan of the corresponding government. Furthermore, since all economic resources were nationalised in the command economy, the central plan usually had a decisive role in local government spending and economic growth. However, with the diversification of investment sources since economic reform, the hierarchical five-year economic plan has actually relaxed, as the central government no longer possesses leverage over local government and private investment. Nowadays, with the transition to a spatial plan, a territorial development strategy is thus entailed in conventional target-oriented plan-making. The new spatial approach indicates that the economic plan not only requires the achievement of growth, but also contains specific spatial regulations, i.e. in order to channel economic growth from developed to underdeveloped areas, or to control development activities in undesirable places. As remarked by the head of NDRC, the five-year plan is now 'more than a text document on strategic industrial development policies, but also a means of spatial regulation regarding where building should occur' (Ma, 2003). In order to achieve these objectives, compulsory policies have been formulated to be enforced on some industrial locations, in addition to general guidance on urban and industrial development in the past. Overall, the newly introduced spatial planning approach is actually acting as the newly sharpened regulative leverage of the central government, as local five-year plans are supposed to be formulated following the central plan. This means that the hierarchical five-year plan has been restored and regulation over local government spending has also been strengthened.

批准。无论是由发改委还是住建部负责,当前区域规划的理念和作用都经历了从发展计划到发展管理的巨大转变。例如,2002年,发改委将"五年计划"(传统的五年经济计划)更名为"五年规划"(五年空间规划),正式宣告了国家规划的新方向。过去,为了开发资源以维持经济增长,各级政府规划委员会都制订了五年经济计划。由于在计划经济时期,政府是唯一的投资者,所以五年经济计划事实上就是相应政府部门的支出计划。此外,在国家掌控的经济中所有经济资源都归国家所有,因此,中央的计划对于地方政府的支出和经济增长往往起着决定性作用。然而,经济改革后,投资来源不断多元化,这种自上而下的五年计划实际上已经松动,因为中央政府对地方政府和私人投资不再具有影响力。如今,随着向空间规划的转变,需要在传统的以目标为导向的规划制定过程中纳入地域发展战略。新的空间规划方法表明,经济计划不仅需要设立经济增长目标,还需要制定具体的空间管理规定,比如,如何让发达地区的经济增长带动不发达地区,或如何控制欠发达地区的发展活动。发改委主任曾指出,现在五年计划"不仅是关于战略性工业发展政策的一个书面文件,对于需要建设的地区来说更是一种空间规划"(马凯,2003)。为了实现这些目标,除了过去制定的关于城市和工业发展的总体指导之外,还出台了强制性政策,在某些工业地区强制执行。总体而言,新的空间规划方法实际上是中央政府最新的调控利器,因为地方政府在制定五年规划时应与中央规划保持一致。这就意味着,自上而下的五年计划重又恢复,同时对地方政府支出的监管也变得更加严格。

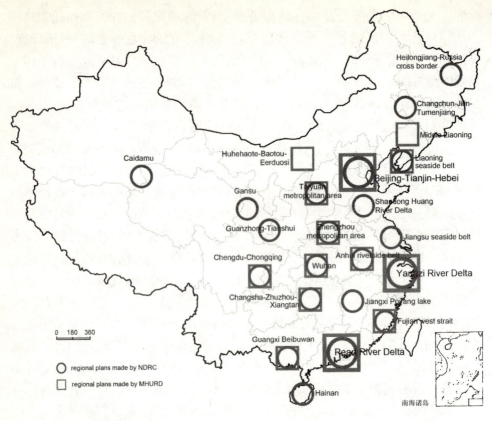

Figure 3.13 The locations of the escalation of regional plans
Source: compiled by the author.

Parallel transformation is also witnessed with regard to the plan-making underneath the MHURD system. Indeed, MHURD prepared the National Urban System Plan (2006-2020) in 2005, which is the first national-level plan on urbanisation and spatial development, to strengthen top-down guidance and regulation. The plan identified existing major urban clusters and potential areas for development across the country, and, hence, formulated differentiated urbanisation strategies to mitigate the over-concentration of population in the coastal area. Based on the overall strategy, an infrastructure framework was provided to stimulate the development of city regions in the central and western districts. Built on overall consideration of the distribution of natural resources and ecological conditions, the plan draws up guidelines on urbanisation and spatial development in individual provincial-level jurisdictions. Within the guidelines, emphasis is placed on core city regions, trans-border areas, and regional and inter-regional infrastructure. Following the preparation of the National Urban System Plan (2006-2020), MHURD intended to launch a

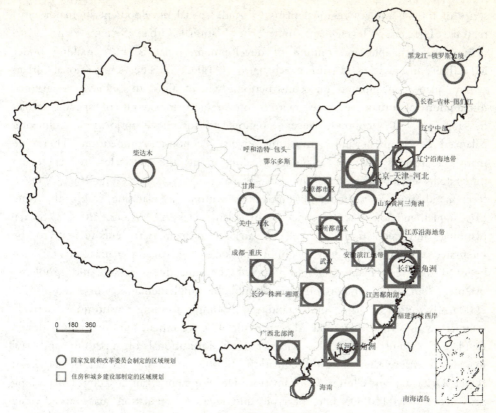

黑龙江-俄罗斯边境

长春-吉林-图们江

辽宁中部

辽宁沿海地带

呼和浩特-包头-
鄂尔多斯

柴达木

北京-天津-河北

甘肃

太原都市区

山东黄河三角洲

关中-天水

郑州都市区

江苏沿海地带

成都-重庆

武汉

安徽沿江地带

长江三角洲

长沙-株洲-湘潭

江西鄱阳湖

福建海峡西岸

广西北部湾

红河-个旧

海南

南海诸岛

○ 国家发展和改革委员会制定的区域规划

□ 住房和城乡建设部制定的区域规划

0 180 360

图3.13 新一轮区域规划涵盖地区

来源:作者编制。

在住建部系统的规划中,我们也看到了相应的转型。事实上,住建部2005年编制了《全国城镇体系规划(2006—2020年)》,这是城市和空间发展方面的第一个国家层次的规划,旨在加强自上而下的指导和管理。该规划划定了现有的主要城镇群和国内具备发展潜力的地区,并据此制定了不同的城市化战略,以缓和沿海地区人口过度集中的问题。为促进中西部地区城市的发展,根据总体战略提供了基础设施建设的框架。根据自然资源分配和生态环境不同的整体状况,还拟定了各省级行政区的城市化和空间发展指导纲要。这些纲要指出,政府的工作重心将放在发展核心城区、跨境地区、区域和跨区域基础设施建设上。《全国城镇体系规划(2006—2020年)》编制完成后,住建部计划发

series of trans-boundary regional plans to guide spatial development in major city-regions. The meso-level plans under the National Urban System Plan try to deliver the principle and outline of development. That is, plan-making under MHURD also witnessed similar changes as NDRC. The conventional urban system plan concentrates on construction, which aims to achieve a rational distribution of urban resources within one region in favour of specific urban developments. In contrast, recent regional plans have prioritised achieving balanced development and eliminating adverse economic competition. There are many discussions in the planning realm about the obstacles to achieving integrated development in China (B. J. Yang, 2004; Chen and Wang, 2006). Yet, in addition to technocratic innovation within the planning realm, the issue of 'implementation' is a concern of plan-makers (Wang, 2004). Spatial planning and regulation, as well as an action plan, are encouraged to be integrated into the regional planning package (Shao and Pan, 2004). It is believed that plan-making should not only be objective-oriented and problem-oriented, but more importantly, it should be implementation-oriented (Zou, 2006). Because of this understanding, leading planning institutions actively interact with MHURD and the provincial government in order to design regulatory measures; they also interact with institutional organisations and law makers to ensure the effect of regulation. In the pioneering project of the Pearl River Delta Urban Cluster Coordination Development Plan, led by Guangdong province and MHURD, different types and levels of regulation space are divided and linked with relevant levels of government and departments; a dedicated government organisation has been established for plan implementation and evaluation and the regional plan has been conferred with statutory status by the provincial People's Congress (Zou and Shi, 2004; Cai and Zhu, 2006; Xu, 2008). Furthermore, the regional plan has been followed by the preparation of a regulatory detailed plan, which is the only type of plan in China that is provided with regulatory devices at the local level (Huang et al., 2007). Overall, the proliferation of regional plans by MHURD demonstrates the renewed efforts exerted by the higher-level governments to legitimise top-down intervention (Xu, 2008: 28), which has been largely weakened since economic devolution.

To sum up, China's territory is now covered by spatial plans by various state agents. The latest practices, driven by central government instead of municipal governments, demonstrate the concern of the central state over sustainability, coordination between regions and the quality of development. However, a sharp increase in planning and planning institutions has also confused the lines of accountability, and may undermine the effect of governance as well.

布一系列跨区域规划，以指导主要城市区域的空间发展。总之，《全国城镇体系规划》的编制过程反映了住建部在制定规划的过程中出现了与发改委类似的转变。传统的城镇体系规划注重建设，并力图实现区域内城市资源的合理分配，以促进特定的城市发展。相反，近来的区域规划则注重实现平衡发展，并消除不利的经济竞争。在规划领域，很多学者都讨论过中国要实现综合发展将面临的障碍（杨保军，2004；陈建华和王国恩，2006）。但除了规划领域技术层面的创新问题之外，规划制定者们还担心"实施"方面的问题（王晓东，2004）。他们鼓励在区域规划组合中纳入空间规划和监管以及行动计划（邵波和潘强，2004）。制定规划时不仅应考虑如何才能实现目标并解决问题，更要考虑怎样才最有利于实施（邹兵，2006）。基于这种理念，一流的规划设计机构在设计监管措施时，一般会事先与住建部和省级政府积极接触，而为了确保监管措施的有效性，它们也会与各体制组织和立法机构进行互动。在广东省政府和住建部牵头的开创性项目《珠江三角洲城镇群协调发展规划》中，对不同类型和级别的监管空间进行了划分，并将其与有关级别的政府和部门相关联；为此，广东省成立了专门的政府机构进行方案实施和评估，省人大也赋予了该区域规划法律效力（邹兵和施源，2004；蔡瀛和朱国鸣，2006；Xu，2008）。此外，该区域规划制定后，还编制了控制性详细规划——在中国，只有这种控制性详细规划才能获得地方监管体系的实际支持（举例详见黄卓等，2007）。总体说来，住建部大量编制和推广区域规划的事实表明，高层政府已经重新开始努力将其自上而下的干预措施合法化（Xu，2008：28），以加强自经济放权以来就放松了的干预工作。

　　总之，由不同国家机构推行的各种空间规划正在中国各地实施。由中央政府而非市级政府主导的最新实践表明，中央对能否实现可持续发展、区域间的协调发展和高质量发展非常关注。然而，规划方案数目的激增和规划机构的大量新建也模糊了管治责任界线，有可能削弱管治效果。

3.10 The features of re-emerged regional governance in China

The above practices, which have already been documented in a plethora of Chinese literature, have illustrated the regional renaissance in China. Nevertheless, the current regional projects in China have shown different dynamics, institutional features and rationales from earlier regional institutions in the 1950s and 1960s. A comparison with previous efforts, as well as with Western regionalism theories and practices, is considered valuable to aid understanding of the current re-emergence of regional governance in China.

3.10.1 State-steered restructuring of territorial governance

The role of the Chinese state is still pervasive and dominant, even after decades of decentralisation. For instance, place promotion and entrepreneurial governance in China is predominantly driven by the central and/or local state rather than the private sector (Wu, 2000b, 2003; Xu and Yeh, 2005; Zhang, 2002b). This is because the bulk of social and economic resources are still possessed by the state. Public participation and partnership with the business sector is only periodic; it is merely a temporary vehicle utilised by the state to materialise its political aims (Zhang and Wu, 2008). Due to the same reason, current city – region restructuring is also largely reliant on the forceful interventions of governments, even though some of the agenda may have initially been triggered by market forces and civil society (Liu et al., 2010). For example, Liu et al. (2010) have documented the trajectory of inter–city coordinated development between two adjacent cities of Guangzhou and Foshan in Guangdong Province. Inter–city transport regionalisation between the two cities had been advocated by local residents for years due to the inconvenience of commuting. However, the issue had not been solved until the active involvement of government began in 2002. Since then, inter–city cooperation between Guangzhou and Foshan has quickly expanded from transport to urban development, environment and the economy.

In the current development, it should be noted that, after the previous state rescaling, decentralised local authorities have acquired their capacity to develop their own state spatial projects and strategies. In other words, the current regional initiatives are articulated by two different mechanisms, i.e. the top-down and bottom-up approach, which is a different situation from the first round of state rescaling. The top – down approach is initiated by the central government. This is very much akin to the 'centrally-orchestrated regionalism' documented in the UK (Harrison, 2008). The bottom-up approach is initiated by the local governments. It should be noted that the mechanism is different

第十节　中国重新出现的区域管治的特点

上述实践已被记载在中国大量的文献中,是中国区域复兴的例证。然而,与20世纪50年代和60年代相比,中国目前的区域项目在动力、体制特征和理念方面都发生了变化。将中国区域管治的现状与过去的工作进行纵向比较,并与西方区域主义理论及实践进行横向比较,有助于理解当前中国区域管治的复兴现象。

一、国家调控下的地域管治调整

即使在放权几十年后,中国政府仍然保持着普遍的影响力和主导权。例如,中国的地方宣传和经营性管治大都由中央和/或地方政府主导,而非由私营部门推动(Wu,2000b,2003;Xu和Yeh,2005;Zhang,2002b)。这是因为国家一直占有着主要的社会和经济资源。公众参与以及与商业部门的伙伴关系都是短暂性的;这只是国家为了实现其政治目的而采取的权宜之策(Zhang和Wu,2008)。出于同样的原因,当前的城市区域重组还是主要依赖政府的强力干预,尽管其中的某些议程最初是由市场力量和民间社会提出的(刘超群等,2010)。例如,刘超群等(2010)记述了广东省内两个相邻城市——广州和佛山之间的协调发展历程。长久以来因为交通不便,两地居民都盼望能早日实现城际交通区域化。但直到2002年政府开始积极参与后,这个问题才得到解决。从此广州与佛山的城际合作由城际交通迅速扩展到了城市发展、环境保护和经济等领域。

在当前的发展进程中,应当注意到,国家尺度重组之后获得分权的地方政府已经有能力自行开发国家空间项目和战略。也就是说,与第一轮国家尺度重组情况不同,现在的区域举措由两种不同机制形成,即自上而下的机制和自下而上的机制。自上而下的区域举措由中央政府发起,很大程度上类似于发生在英国的"中央主导的区域主义"(Harrison,2008)。而自下而上的区域举措由地方政府负责领导实施,但有一点不可忽略,就是中国的这种"自下而上"的

from the notion of 'bottom-up' in the Western context. The resurgent 'new regionalism' literature in Western countries indicates that a new feature of the recent regional practices is the 'bottom-up' mechanism and the preference for 'small government'. In other words, the recent regional practices are fostered by public-private partnership, such as government contracting, outsourcing, privatisation and voluntary collaboration with autonomous institutions in informal networks (Everingham, 2009: 85; Norris, 2001; Savitch and Vogel, 2000; Wheeler, 2002). The involvement of non-public sectors has formed a complex and overlapping governance regime which is a hybrid of cross-jurisdictional, multi-level and networking actions (Everingham, 2009: 85). This is different to the notion of 'bottom-up' in the new regionalism literature; the bottom-up mechanism in China is articulated by the local government with limited participation from civil society, business sectors or NGOs.

3.10.2 Contradictory rationales of the top-down and bottom-up approach

The regional practices respectively led by the central and local governments are actually operated out of distinct motivations. According to the above examination, the central government has initiated exercises such as recentralising land management, formulating spatial plans, launching province-leading county institutional reforms and remaking various regional policies. The package of actions is not rolled out randomly, but rather addresses different and specific problems incurred by insufficient central regulation; for instance, the regional policies in the middle and west regions were launched to quench the discontent of localities regarding the long-running central preference for the coast and balanced central policies between regions. Regional plans and main functional area plans, however, are formulated across the nation in order to reassert central guidance on spatial development and spatial coordination. Furthermore, the reduction of hierarchies of local governments by province-leading-county reform is not only to resolve the fiscal problem of 'prefecture-level city exploiting counties' under the city-leading-county system, but also to strengthen the central regulation in 'far away and unreachable areas' by central government. Likewise, the recentralisation of land management also indicates the up-scaling of certain government functions towards the higher-level to control local discretionary land development. In short, it seems to suggest that uneven development and land politics, the latter in particular, constitute a central position in centrally-orchestrated regional practices. On the one hand, this is different from the setting up of a layer of administrative regions at the founding period of the new People's Republic of China, when it was hoped that regional institutions would help to unify the nation, which was chaotic and

概念与西方语境中的不同。在西方国家出现的"新区域主义"文献中,揭示出近期的区域实践具有"自下而上"作用机制以及偏好"小政府"的新特征。也就是说,近期的区域实践是通过公司伙伴关系实现的,如政府项目承包、外包、私有化,以及与非正式网络中的独立机构进行自愿协作(Everingham,2009:85;Norris,2001;Savitch 和 Vogel,2000;Wheeler,2002)。这些非公共部门的参与导致整个管治机制变得复合而有所重叠,最终成为了一个跨辖区、多级别的联网行动的混合管治体系(Everingham,2009:85)。中国的情况不同于新区域主义文献中的"自下而上"概念,中国自下而上的机制是由地方政府负责操作的,民间社会、商业部门或非政府组织的参与是有限的。

二、自上而下和自下而上机制的冲突

事实上,中央和地方政府是出于截然不同的动机而领导着各自的区域实践的。从上述分析可以看出,中央政府已开始进行各种尝试,如将土地管理权再度收归中央、制定空间规划、启动省管县体制改革以及更新各项已有的区域政策。这一整套行动并非随意制定,而是有针对性地解决了因中央监管措施不足而引发的种种具体问题,比如,出台了中西部区域政策以平息各地对中央政策长期向沿海地区倾斜的不满,并在中央政策的制定过程中兼顾各地区间的平衡。中央为了重申自己在空间开发及空间协调领域的领导地位,统一编制了全国各区域规划及主体功能区规划。除此之外,中央还通过省管县体制改革减少地方的行政层级。这不仅仅是为了解决以往市管县体制下"地级市政府剥削下属县"的税收弊端,而且是为加强中央政府对"偏远地区"的集中监管而采取的一种手段。类似地,土地管理权被再度收归中央也预示着某些政府职能重心的上移,以控制地方政府随意开发土地。简而言之,不均衡的地区发展和土地政治,尤其是后者,似乎在中央主导的区域实践中占据核心地位。一方面,这不同于新中国成立初期行政区域层级的设立,当时那样做是希望能通过区域制度把当时混乱割裂的新生国家统一起来(Donaldson,2010:26)。另

divided (Donaldson, 2010: 26). On the other hand, this is also divergent from the regional motives documented in Western countries, which generally revolve around the containment of urban sprawl, boosting the efficiency of overlapping public services, the improvement of social cohesion, and common concerns over issues such as transportation, environment and quality of life (Everingham et al., 2006; Gleeson, 2003; Jonas and Pincetl, 2006; McCann, 2007; McGuirk, 2007; Purcell, 2007; While et al., 2004). The Chinese experience of concerns about rational land development is closely associated with the present development stage of China, which is in a fast lane of industrial development which consumes a large amount of land for manufacturing.

In contrast, other exercises such as administrative annexations, inter - city associations and local spatial plans have been undertaken by the local governments for different motives. These practices are, to some extent, helpful in terms of expanding administrative boundaries and facilitating inter - city communication and cooperation. However, since the regional practices are generally initiated by the city government alone, they tend to be inward - looking and in pursuit of urban competitiveness. For instance, locally initiated strategic development plans were used as an instrument by the urban entrepreneurial government to enhance structural economic competitiveness (Wu and Zhang, 2007). Even though the local strategic development plans go beyond the boundary of administrative divisions, the relationship between different places is often perceived as fraught with rivalry and hostile. In other words, it was inter-locality competition that served as the motive and rationale for the local governments to initiate such city-region plans (Li, 2008). It is, hence, argued that locally - led cooperation is limited in scope in terms of agenda setting, which is predominantly based on competitive rationales (Zhang et al., 2005). The possibility of economic mutual benefit is crucial to the success or failure of the local cooperation programmes.

3.10.3 Flexible institutionalisation of regional practices and projects

Unlike the Regional Development Agency in the UK, the regional initiatives in China are not formally institutionalised. The central government is using spatial strategies, planning and reshuffling of certain governmental functional structures to deliver the regional perspective, instead of setting up a new tier of government. This is distinguished from the establishment of full - blown regional government in the 1950s, which was even equipped with both governmental and Party institutions. The proliferation of regional plans suggests that formulating these plans has become a major tool for the central government to deliver top-down governance. However, so far, the responsibility

一方面,它与西方国家的区域化动机又不一样,后者主要围绕着遏制城市过度扩张、精简重复的公共服务以提升效率、增强社会凝聚力以及大家共同关切的问题(如交通、环境和生活质量等)来不断推进区域化进程(Everingham等,2006;Gleeson,2003;Jonas和Pincetl,2006;McCann,2007;McGuirk,2007;Purcell,2007;While等,2004)。中国现阶段正处于工业化的快车道上,工业生产耗费大量土地资源,因此,中国政府对合理开发土地表现出了极大的关注。

　　相比之下,地方政府开展行政合并、城际联合和本地空间规划等实践举措则是出于完全不同的动机。这些实践在某种程度上有助于扩大行政边界并促进城际交流与合作。然而,由于这些区域实践大都仅由市政府发起,因而往往都只着眼于自身内部的问题,也只追求提升本市的竞争力。例如,地方制定的战略发展规划通常被经营型市政府用作提升城市结构性经济竞争力的工具(Wu和Zhang,2007)。即便地方战略发展规划跨越了行政区划的界线,不同地区之间的关系仍被认为是充满敌对和竞争情绪的。换句话说,城市间的竞争才是地方政府编制这类城市区域规划的根本动机和原因(李晓江,2008)。因此有学者认为,由地方主导的合作如果以竞争理念为基本出发点,那么能制定的合作议程就很有限(张京祥等,2005)。能否实现经济上的互利互惠是达成地方合作项目的关键。

三、非正式制度下的区域实践

　　与英国区域发展署的做法不同,中国的区域举措并没有正式体制化。中央政府是利用空间战略及某些政府职能架构的规划和重组来呈现区域视角的,而不是增设新的政府层级。这与20世纪50年代建立完善的区域政府的情形构成了鲜明对比,当时的区域政府甚至设有党政双重体制。区域规划数量的激增说明制定这类规划已成为中央政府实施自上而下管治的主要工具。然而,这些战略和政策应当由谁负责实施和监督,又应当如何实现目标,迄今仍

for implementing and monitoring these strategies and policies and how this should be achieved is not well defined.

Similarly, the practices at the local level are also very flexible and basically reliant upon informal inter - local agreements, which seems like the new regionalism approach of 'governance without government'. However, the voluntary approach allows the localities to agree upon certain cooperation arenas which are conceived as economically beneficial. Therefore, the regional issues that would be raised and resolved are very likely to be biased towards the economic realm. Apart from the lack of a comprehensive operation, this flexibility is also offset by the instability of the association and the lack of means of collective action and accountability. Formal networking is not easy to establish in China, generally for two reasons. Firstly, the role of the central state remains indispensable in deciding on the legitimacy of these locally - initiated projects. This is because China's political system is still centralised and hierarchical. The sub-national state has to seek the approval of the central state to obtain support and legitimacy for the meso-level associative governance. Even though planners and academics inside China constantly suggest that a delegated regional organisation or association to handle regional issues is set up, it seems that the central government still does not give much consideration to these suggestions due to concerns regarding the over - complexity of the bureaucratic structure and ever-increasing bureaucratic costs. As a consequence, the informal institution based on the mayors' association and regional forum causes the regional mechanism to lack binding capability and enforcement power. Secondly, China's political system is currently built with five levels of administrative ranks. The strictly defined hierarchy of ranks also undermines the basis of horizontal networking. Currently, the mayors' association or regional forum is only attended by prefecture - level jurisdictions, which means the vast number of county - level units (including counties, county - level cities and city districts) are just represented by their upper-level administrations. The lack of participation in these regional activities causes the county-level units to feel that regional issues are irrelevant to them. Moreover, even if these county-level units were involved in some cooperative agenda, they could not make decisions themselves, but would have to ask for instruction from prefecture - level governments. Overall, unlike the experiences in Western countries, there is actually no power reshuffling towards the regional level in the case of China's regional make-up.There is no sign to suggest the central government will grant the regional level the power to make decisions. Nor is there any indication that the local governments will concede certain authority to the regional-based organisations for the sake of regional interests. As a result, the opportunity for and efficiency of city - networking is fundamentally undermined. In this sense,

未明确界定。

同样,地方一级的实践也表现出了很高的灵活性,这些实践基本都依据非正式的地方间协议开展,这看上去像是新区域主义所说的"无政府管治"的做法。但是,在自愿原则下,各地区只愿意在某些能产生经济效益的领域达成一致。因此,区域问题的提出和解决很可能会偏向经济领域。但是除了缺少全方位的运作之外,这种灵活性还受到协作关系不稳定以及缺乏联合行动的途径和问责制的制约。但是,目前在中国还很难建立正式的区域网络。第一,地方发起的区域项目的合法性仍须由中央政府决定。这是因为中国的政治体制依旧是中央集权的等级制体系。各省市政府必须寻求中央批示才能获得政府间联合管治所需的支持和合法性。尽管中国的城市规划者和学界一直在建议建立一个中央授权的区域组织或联盟来处理区域问题,但中央政府似乎仍未对这些建议予以考虑,原因之一是担心目前的官僚架构已经过于庞大,并且政府运作成本也在日渐增长。所带来的后果是,以市长协会和区域论坛为基础的非正式体制导致区域机制缺乏约束力和执行力。第二,中国目前政治体制中的行政架构分为五个等级。严格的等级制度也破坏了横向协作的基础。目前,只有地级行政辖区才能参加市长协会和区域论坛,这意味着许多县级单位(包括县、县级市和市辖区)都只能由他们的上级行政领导代表参与。县级行政单位在区域性活动中缺乏参与度,会使它们感到区域事务与己无关。再者,即使这些县级单位参与了某些合作议程,它们也没有自主决策权,只能向地级市政府寻求指导意见。综上所述,当前中国的区域重塑过程中实际上并没有发生区域层面上的权力重组,这是不同于西方国家的实践经验的。没有迹象表明中央政府会给予地方政府自主决策权;也没有迹象表明地方政府会为了实现区域利益而将某些权力让给区域性组织。这从根本上破坏了城际合作的

even though the consolidation approach, for example, the administrative adjustment of annexations of suburban counties and county-level cities into prefecture-level cities, has its own problems, this unified government approach seems to be, at least at present, the only formalised institutional option in China. Even though city-county consolidation is very difficult to pass through referendum in Western countries, the approvals process for administrative annexation is relatively easier in China (Zhang and Wu, 2006: 5) because China has a centralised political system.

3.11 Conceptual framework for the transformation of regional governance in China

Initially, some literature interpreted the phenomenon of 'new regionalism' from the perspective of the diminishing role of the state (Ohmae, 2004). It seems the renewed regional practices, which favour flexible and voluntary arrangements, are the improved approach from the past crude metropolitan administrative reform (Lefvere, 1998: 16 - 20). However, it is questionable whether 'the institutional ensembles themselves [...] [can be] automatically assumed to be a pre-given part of the explanation' (MacLeod and Goodwin, 1999a: 697). It is argued that these institutional choices themselves need to be explained, rather than assumed as if they were ontologically and epistemologically given, in order to advance a deeper analysis (ibid). Here, for the same purpose, Brenner's framework of 'new state space' (2004b), which is drawn from Jessop's state-theoretical work, is employed to understand changing urban and regional governance in China.

3.11.1 Changing central-local relationship as a re-scaling of state spatiality

The previous sections illustrated the changes in the central-local relationship and the shift of regional policies in China from 1949 to present. Fiscal decentralisation and economic devolution have entailed a fundamental transformation of government structures and central-local relationships. Certainly, local governments are no longer the passive agents of the central state; they are directly involved in shaping and propelling local development (Oi, 1995; Walder, 1995; Zhu, 2002). However, the downscaling of governance does not necessarily mean the relaxation of central state control or the hollowing out of the state (Wu, 2002). In the Chinese case, the central government is 'tooling' urban entrepreneurialism (Jessop et al., 1999), or even becoming involved in the building of the entrepreneurial city, to enhance the structural competitiveness

机遇和成效。就此而言,尽管整合措施(如将一些郊县和县级市并入地级市的行政调整)有其自身的问题,但这一做法似乎是中国目前所能采取的唯一一种正式体制方案。虽然县市合并在西方国家难以通过公民投票实现,但这一行政合并在中国却相对容易通过(Zhang 和 Wu,2006:5),因为中国拥有中央集权的政治体制。

第十一节 解释中国区域管治转型的概念框架

最初,一些文献从国家的作用日渐弱化这一角度阐释"新区域主义"现象(如 Ohmae,2004)。从表面上看,赞成灵活和自愿协商的新区域主义实践是对过去粗糙的都市行政改革的一种改良措施(Lefvere,1998:16-20)。然而,是否"制度组合本身……(就可以)被自动认为是不言而喻的解释",仍值得质疑(MacLeod 和 Goodwin,1999a:697)。有人认为,为了进行更深入的分析,这些制度的选择本身是需要作出解释的,而不能假设它们在本体论和认识论上已经存在(同上)。在这里,出于同样的目的,笔者采用 Brenner 从 Jessop 的国家理论著作中提取的"新国家空间"理论框架(2004b)来阐释中国城市和区域管治的变化过程。

一、中央与地方关系的变化表现为国家空间尺度的重组

前面几节列举了 1949 年至今中央与地方关系的变化及区域政策的转变。财政权力和经济权力下放导致了政府结构和中央与地方关系的根本性转型。理所当然地,地方政府不再是中央政府的被动代理机构,他们直接参与了规划和推动地方发展(Oi,1995;Walder,1995;Zhu,2002)。但是管治权力下放并不一定意味着中央放松了对地方的控制或国家权力中空(Wu,2002)。在中国,中央政府把城市经营主义"作为工具"(Jessop 等,1999),甚至参与到经营型城市的建设过程中,以此来提高中国在世界舞台上的结构竞争力(Wu,2003)。

of China's place on the global stage (Wu, 2003). Even though the state retreated from direct interventd social reproduction, the entrepreneurial project legitimises the state to restore its intervention in economic spheres to promote and sustain development (ibid: 1694). It is therefore argued that the power decentralisation process is in actuality a re-territorialisation of the state, rescaling the state's functionality from the predominant national level to the level of localities (ibid: 1695). A contentious process of power reshuffling between levels of state is underlying the broad scheme of decentralisation (Hsing, 2006) and the central-local relationship is not a zero-sum game, but has become all the more complicated and interactive (Li, 1997). Put in the language of state spatiality, this represents a rescaling of state power at a multitude of scales.

The concept of 'state spatiality', i.e. the multi-scalar institutional organisation of state capacity (Brenner, 2004a: 452-453), is highly relevant here. Brenner extended Jessop's state-theoretical theory to 'a spatialised and scale articulated conceptualization of statehood' (2004b: 89). As defined by Brenner, state spatiality 'combines both the geographical configuration of a state's territory (its external and internal boundaries and the territorial organization of its political and administrative system) and the spatial dimensions of the state's intervention in socioeconomic processes within that territory, including both spatiality targeted interventions and indirect spatial effects of aspatial actions' (Breathnach, 2010: 1180). 'State projects' refers to projects that mobilise changes of state apparatus, whereas 'state strategies' relates to general state interventions that regulate the economy and civil society (Brenner, 2004: 87-88; MacKinnon and Shaw, 2010: 1228; Varro, 2010: 1256). That is, the state has no essential form, but constantly changes through the launch of state projects and state strategies.

Based on the study of the changing central-local structure and regional policies in China, Table 3.9 summarises the basic features of China's changing state spatiality. During the socialist economy, centralised decision-making was the single layer of state spatial regulation. The overarching goal was to redistribute resources and production forces to the lagging and remote regions and thus to redress the marked regional inequality in the national economy. As a consequence, the institutional framework of the era entailed a unified national system of material rationing and financial sharing, in which local political institutions and policies were compliant to the national command. The localities 'have neither the incentive for 'entrepreneurial' endeavour nor the capacities and conditions to initiate such activities' (Wu, 2003: 1679).

即使国家不再直接干预社会再生产,也能通过参与经营型项目而重新以合法地位干预经济领域,以促进和保持发展(WU,2003:1694)。因此,有观点称权力下放的过程实际上是国家的地域重组,把国家的功能从居于支配地位的国家层面下放到地方层面(同上:1695)。宽泛的权力下放计划的实质是国家各层级之间你争我夺的权力重组过程(Hsing,2006),而且中央与地方的关系并非零和游戏,而是变得越来越复杂和具有互动性(Li,1997)。用国家空间尺度的措辞来表述,这就代表着诸多不同尺度的国家权力的重组。

"国家空间尺度"代表着国家权力的多尺度制度化组织(Brenner,2004a:452-453),这个概念在此非常重要。Brenner将Jessop的国家理论扩展成"具有空间性和尺度化的国家概念"(2004b:89)。如Brenner所定义,国家空间尺度"既是指国家地域的地理形态(其外部和内部边界以及国家政治行政体系的地域性组织),也是指国家在该地域内对社会经济活动进行干预的空间维度,包括以空间为目标的干预以及非空间行为产生的间接空间效果"(Breathnach,2010:1180)。"国家项目"指的是促使国家体制变化的项目,而"国家战略"是指管理经济社会和民间社会的一般国家干预(Brenner,2004:87-88;MacKinnon和Shaw,2010:1228;Varro,2010:1256)。这就是说,国家没有固定的形态,而是随着国家项目和国家战略的启动而不断变化的。

根据对中国变化中的中央与地方关系和区域政策的研究,表3.9总结了中国国家空间尺度变化的基本特点。在社会主义计划经济时期,中央决策是国家空间治理的唯一层面。其首要目标是将资源和生产力再分配到落后和边远地区,以解决国民经济中显著的区域间发展不均衡问题。结果,这一时期的制度框架产生了一个全国统一的物资配给和财政共享的制度,在这一制度下地方政府和政策完全服从国家指令。地方政府"既没有动机尝试'经营型'活动,也没有能力和条件发起这样的活动"(Wu,2003:1679)。

Table 3.9 Changing state spatiality from 1949 to the present

	Socialist state (1949-1978)	State in early market reform (1979-2000)	State in post-WTO market society (2001-present)
Geo-economic and political context	Centrally-planned economy; Cold war; Pursuit of self-reliance	Decentralisation and market-oriented economy; Pursuit of economic growth; GDP growth is of overriding importance	China as a world manufacturing workshop; 2008 global economic recession; Building of a 'harmonious society'; Pursuit of sustainable development
State spatial projects	Centralisation of state regulation; Uniform and standardised administrative and bureaucratic coverage; Localities as a transmission belt to deliver administrative commands	Economic and political power devolution to urban governance; Asymmetrical devolution and diversities of practices in different regions, provinces and cities; Coastal area as a forerunner in decentralisation scheme; Open cities and economic development zones as a field of experiment on government bureaucratic reform oriented to market economy	Recentralisation in respect of some state functions, e.g. land management; Upscaling of administration from urban level to the regional level, e.g. the province-leading-county administrative reform; Administrative experimental zones under diverse titles across the whole national territory, e.g. Tianjin, Shenzhen and Pudong in the coastal area as comprehensive reform areas, Chengdu-Chongqian (Chengyu) in the west as an urban-rural coordinated development reform area, Wuhan metropolitan area and Changsha-Zhuzhou-Xiangtan (Changzhutan) in middle China as a reform area to promote environmental-friendly development; Inter-city economic cooperation associations are pursued in some key regions, such as Yangtze River Delta and Pearl River Delta
State spatial strategies	Privileging of a single national scale; Taking all regions into account like when playing chess (quanguo yipanqi); Egalitarianism	Urban units as the predominant scale for socio-economic activities; Re-globalising Shanghai to bring China back to the global economy stage; Uneven regional policy to allow some regions and some people to become rich first	Urban regions around the core economic city (cities) as the scale for socio-economic activities; City-regions (urban and town clusters) as the key form to promote urbanisation, economic development and to engage in global distribution of labour; Coordinated development between regions

Source: compiled by the author.

表3.9 1949年至今国家空间尺度的变化

	社会主义计划经济时期 (1949—1978)	早期市场经济改革时期 (1979—2000)	加入世贸组织后的市场化社会主义时期 (2001至今)
地缘经济和政治背景	中央计划经济； 冷战； 追求独立自主	权力下放和市场导向经济； 追求经济增长； GDP增长高于一切	中国成为世界制造工厂； 2008年全球性经济衰退； 建设"和谐社会"； 追求可持续发展
国家空间项目	集中的国家管理； 标准统一的行政和官僚体制覆盖； 地方政府成为转达行政命令的传送带	经济和政治权力下放到城市管治； 不同区域和省市不对称的权力下放和多样化的做法； 权力下放计划在沿海地区最先实行； 开放城市和经济开发区成为以市场经济为导向的政府官僚体制改革的试验场	某些国家职能重新收权，如土地管理； 行政管理尺度从城市升级到区域，如进行"省管县"行政改革； 在全国范围内成立了名目不同的行政实验区，如在沿海的天津、深圳和浦东进行全面改革，西部的成都和重庆(成渝)进行城乡协调统筹发展的改革，在中部的武汉城市圈和长沙—株洲—湘潭(长株潭)地区推行环境友好型发展； 在一些重点地区建立城际经济合作，如长江三角洲和珠江三角洲地区
国家空间战略	赋予单一国家尺度以特权； 统筹考虑所有区域，全国一盘棋； 平均主义	以城市单位为主导尺度开展社会经济活动； 通过上海的国际化使中国重回世界经济舞台； 推行不均衡的区域政策，允许一部分地区和一部分人先富起来	以重点经济城市(城市群)周围的城镇区域为尺度开展社会经济活动； 将城市区域(城区和乡镇集群)作为推进城市化、加快经济发展和参与全球劳动力分配的主要形式； 区域协调发展

来源：作者编制。

Since economic reform, the equalisation strategy has given way to economic efficiency. Preferential treatment was given to the coastal area, which is more competitive compared to the interior. Moreover, decentralisation and market reform has been engineered in order to unleash individual and local initiatives. Based on the socialist urban - rural division of labour, urban administrative units, which used to be concentrated with previous industrial assets, were given more support in terms of administrative and economic resources in order to build the urban economy as the growth pole of the region and thus to promote regional development. Along with the power devolution to the localities, fiscal pressure and a GDP - based cadre promotion system also became virtual incentives for various tiers of local government to stimulate economic growth. As a corollary, municipal government has become the major agent which is directly involved in promoting local development and the urban economy has turned to be the dominant engine of the national economy.

As of 2000, regional policies have been rejuvenated after a period of marginalisation. Following the publication of 'West Development', 'Northeast Regeneration' and 'Central Revival', the interior region seems to have been given more attention by the state. However, the difference between recent regional polices and the previous regional equalisation policy in the socialist era is that efficiency is still prioritised in the latest strategies. Only some city-regions with potential economic competitiveness are selected and highlighted; for example, some specific projects such as Chengdu-Chongqian (Chengyu) in the west,Wuhan metropolitan area and Changsha-Zhuzhou-Xiangtan (Changzhutan) in the central region have been launched following the grand regional policy. The top-down regional plans initiated by the central government and the bottom-up inter-city association promoted by the higher-level governments are also concentrated in some particular regions such as YRD, PRD and Bohai Sea Rim. Overall, new state spatiality at the regional scale is just emerging in contemporary China.

3.11.2 Conceptualising the regional renaissance in China: the transformation of state selectivity

State spatial selectivity demonstrates the 'state['s] strategic tendency to privilege certain places [and/or groups] through spatial projects and strategies' (Varro, 2010: 1256), which is structurally inscribed under a certain context and timeframe. According to Brenner, state spatiality 'is never permanently fixed but, like all other aspects of the state form, represents an emergent, strategically selective, and politically contested process' (Brenner, 2004a: 89). The evolution of state spatiality is mobilised through state spatial projects and state spatial

改革开放以来,平均主义的战略被经济效益取代。沿海地区受到特惠待遇,相比内陆地区更具竞争优势。此外,为了激发个人和地方的积极性,中央还启动了权力下放与市场改革。根据社会主义的城乡劳动分工,城市行政单位由于集中工业资产而在行政和经济资源方面获得更多支持,以便将城市经济建设为该区域的经济增长标杆,以此推动区域发展。随着行政管理权力的下放,财政压力和以国内生产总值为考量的干部提拔标准实际也成了各级地方政府推动经济增长的主要动力。因此,市政府必然成为直接参与地方发展建设的主要作用者,城市经济则成为国家经济的主导引擎。

自2000年起,区域政策在一段时期的边缘化后重焕生机。随着"西部大开发"、"振兴东北"以及"中部崛起"项目的启动,国家似乎对内陆地区给予了更多的重视。然而,近期的区域政策与早先社会主义计划经济时期的区域平均主义政策的不同之处在于,近期的战略把效率放在了首位。只有部分具有潜在经济竞争力的城市区域入选并得到了重视;例如,根据大区域政策开展的一些具体区域项目,如西部的成都—重庆(成渝)项目,中部地区的武汉城市圈项目和长沙—株洲—湘潭(长株潭)项目。由中央政府制定的自上而下的区域规划和由上级政府推动的自下而上的城际联盟项目在一些特定区域也比较集中,如长江三角洲地区、珠江三角洲地区和渤海地区。总的来说,目前中国区域尺度的新型国家空间正在不断涌现。

二、解析中国的区域复兴:国家空间尺度选择的转变

国家空间尺度选择体现的是在一定情形下和一定时期内"国家通过实施空间项目和战略优先发展某些特定地区(和/或团体)的战略倾向"(Varro,2010:1256)。Brenner认为,国家空间尺度"从来都不是一成不变的,它和国家形式的其他所有方面一样,是一种亟待解决的、具有战略选择性和政治竞争性的过程"(Brenner,2004a:89)。国家空间尺度的演变是各种社会力量通过国家空间项目和国家空间战略推动发展的(同上)。例如,Brenner(2004a,b)通过国

strategies by diverse social forces (ibid). For example, Brenner (2004a, b) investigated changing urban governance through the lens of changing state spatiality. It is conceived that spatial Keynesianism, the centralised, redistributive and uniform administrative system, was destabilised by de-industrialisation and the crisis of North Atlantic Fordism. As a consequence, the local managerialism is contested by urban entrepreneurialism. That is, selectivity is transformed towards decentralisation and the customisation of state administrative arrangements, and the localisation and differentiation of national political-economic spaces (Brenner 2004a: 214). The resurgence of new spatial strategies and projects in China also demonstrates the tendencies of changing state selectivity. The selectivity is transformed towards recentralisation in administrative arrangements and regionalisation in political-economic space (Table 3.10). That is, another scale at the regional level is emerging in the contours of China's state spatiality through centrally orchestrated strategies and bottom-up collaboration. However, compared to the regional intervention in the era before economic reform, the current regional initiatives show the distinct features of customisation and concentration on certain areas (Table 3.10). In other words, in comparison with past national redistributive policies and administrations, the current regional strategies and projects are quite differentiated at the territorial dimension.

Table 3.10 The transformation of state spatial selectivity in China since 2000

	State spatial projects	State spatial strategies
Scalar dimension	Re-centralisation of part of the state functions: Re-concentration of political authority towards the higher-level of government, e. g. recentralisation of land management, province-leading-county administrative reform This enhances the regulatory responsibilities of central and provincial tiers of state power	Resurgence of regional strategies: Regional scale is mobilised by all kinds of regional plans and regional policies Regional scale is privileged by the state to enhance concentrated industrial development and urbanisation and to address enlarging inter-regional disparity by promoting growth in certain major urban regions
Territorial dimension	Customisation: Expansion of urban administrative boundaries, experiments on inter-city association,especially in the coastal area; Administrative experimental zones under diverse titles across the whole national territory This entrenches the customised, place-specific institutional arrangements since the economic reform	Concentration: Promoting agglomeration, e.g. regional plans and policies are transforming urbanisation from the development of small, medium and large cities in favour of the development of city-regions This contributes to the concentration of infrastructural investment towards key urban and regional development pathways, for example, the recent development of the high-speed railway network

Source: compiled by the author.

家空间尺度变化的视角探讨了城市管治的变化。他认为,空间凯恩斯主义这种集权的、再分配的、统一的行政系统,受到去工业化和北大西洋福特主义危机的冲击而难以稳定。因此,地方管理主义面临城市经营主义的挑战。也就是说,国家空间选择转向了权力下放和国家行政安排的定制化,以及国家政治经济空间的地方化和差异化格局(Brenner 2004a:214)。中国新型空间战略和项目的出现也体现了国家空间尺度选择的变化趋势,转向了行政安排的重新集中和政治经济空间的区域化(表3.10)。这意味着通过中央制定的战略和自下而上的协同合作,中国国家空间尺度框架在区域层次上出现了一个新的尺度。然而,与经济改革之前的区域干预相比,目前的区域举措显示出了在某些领域的定制化和集中化的鲜明特性(表3.10)。换言之,与之前的国家标准的再分配政策和行政管理方式相比,目前的区域战略和项目在地域层面上差别化非常大。

表3.10 2000年以来中国国家空间尺度选择的转变

	国家空间尺度项目	国家空间尺度战略
尺度层面	**部分国家职能收权:** 行政权重新向上级政府集中,如土地管理重新集权;省管县行政改革 加强了中央和省级行政权力的监管职责	**区域战略复兴:** 区域尺度的发展受到各种区域规划和区域政策的推动 国家赋予区域尺度以特权,集中力量推动工业发展和城市化进程,并通过促进主要城市区域的发展来解决日益扩大的区域间差距
地域层面	**定制化:** 拓展城市的行政界线,开展城际联合试点工程(特别是在沿海地区); 在全国范围内建立名目不同的各种行政实验区 加强了经济改革以来的定制化、具有地方特色的体制安排	**集中化:** 提高集聚规模,如制定区域规划和政策使城市化从发展大中小城市转变为发展城市区域 促进了基础设施投资向主要城市和区域的发展通道集中,如近年来的高速铁路网建设

来源:作者编制。

According to Brenner (2003b), the increasing inter-locality competition and enlarging uneven development is conceived as the driving force for the articulation of the new selectivity from urban entrepreneurialism towards new regionally-focused projects and strategies (Brenner, 2003b: 212). The similarly changing trajectory seen from the planning policies also demonstrates that institutional fragmentation is another factor leading to regional renaissance. Allmendinger and Tewdwr-Jones (2000: 714) documented that regional planning in the UK was made difficult by the downscaling of governance;for example, the privatisation of public utilities, and the emergence of semi-commercials and quangos. The resultant fragmented state spaces, based on individual institutions, were replaced by regional planning governance to make up for regional coordination. In contrast, the transformation of state spatiality in China has developed under a different local context (Table 3.11). During the socialist period, a redistributive regional policy was a necessary state governance strategy under the state-led industrialisation adopted by the planned economy (Wu and Zhang, 2010: 62).Under the catching-up industrial policy, the predominant role for the state in the socialist economy was to guarantee the low cost and high profit of industries by means of controlling production resources,product procurement, labour forces, labour mobility and urbanisation. As a consequence, resource-rich regions were made to sell their resources at a compulsory low price to production regions to facilitate rapid industrialisation. In turn, revenue remitted by the production regions was transferred to the resource-rich regions to sustain the regional division of labour. This differs from the Keynesian Welfare State, which strives to standardise industrial and infrastructure investment throughout the nation in order to support mass production and consumption to solve the crisis of oversupply andstabiliseindustrial growth (Brenner, 2004b); the socialist state was characterised by constrained consumption and extensive expansion of means of production to accelerate the industrialisation process (Wu et al., 2007). Therefore, the organised division of labour between regions, urban and rural areas in actuality,created inequality inherent in different regions and industrial sectors. Although the strategic relocation of heavy industries to the interior region under the Cold War did transfer the production capacity from the coast to the inland area to some extent, production efficiency was not correspondingly transferred. Eventually, the economic inefficiency of state-led industrialisation and industrial relocation starved national revenue and enlarged the deficit.

Brenner(2003b)认为,日趋激烈的地区间竞争和不断扩大的不均衡发展推动了国家空间选择的新转向,由城市经营主义转向以区域为中心的新的项目和战略(Brenner,2003b:212)。在规划政策中所见到的相似变化轨迹也表明,机构管理碎片化也是推动区域复兴的一个动因。据 Allmendinger 和 Tewdwr-Jones(2000:714)的研究表明,英国的区域规划因管治权力下放而困难重重;比如公共设施私有化,以及半商业化和准政府机构的出现。以个体机构为基础的国家空间因此碎化严重,从而被区域规划管治所取代,以弥补区域协作的缺失。形成对比的是,在中国国家空间尺度的转变是在一种不同的地方背景下形成的(表3.11)。在社会主义计划经济时期,再分配的区域政策是计划经济条件下由国家主导的工业化必不可少的国家管治战略(Wu 和 Zhang,2010:62)。在以赶超为目的的工业政策指导下,国家在发展社会主义经济中的主要作用就是通过控制生产资源、产品采购、劳动力、劳动力流动和城市化来保障工业的低成本和高收益。因此,资源丰富的地区被强制要求以低价向生产地区出售资源,以推动其工业化快速发展。反过来,生产区域的工业收益回流到资源丰富区,以保证区域劳动分工的稳定。这种方式与凯恩斯福利国家理念不同,后者致力于为全国范围内的工业和基础设施投资设立标准,支持批量生产和消费以解决供应过剩危机,使工业稳定增长(Brenner,2004b);而社会主义国家则是限制消费和生产手段的扩展,以加快工业化进程(Wu 等,2007)。因此,区域间有组织的劳动分工,即城乡劳动分工,造成不同区域和不同工业部门内在的不平等。虽然冷战时期重工业由沿海地区向内陆的战略转移确实在一定程度上转移了生产力,但是生产效率却并未相应转移,最终造成国家主导的工业化经济效率低,工业转移使国家财政陷入困境,赤字增加。

Table 3.11 Transformation of regional governance in China

Period	Form of state spatial selectivity	Form of urban and regional governance	Major conflicts and contradictions
1949-1978	Single scale of nation state	State managerialism; City and regionalinstitutions as implementation belts	Urban-rural dualism; Regional inequalities based on socialist internal division of labour
1979- 2001	Decentralise economic governance and planning powers etc. to lower layers of government; and also subcontract and divide responsibilities to lower levels; multi-scales of state (mainly: local and central)	Urban entrepreneurialism; Economic development is predominantly led and funded by city government;	Fierce inter-city competition; Uncoordinated and redundant infrastructure development; Environmental degradation, especially encroachment of rural land
2001- present	The recentralisation of some state functions, such as land management; The downscaling of the central state to the regional level to strengthen its intervening role; The upscaling of the local state to the regional level to build regional competitiveness multi-scales of state (local and central, with the making of regions)	Re-asserting a city-regional scale; Regional scale as a layer of 'soft institution' without building up a substantial level of regional government or mechanism	The city-region as an 'imagined community' which continues to see conflicting and diverse interests; Region-building is achieved through both top-down and bottom-up processes, but the central government lacks full commitment towards a region; and local governance lacks a participatory political legitimisation process

Source: compiled from Wu and Zhang (2010: 61).

It is under this context that it was believed China's economy was in urgent need of market mechanism and power decentralisation to unleash individual and local initiatives to increase productivity by means of competition. Therefore, the state orchestrated administrative and fiscal decentralisation laid down the institutional foundation and economic motivation for entrepreneurial urban governance. In short, decentralisation is a state strategy. As commented by Wu and Zhang (2008: 150), 'the central government purposely uses it as an incentive for local government to promote local growth'. However, urban entrepreneurialism is problematic in that the centrally induced strategy is a fragmentarily organised project (Brenner, 2003b: 210). As a consequence, locally-initiated industrial development has resulted in environmental degradation, redundant development and enlarging regional inequality. Fast-speed industrial expansion has created great demand for land and water resources. Accelerated consumption has already reached a

表3.11 中国区域管治情况的转变

时期	国家空间尺度选择的形式	城市及区域管治形式	主要冲突和矛盾
1949—1978	单一的国家尺度	国家管理主义；城市以及区域机构作为外围执行机构	城乡二元结构；社会主义内部劳动分工造成不均衡区域发展
1979—2001	经济管治权力和规划权力等下放到次级政府；责任也相应分包并下放到次级政府；国家尺度多层化（主要是地方和中央）	城市经营主义；经济发展由市级政府主导并提供资金	城市间竞争激烈；基础设施建设规划混乱，重复开发；环境恶化，尤其是侵占农村土地
2001至今	某些国家职能收权，比如土地管理权；中央政府权力下放到区域层级，加强其干预作用；将地方政府提升到区域层级，以提高区域竞争力；国家尺度多层化（地方和中央，以及正在形成的区域）	巩固城市区域尺度的地位；区域尺度作为'软制度'存在，不建立实质的区域政府或机制	城市区域作为"虚拟社区"继续面临利益冲突和矛盾；区域建设通过自上而下或自下而上的过程得以完成，但中央政府未对区域发展做出充分的承诺；地方政府也未能参与政治立法进程

来源：Wu和Zhang编制（2010:61）。

　　正是在这样的背景下，人们认为中国的经济迫切需要引入市场机制，进行权力下放，以调动个人和地方的积极性，在互相竞争中提高生产力。因此，国家作出了行政和财政权力下放的安排，为经营型城市管治建立制度基础，提供经济动力。总之，权力下放是一种国家战略。正如Wu和Zhang（2008:150）所指出的，"中央政府有目的地把它作为激励地方政府促进地方发展的举措"。然而，城市经营主义也有问题，因为战略是中央制定的，但实施项目却组织零散（Brenner，2003b:210）。结果，地方自发的工业发展导致了生态恶化、重复开发和区域贫富差距加大。高速发展的工业扩张需要更多土地资源和水资源。

threshold which threatens the environment. It is documented that China has lost arable land at an astonishing rate, leaving per capita arable land in some areas under 0.8 *mu* (1 *mu* equals to 0.06666667 hectare), which is the warning line recognised by the United Nations (State Council Development and Research Institute, 2008: 97). It is also indicated that over 400 cities in China are confronted with water shortages due to the excessive industrialisation (ibid). Blind industrial development in environmentally‑sensitive regions has generated even greater damage. In addition, whereas economic inefficiency was induced by low productivity and in‑coordination in the centrally‑planned system, the market‑oriented economy in China remains inefficient due to continuous development and over‑competition. Finally, the inter‑provincial Gini‑coefficient of GDP in China has increased from 0.347 in 1978 to 0.386 in 2004, an increase of 11.3 percent (ibid: 98); in terms of public services, the discrepancy is even more considerable. For example, only a third of the student dormitories in the central and western regions reach the national standard according to the statistics (ibid). These figures just demonstrate the social and environmental problems that are confronting contemporary China. In other words, the land, environmental, economic and social problems caused by excessive industrial development under urban entrepreneurialism are the major factors that contribute to the recent regional renaissance in China.

3.11.3 The production of regional scale and inter-scalar politics

The form of spatial selectivity is only representative of actions and does not necessarily entail a straightforward replacement of the latter with the former (Deas and Ward, 2000).The changing process is highly contested by diverse powers and is embedded upon an 'institutional product of earlier rounds of regulatory experimentation and socio‑political struggle' (Brenner, 2004b: 94). Therefore, it is important to recognise the 'politics of scale' in understanding the process of changing state spatiality and scale making. The concept of 'politics of scale' relates to the proposition that geographical scales, whether urban, regional, national or global, are not pre‑given, but are socially constructed and politically contested (Brenner, 2002: 4, note 1). The concept, on the other hand, also indicates that the state has no power by itself, but is mediated through a set of institutional ensembles by social forces (MacKinnon and Shaw, 2010: 1228). The process‑based approach and agency perspective is helpful to avoid the mistake of the regulational and structuralist 'top‑down' approach which is framed around the general and abstract tendency of economic Fordism to post‑Fordism. In conceiving the state agency, the territorial approach considers the space is articulated by multi‑levels of state, while the relational

消费的快速增长已经对环境构成了威胁。据记载,中国的可耕地快速流失,在某些地区人均可耕地面积低于联合国规定的0.8亩的警戒线(国务院发展研究中心,2008:97)。还有数据表明,在中国有400多个城市因为过度工业化而正在遭遇水资源短缺(同上)。在环境脆弱地区盲目发展工业已经造成了更严重的破坏。此外,生产率低下和中央计划体系缺少协调造成了经济效率低下,而中国以市场为导向的经济仍然由于持续开发和过度竞争而难以提高效率。最后一点,中国省际之间的国内生产总值基尼系数已经从1978年的0.347增长到了2004年的0.386,增幅11.3%(同上:98);在公共服务方面这个变动更为显著。例如,有数据显示中西部地区只有三分之一的学生宿舍达到国家规定的标准(同上)。这些数据表明了当今中国正在面临的社会与环境问题。换言之,在城市经营主义指导下的工业过度发展带来的土地、环境、经济和社会问题是促使近年来中国区域复兴的主要动因。

三、区域尺度的形成和尺度间政治

国家空间选择的形式仅代表行动本身,并不代表结果(Deas 和 Ward,2000)。这一转变的过程不仅受到多种力量的激烈挑战,而且始终根植在"之前一轮又一轮管理试验和社会政治斗争的制度产物"之上(Brenner,2004b:94)。因此,探讨"尺度政治"对于理解国家空间尺度的变化和尺度形成的过程是十分重要的。"尺度政治"的概念涉及的观点是,任何地理尺度,无论是城市、区域、国家还是全球的尺度,都不是预先设定的,而是在社会因素促使下构建起来的,并且受到政治力量的挑战(Brenner,2002:4,注释1)。另一方面,这一概念也表明国家本身是没有力量的,实际上是各种社会力量在透过一系列国家制度机构发挥作用(MacKinnon 和 Shaw,2010:1228)。这一以过程为基础的研究方法以及考察动因的视角有助于避免管制和结构主义者基于经济福特主义向后福特主义发展转变的一般抽象理论而得出的"自上而下"的国家空间尺度重塑的解释。针对国家能动性的问题,地域论者认为空间是国家不同级政

approach emphasises the local political actors which participate from a range of overlapping political networks (Allen and Cochrane, 2007). Yet, it is argued by Sonn (2010: 1204) that it is also important to view the state as an organisation composed of 'multiple sub - organizations, such as various departments, agencies and offices that have different, sometimes conflicting interests, than a monolithic entity'. In addition to the argument on new state spaces and agency, it is, on the other hand, suggested that the transformation of new state spaces could be driven not only by economic projects, but also political, cultural, social and environmental projects (Jonas and Ward, 2007). Brenner (2002: 4, note 1) has deployed the term 'new politics of scale' to 'underscore the ways in which the scalar organisation of capitalism is itself becoming an important stake of ongoing sociopolitical struggles'. It is hence argued that the development of new state spaces, which are the fusion of existing and evolving projects, are filled with uncertainties (Allmendinger and Tewdwr-Jones, 2000).

The above theoretical perspective is very helpful in terms of perceiving the dynamics in the building of regional scale in China. In conceiving the emergence of regionalisation, Xu (2008), Xu and Yeh (2011) and Yeh and Xu (2008) attempted to understand the changes in regional cooperation from the transformation of the regime of accumulation. It is suggested that 'regional cooperation is needed to overcome the hurdle of capital accumulation' (Yeh and Xu, 2008: 413). In the pre - reform socialist regime, regional policies and cooperation strategies were developed to 'enforce central planning so that the state could enhance its capacity to divert the accumulated surplus from organised socialist industrialisation to the new expansion of production' (Xu, 2008: 161). In the post - reform regime, however, regional governance and strategic planning was initiated to achieve administrative efficiency or economic rationality, which is undermined by downscaled state function and entrepreneurial strategies (ibid: 162). In a word, regionalisation is explained as part of the wider process of changing state spatial strategy in response to economic restructuring after economic reform. Although the analyses of the changing rationales of regional cooperation in these studies (Yeh and Xu, 2008: 413) are acceptable, the explanation is problematic from two aspects. Firstly, the theorisation privileges economic factors over other elements, such as land politics and the environmental crisis in China after extensive decentralisation and entrepreneurialism. This also matches the criticism of the empirical conceptualisation made by Brenner (2004b). Even though Brenner (2002; 2004b) initiated a comprehensive conceptual framework to theorise changing urban governance and the rescaling of statehood, Brenner's empirical analysis of changing statehood in Western European countries (2004b) is criticised from the point of view that 'accumulation strategies are consistently privileged over

府作用形成的,而关系论者则强调空间是地方政治作用者从一系列重叠的政治网络中参与进来的(Allen 和 Cochrane,2007)。然而,Sonn(2010:1204)认为也必须将国家视作一个由多重机构组成的组织,包含"多重的次级组织,例如利益不同甚至有利益冲突的各个部门、机构和办公室,而不是一个单一体"。除了围绕新国家空间和能动性的争论之外,也有学者认为,新国家空间的转变不仅可以由经济项目推动,同时也受到政治、文化、社会和环境项目的推动(Jonas 和 Ward,2007)。Brenner(2002:4,注释1)提出了"新尺度政治"的术语,以"强调资本主义的尺度组织形式本身如何在持续的社会政治斗争中成为一个重要的利益体"。因此有学者认为,新国家空间的发展是现有项目和正在生成的项目融合的过程,其中充满了不确定因素(Allmendinger 和 Tewdwr-Jones,2000)。

上述理论视角对于理解中国区域尺度形成的动态过程颇有裨益。在思考中国区域化的出现时,Xu(2008)、Xu 和 Yeh(2011)以及 Yeh 和 Xu(2008)试图从资本积累体制的转变这一视角来解释区域合作的变化。他们认为"需要区域合作是为了克服资本积累的障碍"(Yeh 和 Xu,2008:413)。在改革前的社会主义体系中,区域政策和合作战略的制定都是为了"执行中央计划,从而使国家能增强将积累的剩余资产从有组织的社会主义工业化转移到新的生产扩张的能力"(Xu,2008:161)。然而在改革后的社会主义体系中,国家启动了区域管治和战略规划来实现高效行政或理性经济,但是这受到了国家管理职能下放和经营主义战略的干扰(同上:162)。总之,区域化被解释为应对经济改革后的经济重组而出现的更大规模的国家空间战略变化过程的一部分。尽管这些研究(Yeh 和 Xu,2008:413)关于区域合作目的转变的分析是可以接受的,但是他们的理论阐述在两个方面存在问题。首先,这一论述将经济因素置于其他因素之上,例如没有考虑中国在大范围的权力下放和政府企业化后出现的土地政治和环境危机等因素。这也与 Brenner 对经验主义概念化的批判不谋而合(2004b)。尽管 Brenner(2002;2004b)提出了一个全面的概念框架来阐述城市管治的变化和国家尺度的重组,但是他对西欧国家的国家尺度变化的实证分析(2004b)也遭到了批判,批评者的观点认为在 Brenner 的分析当中"经济积累战略总是被置于社会主要项目之上"(Oosterlynck,2010:1156)。换言之,

hegemonic projects' (Oosterlynck, 2010: 1156). That is, the potential connection with issues concerning social reproduction is missing from the analysis (Walks, 2006: 228). Secondly, the explanation seems to suggest that the regional level is a pre-given scale of statehood. It is suggested that the politics of regional cooperation are due to the loose approaches to forge regional cooperation, which hence makes regionalisation subject to political influence (Yeh and Xu, 2008: 414). However, as the above theoretical perspective implies, this chapter argues that the regional scale is not yet consolidated and well-established, and the politics just show the tensions throughout the regional-scale making process. Overall, the 'new politics of scale' concept, the process-based approach and the agency perspective are particularly useful for addressing cases in China because these conceptual tools embed the analysis in the context of contested territorial politics, rather than treat it as a necessary outcome of economic restructuring.

Furthermore, the scalar tension in China is different from that of the UK and other Western countries. The latter are more democratised societies. The building of new state scalar architecture involves powers both within and outside the government. For example, the scalar tension in the case of waste management in the UK is manifested in the struggle over the terms of engagement (Davoudi, 2009: 147-148); whereas, the regional initiatives in China are articulated by the government, at both the central and local level, with the involvement of various divisions and departments. Furthermore, the tensions revolve around independent driving forces and the incompatible rationales between the centrally-launched and locally-initiated projects. The programmes launched by the central state are intended to be re-regulated through the level of regional governance to tackle the problems caused by earlier and ongoing entrepreneurial development across localities. In other words, the central government is motivated by government capacity problems, which is characterised by land loss and environmental degradation, excessive competition in manufacturing development and national economy safety, uneven development and social polarisation. By contrast, the intention for the local states to initiate bottom-up cooperation is largely for the sake of urban competitiveness and competition with other regions. That is, economic growth and economic benefits are still the main concern for the local governments. As the civil society and business sector are barely involved within the current regional programmes, the scalar tension is thus mainly articulated between the central and local governments, and between the divisions of ministries.

这一分析忽视了与社会再生产相关问题的潜在联系(Walks,2006:228)。其次,他们的理论解释似乎认为区域层级是个预设的国家尺度,但由于开展区域合作的方式没有制度化,所以导致区域化受到了政治因素的影响(Yeh和Xu,2008:414)。然而,正如上述理论视角所表明的,本章的主要观点是区域尺度并非已经稳固存在或已经建立完善,而这个过程中的政治因素正说明了区域尺度形成过程中始终存在着矛盾紧张的关系。总之,"新尺度政治"的概念、以过程为基础的研究方法以及考察动因的视角,对于探讨中国的案例特别适用,因为这些概念工具是在有竞争的地域政治背景下分析区域的形成,而不是只把它当作经济结构重组的必然结果来看待。

此外,中国的尺度紧张关系不同于英国和其他西方国家。后者是更加民主的社会,因而建立新的国家尺度结构涉及政府内部和外部的权力。例如,英国废物管理中的尺度紧张关系表现为围绕参与条件的争夺(Davoudi,2009:147-148);而中国的区域项目都是由政府操控的,包括中央政府和地方政府,其中还牵涉到诸多不同的部门。中国的尺度紧张关系源于不同的驱动力,如中央启动的区域项目和地方发起的区域项目之间不相容的理念。中央政府启动区域项目的目的是试图通过区域管治的层面来重新管理解决地方早期及当前经营型发展中所出现的问题。换言之,中央政府的动机在于要解决权力下放后政府管治能力的种种问题,例如对土地流失、环境的恶化、制造业发展中的过度竞争、国家经济安全、发展不均衡以及社会两极分化等问题的管理。与此不同的是,地方政府发起自下而上的合作的主要意图是要解决城市竞争力以及与其他区域竞争的问题。也就是说,经济增长和经济利益仍然是地方政府主要关心的问题。由于民间社会和商业部门很少参与到目前的区域项目中,尺度紧张关系主要表现在中央政府与地方政府之间以及不同部门之间。

3.12 Conclusion

The chapter develops a thorough overview of China's changing regional governance at different stages since 1949. Particular attention is paid to recent changes at the regional scale. It is discovered that China is now experiencing regional renaissance after decades of downscaling of governance since 1978. Through the investigation of the various policies and practices in the emerging regional governance, the leading actors, the underpinning rationales, the implication of regional governance, and the extent of implementation are examined.Based on the extensive analysis, the characteristics of the re-emerged regional governance are summarised.

The current second wave of regional practices in China is qualitatively different from the regional governance in the socialist period. Firstly, the regional programmes are mainly in the form of inter-city associations, regional planning or regional policies rather than a formal tier of regional administration. Secondly, the contemporary regional initiatives are focused on particular regions instead of being a nationally uniform administrative system. Thirdly, the launch of regional strategies is not motivated by redistribution and equalisation, but is promoted by the requirement of resolving locally-specific crises or problems. Furthermore, the current regional activities are not only orchestrated by the central state, but are also articulated by the local government. Therefore, the re-emergence of regional governance in China is more complex, since the emerging regional scale is intertwined with different leading actors and different rationales. The locally-initiated regional projects are intended to strengthen local endogenous growth opportunities and urban economic competitiveness. However, the initiatives led by the central government aim to manage the long-standing inter-locality adverse competition, in-coordinated and redundant development, and the enlarging inter-regional inequalities and tensions.

The notion of 'state spatiality' and 'state selectivity' is useful when perceiving the emerging regional governance from the perspective of the political economy and changing statehood. From the recent changes of governance, it is shown that state selectivity is oriented towards recentralisation and the resurgence of the regional scale, which is characterised with customisation and concentration. However, it is argued that the changing state spatiality in China is not triggered by the changes to the wider political economy, for example, the global economic restructuring and economic recession experienced in Western countries, but is provoked by China's territorial politics, i.e. in order to manage the long-standing problems of urban entrepreneurial development such as excessive economic competition, waste of land resources, rising environmental concerns and requests for sustainable

第十二节　结论

　　本章综述了自1949年以来中国经历的不同时期区域管治的变化。重点关注了近期区域尺度的变化。研究发现中国自1978年开始实行了几十年的区域管治下放之后,如今正在经历区域复兴。通过对新兴区域管治中各项政策和实践案例的研究,本章主要探讨了这一过程中的主要作用者、基本理念、区域管治的含义以及实施的范围。根据大量的分析,本章总结了区域管治重新兴起的特点。

　　中国目前正在经历的第二波区域管治的做法与社会主义计划经济时期的区域管治存在本质的区别。首先,区域构成主要表现为城际联合组织、区域规划或区域政策的形式,而没有建立正式的区域行政层级。第二,目前的区域项目主要是针对特定的区域,而不是全国范围。第三,发起区域战略的动机并不是要解决再分配和区域平衡问题,而是为了满足解决地方特有的危机或问题的需要。此外,目前的区域活动不仅受到中央政府的指挥,还有地方政府的参与。因此,区域管治在中国的复兴变得更加复杂,因为新出现的区域尺度牵涉到不同作用者和不同理念的影响。地方发起的区域项目主要是为了增强地方的内生性增长机遇和城市的经济竞争力。然而,中央政府采取的区域措施则旨在管理地方上长期存在的恶性竞争、不协调发展和过度开发,以及区域之间日益扩大的发展不平衡和紧张关系。

　　"国家空间尺度"和"国家空间尺度选择"两个概念对从政治经济学和国家尺度变化的角度来研究新兴的区域管治非常有用。从管治的最近变化可以看出,国家空间尺度选择的主要导向是重新收权和区域尺度的复兴,并具有定制化和集中化的特点。然而,本研究认为中国的国家空间尺度变化并不是由更大范围的政治经济变化引起的,例如全球经济重组和西方国家经历的经济衰退,而是由中国的地域政治引起的,即是为了解决城市经营型发展所带来的长期问题,如过度的经济竞争、土地资源浪费、日益严重的环境问题以及可持续

development. Furthermore, in order to illuminate the actual mechanism and process of regional - scale making, special attention is given to exploring the agency and politics underlying each specific regional project. It is established that the implementation of contemporary regional programmes is confronted by many challenges and tensions in practice. To sum up, the Chinese case of changing regional governance demonstrates that governance is not the automatic product of an economic accumulation regime, but is closely associated with local politics. In order to further illustrate the mechanism and inter - scalar tensions, in-depth case studies are to be conducted in the following chapters.

发展的需求。此外,为了阐明区域尺度形成的实际机制和过程,本章特别关注了每个具体区域项目背后的动因和政治因素。它们反映出目前区域项目的实施遇到了许多挑战和压力。总而言之,中国的区域管治变化表明区域管治并不是经济积累体制的自然产物,而是与地方政治密切相关的。为了进一步阐明这一机制以及尺度间的政治,下面几章将进行深入的案例研究。

第四章

CHAPTER FOUR

Research Framework and Methodology

4.1 Research tasks and objectives

As declared in section 1.2, the overall aim of the study is to highlight the new phenomenon of re-emerging regional governance in China after decades of decentralisation, and to analyse the changing regional configurations in China, and account for the mechanisms which brought about these transformations and the nature of the changes. The research intends to add China's experience to the current Western theory of changing local governance, which is mostly generalised from Western European and North American studies.

In order to realise the aim of the research, the following tasks are outlined:

1. To establish the theoretical perspectives to be taken by the research by reviewing Chinese and overseas literature to ascertain the gap in the theoretical and empirical knowledge in China on regional governance;

2. To identify and examine the different stages of changing regional configurations, central-local state relationships, and the political context in China from 1949 to the present day; to summarise the different features of regional governance in different periods;

3. To examine different actors behind and different rationales for region-building, and account for the dynamics of the emerging regional governance with the empirical study of the area of the YRD region;

4. To examine in what sense is there a 'new state space' created by the current practices articulated at the regional level in the YRD.

4.2 Research focus and definition

The focus of the study is the ongoing process of the emerging regional governance associated with different actors and practices. Due to the remarkably different context between China and the dominant western countries, it is deemed necessary to define the use of the term 'region' and 'governance' in Chinese context, which constitute as the essential research subject of the study.

According to the context chapter (chapter three), the landscape of the state power of China has been greatly transformed, compared to that in the socialist period. The authority is no longer centralised at the national state, i.e. the central government, but has been decentralised to the provincial government, city and county government, and even town and village governments at the lowest layer of the China's government structure. In the meantime, the absolute control of the state administrative system is gradually

第四章　研究框架和研究方法

第一节　研究任务和研究目标

如第一章第二节所述,本研究的总体目标是突出中国权力下放几十年后再度兴起的新的区域管治现象,分析中国区域格局的变化,并解释引起这些变化的机制和变化的本质。本研究有意用中国的经验扩充当前以西欧和北美研究为主的西方地域管治变化理论。

为了达到本研究的目的,具体列出以下研究任务:

1. 梳理国内外文献,确立本研究所采用的理论视角,论证国内在区域管治问题上存在的理论知识和经验知识的不足;

2. 鉴别和研究不同时期区域格局、中央与地方政府关系,以及中国1949年至今政治背景的变化,并总结不同时期区域管治的不同特点;

3. 研究区域形成背后不同的作用因子和原因,并以长三角地区的案例研究来说明当前兴起的区域管治的动力机制;

4. 研究长三角目前的区域项目在何种程度上产生了"新的国家空间"。

第二节　研究重点和相关定义

本研究的重点是正在兴起的区域管治的过程及其不同的作用者和实施项目。因中国与主要西方国家之间存在显著的背景差异,所以有必要在中国背景下界定"区域"和"管治"这两个概念的涵义。这两个概念也是本研究的核心主题。

据第三章所述,中国国家权力的状况相比社会主义计划经济时期有了很大变化。权力不再集中于国家层面,也就是中央政府,而是下放到了各省、市、县政府,甚至下放到中国政府权力结构最基层的乡镇政府。与此同时,国家行政管理体系对经济社会的绝对控制也随着市场化、外资引入和全球经济一体化的进程而逐渐瓦解,尽管中国商业精英和民众社会的力量还十分微弱。上

disintegrating through marketisation, the introduction of foreign investment and the integration with the global economy, even though China's business elites and civil society are still very weak. The two major aspects of change set the context for the use of 'governance' in China, which indicates the remarkable transition away from absolute central government control.

There has been a proliferation of studies on Chinese localisation and the changing urban governance (Oi, 1995; Walder, 1995; Wu, 2002, 2003; Wu et al., 2007; Zhang, 2002b), and the consequent local fragmentation and competition between each administrative level from provincial to the basic units (Chien and Gordon, 2008; Zhao and Zhang, 1999). However, the findings of chapter three have demonstrated the rising regional practices in the contemporary China. As documented in the previous chapter, the current practices are present at all kinds of different regions with a variety of geographical scales and boundaries. This is in part because of the fact that China does not have a formal level of regional government structure after the economic reform, neither an official definition on what constitutes a 'region'. Due to the reality, 'region' is loosely used in the research and implies all kinds of trans – border practices designed to tackle issues across administrative boundaries. The new phenomenon of regional governance in China hence refers to the tendency of a new level of sub – national governance beyond localisation and bounded administrative borders.

4.3 Research questions

The dominant role played by the Chinese state makes the conceptual framework of 'new state spaces' proposed by Brenner (2004b) applicable to conceptualises the resurgence of regional exercises in China. In section 3.11, the research argues that the contemporary regional process is indicative of a changing geography of state power in China, i.e. the rescaling of statehood to build a new regional state space. With this as a foundation, the core of the research studies the 'intention' to create the new state space and how the space is developed.

As informed by the theoretical perspective derived from the western literature review, the study on the agency, the rationale and the context behind the formation process is essential to understand the intention of the production of regional spaces, and to unravel the nature of the changing landscape of governance. Henceforth, the following questions are addressed in the remainder part of the research.

1. Who is articulating the current regional practices?
2. For what purposes are the agents promoting these regional practices?

述这两方面的变化是本研究决定使用"管治"一词的背景,即体现中国社会已不再处于中央政府的绝对控制之下。

有关中国的地方化和城市管治变化已经有了大量的研究(如 Oi,1995;Walder,1995;Wu,2002,2003;Wu 等,2007;Zhang,2002b),对随之出现的从省到基层的各个行政单元的地方碎片化以及相互竞争也有不少研究(如 Chien 和 Gordon,2008;Zhao 和 Zhang,1999)。但是本研究的第三章展现了当前中国正在兴起的区域管治实践。如第三章所述,目前的实践发生在各种尺度和边界范围的区域空间上,这其中的一部分原因是中国在经济改革后还没有设立一个正式的区域政府层级,对"区域"的构成也没有官方的定义。基于这样的现实,"区域"一词在本研究中的使用较为灵活,可泛指所有为处理跨行政边界问题而设的跨界政策或项目。因此,中国新出现的区域管治现象是指一种超越地方化和行政边界束缚的新的次国家层级的管治。

第三节　研究问题

由于中国的政府发挥着主导作用,我们可以采用 Brenner(2004b)提出的"新国家空间"的理论框架来阐述中国再度出现的区域尺度的管治。第三章第十一节的研究认为,当前的区域进程揭示了中国国家权力的地理变化,即国家尺度的调整,从而构建新的区域国家空间。在此基础上,本研究的核心内容是探索构建新国家空间的"意图"和空间形成的过程与方式。

由西方文献的理论观点可知,研究区域形成背后的动因、缘由和背景有助于理解构建区域空间的意图,进而揭示管治变化的实质。因此,本研究接下来的部分将探讨以下问题。

1. 谁在推行当前的区域项目?
2. 作用者推行这些区域项目的目的是什么?

3. What are the conditions that have led the agents to shift from previous practices of decentralisation and localisation to recent attempts at regional governance?

4. What is the defining features of the contemporary practices of regional governance?

5. What politics are exposed in the process of governance building?

6. To what extent have contemporary regional state spaces developed in China?

The above research questions directly respond to the call for in-depth study on the transformation processes under way within places in the development of new regional state spaces in different parts of the world. This is deemed preferable to an approach based upon assumptions about the dominance and mechanisms of a top-down approach and general global context (Jonas and Ward, 2002, 2007). The research also fills the empirical gap in the understanding of the dynamics of changing regional governance in China in the existing literature.

4.4 Case study approach and case selections

The case study approach is adopted to examine the ongoing process of the emerging regional governance in the real-life context. This is because a case study strategy is adept in examining contemporary events and delving into the 'how' and 'why' questions (Yin, 1994: 9).

One critical case, the evolution of regional governance in the Yangtze River Delta (YRD) region, is examined to offer an understanding of the dynamics of region building. Located in the eastern coast area and centred on Shanghai, YRD is one of the first regions to be exposed to opening-door policies and market-oriented economic reform. Many practices of decentralisation were foremost launched here and then spread to the other parts of the country. The YRD is also a region with a long history of regional institutional development. With the abolition of formal mega-region tiers of authorities in the planned economy, attempts to form a flexible network were made, either with state encouragement or spontaneously. However, the regional regime remained mostly nominal throughout the 1980s and 1990s. However, since 2000, the regional cooperation and development of YRD has again been highlighted in both local and national policy. The ups and downs of regional policy in the area and the complexity of actors associated throughout the process make the region an appropriate area for case study.

In this case, the regional governance development is examined from the two aspects of the changing economics and politics. As the findings of chapter

3. 什么样的情形造就了作用者从先前的权力下放和地方化转向现在的区域管治?

4. 当前区域管治实践的基本特征是什么?

5. 管治形成过程中会遇到哪些政治因素?

6. 中国当前的区域国家空间已经发育到了什么程度?

上述研究问题体现了要深入研究不同地区新区域国家空间的形成过程;而不是预先假设有自上而下的主导机制或全球背景的影响(如Jonas和Ward,2002,2007)。本研究也可以填补现有文献中理解中国区域管治变化机制的实证研究空白。

第四节　案例研究方法和案例选择

本书采用案例研究的方法来考察新出现的区域管治在现实背景下的形成进程。这是因为案例研究方法更利于研究当前正在发生的事件,更利于深入探究"如何"和"为什么"的过程问题(Yin,1994:9)。

本研究以长三角地区为案例研究区域,分析了长三角地区区域管治的演变过程,以解析区域构建的动力机制。长三角位于东部沿海地区,以上海为中心,是最早实行开放政策和市场经济改革的地区之一。许多权力下放的实践最早都是在这个地区启动,然后才普及全国其他地区。长三角还有着悠久的区域体制建构的历史。随着计划经济时期的大区建制的撤销,出现了建立灵活区域体制的尝试,其中有些是受国家鼓励设立的,有些则是自发的行为。但是八、九十年代的区域政体大多有名无实。自2000年以来,长三角的区域合作和发展再次受到地方和国家政策的重视。这个地区区域政策的起起伏伏以及整个进程中所关联的复杂的相关作用者,使得这个区域成为了理想的案例研究对象。

本研究将从经济变化和政治变化两方面研究案例区域的区域管治发展。如第三章的研究发现所示,现今的区域管治实践是由两个不同的作用者推动

three has indicated that the practices of recent regional governance are operated by two contrasting actors: the sub-national level governments at and below provincial governments, and the central government. Two embedded case studies are undertaken to demonstrate two different leading agents and their contrasting rationales and dynamics underlying the tentative regional governance. Firstly, a trans-border area between Jiangsu and Shanghai, i.e. the area between the county-level city in the region, Kunshan, and the Jiading district of Shanghai, is selected as the in-depth case study to focus on changing regional governance at the local level. Secondly, the recently formulated regional plans of the YRD are selected to study regional governance initiated by the central state, in which regional plans are utilised as the crucial device to deliver regional intervention and thus act as a contributor to changing territorial governance. The case selections are also closely related to the feasibility of data collection and fieldwork, which will be further discussed in data acquisition section.

4.5 Data acquisition and analysis

Data has been collected from both primary and secondary sources during the last four years. A pilot fieldtrip was conducted from January to March 2009, and intensive fieldwork was undertaken from February to May in 2010. Bookstores, local libraries of cities and universities, and personal contacts and visits are the main source of secondary data. Primary data has been collected through interviews to provide in-depth information on case studies.

4.5.1 Secondary data: documents and numeric data

In the study, documents refer to any printed or written information. They are collected for three main purposes; the first is to gather the general documentation on the changing regional policies and administration in China. Longitudinal materials dated from 1949 to the present day include regional policies, regional administrations, administrative changes, and regional plans, etc. Data sources are mainly from existing studies and documentation in the form of articles and monographs; official publications of regional policies, National Five-Year Plans, and administrative handbooks; as well as fresh news and reports from newspapers or websites. In this section, data collection on the recent regional transformation is most critical, since they represent the latest developments and have not yet been systematically compiled in either domestic or overseas studies. With regard to data processing, qualitative analysis is deployed to carry out policy review and document compilation in accordance with the different stages.

的:一是省级及省级以下的地方政府,一是中央政府。本书采用两个案例研究来阐释区域管治实践中不同的主导因素及其不同的目的和动力机制。首先,选定苏沪间的一个交界地区,即县级市昆山与上海市嘉定区之间的一个地区作为深入研究案例,关注地方层面的区域管治变化。其次,选择最近编制的长三角区域规划来研究中央政府发起的区域管治,其中区域规划被作为实施区域干预的重要工具,是促进地域管治变化的重要因素。选择这两个案例也与数据收集和实地调查的可行性密切相关,这将在数据采集一节中进一步讨论。

第五节　数据采集及分析

第一手和第二手资料的采集工作是在 2007 至 2011 年的四年当中完成的。2009 年 1 月至 3 月进行了首次实地考察,2010 年 2 月至 5 月进行了深入实地考察。第二手资料主要来自书店、所在城市的图书馆和大学图书馆,以及人物访谈过程中获得的内部材料等。第一手资料主要通过采访获得,为案例研究提供了深入的资料。

一、第二手资料:文献和数据

本研究中所述的文献是指所有印刷或书面材料。收集此类文献主要出于三个目的。其一是收集中国区域政策及行政体系变化的基础文献资料。自 1949 年至今的纵向资料包括区域政策、区域行政体系、行政体系变化及区域规划等。此类资料的来源主要是现有的研究论文和专著;官方出版的区域政策、国家五年规划(计划)、行政区划手册;报纸或网络上刊载的最新相关新闻和报道等。有关近期区域转型的资料收集最为重要,因为这些资料反映了最新的发展现状,而且国内外的研究都尚未对这些资料做过系统的整理。就资料处理而言,本研究主要采用的是定性分析的方法,按不同阶段对资料进行了政策综述和文献汇编。

The second purpose is to present the transformation of the case study area of the YRD. This mainly contains two datasets: territorial administrations and economic development. Consequently, maps of administrative divisions and changing regional administrations, and chronological data on the changes in administrative units, structures, and jurisdiction areas at the county level have been collected from administrative handbooks and statistical yearbooks. Moreover, data of industrial output, percentage of industries and from the tertiary sector, which indicate the facets of regional economic development, have been produced or collected from Jiangsu, Zhejiang, Shanghai Statistic Yearbooks and Chinese City Statistic Yearbooks. Some data may have been compiled by the author from various sources such as websites, reports and books, for instance, the distribution of economic zones. Furthermore, quantitative analysis via Excel and MapInfo is applied to visualise the changes in the governance structure and the spatial implications.

In addition, secondary data has been collected for the in-depth case studies of the changing relationship between Shanghai and Jiangsu, and the YRD regional plans, which are employed to illustrate the trajectory of YRD regional governance development in a vivid and detailed way. For the trans-border case on the side of Kunshan, a good foundation was established by existing studies on Kunshan and my experience in Kunshan during January, 2008 due to a local planning project. Materials such as the digital Kunshan administrative map, statistical yearbooks, the Kunshan master plan and Kunshan concept plan have already been collected through the planning project. However, further collection was made during the fieldwork of the most recent materials such as the newly approved master plan and statistical yearbooks to keep data up to date. On the other side of the border area of Anting town, Jiading district, Shanghai, materials of maps, planning documents and government policies were collected during the visit to the local planning bureau and economic zone development corporation.

With regard to the recent YRD regional plan, planning documents have been collected from open sources such as government websites, and from personal contacts with reference to unpublished texts. Materials on the historical development of YRD regional governance have been compiled from various publications including articles, reports and monographs.

4.5.2 First-hand data: semi-structured interviews

Secondary data are best to trace and document historical transformation and economic development because statistical books, monographs and articles published over the years contain abundant information and numeric data to illustrate progress, while documents and policies are able to provide specific

收集材料的第二个目的是展现案例研究对象长三角地区的转型状况,其中主要包括两类资料:行政体系和经济发展。因此,作者从行政区划手册和统计年鉴中收集了行政区划图、区域行政变化的相关图表以及县级以上行政单元、行政机构和管辖范围变化等各方面的编年资料。此外,还根据江苏、浙江、上海各省市的统计年鉴及《中国城市统计年鉴》采集或整理了反映区域经济发展状况的工业产出、行业比重及第三产业的相关数据。其中有些数据是作者根据网站、报告和书籍等各种来源汇编的,例如经济开发区分布等。本书利用Excel和MapInfo等软件对此类数据进行了定量分析,以便直观地反映管治结构的变化及对地理空间的影响。

此外,所收集的第二手资料还用于对上海、江苏之间的变化关系及长三角区域规划两个案例的研究,以便生动而详尽地展现长三角区域管治变化的轨迹。对于跨边界案例研究中的昆山部分,现有有关昆山的研究文献以及笔者于2008年1月在昆山参与的一个当地规划项目为展开研究提供了良好的基础。在笔者参与规划项目期间,就已收集了电子版的昆山行政区划图、统计年鉴、昆山总体规划方案及昆山概念规划图等资料。不过,为及时更新资料,此后笔者又进行了实地考察,进一步收集了最新资料,比如最新批准的总体规划方案和最新统计年鉴等。有关边界另一边的上海嘉定区安亭镇的地图、规划文件及政府政策等资料,是通过走访当地的规划局和经济开发区收集获得的。

有关近期长三角的区域规划,相关的规划文件是通过政府网站等公开来源收集的,也有部分资料是通过个人渠道索取的未发表的文字记载。关于长三角区域管治发展历史的资料则是根据论文、报告及专著等各类出版物汇编而成的。

二、第一手资料:半结构化访谈

由于多年来出版的年鉴和论文著作中含有大量反映区域发展进程的信息和数据,而各类文件和政策则能够提供针对各个项目的具体信息,因此第二手资料最适宜于追踪和记载历史变革和经济发展的状况。但是,第二手资料无

information on individual projects. However, the secondary data are not capable of providing information on the most recent developments and unpublished stories. Therefore, qualitative interviews are used to enrich information generated by the secondary data, and also to give evidence of information that cannot be retrieved through secondary data.

Semi – structured interviews were arranged for the two embedded case studies. The semi – structured interview technique is employed because of its strength in eliciting views and opinions from people who are rich in relevant experiences. Moreover, it also allows 'the interview to have more latitude to probe beyond the answers and thus enter into a dialogue with the interviewee' (May, 1997: 111). The proper design of interview questions is critical to the acquisition of information; threads of interview questions should be formulated according to the theory questions that the research aims to answer (Wengraf, 2001: 73). In the research, analysis of the interview transcription is based on themes, and insights are quoted to capture the points.

In total, 43 in – depth face – to – face semi – structured interviews were conducted, 10 were made during the pilot fieldtrip and 33 were held during the second fieldtrip.All interviews were conducted in the interviewees' offices, lasting from 30 minutes to 2 hours. Unfortunately, interviews made on the first fieldtrip were not recorded, but notes were taken. All 33 interviews later on were recorded and transcribed during the fieldtrip.The questions asked during interviews are attached in Appendix 1. Many experts were drawn from existing connections established during years of study in China, but some new contacts were also made during the research by means of references from supervisor and other experts.

The 10 interviews made on the pilot fieldtrip helps the study to gather a general knowledge about all the emerging practices at the regional level, and also helps to make decisions on the research design, particularly on choices of case studies and future methods. Due to the researcher's background in planning school and the involvement in live planning projects during the education, the 2 planning and development strategy - related cases of Kunshan (Jiangsu) and Jiading (Shanghai) and the Yangtze River Delta are selected. This is because the researcher is familiar with the plan–making process and can precisely target the relevant people to be recruited, who can be generally categorised into three types of people, that is, academics, planners and government and planning officials. In China, the planning and strategy making process is not only heavily involved by government officials of both senior civil servants and routine practitioners who are working in the relevant departments, and planning professionals who undertake the project, but also academics in the planning school. Academics often directly participate in planning projects and

法提供反映最新发展状况的信息,也不能提供未公布的动态。因此,本书采用定性采访的方法来充实二手资料的不足,同时也为无法从第二手资料中获取的信息提供依据。

本书的两个案例研究都安排了半结构化访谈。这种访谈的优势在于能够引出具有丰富相关经验的受访者的观点和意见。此外,这种方法还能够"通过追问的形式与受访者展开对话"(May,1997:111)。因此访谈问题的合理设计对获取信息至关重要;访谈问题的线索应根据研究所意图解答的理论问题合理编排(Wengraf,2001:73)。在本研究中,访谈记录被按主题类别进行了分析,有些直击要害的见解则直接引用。

本研究总计进行了43次面对面的半结构化深入访谈,其中10次是在首次实地考察期间进行的,33次是在第二次实地考察期间进行的。每次访谈都是在受访者的办公室进行,持续时间从30分钟到2小时不等。遗憾的是,第一次实地考察期间的访谈未进行录音而只做了访谈笔记;后期的33次访谈均有录音,并在实地考察期间根据录音记录成文。访谈中所提的问题见附录一。受访的许多专家都是作者在中国求学期间已经认识的,但也有一些是在此次调研中通过导师或其他专家推荐而新认识的。

首次实地考察期间所进行的10次访谈不仅使作者对区域层面新兴的实践积累了总体上的认识,同时也帮助作者最终确定了本研究的研究设计,尤其是在选择案例和确定接下去的研究方法方面。鉴于作者的规划专业背景,以及在求学期间参与过实际规划项目的经历,因此最终选择了昆山(江苏省)和嘉定(上海市)以及长三角地区这两个与规划和发展战略相关的案例。这是因为作者熟悉规划编制的过程,并且能够准确地找到相关参与人员进行访谈,包括学者、规划师及政府规划官员。在中国,参与规划和战略制定的人员往往有大量的政府官员(既有高层领导也有在相关部门任职的日常工作人员)、承担项目任务的专业规划人员,还有规划院系的专家学者。专家学者通常直接参与规划项目,并在起草规划方案时扮演重要角色,而非仅仅只是顾问。因此,中

play a leading role in drafting plans rather than merely work as consultants. Therefore, planning academics in China have long established links with the government and are very familiar with the process of plan-making. The list of interviewees is attached in Appendix 2. In the case of Kunshan (Jiangsu) and Jiading (Shanghai), an overall 19 interviews were made to both sides of trans-border region, with 2 academics, 7 planners and 10 government officials; while in the case of the Yangtze River Delta, 16 interviews were made, with 9 academics, 6 planners, and 1 government officials. Although the research was intending to cover all types of people who participated in or are well informed regarding the recent events and planning issues, the achievement in the second case study is slightly poor in terms of approaching government officials.

One of the main disadvantages of interviews is difficulty in gaining access to the interviewees. The potential interviewee may not be available or may not want to cooperate. This is especially the case in the second case study of the YRD regional plan because the plan is overseen by the central ministries, where the civil servants are highly-ranked. Originally, 4 officials in the central ministries were targeted. Even though strenuous efforts were made, the results were disappointing even with contacts and references. They were either too busy to make an arrangement, or did not respond to enquiries regarding the possibility of an interview, or simply refused to participate. For example, neither the senior official nor the civil servant from the National Development and Reform Commission (NDRC) nor the person from the Ministry of Housing and Urban and Rural Development (MHURD) who is in charge of YRD regional plan making was available for interview, despite several attempts to meet. Finally, only one other official, the chief of the section of urban development in MHURD, was approached with the help of contacts. And this is the only official interviewed in the central ministries. Therefore, great efforts were made to obtain the missing information from alternative sources. For example, talks, interviews or speeches made by officials on public occasions were collected from various resources such as the government's official website, news portal websites, newspapers, news or academic journals or personal contacts. Meanwhile, as many interviews as possible were conducted with academics, senior planners and others involved in the YRD regional plan preparation. For ethical considerations, the location of some of the interviewees is removed in the text due to the sensitivity of the comments or at the request of the interviewe.

国的规划专业学者同政府之间的合作由来已久,他们对规划制定的过程非常熟悉。受访者名单见附录二。在昆山(江苏省)和嘉定(上海市)案例中,笔者在苏沪边界的两地共进行了19次访谈,其中学者2次,规划师7次,政府官员10次;在长三角案例中共进行了16次访谈,其中学者9次,规划师6次,政府官员1次。虽然本研究力图涵盖所有参与过或熟知最新发生的区域项目和相关规划的人员,但是第二个案例中对政府官员的访谈资料仍略显匮乏。

　　访谈的一个主要难点在于得到受访者的配合。潜在的受访者有的可能无法应约,有的可能不愿意接受访谈。这种情况在长三角区域规划的案例研究中尤其突出,因为这个规划是由中央部委的高层官员直接主管的。尽管费尽周折,结果仍令人失望。他们或者太忙无法安排,或者不回复可否接受采访的询问,或者直接拒绝参与。例如,国家发改委高层官员和公务员,以及住建部负责长三角区域规划制定的官员均未能接受采访。最后只能在熟人的帮助下找到了另外一位住建部的官员,这也是案例中唯一采访到的中央部委官员。因此,笔者努力通过其他途经获取研究所需要的资料。比如,从政府官网、新闻门户网站、报纸、新闻或学术期刊、个人联系等来源收集了中央部委官员在公共场合的谈话、采访或演讲。同时,笔者尽可能多地采访了参与长三角区域规划编制工作的学者、资深规划师以及其他相关人员。出于学术道德的考虑,鉴于有些评论内容的敏感性或者应受访者的要求,本书略去了某些受访者的所在地信息。

第五章

CHAPTER FIVE

The Development of the Yangtze River Delta in China

5.1 Introduction

Under the centrally planned system prior to 1978, China was ruled under a command economy. There was no natural economic flow or monetary regionalisation during that time. Arbitrary spatial labour divisions were distinguished between cities and rural areas, with cities intended to develop industries and villages to develop agriculture. For example, Shanghai and the neighbouring county, Kunshan, were rarely related to each other and were even managed by separate urban and rural systems. During the socialist period, Shanghai was the most important manufacturing city in China. Shanghai's products were appropriated all over the country under the central command. In contrast, Kunshan, the rural county, was mainly engaged in agricultural activities and farming. It is not until the start of the economic reform that horizontal economic connections began emerging between enterprises and cities, under the encouragement of the central government. The increasingly integrated regional economy with intense flows of trade, people, traffic, logistics and capital is a new phenomenon in China.

However, there is little research on the development of economic regionalisation and the consequently changing inter-city economic relationship in China in either Chinese-or English-language literature. Although some literature exists on the changing cross-border economic relationship between Hong Kong and Guangdong (Ash and Kueh, 1993; Shen, 2002, 2003; Yang 2004, 2005a; Yeh, 2001), the inter-relationship between Hong Kong and the PRD region is peculiar to mainland China in that the area includes one special administrative region, i.e. Hong Kong. The special framework of 'One Country, Two Systems' between the two areas increases the regional economy in the sense of 'transnational' regionalisation under economic globalisation. In contrast, the majority of the existing regional literature in China mainly focuses on the issue of regional economic development and the consequent economic and spatial transformation (Chen, 2007; Eng, 1997; Lin, 1997, 2001ab; Lo, 1989; Ma and Fan, 1994; Shen et al., 2002; Sit and Yang, 1997; Wei, 2002, 2010; Wei et al., 2009). Zhao and Zhang (2007) described the regional polarisation with strong outward linkages as global city-regions. It is widely acknowledged that FDI and local government are the indispensable driving forces which stimulate the regional economic development (Chien, 2007; Wang and Lee, 2007; Wei, 2002; Yang, 2009; Zhao and Zhang, 2007).

第五章 中国长三角地区的发展

第一节 引言

在1978年前的中央计划经济体制时期,中国实行的是指令性经济。在那个时期,没有自然的经济流动,也没有形成货币区域化。城乡之间有着硬性的劳动分工,城市集中发展工业,农村则全力发展农业。以上海市和相邻的昆山县(现为昆山市)为例,两地之间没有什么联系,甚至在行政管理上分属城市和农村两个彼此独立的体制。在社会主义计划经济时期,上海是中国最重要的制造业城市。上海制造的产品在中央的指令下向全国各地调配。相反,昆山作为农业县,主要从事与农业相关的活动。直到经济改革开始,在中央政府的鼓励下,企业和城市间才逐渐出现横向的经济联系。随着贸易、人员、交通、物资、资本的密集流动,地区经济整合日益增强,成为了中国的一个新现象。

然而,无论是在中文还是英文的文献中,都很少有关于中国的经济区域化发展及由此产生的城际经济关系变化的研究。虽然有一些文献涉及了香港与广东之间的跨境经济关系的变化(Ash 和 Kueh,1993;Shen,2002,2003;Yang,2004,2005a;Yeh,2001),但是香港与珠三角之间的关系对中国大陆来说是一个特例,因为香港是一个特别行政区。"一国两制"的特殊架构使该地区的区域经济更像是经济全球化背景下的"跨国"经济区域化。在中国现有的区域研究文献中,大多数主要着眼于区域经济发展及其引发的经济和空间变革的问题(Chen,2007;Eng,1997;Lin,1997,2001ab;Lo,1989;Ma 和 Fan,1994;Shen 等,2002;Sit 和 Yang,1997;Wei,2002,2010;Wei 等,2009)。Zhao 和 Zhang(2007)将高度外向化的区域极化现象描述为中国的全球城市区域。目前普遍认为,外商直接投资和地方政府的支持是区域经济发展不可或缺的推动力(Chien,2007;Wang 和 Lee,2007;Wei,2002;Yang,2009;Zhao 和 Zhang,2007)。

However, the recent Western literature on city-regions has transcended the focus on the physical agglomeration and spatial clustering of economies, and extended the analysis to the functional connectivity within the region (Hall, 2009: 804). That is, the concept of the city-region is not merely defined as a continuously urbanised area, but also 'on the basis of what Manuel Castells has called the "space of flows"' (ibid). Hall and Pain (2006) studied the cluster of cities in Europe and defined the functional polycentric region as a new form of urbanisation, which is organised by networks that are clustered around one or more large central city. It is documented that 'these places exist both as separate entities, ... and as parts of a wider functional urban region connected by dense flows of people and information along motorways, high-speed rail lines, and telecommunications cables' (Hall, 2009: 806). It is suggested that the vibrant regional economy is drawn from the new functional division of labour within and between the networks (ibid).

The insufficient attention paid to the changing cross-boundary relationships between cities and provinces in China (except for Tang and Zhao, 2010; Zhang, 2006) provides a gap for research to examine the regionalisation process developing in China. The chapter attempts to illustrate the development of the regionalisation of the YRD region and the changing economic inter-relationship between the cities. It not only draws upon the great quantity of literature on the economic development of the YRD region to illustrate the implication of the economic development to the changing inter-city economic relationship, but also extends the analysis forward to the new development of functional connectivity between the cities in recent years. It is argued that the YRD has become virtually regionalised since the 1990s through two stages. In the 1990s, the region was developing into an export-oriented manufacturing belt with close relationships with foreign markets and investment. Cities within the dynamic region were increasingly inter-related to each other, not only in the sense that they were in sympathy with foreign markets, but also in that they were confronted with common regional issues such as housing problems, traffic congestion and environmental degradation after years of urban expansion. Since the beginning of the 2000s, the regionalisation of the YRD has stepped into a new stage. Cities in the region at different development stages are beginning to develop functional division of labour between one another. The new development pattern is driven by both government push and market pull, and facilitated by improved regional transport.

The chapter is organised according to the different development stages of economic regionalisation. In addition to the existing YRD literature and monographs, Shanghai, Jiangsu and Zhejiang statistical yearbooks have been collected. By making use of MapInfo, maps based on county-level jurisdictional

然而,近来研究城市区域的西方文献不再局限于经济的物理和空间集聚,而是将研究重心扩大到了区域内的功能联系(Hall,2009:804)。这意味着城市区域这个概念不仅表示不断城市化的区域,而且是"建立在 Manuel Castells 提出的'流的空间'基础上"的(同上)。Hall 和 Pain(2006)研究了欧洲的城市群分布,并将功能性多中心区域定义为城市化的一种新模式,这种区域的组织形式是由一个或多个大型中心城市形成的城市群网络。有文献提出,"这些地区既作为独立的实体存在……同时也是更广阔的功能性城市区域的一部分,它们被高速公路、高速铁路和电信电缆所传输的密集的人流和信息流联系了起来"(Hall,2009:806)。由此可见,各个网络内和网络间的新型劳动分工推动了区域经济的蓬勃发展(同上)。

中国城市与省份之间的跨境关系变化并未受到足够的重视(除了唐子来和赵渺希,2010;Zhang,2006),因此关于中国区域化进程发展的研究还略显不足。本章旨在描述长三角地区的区域化发展进程以及城市间的经济关系变化。本章不仅借鉴了大量有关长三角地区经济发展的文献来阐述城市间不断发展的经济关系,还进一步分析了近几年来城市间职能联系的新发展。本章认为,长三角地区实际上从20世纪90年代起就已经进入了区域化的发展,并经历了两个阶段。20世纪90年代期间,该区域逐渐形成了一条与外国市场和投资紧密联系的出口型制造业产业带。在这个充满活力的区域中,城市之间的联系也越来越紧密,这不仅表现在它们都看好外国市场,而且在经过若干年的城市扩张后,它们都面临着相同的区域性问题,比如住房问题、交通拥堵和环境退化等问题。自21世纪初以来,长三角的区域化进入了新的阶段。区域内处于不同发展阶段的城市之间开始出现职能分工。新型发展模式在政府的推力和市场的牵引力作用下得到发展,区域交通的改善也为发展提供了便利。

本章根据经济区域化的不同发展阶段进行组织。除了现有的关于长三角地区的研究文献和专著之外,还收集了上海、江苏和浙江的统计年鉴。通过使

units (except Shanghai, where data of districts and counties cannot be accessed) have been compiled in order to illustrate the transformation of the YRD development.

5.2 The development of the regional economy in the YRD in the 1980s

Distinguished from town development in the PRD, the growth of the YRD in the 1980s was largely not fuelled by foreign (overseas Chinese) investment and manufacturing exports. In contrast, the local development of town and village enterprises (TVEs) played a key role in the regional growth of the YRD throughout the take-off period of economic reform. As shown by the spatial distribution of industrial output value in the YRD in 1990 in Figure 5.1, manufacturing was no longer merely dominated by the provincial capital cities or main cities such as Hangzhou, Ningbo of Zhejiang province, Suzhou, Wuxi, Changzhou and Nanjing of Jiangsu province. The counties or county-level cities such as Wujiang, Changshu and Zhangjiagang under the Suzhou prefecture-level city; Xishan, Jiangyin under the Wuxi prefecture-level city and Wujin under the Changzhou prefecture-level city also performed a strong role in industrial production. This was due to the fact that TVEs had strongly driven rural industrialisation, especially in southern Jiangsu of Suzhou, Wuxi and Changzhou in the 1980s (Ma and Fan, 1994), which is also known as the 'Sunan Model' (Marton, 2000). It is documented that, during the period from 1978 to 1994, industrial output in Suzhou and Wuxi city region increased 44.1 times and 34.6 times respectively, much higher than the 7.3 times in Shanghai and 15.6 times which was the national average (Shen and Ma, 2005: 765). The 'Sunan Model' is actually a kind of collectivism built on the institution of production brigade in the socialist economy. The thriving growth of towns occurred without the financial or policy assistance of the central government; rather, it was driven by local initiatives of the county, township and town government, or rural entrepreneurs (Ma and Fan, 1994: 1642). In a word, the disappearance of the arbitrary division of labour between urban and rural areas, as well as the lessening control of the central government on the economy with the inception of economic reforms, had contributed to the influx of TVEs and the emancipation of the rural industrialisation.

用MapInfo地理信息系统软件编制了基于县级管辖单位的地图(上海除外,无法获取其所辖区县的数据),用于阐述长三角地区的发展转变过程。

第二节　20世纪80年代长三角区域经济的发展情况

与珠三角城镇发展不同,20世纪80年代长三角地区的发展在很大程度上并非依靠外国(海外华人)投资和制造业出口。相反,在经济改革的初始阶段,乡镇企业自始至终都在长三角地区的发展中扮演着关键角色。图5.1的1990年工业产值空间分布图显示,制造业已不再是只由省会城市和主要城市(如浙江省的杭州和宁波,以及江苏省的苏州、无锡、常州和南京等)占据主导地位。地级市苏州所辖的吴江、常熟、张家港,地级市无锡所辖的锡山和江阴,以及地级市常州所辖的武进等县和县级市,也都在工业生产中发挥了重要作用。这是因为乡镇企业强有力地促进了农村地区的工业化,其中80年代在苏南地区的苏州、无锡和常州发生的情况尤为显著(Ma和Fan,1994),这也就是后来为人熟知的"苏南模式"(Marton,2000)。资料显示,1978年至1994年,苏州市和无锡地区的工业产值分别增长了44.1倍和34.6倍,远高于上海的同期增幅7.3倍和全国的平均增幅15.6倍(Shen和Ma,2005:765)。"苏南模式"实际上是一种建立在社会主义经济生产大队制度上的集体所有制。这些城镇的繁荣发展并不是在中央政府的财政和政策支持下实现的;相反,是靠县和乡镇政府或农村企业家在当地采取的积极举措推动起来的(Ma和Fan,1994:1642)。简而言之,随着经济改革的开始,硬性的城乡劳动分工消失,中央政府对经济控制的放松,促进了乡镇企业的涌现和农村工业化的自由发展。

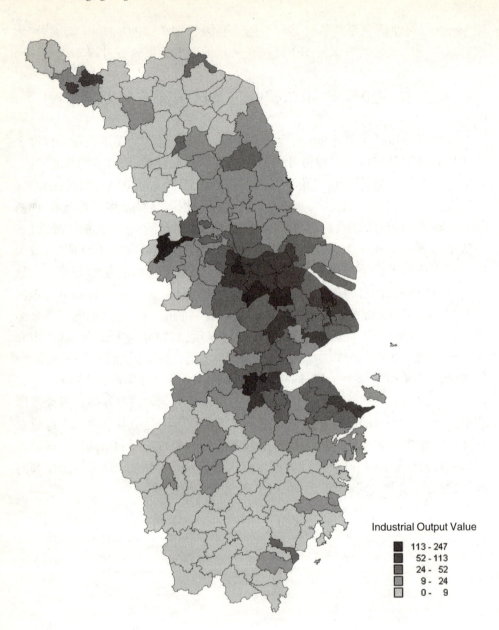

Figure 5.1 The spatial distribution of gross industrial output value in the YRD (1990)

Source: Jiangsu Statistical Bureau, 1991; Shanghai Statistical Bureau, 1991; Zhejiang Statistical Bureau, 1991.

Note: Due to the data availability, the total amount of industrial output rather than the per capita GDP is used here for illustration.

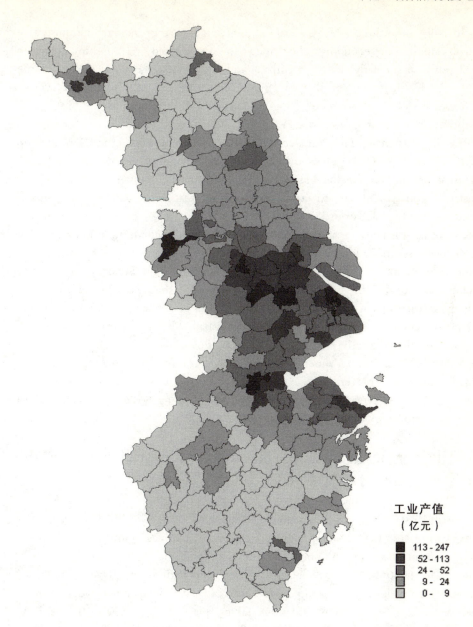

图5.1 长三角地区工业总产值的空间分布(1990)

资料来源:江苏省统计局,1991年;上海市统计局,1991年;浙江省统计局,1991年。

注:由于获取数据的途径受限,此图示中使用的是工业总产值数据,而不是人均国内生产总值数据。

In the meantime, the gradual elimination of the central administrative controls upon the economy also fused the segmented relationships between jurisdictions, particularly between urban and rural areas. For example, in the YRD, it is documented that a significant number of town and village enterprises (TVEs) in southern Jiangsu managed to develop business links with enterprises in other regions, over a half of which were state-owned enterprises (SOEs) in Shanghai (The Yangtze River Delta Urban Economic Coordination Office, 2007: 27). These TVEs mainly undertook the initial processing or labour-intensive production for the big SOEs. Apart from the transfer or expansion of industries from Shanghai to this developing area, the outflow of capital, technology and trade from Shanghai was also very strong. At that time, the manufacturing capacity in the peripheral towns lagged behind to the extent that the majority of the equipment was transferred from Shanghai's enterprises, and engineers were also borrowed from Shanghai's factories on Sundays (ibid). The development of TVEs in Kunshan was exactly the case in point. The industrialisation of Kunshan started by attracting Shanghai's investment, equipment, engineers and brand names (Kunshan Planning Bureau, 2010: 4). Overall, shortly after the economic reform, flows of investment, trade, and people were just about to emerge after a long term of stiff economy under the central command. Nevertheless, interactions during this time remained very limited and were even influenced by residual planning orders due to gradual and partial reform in the 1980s.

5.3 The regionalisation of manufacturing production in the YRD since the 1990s

After 1990, the regional economy in the YRD developed at a spectacular speed owing to the opening up of Pudong. The economy was gradually deviating from the state-sponsored development and the collectively-led 'Sunan Model'. In contrast, the development since the period has shown combined influences from local states and global forces. The development transition is contextualised in several transformations taking place in the YRD or even the whole country. First of all, the pillar of the region's economy, the development of TVEs, was confronted with dwindling profits, especially after the mid-1990s. It is documented that 22 percent of the total number of TVEs in Jiangsu province lost money in 1995; and overall industrial output in Suzhou, Wuxi and Changzhou prefecture-level city dropped precipitously in 1995 and 1996 (Shen and Ma, 2005: 765-766). As a result, drastic privatisation of collectively-owned enterprises occurred from the mid-1990s to the early 2000s in order to

　　同时,随着中央政府对经济的行政控制逐渐减弱,各个辖区之间被割裂的关系也开始恢复,尤其是在城乡之间。例如在长三角地区,资料显示,苏南地区的大批乡镇企业与其他地区的企业成功建立了业务往来,其中一半以上是上海的国有企业(长江三角洲城市经济协调会办公室,2007:27)。这些乡镇企业主要为大型国有企业进行产品初加工,或承担劳动密集型产品的生产。除了工业从上海向这些发展中地区大规模转移或扩张之外,还有大量的资本、技术和贸易也从上海流向这些地区。当时,周边城镇的制造能力相当落后,多数设备需从上海企业运来,还要向上海的工厂借调工程师周日来加班(同上)。昆山乡镇企业的发展就是一个典型案例。昆山的工业化始于从上海引进投资、设备、工程师和品牌(昆山市规划局,2010:4)。大体上,经济改革开始后不久,僵化的经济摆脱了中央指令的长期束缚,投资、贸易和人员的流动迅速涌现。尽管如此,由于20世纪80年代的改革还只是渐进式的局部改革,这一时期的流动性仍然有限,并且受到残余的计划指令的影响。

第三节　20世纪90年代以来长三角地区制造业生产的区域化

　　1990年后,浦东的开放使长三角的区域经济得以高速发展,逐步摆脱了国家扶持的发展模式和集体所有制主导的"苏南模式"。相比之下,这一时期开始的发展显示了地方政府和全球化力量的综合作用。这种发展的转型是以长三角地区乃至全国发生的一些变革为背景的。首先,作为区域经济支柱的乡镇企业出现利润下滑,这一现象在20世纪90年代中期之后尤为明显。据文献记载,1995年,江苏共有22%的乡镇企业出现亏损;1995至1996年,苏州、无锡和常州三个地级市的工业总产值出现大幅下降(Shen和Ma,2005:765-766)。因此,从20世纪90年代中期至21世纪初期,为遏制农村经济的下滑,集体所有制的乡镇企业进行了大规模的私有制改革。据报道,20世纪90年代中期,苏南地区70%左右的乡镇企业实现了私有化,截至2000年,该地区超过95%的乡镇

reverse the downturn of the rural economy. It was reported that about 70 percent of TVEs in southern Jiangsu were privatised in the mid-1990s, and by 2000 more than 95 percent had practiced the property rights reform (Chen, 2005: 73), which virtually terminated the Sunan model. Parallel to the declining performance of TVEs was the opening up of Pudong, Shanghai in 1990. With the launch of the national strategy equivalent to that of the Shenzhen Special Economic Zone of the PRD, the YRD followed the PRD to adopt preferential policies to FDI and globalisation. With the infusion of foreign capital, TVEs lost their competitiveness even after the property rights reform. Henceforth, local governments gave higher priority to foreign invested enterprises than private ones. Consequently, a significant increase in the amount of overseas investment in YRD was seen from 1992 (Figure 5.2). Although influenced by the 1997 Asian Financial Crisis, the volume of foreign investment did not shrink sharply.

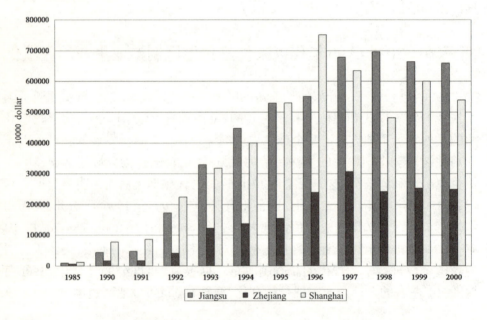

Figure 5.2 The foreign capital actually utilised in the YRD (1990—2000)
Source: National Statistical Bureau, 2001.

The transformation of the local economy has been intensively researched in the existing literature especially that based on the Suzhou municipality, the globalising region in the southern Jiangsu province, which used to be the prototype of the 'Sunan Model'. It is claimed that Suzhou had undergone a dramatic transformation, from an economy based on SOEs and TVEs towards

企业实行了所有制改革(Chen,2005:73),这实际上宣告了苏南模式的终结。1990年,就在乡镇企业逐渐衰落的同时,上海浦东踏上了开放之路。新的国家战略的出台,使浦东具有了和珠三角地区的深圳经济特区一样的地位。长三角地区效仿珠三角,为外商直接投资和全球化提供政策优惠。外国资本的流入,使乡镇企业丧失了竞争力,即使所有制改革之后也无法挽回颓势。从此,地方政府的关注重心从私营企业转向外商投资企业。结果,长三角地区的海外投资额从1992年起出现显著增长(图5.2)。即使在1997年亚洲金融危机的打击之下,该地区的外商投资额也没有大幅降低。

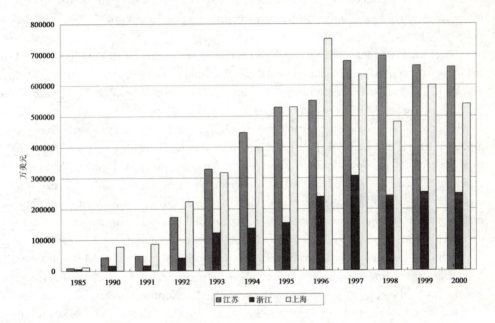

图5.2 长三角地区实际利用外资情况(1990—2000)

资料来源:国家统计局,2001年。

　　地方经济的转型在现有文献中已得到广泛探讨,其中以苏州市为案例的研究尤为集中。苏州是江苏省南部最具全球化特征的地区之一,曾被视为"苏南模式"的典范。有学者称,苏州的经济经过了大规模的转型,已经从依靠国有企业和乡镇企业的经济模式转变为主要依赖对内投资和出口贸易的经济模式(Wei,2002;Wei等,2009)。地方经济的重新定位大大影响了行政区间的关系和政企关系。随着众多市县将焦点转向吸引外资和生产全球商品,原有的国有企业与乡镇企业的合作关系已被平行的竞争关系所取代。另一方面,乡

one heavily dependent upon inward investment and export trade (Wei, 2002; Wei et al., 2009). The re-orientation of the local economy made a great impact upon the inter-jurisdictional and government-business relationships. As a considerable number of cities and counties had turned to foreign investment and the production of global commodities, the previous SOE-TVE cooperation had been replaced by parallel and competitive relationships. On the other hand, the TVE property rights reform made a legal separation of village administrations and business corporations, and led to a divergence between political leadership and corporate leadership, which used to be intertwined in the TVEs (Chen, 2005: 79). As a consequence, the local governments made a profit from the collection of management fees and taxes and the lease of land use rights, instead of directly from the turnover of corporations (Shen and Ma, 2005: 770).

The development path of the YRD shares some similarities with the PRD in light of externally-driven regional development (Chen, 2007; Wei et al., 2009: 424). However, according to Yang (2009), the PRD region is driven by foreign (Chinese) investment without active local initiatives, while the YRD is fostered by local governments with explicit proactive strategies of globalisation. The active role of local governments is mainly demonstrated by their initiatives in development zone establishment and pro-business institution building (Wang and Lee, 2007). A considerable amount of land has been set aside by the local governments as development zones, and well-developed infrastructures and preferential policies are provided in order to attract industries, particularly foreign-invested enterprises. Such a development model, centred on development zones and institutional innovation, is coined as the 'Kunshan Model', a prototype based on a county-level city under the Suzhou municipality, which took the initiative to set up its own development zone in 1985 and adopted the globalisation strategy in the early 1990s, far ahead of Suzhou city (Chien, 2007; Wang and Lee, 2007: 1878-1879). At the beginning of economic reform, Kunshan was merely a small county not only in terms of administrative ranks, but also with regard to economic base. However, with the opening up of Shanghai and the Yangtze River Delta, Kunshan has led the way in driving local economic development by local-state initiated globalisation (Wei, 2002). In addition to 'free' land and tax exemptions in its development zones, Kunshan also tailored its local institutions to cater for business requirements for speed and flexibility (Wang and Lee, 2007; Chien and Zhao, 2008). The fostering of an IT global production network plus a pro-business environment have transformed Kunshan into a close competitor to the giant city of Shanghai to attract big name enterprises or even the top 500 transnational corporations, particularly since the new millennium (Wu and Phelps, 2008: 474).

镇企业的所有制改革使乡镇的行政管理与企业经营在法律上实现脱钩,并使乡镇企业中原本混为一体的政治领导和企业领导实现两权分离(Chen,2005:79)。因此,地方政府不再直接接收企业的营业利润收入,而是通过向企业收取管理费、征税和出租土地使用权等途径获得政府收入(Shen和Ma,2005:770)。

长三角地区的发展也受到了外力的推动,在这一方面与珠三角的发展有一些相似之处(Chen,2007;Wei等,2009:424)。但是,Yang(2009)认为珠三角的发展主要受到的是外国(海外华人)投资的推动,地方本身并没有采取积极行动,而长三角的发展则受到地方政府积极明确的全球化战略的扶持。地方政府的积极作用主要表现在大力推动开发区建设和建立有利于商业的制度(Wang和Lee,2007)。地方政府划拨大片土地作为开发区,提供良好的基础设施,同时给予政策优惠,吸引企业,尤其是外资企业进驻。这种以开发区和体制创新为核心的发展模式,被称为"昆山模式"。作为苏州市管辖下的一个县级市,昆山在1985年率先创建了自己的开发区,并早在20世纪90年代初就实行了全球化战略,起步时间远远早于苏州市(Chien,2007;Wang和Lee,2007:1878-1879)。在经济改革初期,无论从行政级别还是经济基础上来看,昆山都只是一个小县城。但是,随着上海和长三角的开放,昆山凭借地方政府开创的全球化战略,成为了促进地区经济发展的领头羊(Wei,2002)。昆山不仅在开发区内提供"免费"土地,给予免税优惠,还调整了地方制度以快速、灵活地迎合商业需求(Wang和Lee,2007;Chien和Zhao,2008)。如今,昆山所培育的全球IT生产网络以及利商环境已经使这个县级市在吸引大牌企业,乃至世界500强公司方面,足以与大都市上海相抗衡,尤其是在进入新千年之后(Wu和Phelps,2008:474)。

Consequently, the spatial economic structure in the YRD region is becoming more polycentric, with counties and towns at the margin of the metropolis of Shanghai achieving the fastest growth. This is because the peripheral region owns a vast amount of land available at a low price, offers more lax and flexible regulations, and enjoys geographical adjacency to Shanghai. However, the polycentric economic structure is generally characterised by a similar industrial structure predominated by manufacturing industries. Figure 5.3 shows that over a half of the GDP of Shanghai and neighbouring southern Jiangsu and northern Zhejiang was constituted by secondary industries in 1995. Although the inter-city interactions are booming in terms of logistics, capital, migration, business and so on, the functional division of labour among the cities is still relatively weak. Striking evidence is the widespread construction of development zones and the reduced cost of industrial land, priced to attract investment. In the 1980s, the industrial development zone was only a specific parcel of land approved by the central government to attract foreign investment. There were only fourteen economic and technological development zones in China in 1984. However, a great quantity of development zones has been set up by the local governments since the 1990s. There is a boom in development zones at different levels, depending on their supervising jurisdictions, ranging from 'national' economic zones to 'municipal' development zones, to 'county' and 'town and village' ones. According to Tao et al. (2010: 2218), the total number of development zones in China arrived at 3,837 by 2003, only 6 percent of which were founded by the central government, and 27 percent of which by the provincial governments. The total number almost doubled in the following years, rising to as many as 6,015 in 2006. The situation is similar in the case of the YRD. According to Yang (2001), the number of development zones in Shanghai, the south and middle of Jiangsu and the north of Zhejiang was only 17 in 1991, while the number soared to 74 in 1993, which did not even include those approved by the counties and cities themselves (Yang, 2001: 125). Figure 5.4 demonstrates the widespread nature of development zones in the YRD region.

在此背景下,长三角地区的空间经济布局正朝着多中心化的方向发展,其中位于上海大都市周边的县和镇发展最快。其原因在于,这些周边地区可提供大量廉价土地,规章制度更为宽松灵活,并且具有毗邻上海的地理优势。然而,多中心的经济格局仍是以制造业为主导的工业结构为总体特征的。图5.3显示,1995年上海及邻近的苏南和浙北地区的国内生产总值中超过半数来自于第二产业。尽管就物流、资本、人口迁移和商业等因素而言,城市间的交流越来越频繁,但城市间的职能性劳动分工仍然较为欠缺。很明显的一个例子是,为吸引投资,各地纷纷设立开发区并降低工业用地的价格。在20世纪80年代,开发区还只是由中央政府批准,专为吸引外商投资而设立的一个特定地域。1984年,全国仅有14个经济技术开发区。但是从20世纪90年代起,全国各地涌现出了一大批由地方政府设立的开发区。各级政府依据各自的监督管辖权纷纷设立起不同层级的开发区,包括"国家级"经济开发区、"市级"开发区,甚至还有"县级"、"村镇级"开发区。根据Tao等(2010:2218)的统计,截至2003年,中国开发区的总数达到了3,837个,其中只有6%是由中央政府设立的,27%由省政府设立。在随后几年内,开发区的总数几乎翻番,在2006年达到了6,015个。类似的情形也出现在长三角。杨桂山(2001:125)指出,1991年,上海、苏南、苏中和浙北的开发区总数仅为17个,到1993年则飙升至74个,其中还不包括那些由各县市自行批准设立的开发区。图5.4显示了长三角地区开发区广泛分布的特性。

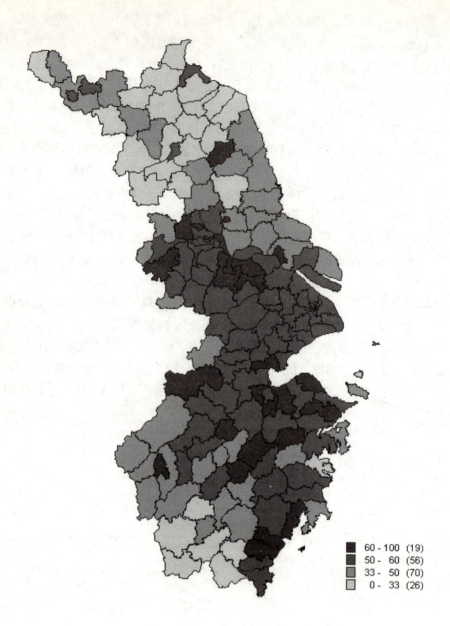

Figure 5.3 The regionalisation of manufacturing production
in the YRD region (the percentage of secondary industry in 1995)

Source: Jiangsu Statistical Bureau, 1996; Shanghai Statistical Bureau, 1996; Zhejiang Statistical Bureau, 1996.

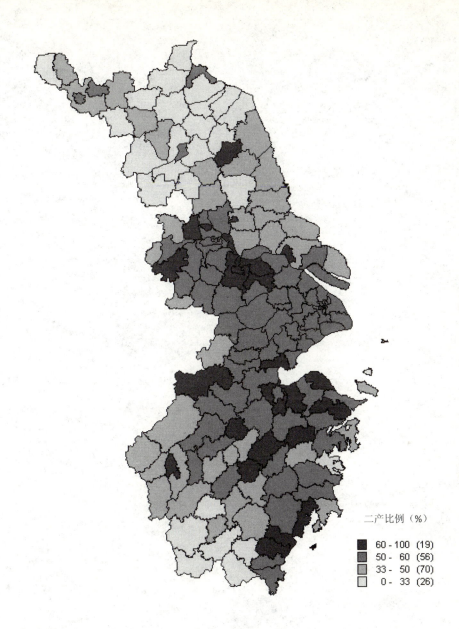

二产比例（%）

■ 60 - 100 (19)
▩ 50 - 60 (56)
▨ 33 - 50 (70)
□ 0 - 33 (26)

图5.3 长三角地区制造业生产的区域化(1995年第二产业的比重)

资料来源:江苏省统计局,1996年;上海市统计局,1996年;浙江省统计局,1996年。

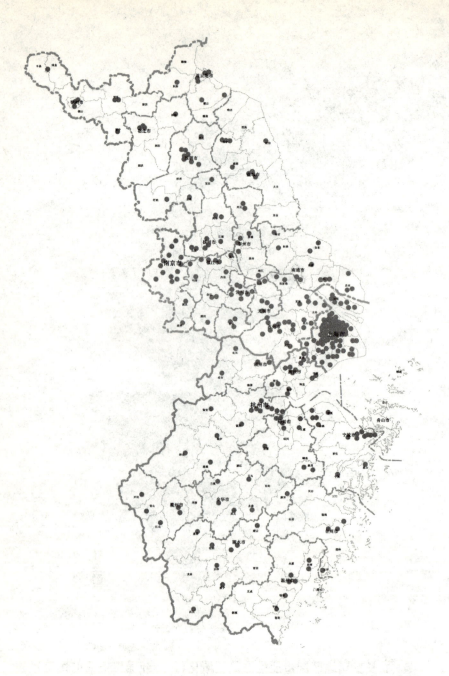

Figure 5.4 The widespread nature of development zones in the YRD
Source: compiled from YRD investment attraction website, http://www.c3j.com.cn/
c3jmap.asp; China development zone website, http://www.cadz.org.cn/index.jsp.

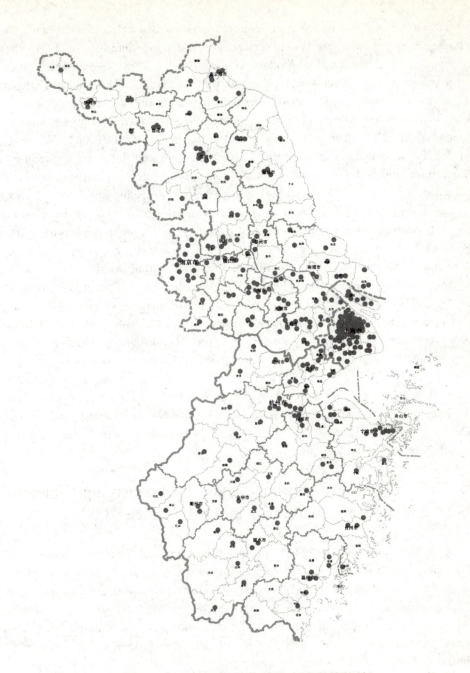

图5.4 长三角地区开发区广泛分布的特性

资料来源:根据长三角招商引资网 http://www.c3j.com.cn/c3jmap.asp 和中国开发区网 http://www.cadz.org.cn/index.jsp 汇编整理。

To summarise, the opening up policy and attraction of investment has had a homogenising impact on local economies. With the infusion of FDI, the development of manufacturing production soon spread from major central cities to the wider region around Shanghai and the nearby area of southern Jiangsu and northern Zhejiang. The spill over of manufacturing to the neighbouring towns and counties formed a partially regionalised production network in the region (Chen, 2007: 189–190). That is, the former SOE–TVE link has been replaced by a global–local production network or some local–local supplier–manufacturer links. Despite the network relationship, fierce competition exists between cities at the same hierarchy or late-comers struggling into the network or cities trying to move upwards in the division of labour. The regionalisation of manufacturing development served as a catalyst for growth and turned the YRD into a dynamic region in the national economy. For example, it is documented that, in 1993, the density of industrial output in the core area of the YRD region was 12,370,000 *yuan*/km^2, which was 7.3 times the national average; and the GDP of the area accounted for 18 percent of the GDP of all the cities in the country (National Statistical Bureau, 1994: 529, 531). In a word, the foci of foreign investment and the regionalised production chains have stimulated and sustained an unprecedented booming economy in the region of the YRD (Chen, 2007). However, the physically extended metropolitan area has also posed huge pressure on land consumption and environmental sustainability; for example, air quality deteriorated and water pollution occurred. That is, the region was beginning to suffer the negative externality of economic agglomeration.

5.4 Industrial restructuring and the emerging integral labour and housing market in the YRD since 2000

With the accession to WTO, manufacturing in the YRD has risen once more since 2000 (Figure 5.5). Manufacturing in counties and county-level cities around Shanghai, Hangzhou and Nanjing achieved spectacular development and the proportion of secondary industry accounted for over 60 percent in 2005. However, manufacturing distribution has demonstrated two features that are distinct from those of the 1990s. First of all, the proportion of secondary industries of the central cities of Shanghai, Hangzhou and Nanjing began to drop to less than a half of total GDP. Secondly, manufacturing development gained a notable growth in the area south of Zhejiang and north of Jiangsu, which has previously lagged behind in this aspect. The rise of manufacturing in this area was even more marked in 2009. The percentage of manufacturing of

总而言之,开放政策和招商引资对地方经济产生了一致的影响。随着外商直接投资的涌入,制造业生产迅速从主要的中心城市向上海外围区域以及苏南、浙北的周边区域扩展。制造业向周边的县和乡镇扩张,在该地区形成了一个半区域化的生产网(Chen,2007:189-190)。换言之,原有的国有企业与乡镇企业链已被一个全球与地方生产网络,或是某些地方与地方间的供应制造链所取代。尽管共存于同一网络之中,辖区相互之间依然存在着激烈的竞争;它们不仅表现在同一层级的城市之间,还表现在后来者的竞争追赶,以及原生产网络中城市向劳动分工上游转型的竞争。制造业发展的区域化促进了经济增长,使长三角成为了国家经济建设中的一个活跃区域。例如,据文献记载,1993年长三角核心地区的工业产值密度为1,237万元/平方公里,是全国平均水平的7.3倍;该地区的国内生产总值占全国所有城市国内生产总值的18%(国家统计局,1994:529,531)。简而言之,通过大力吸引外资和发展区域化生产链,长三角地区获得了前所未有的经济持续繁荣。然而,大都市地区不断向外扩张绵延,也为土地消耗和可持续环境保护带来了严峻的挑战,例如出现了空气质量下降、水污染等问题。换言之,该区域开始承受经济集聚带来的负面外部影响。

第四节　2000年以来长三角地区的产业结构调整及新兴的劳动力和房地产一体化市场

自从中国加入WTO后,长三角的制造业从2000年开始再度腾飞(图5.5)。上海、杭州和南京周边的各县及县级市的制造业发展迅速,第二产业所占比重在2005年超过60%。然而,制造业的分布显示了与20世纪90年代不同的两个特点。第一,在上海、杭州和南京这些中心城市中,第二产业占国内生产总值的比例逐步下降到不足50%。第二,浙南和苏北地区的制造业摆脱了之前相对滞后的局面,获得了显著发展。该地区制造业的崛起在2009年尤为

the majority of cities in the area reached over 45 percent of GDP in 2009, with none falling below 33 percent. Overall, it seems that while some of the cities in the wider region have just started the process of industrialisation, the major cities of the region such as Shanghai, Hangzhou and Nanjing are beginning industrial restructuring in the meantime.

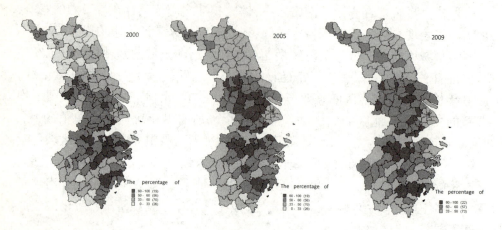

Figure 5.5 The spread of manufacturing development to the wider region of the YRD (the percentage of secondary industry of 2000, 2005 and 2009)

Source: Jiangsu Statistical Bureau, 2001, 2006, 2010; Shanghai Statistical Bureau, 2001, 2006, 2010; Zhejiang Statistical Bureau, 2001, 2006, 2010.

The de-concentration of industrial development and the industrial restructuring within the YRD are driven by both government push and market pull. On the one hand, the manufacturing environment in YRD began to change after a period of extraordinary development, especially over the most recent two years. Regionally speaking, a low-cost labour shortage has emerged in the area (Chen, 2007: 193). The demand for manpower has led to 'high turnovers, rising salaries, and shrinking margins' for the local manufacturing businesses (ibid). Additionally, some of the cities and counties that developed first in the region are on the verge of using up their land quota under the stringent central land policies. For example, the 'small' county-level-city Kunshan, beside the Shanghai metropolis, is said to be likely to run out of land for industrial use in the near future in its latest master plan (2007-2020). It is analysed that only 128.9 km^2 of land area is physically left, besides lake and compulsory agricultural land. If the industrial land grows in accordance with the average speed of about 22 km^2 every year that occurred from 2000 to 2008, then the left land area of 128.9 km^2 could only last for five to six years. Therefore, it is

突出。2009年,该地区大多数城市的制造业都为当地创造了45%以上的国内
生产总值,无一低于33%。总而言之,当整个大区域刚刚开始工业化进程时,
上海、杭州和宁波等主要城市已经着手进行产业结构调整。

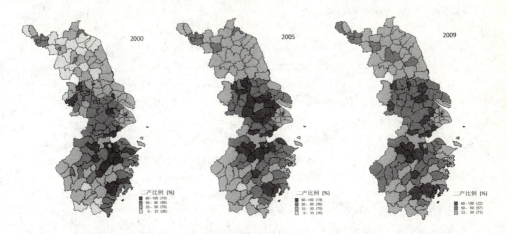

图5.5　制造业向长三角的外围地区扩散发展
(2000年、2005年及2009年第二产业的比重)

　　资料来源:江苏省统计局,2001年,2006年,2010年;上海市统计局,2001年,2006年,2010
年;浙江省统计局,2001年,2006年,2010年。

　　长三角地区工业发展的多中心模式和产业结构的调整主要受到政府推动
和市场拉动两方面的作用。一方面,长三角的制造业环境在经过一段时间的
突飞猛进后开始有所转变,其中最近两年的改变尤为明显。就整个区域而言,
廉价劳动力短缺的问题已经出现(Chen,2007:193)。对人力的需求已经导致
本地的制造业面临“人员流动加快,工资上涨和利润缩水”(同上)等问题。除
此之外,在严格的中央土地政策控制下,该地区一些率先发展起来的城市和县
镇濒临土地配额耗尽的边缘。以毗邻大都市上海的“小”县级市昆山为例,根
据最新的昆山市总体规划(2007—2020年),在不远的将来,昆山可能会面临无
地可用于工业生产扩张的尴尬境地。分析指出,除去湖泊及基本农田用地,昆
山实际仅存128.9平方公里土地可用于开发。如果工业用地继续按照2000至
2008年平均每年22平方公里的速度扩张,那么剩余的128.9平方公里土地仅

suggested that it is urgent for Kunshan to attract more profitable manufacturing enterprises to replace some of the existing low-end industries in order to sustain economic growth. In a word, the constraint of land resources has become the common challenge for many cities, especially for those which have been developing their manufacturing sector since the 1990s. As a result, industrial upgrading has been turned from a discursive slogan into real pressure. For example, the interviewee from Anting, Shanghai mentioned that:

> We would not consider small or lower-end manufacturing projects any more because these projects would not bring big revenue, but only huge land consumption. We were even considering relocating some less - valued industrial projects from our development zones to other cities. These potential or existing projects would be recommended to move to lagging areas such as the northern part of Jiangsu. Cities from northern Jiangsu would also come to Anting to attract projects that we don't want anymore. (Interview, government official, Anting, April 20, 2010)

Nationally speaking, it is reported that the manufacturing sector is leaving hubs along the coast, such as the YRD, to go to inland areas for cheaper labour forces, lower investment costs, and improved logistics and infrastructure. It is estimated that production costs are 10% higher in the coastal regions. For example, it is said the minimum monthly wage in Shanghai is 1,120 *yuan* while in Anhui is just 720 *yuan* (*Financial Times*, August 4, 2010, p.9). As a result, some rural backwaters in the centre and west of China, which hardly received any direct investment from overseas or other provinces, are now booming with inward investment. For instance, Anhui Province, which used to be the labour supply to the south and east coast, is now receiving industries that moved from the urbanised coast. The inland shift significantly gathered pace over the past two years owing to government investment in interior infrastructure, such as the high - speed railway system, since the global financial crisis (*Financial Times*, October 27, 2010, 3). Overall, the notably improved infrastructure and the lower production costs have changed the outlook for manufacturing in inland China and, moreover, challenged the advantage enjoyed by the coast, for example, the YRD region in manufacturing development. Manufacturing development is beginning to disperse from the core area around Shanghai to the periphery of the YRD region or even to inland China (Chen, 2007: 183).

On the other hand, the service sectors are also developing fairly fast in the region, accompanying the growth of manufacturing. Industrialisation is due to bring an increase in average wages, and higher consumer spending would be expected as a result. Henceforth, demand for services such as housing, catering,

可维持6年时间。因此,当务之急是引进利润更高的制造企业替代部分低端工业企业,以保持经济的持续增长。总而言之,土地资源的限制成为了许多城市共同面临的一大挑战,尤其是从20世纪90年代起就开始发展制造业的城市。因此,产业升级不再是一句空喊的口号,而是现实的压力所迫。一名来自上海安亭的受访者称:

> 我们不会再考虑小型或低端的制造业项目,因为这些项目不仅不能带来高额收益,还会消耗大量土地资源。我们甚至在考虑是否将部分价值较低的工业项目从安亭开发区迁移到别的城市。我们建议把这些现有或潜在的低端项目转移到其他发展相对落后的地区,比如苏北地区。苏北地区的城市也可以来安亭引进一些我们不再需要的项目。(与安亭政府官员的访谈,2010年4月20日)

就全国而言,有报导称制造业正从沿海中心城市,比如长三角地区,转向内陆地区,因为那里的劳动力更廉价,投资成本更低,并且物流和基础设施都已经得到改善。据估计,沿海地区的生产成本要高出10%。以最低月工资为例,上海是1,120元,而安徽则仅为720元(《金融时报》,2010年8月4日,第9版)。因此,在中国中西部地区,一些以往无法获得海外和其他省份直接投资的闭塞农村,随着对内投资的注入,也获得了蓬勃发展。比如安徽省曾是向东部和南部沿海城市输送劳动力的大省,而现在则在着力引进来自沿海城市化地区的工业。自从全球金融危机以来,由于政府开始对高铁系统等内地基础设施加大投入,工业向内地城市转移的步伐在过去两年中显著加快(《金融时报》,2010年10月27日,第3版)。总之,基础设施的显著改善和生产成本的低廉,使中国内地城市制造业的前景大为改观,使沿海城市的独有优势受到了挑战,比如长三角地区的制造业发展已开始从上海周边的核心地区向长三角地区的外围甚至内陆地区转移(Chen,2007:183)。

另一方面,随着制造业的发展,该地区的服务业也获得了高速发展。工业化将拉高平均工资的水平,并因此带动消费支出的增长。相应地,对于住房、餐饮、零售、家政、理发等服务业的需求也将随之增长,第三产业占国内生产总

retailing, housekeeping, hairdressing and so forth will grow, which is manifested by the increase in the rate of tertiary industry in GDP. Figure 5.6 shows the development of tertiary industry in YRD from 1995 to 2009. In 1995, tertiary development in most of the region was below a third of the GDP, without a single city above the rate of 50 percent. In 2000, the central cities of Shanghai, Nanjing and Hangzhou became the only three cities in which the tertiary proportion rose above 50 percent. In the meantime, the increase in tertiary development was also conspicuous in southern Jiangsu. In 2005, the tertiary rate of Nanjing and Hangzhou dropped below 50 percent due to administrative annexation with neighbouring counties. In 2009, the tertiary percentage of Shanghai, Nanjing, Hangzhou and Ningbo again reached over 50 percent and the tertiary development of the majority of cities in the region reached over a third of GDP. The increase of the proportion of the tertiary industry not only represents an increase in the untradable services, but also the emerging market for producer services. For instance, the role of Shanghai as the regional business centre has been largely strengthened since 2000. For example, the headquarters of many industrial enterprises were based in Shanghai, but the companies set up manufacturing factories in neighbouring secondary cities such as Suzhou. It is documented that Suzhou has attracted a total capitalisation of over $5 billion from Shanghai-based industrial companies since 1999, which turns Shanghai into the largest investor in Suzhou (Chen, 2007: 187). Tang and Zhao (2010) compared the urban network within the metropolitan region around Shanghai in 1995 and 2005, and found that these cities are gradually shifting from parallel industrial production to division of labour in accordance with chain of value. Throughout the decade, Shanghai, Nanjing and Hangzhou were largely occupied by technology-intensive manufacturing and producer services. Shanghai, in particular, performed as the headquarters for home and overseas businesses and acted as the gateway city for the region, with ample linkages to the outside world. Overall, industrial development has been much more diversified since 2000 compared to that of the 1990s. The emergence of a further division of labour within manufacturing, as well as the development of service sectors, has created more scope for complementary cooperation.

值比重不断提高便证明了这一推论。图5.6显示了从1995年到2009年长三角区域第三产业的发展。1995年,该区域大部分地区的第三产业占国内生产总值比重都不足1/3,各城市的这一比重都不超过50%。2000年,只有上海、南京和杭州这三个中心城市的第三产业比重超过50%。与此同时,江苏南部的第三产业也得到了显著发展。2005年,在与相邻县镇实行行政合并后,南京和杭州的第三产业比重降低到50%以下。2009年,上海、南京、杭州和宁波的第三产业比重再次超过50%,该区域其他大多数城市的第三产业占国内生产总值比重也都超过了1/3。第三产业比重的增长不仅显示了服务业的增长,也表明了生产性服务业新兴市场的崛起。举例而言,自2000年起,上海作为区域商业中心的地位大大增强,许多工业企业都把总部设在上海,把制造厂设立在相邻的二线城市,比如苏州。资料显示,1999年以来,苏州从总部位于上海的工业企业引进的资本总额超过50亿美元,上海因此成为苏州最大的投资来源地区(Chen, 2007:187)。唐子来和赵渺希(2010)比较了1995年和2005年围绕上海形成的城市密集区域内的城市网络后发现,这些城市逐渐从平行的工业生产关系转变为根据价值区段进行划分的劳动分工关系。这十年间,落户上海、南京和杭州的企业主要集中在技术密集型制造业和生产性服务业领域,尤其是上海,吸引了众多国内外企业的总部纷纷入驻,成为长三角地区的门户城市,与外界的联系非常广泛。总之,与20世纪90年代相比,2000年以来工业发展日趋多样化。制造业中劳动分工的进一步深化以及服务业的发展为互补合作创造了条件。

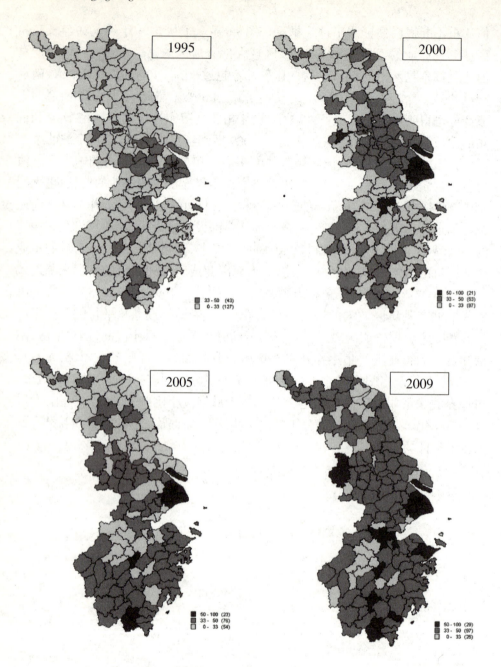

Figure 5.6 The development of tertiary industry in the YRD region
(the percentage of tertiary industry of 1995, 2000, 2005 and 2009)

Source: Jiangsu Statistical Bureau, 1996, 2001, 2006, 2010; Shanghai Statistical Bureau, 1996, 2001, 2006, 2010; Zhejiang Statistical Bureau, 1996, 2001, 2006, 2010.

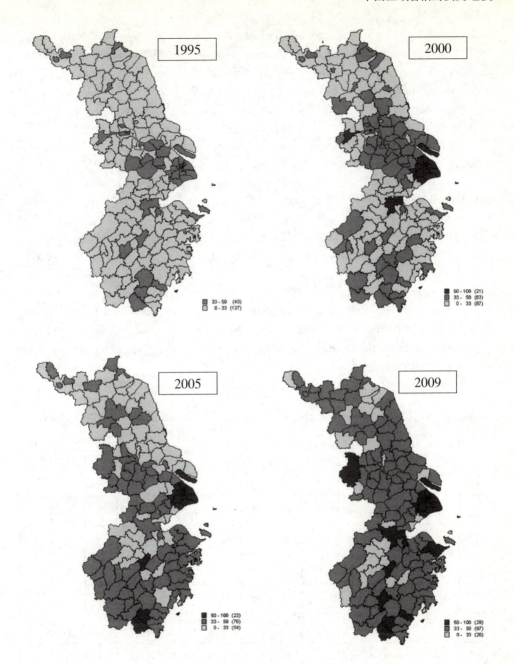

图5.6 长三角地区第三产业的发展

(1995年、2000年、2005年及2009年第三产业的比重)

资料来源:江苏省统计局,1996年,2001年,2006年,2010年;上海市统计局,1996年,2001年,2006年,2010年;浙江省统计局,1996年,2001年,2006年,2010年。

Furthermore, the functional division is facilitated by the dramatically improved inter-city and regional transport within the YRD region. Particularly in recent years, the building of a railway network instead of highway construction has been prioritised by the central government. The National Transport Ministry started to build an inter-city high-speed railway between Nanjing-Shanghai, Hangzhou-Shanghai and Nanjing-Hangzhou in 2007. The high-speed railway line between Nanjing-Shanghai was put into use on July 1, 2010, while the Hangzhou-Shanghai line began operating on Oct. 26 in 2010. As a consequence, the travel time from Nanjing to Shanghai only takes 73 minutes, whereas from Hangzhou to Shanghai only takes 45 minutes. The direct Nanjing-Hangzhou line also operated on March 28, 2013, which takes only 50 minutes compared to the current travel time of 3 hours on the expressway. Table 5.1 shows the current frequency of the high-speed railway within the YRD. At peak times, inter-city trains between Nanjing and Shanghai leave every 5 minutes. The operation of the reliable and fast inter-city transport makes one-day return not only possible, but much more convenient than before in the YRD region. This will enormously facilitate daily commuting within the region, besides the existing large number of business trips and logistics.

As demonstrated by Table 5.1, many small cities around big cities such as

Table 5.1 The frequency of the high-speed rail line within the YRD region

	Shang hai	Nan jing	Wu xi	Su zhou	Chang zhou	Zhen jiang	Kun shan	Dan yang	Hang zhou	Jia xing	Hai ning	Jia shan	Tong xiang	Yu hang
Shang hai	—	65	49	44	37	33	46	24	50	20	1	6	6	7
Nan jing	64	—	36	40	36	30	32	21	5	1	0	2	0	1
Wu xi	44	41	—	36	31	27	28	16	5	1	0	2	0	1
Su zhou	58	29	27	—	22	20	41	11	5	1	0	2	0	1
Chang zhou	38	35	30	33	—	25	26	19	5	1	0	2	0	1
Zhen jiang	30	33	21	24	25	—	22	9	4	0	0	2	0	0
Kun shan	50	33	31	28	25	23	—	16	3	0	0	2	0	0
Dan yang	21	24	18	17	14	15	12	—	1	0	0	0	0	1
Hang zhou	50	5	5	5	5	3	4	2	—	16	1	9	14	8
Jia xing	16	4	4	4	4	2	3	2	20	—	1	0	2	4

　　此外,长三角地区的城际和区域交通的显著改善也促进了职能分工。特别是近些年,中央政府将铁路网建设作为优先工作,排在了公路建设之上。国家交通部从2007年开始投入建设南京至上海、杭州至上海和南京至杭州的城际高铁。2010年7月1日南京至上海的高铁线路投入使用,2010年10月26日杭州至上海的高铁线路投入运营。这使得从南京到上海最短只需73分钟,而杭州到上海只要45分钟。南京至杭州的直达高铁线路也于2013年3月28日通车,南京到杭州将只需50分钟,而目前高速公路需用时三个小时。表5.1列出了长三角地区目前的高铁发车频率。高峰时,南京和上海间的城际列车每五分钟一班。可靠、快速的城际交通运营不仅使长三角地区内的单日往返成为可能,而且要比以前方便得多。除了目前频繁的商务旅行和物流运输之外,这也将大大方便人们日常的交通出行。

　　如表5.1所示,上海、杭州和南京等大城市周围的很多小城市已经变成高

表5.1 长三角区域内高速铁路发车频率

	上海	南京	无锡	苏州	常州	镇江	昆山	丹阳	杭州	嘉兴	海宁	嘉善	桐乡	余杭
上海	—	65	49	44	37	33	46	24	50	20	1	6	6	7
南京	64	—	36	40	36	30	32	21	5	1	0	2	0	1
无锡	44	41	—	36	31	27	28	16	5	1	0	2	0	1
苏州	58	29	27	—	22	20	41	11	5	1	0	2	0	1
常州	38	35	30	33	—	25	26	19	5	1	0	2	0	1
镇江	30	33	21	24	25	—	22	9	4	0	0	2	0	0
昆山	50	33	31	28	25	23	—	16	3	0	0	0	0	0
丹阳	21	24	18	17	14	15	12	—	1	0	0	0	0	1
杭州	50	5	5	5	5	3	4	2	—	16	1	9	14	8
嘉兴	16	4	4	4	4	2	3	2	20	—	1	0	2	4

Continued

	Shang hai	Nan jing	Wu xi	Su zhou	Chang zhou	Zhen jiang	Kun shan	Dan yang	Hang zhou	Jia xing	Hai ning	Jia shan	Tong xiang	Yu hang
Hai ning	1	0	0	0	0	0	0	0	1	1	—	0	0	0
Jia shan	9	1	1	1	1	1	1	0	6	2	0	—	1	0
Tong xiang	14	1	1	1	1	1	1	0	6	0	0	6	—	1
Yu hang	8	2	2	2	2	1	2	1	7	7	0	0	1	—

Source: compiled from www.shike.org.cn (accessed on Dec. 23, 2010).

Shanghai, Hangzhou and Nanjing have become the main stops on the high-speed rail line. For instance, the shuttle service runs 50 times between Kunshan and Shanghai every day. With the development of the fast link, the housing prices of these small cities have also rocketed. It is said that many young residents who are working in Shanghai are very interested in property in the smaller cities along the high-speed rail line, which offer a better environment and lower housing prices compared to Shanghai. In the past, the decentralisation of Shanghai's population was only directed to the suburban districts of Shanghai, but now Shanghai could develop an integral housing market within outer-suburbs such as Songjiang and Jiangding, as well as the nearby secondary cities such as Jiashan, Jiaxing, and Kunshan, due to the improvement of regional transport. As a result, the region will not only benefit from economically networked clusters surrounding Shanghai, but is also going to possess an inherently integral housing and labour market. In other words, there is wider scale for spatial and functional division of labour between cities within the region. The surrounding region could not only develop manufacturing, but also residential and service industries owing to the enhancement of transport connectivity.

5.5 Conclusion

This chapter analyses the development of the regional economy and the regionalisation process of the YRD region before and after the economic reform. During the planned system, the regional economy in the YRD was segmented between jurisdictions and economic sectors. Ruled under the central command, there was no natural economic flow in the local economies. After economic reform, horizontal economic linkages were advocated by the central government, and the arbitrary division of labour between urban and rural areas

	上海	南京	无锡	苏州	常州	镇江	昆山	丹阳	杭州	嘉兴	海宁	嘉善	桐乡	余杭
海宁	1	0	0	0	0	0	0	0	1	1	—	0	0	0
嘉善	9	1	1	1	1	1	1	0	6	2	0	—	1	0
桐乡	14	1	1	1	1	1	1	0	6	0	0	6	—	1
余杭	8	2	2	2	2	1	2	1	7	7	0	0	1	—

资料来源：根据网站 www.shike.org.cn 汇编（网站访问日：2010年12月23日）。

铁线路的主要站点。比如，昆山和上海之间每日的短程往返车次有50次。随着高速铁路的发展，这些小城市的房价也一路飙升。据称，许多在上海工作的年轻人对高铁沿线的小城市住房表现出极大的兴趣；与上海相比，这些小城市的环境更舒适、房价更低。过去，上海人口只是向本市郊区扩散，但现在上海有望发展成为一个涵盖远郊区县（如松江和嘉定）以及邻近二线城市（如嘉善、嘉兴和昆山）的综合性房地产市场，这都得益于区域交通的改善。因此，长三角地区不仅能从上海周边的经济网络化集群发展中获益，还将形成一个整合的房地产和劳动力市场。换言之，长三角区域内城市的分工合作将有更大的空间。由于交通连通性得到了改善，周边地区在发展制造业的同时，还可以发展房地产业和服务业。

第五节　结论

本章分析了经济改革前后长三角地区经济发展的历程和该地区的区域化过程。在计划经济时期，长三角地区的区域经济存在行政管辖区与经济部门之间的分割。受中央指令的约束，各地方经济体内不存在自然的经济流动。经济改革之后，中央政府大力提倡横向经济联系，废除了城乡之间硬性的劳动

was also abolished. In the context, many TVEs in the rural area began to develop business links with SOEs in the central cities, and the division of labour began to evolve between urban and rural areas in terms of manufacturing. The previous pattern of cities developing industries and villages developing agriculture was broken by cities providing technology and engineering and villages undertaking initial processing. Overall, horizontal economic flows were just emerging in the 1980s after the economic reform.

In the 1990s, spectacular regional growth was witnessed in the YRD region due to the opening up of Pudong, Shanghai and the infusion of foreign investment. The development model based on supply - side policies such as effective administration, lax development policies and land management to attract foreign investment became widespread in the region, from urban to rural areas. The development of TVEs suffered disadvantages due to its own problems and outside challenges from foreign investors. The extensive development of export-oriented manufacturing soon turned the YRD into another economic hub similar to the PRD. The regionalisation of manufacturing development made the region more and more polycentric in spatial structure in terms of industrial structure, GDP growth, inward investment, industrial output and so forth. To some extent, the development of economic flows and logistics brought the cities within the region into regionalised production chains. Furthermore, cities within the region were also experiencing some common problems such as environmental degradation and land encroachment after the excessive manufacturing development. To sum up, the extended metropolitan region of the YRD was formed by the 1990s with the phenomenal process of industrialisation from primary industries. The physical or morphological phenomenon of urban expansion is not only due to urbanisation and suburbanisation, but also to the entrepreneurial development of individual cities. Industries began to be clustered in some core areas such as the development zones of the cities due to the active role of the local government. Some manufacturing towns around the major cities have become dynamic and competitive manufacturing clusters for certain specialised products for both global and regional markets (Chen, 2007: 190). However, fierce competition also exists between these clusters, such as the competition in IT manufacturing between Suzhou and Kunshan (Wang and Lee, 2007). This is because the clusters were mainly oriented to global manufacturing and did not possess close inter-relationships.

Since 2000, the regionalisation of the YRD region has reached a new stage. The cities in the wider region started rapid industrialisation, while the central cities in the region began industrial restructuring. The different development stages of the cities provide the scope for vertical cooperation

分工。在此背景下,农村地区很多乡镇企业开始与中心城市的国有企业建立起业务联系。在制造业方面,城乡间的劳动分工逐步发生变化,打破了传统的"城市发展工业"、"乡村发展农业"的模式,转变为由城市提供技术和工程设计,由乡村从事初加工的模式。总体而言,经济改革之后,上世纪80年代横向经济流动还只是刚刚兴起。

上世纪90年代,上海浦东的对外开放和外资注入带动了长三角地区的经济迅猛增长。长三角地区内的城乡开始广泛推广以供给刺激政策为基础的发展模式,比如有效的行政治理、宽松的发展政策和土地管理,目的是吸引外商投资。因为受到自身体制问题的困扰和来自国外投资者的外部竞争,乡镇企业的发展遭受到挫折。出口导向型制造业得到广泛发展,使长三角地区迅速转变成了类似于珠三角地区的另一个区域经济中心。制造业发展的区域化使长三角地区在产业结构、国内生产总值增长、对内投资、工业产值等方面逐渐呈现出空间结构多中心化的趋势。在某种程度上,经济流和物流的发展将长三角地区的各个城市凝聚成了区域化的生产链。此外,这些城市在经历了制造业的过度发展之后,也面临一些普遍问题,如环境恶化和土地侵蚀。总之,随着工业化的广泛推进,到上世纪90年代,长三角地区形成了范围更广的大都市区域。城市的地域或形态扩张现象不仅源于城市化和郊区化的发展,也是由于各个城市的企业式发展。在地方政府的积极作用下,工业逐渐向部分核心地区聚集,如各个城市的开发区。大城市周边的部分制造业城镇已经成为活跃而又颇具竞争力的制造业集群,为全球和区域市场生产某些专门产品(Chen,2007:190)。但这些集群之间也存在着激烈的竞争,比如苏州和昆山在信息技术制造业方面的竞争(Wang和Lee,2007)。这是因为这些集群都主要面对全球制造业市场,而且相互间的联系并不紧密。

自2000年以来,长三角地区的区域化步入新的阶段。在该区域中,更大范围内的各个城市开始进入快速工业化的进程,而中心城市则开始着手产业结构调整。由于这些城市处于不同的发展阶段,因此为区域内的服务业和制造

between the service sector and manufacturing within the region. Meanwhile, functional connectivity is also facilitated by improved regional transport such as the operation of a high-speed rail line within the region. In addition, the fast inter-city link also makes daily commuting between central cities and the surrounding small cities more convenient, which would facilitate the new 'suburbanisation' that is common in Western countries, where people working in large and central cities live in the surrounding small cities. Overall, a more complicated pattern of functional connectivity is just developing in the YRD region.

The analysis in the chapter extends the previous YRD overview on economic development and regional transformation forward to the recent stage beyond excessive competition and spatial polarisation. It is argued that the regionalisation of the YRD region is entering a new stage and economic and functional integration is just emerging in the YRD region after decades of market development after economic reform. The development tendency may match with the new urbanisation form of polycentric mega city-region thesis proposed by Hall and Pain (2006). In the Western literature, the transition to the new form of metropolis is suggested to be fed by 'economic restructuring, digital telecommunications, demographic shifts, and neoliberal policies' (Lang and Knox, 2009: 790), while in China, some of the intriguing factors may be the same as those in Western countries such as the development of digital technology and regional transport. However, at the same time, what is different in China is that the dispersal of urbanisation to the wider region is not triggered by rising costs in the central cities in terms of services and businesses, but is due to the rising costs of labour and land in manufacturing. The service economy and integrated housing and labour market are just developing in China. It is argued that the ever-increasing commuting and business flows will be the main driver for integrated economic development. Nevertheless, the development of an economically integrated region does not mean that the region is functioning as a coordinated actor. In fact, the region comprises a complexity of local actors. The following two chapters will examine the process of regional governance and planning development in the YRD region.

业的纵向合作提供了空间。同时,随着区域内高铁线路的投入运营,区域交通得到改善,加强了区域内的功能连通。另外,快速的城际交通也使得中心城市与周边小城市间的日常交通更加便捷,从而带动了新一轮的"郊区化"。这种"郊区化"现象在西方国家较为常见,人们倾向于在大城市和中心城市工作,但在周边小城市居住。整体而言,长三角地区内部更为复杂的功能联系才刚刚开始发展。

　　本章延伸了早期关于长三角地区经济发展和区域转型的研究,指出现有区域发展正在超越过去过度竞争和空间极化的阶段。本研究认为长三角地区的区域化正在迈入一个新的阶段:经过经济改革之后几十年的市场发展,经济和功能整合正在长三角地区兴起。这一发展趋势可能与 Hall 和 Pain(2006)提出的多中心巨型城市区域理论中的城市化新形式相吻合。在西方文献中,向新型大都市的转变被认为是受到"经济重组、数字通讯、人口结构转变和新自由主义政策"的刺激(Lang 和 Knox,2009:790),而在中国,其中有些启动因素可能与西方国家相同,例如数字技术和区域交通的发展。但同时也存在着不同之处,即中国的城市化之所以向更广泛的地区扩散,并不是由于中心城市服务和商业成本不断上升引起的,而是由于制造业的劳动力和土地成本攀升所致。中国的服务经济以及一体化的房地产和劳动力市场还只是刚刚起步。本研究认为,交通和商业流动的日益频繁将成为该区域经济联动发展的主要动力。尽管如此,经济上的一体化并不意味着该区域将成为一个行动一致的整体。实际上,该区域中存在着各级地方行动主体。接下来的两章将分析长三角地区的区域管治和规划发展过程。

第六章

CHAPTER SIX

The Changing Relationship Between Shanghai and Jiangsu: The Emergence of Inter-locality Collaboration

6.1 Introduction

In the centrally-planned economy during the Socialist period, inter-city relationships were not spontaneous, but were decided by the economic plan and central command. After market reform in 1978, economic mobility developed with increasingly intense flows of trade, people, traffic, logistics and capital. Nevertheless, the natural market flow was hampered by artificial blockades and adverse competition between cities or provincial governments (Chien and Gordon, 2008; Zhao and Zhang, 1999). However, recently, a regional discourse of inter-city cooperation has appeared in both governmental reports and Chinese academic literature (Hong, 2009; Ji et al., 2006; Tao, 2007; Wang, 2008; Wang, 2009; B. J. Yang, 2004; Zhang et al., 2007; Zou and Shi, 2004). The emergence of a regional agenda to some extent represents the policy response to the pervading conflicts and competition between different jurisdictions. Meanwhile, there is an emerging body of literature from overseas researchers documenting the initiatives of regional governance in China (Luo and Shen, 2009; Wu and Zhang, 2009, 2010; Xu, 2008; Xu and Yeh, 2010, 2011; Yeh and Xu, 2008; Zhang, 2006; Zhang and Wu, 2006). For example, Zhang (2006) suggests that Chinese cities are experiencing a change from inter-city competition to regional collaboration. However, Zhang's paper does not answer to what extent collaborative regional governance departs from previous individually based urban entrepreneurialism.

Rather than assuming that regional governance is established in China, this chapter seeks to investigate the actual transformation process of regional governance. For the purpose, it is considered important to distinguish the process of economic regionalisation and the development of regional political institutions. The distinction is helpful to understand the nature of Chinese emerging regional space. Jones and MacLeod (2004) distinguished the process by 'regional (economic) space' and 'space of regionalism'. The latter is dealt with from the governance perspective, following the 'old' political regionalism between the 1960s and 1970s, when the establishment of regional government was witnessed across many Western countries. However, the former is associated with the 'new regionalism' literature, in which it is conceived that the region is the unit of economic agglomeration in the post-Fordist and knowledge

第六章　上海与江苏的关系变化：地区间合作的兴起

第一节　引言

在改革开放前的社会主义时期，城市间的关系不是自发形成的，而是由经济计划和中央指令决定的。1978年市场改革以后，随着日益频繁的贸易往来、人员和资金的流动，以及日益发达的物流和交通运输，经济流动性有所提高。尽管如此，市场的自然流动却阻碍重重：有人为的封锁，也有城市之间或省政府之间恶性竞争的影响（Chien 和 Gordon，2008；Zhao 和 Zhang，1999）。然而，最近的政府报告和中国学术文献中均谈及城市间合作的问题（洪世健，2009；纪晓岚等，2006；陶希东，2007；王川兰，2008；王枫云，2009；杨保军，2004；张颢瀚等，2007；邹兵和施源，2004）。区域议程的出现在某种程度上是对广泛冲突和不同辖区间竞争的政策回应。与此同时，出现了一批海外研究者撰写的文献著作，详细记载了中国区域管治的举措（Luo 和 Shen，2009；Wu 和 Zhang，2009，2010；Xu，2008；Xu 和 Yeh，2010，2011；Yeh 和 Xu，2008；Zhang，2006；Zhang 和 Wu，2006）。例如，Zhang（2006）指出中国城市正在经历从城市间竞争到区域合作的转变。但是，Zhang 的论文中并未回答区域协作管治是否脱离了先前基于个体的城市经营主义。

本章并不认为区域管治模式已在中国建立，只是试图研究区域管治转型的实际过程。为此，区分经济区域化进程与区域政治制度的发展十分重要。两者的区别有助于人们理解中国新兴区域空间的本质。Jones 和 MacLeod（2004）使用"区域（经济）空间"和"区域主义空间"的概念来区别这两个过程。后者从管治视角出发，依照的是20世纪60、70年代间的"旧"政治区域主义，当时众多西方国家都建立了区域政府。而前者则与"新区域主义"文献有关，此类文献将区域设想为后福特主义和知识经济中的经济集聚单位（Krugman， economy (Krugman, 1991; Scott, 2001; Storper, 1995). The chapter then highlights that 'the formation of any given regional map is reflective—and indeed constitutive—of an unevenly developing, often overlapping and superimposing mosaic of economic practices, political mobilizations, cultural performances and institutional accomplishments' (Jones and MacLeod, 2004: 433). That is, in the meantime, the formation of a region is socially and politically constructed to manage local conflicts and struggles (Jones, 2001; Jones and MacLeod, 1999; Jonas and Ward, 2007; Ward and Jonas, 2004).

The distinction helps to investigate emerging cooperation and integration practices in China by disentangling regional economic development and regional institutional development. Following the work of Jones and MacLeod (2004), this chapter aims to answer the following questions through a case study of the YRD region: is there inter-city cooperation in China? What is the scope of these practices? How intensive are these collaborations? What are the conditions that led to the change from development based on individual cities to cooperation between different cities? This study focuses on the border region between Shanghai and Jiangsu province to examine the trajectory of a changing inter-city relationship.It is then argued that although the development of regional economics is where the discursive regional governance is embedded, it does not necessarily mean that the development of regional governance is well established in reality.

The location of the cross-border region is illustrated in Figure 6.1. The city of Kunshan in Jiangsu borders the Jiading district of Shanghai. Kunshan is one of the six county-level cities beneath the municipality of Suzhou. Before the 1990s, Kunshan developed slowly and was mainly engaged in agricultural production. However, the rural county was transformed into a manufacturing district in subsequent years through attracting foreign investment and export-oriented industries. The Jiading district, located west of the city proper of Shanghai, is a suburban district of Shanghai municipality. Jiading used to be a county led by the Shanghai municipality, and was converted from a rural county to a suburban district in 1992. The key industry of Jiading has been involved in auto-manufacture since the development of a joint venture with Volkswagen in Jiading in 1985. Because these places focused on different economic and industrial specialisations and their built-up areas were relatively compact and separated by a vast rural hinterland, the relationship between the counties of Kunshan and Jiading was very loose in the 1980s. However, the relationship between the two became very tense at the turn of the new millennium, as Shanghai decided to take advantage of its vast suburban area to sharpen its edge in attracting foreign investment. Consequently, the cross-border region of Kunshan and Jiading was turned into a battlefield for developing

1991；Scott，2001；Storper，1995）。本章继而强调了"任何既有区域空间的形成都反映了（事实上构成了）经济、政治、文化和制度的不均衡、交错重叠发展"（Jones 和 MacLeod，2004：433）。也就是说，区域的构成不仅是经济发展的结果，同时也是社会和政治环境塑造的结果，以解决地方的冲突和争斗（Jones，2001；Jones 和 MacLeod，1999；Jonas 和 Ward，2007；Ward 和 Jonas，2004）。

这一区分理清了区域经济发展和区域制度发展的概念，有助于研究中国新兴的合作与一体化实践。依据 Jones 和 MacLeod（2004）的上述理念，本章旨在通过长三角地区的案例研究回答以下问题：中国存在城市间的合作吗？此类合作的领域有哪些？合作程度如何？哪些条件导致了城市由各自发展转向城市间的合作发展？本研究以上海市与江苏省的交界地区为重点研究对象，来审视城市间关系变化的轨迹。随后本章指出，尽管区域经济的发展促使了区域管治讨论的出现，但这并不意味着现实中区域管治已经建立成熟。

交界区域的位置详见图 6.1。江苏省的昆山市与上海市的嘉定区相邻。昆山是苏州市下属的六个县级市之一。20 世纪 90 年代以前，昆山发展缓慢，主要从事农业生产。然而，随后几年通过吸引外资和发展出口导向型产业，昆山由农业城市转变成了工业区。嘉定区是上海市西面的郊区。嘉定曾经是上海市的下属县，1992 年从上海下属县转变成市郊的辖区。自 1985 年与德国大众合资的上海大众设在嘉定以来，汽车制造业就成为了嘉定的支柱产业。由于昆山和嘉定侧重的经济和产业领域不同，建成区相对紧凑且中间又隔着一大片农村地区，所以在 20 世纪 80 年代，昆山各县与嘉定县的关系十分松散。然而，进入 21 世纪后两地之间的关系变得十分紧张，原因在于上海决定利用其广大郊区来加强吸引外资的优势。结果昆山和嘉定交界的地区变成了两地竞

export-oriented industries. Nevertheless, initiatives to promote regionalisation are more recently being witnessed within this very region, especially between the town of Huaqiao under the city of Kunshan and the town of Anting under Jiading district. Therefore, the border region offers a very good case to understand the emergence of a regional agenda and its underlying dynamics.

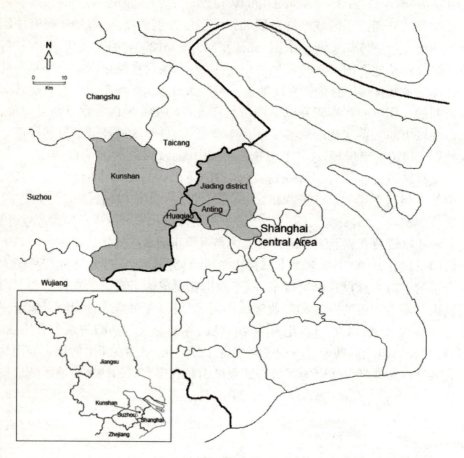

Figure 6.1 The border area between Shanghai and Jiangsu
Source: compiled by the author.

The chapter is organised as follows. First of all, the rivalry and competition at the border of Shanghai and Jiangsu is documented. Secondly, the new phenomenon of cooperative development is scrutinised. The scope of collaboration and collaborative practices is described, and the intensity of collaboration is assessed. The next section explains why local governments changed from engaging in hostile competition to seek collaboration. Then, the characteristics and dynamics of emerging regional governance in China are

相发展出口导向型产业的战场。尽管如此,在这个交界地区,尤其是在昆山市下属的花桥镇和嘉定区下属的安亭镇之间,最近出现了越来越多推动区域化的举措。因此,这个交界地区对研究区域议程的兴起及其根本推动力提供了一个很好的案例。

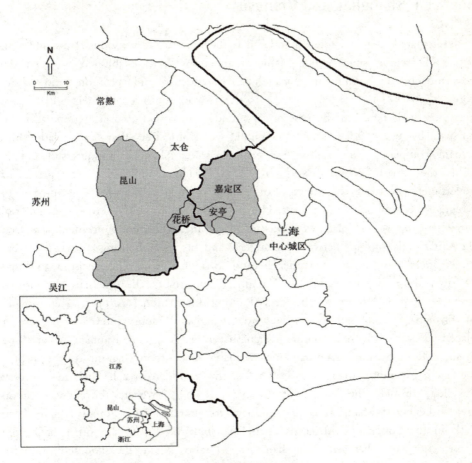

图6.1 上海与江苏交界地区

来源:笔者编制。

本章的内容结构如下。首先,记述了上海与江苏在交界地区的对立竞争状况。其后,审视了两地间合作发展的新现象,并描述了合作的范围及合作开展的活动,评估了合作的紧密程度。接下来解释了地方政府为何不再搞恶性竞争转而寻求合作。然后,总结了在中国兴起的区域管治的特点和推动力。

summarised. Finally, the chapter concludes that the politics around region building in China do not depart substantially from local entrepreneurialism.

6.2 Rivalry in manufacturing projects in the border area between Shanghai and Jiangsu

Integrated regional development has become a very popular discourse in the YRD region since 2000. Many organisations were established between the governments or within the academics to discuss and promote inter - city cooperation (Zhang et al., 2008: 155). However, the agreements that have been reached tend to be rhetorical (ibid). In other words, cooperation is pursued by every government on public occasions, but inter - city relationships remain competitive in reality. For example, after Shanghai's successful bid to hold the 2010 World Expo in 2002, Jiangsu and Zhejiang provincial government declared the strategy of jointly holding the Expo as a pledge to integrated economic development (Lu and Shi, 2008: 160). However, no real agreement or action plan was put in place after the pronouncement. In fact, the inter - relationship between Shanghai and its neighbouring provinces were under great pressure at the time, because Shanghai made the decision to build its own deep - water seaport in Yangshan, and move the international airlines from Hongqiao Airport to the new Pudong International Airport. The moving of Shanghai's international airlines to Shanghai Pudong International Airport placed export - oriented southern Jiangsu at a great disadvantage. The time distance from Suzhou, Kunshan and Wujiang in southern Jiangsu to the airport increased by more than two hours, as the route to reach the new airport travelled through the city centre (ibid: 275). However, the new location greatly benefited Shanghai's IT industry, for instance, the Songjiang Hi - Tech Park in the Songjiang district of Shanghai (ibid: 175). On the other hand, the construction of Shanghai Yangshan seaport also raised the competition with Beilun port in Ningbo, Zhejiang (Lu and Shi, 2008: 274; Zhang and Wu, 2006: 10). Under pressure, Zhejiang province built Kuahai Bridge from Ningbo to Jiaxing, which cost more than 1.85 billion *yuan*, in order to improve the accessibility of Beilun port (Zhang et al., 2007: 314-317). Henceforth, Jiangsu and Zhejiang claimed the giant Shanghai was not cooperative at all in economic integration. The above cases demonstrate that inter-city relationships are still very tense, especially in terms of economic development, for example, in manufacturing development, investment attraction, and strategic infrastructure construction. The following section examines the case of 'Project 173' and the consequences that it caused to illustrate the strained relationship during the period.

最后,本章得出结论,围绕中国区域建设的政治因素实质上并未脱离原先的地方经营主义。

第二节　苏沪交界地区在制造业项目上的竞争

区域一体化发展自2000年以来成为了长三角地区的流行语。政府间或学术界成立了许多组织来讨论和推进城市间的合作(张京祥等,2008:155)。然而,达成的协议不免流于形式(同上)。换言之,在公开场合所有政府都在寻求合作,而实际上城市间的关系仍充满竞争。例如,上海于2002年成功申办2010年世界博览会后,江苏和浙江两省政府当即宣布共同举办世博会的战略,以确保取得一体化经济发展(陆阳和史文学,2008:160)。然而,宣布之后两省并未真正落实任何协议或行动计划。事实上,当时上海与邻省之间的关系正承受着巨大的压力,原因是上海决定在洋山建立自己的深水港,并将国际航线从虹桥机场转移至新建的浦东国际机场。上海国际航线向浦东国际机场的转移使得以出口为导向的苏南地区处于非常不利的地位。位于苏南的苏州、昆山和吴江到浦东国际机场的时间比到虹桥机场增加了两个多小时,因为从这些城市到达新机场的路线需穿过上海市中心(同上,2008:275)。然而,新机场的位置为上海的IT产业带来了很大优势,比如位于上海松江区的松江高科技园区就大受其益(同上,2008:175)。另一方面,上海洋山港的建立也使其与浙江宁波北仑港的竞争更加激烈(陆阳和史文学,2008:274;Zhang和Wu,2006:10)。迫于压力,浙江省建造了从宁波到嘉兴的跨海大桥,耗资高达18.5亿元,以使北仑港的交通更为便利(张颢瀚等,2007:314-317)。自此以后,江苏和浙江均谴责实力雄厚的上海在经济一体化方面根本没有展现出合作的态度。上述案例表明城市间关系仍旧十分紧张,尤其是在经济发展方面,如制造业发展、招商引资和战略性基础设施建设等领域。下一节将分析"173工程"的案例及其产生的后果,以阐明当时的紧张关系。

6.2.1 The launch of 'Project 173' by Shanghai

The so-called 'Project 173' was launched by Shanghai in 2003. 'Project 173' refers to three development zones with a total area of 173 square kilometres in suburban Songjiang, Qingpu and Jiading districts (Figure 6.2). The development of 'Project 173' originated from the rival relationship between Shanghai and Kunshan with regard to attracting overseas investment. In contrast to spectacular industrial development in neighbouring cities, Shanghai felt itself to be marginalised in the competition for foreign-invested manufacturing industries. The municipal government had striven to promote the development of the tertiary sector in the central city in order to build itself into a global city before 2000, and did not place much emphasis on manufacturing development in the suburbs. As a result, manufacturing industry in Shanghai did not see fast growth, compared with other neighbouring cities. The suburban districts enjoyed few preferential policies from the municipal government of Shanghai. With the slow growth of manufacturing industries, Shanghai's GDP growth rate and FDI lagged behind those of the municipality of Suzhou (Table 6.1). Under these circumstances, Shanghai launched 'Project 173' in 2003 in order to enhance its attractiveness for overseas investment and maintain double-digit GDP growth.

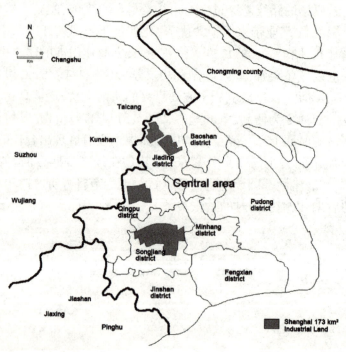

Figure 6.2 The location of Project 173 in Shanghai

Source: compiled by the author.

一、上海启动"173工程"

上海于2003年启动了所谓的"173工程",计划在上海市郊的松江、青浦、嘉定三区设立试点开发区(图6.2),因三地的总面积为173平方公里,故称"173工程"。这一项目的启动源于上海与昆山在吸引外资方面的竞争。面对相邻城市迅猛的工业发展,上海感到自己在外资制造业的竞争中处于边缘化的境地。上海市政府为把上海建设成为国际化城市,在2000年以前一直致力于推动中心城区第三产业的发展,并没有对郊区的制造业给予重视,也没有向其提供优惠政策,致使上海的制造业发展不及周边其他城市。由于制造业发展缓慢,上海的国内生产总值增长率和外商直接投资额均落后于苏州市(表6.1)。在此种情形下,为了提高自身吸引外资的能力并将GDP增长率维持在两位数,上海在2003年启动了"173工程"。

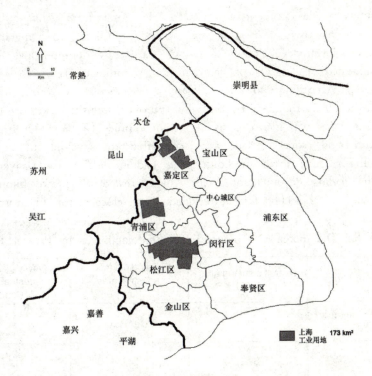

图6.2 上海"173工程"开发区位置

来源:笔者编制。

Table 6.1 GDP growth rate and FDI in Shanghai, Jiangsu and Suzhou

Year	GDP growth rate (%)			FDI (100 million USD)		
	Shanghai	Jiangsu	Suzhou	Shanghai	Jiangsu	Suzhou
1990	3.5	8.2	14.7	1.77	1.4	0.34
1995	14.3	15.4	25.3	32.5	47.8	23.3
2000	11.0	10.6	13.4	31.6	64.2	28.8
2001	10.5	10.1	14.3	43.9	71.2	30.2
2002	11.3	11.7	18.2	50.3	103.7	48.1

Source: Shanghai Statistical Yearbook (2002, 2004); Jiangsu Statistical Yearbook (2009); Suzhou Statistical Yearbook (2007).

These three development zones were not built from scratch, but were based on existing town-level industrial districts. 'Project 173' upgraded these former town-level development zones to the status of municipal level and further allocated a significant amount of additional land for industrial development. According to the Shanghai Municipal Government No.37 Document in 2003, the area of officially approved industrial land in the three development zones was increased by about three times (Table 6.2). In order to create extra land, some towns were converted to development zones. For example, the original town of Loutang in Jiading district was converted into part of the Jiading development zone, which created 32 square kilometres of industrial land. Over 40,000 former residents were relocated for this reason.

Table 6.2 The increase of planned industrial land area by Project 173

development zone	Overall planning area (km²)	Existing planned industrial area (km²)	Newly planned industrial area (km²)
Qingpu experimental development zone	56.2	16.2	40
Jiading experimental development zone	57.2	24.8	32.4
Songjiang experimental development zone	59.8	20.6	39.2
Total	173.2	61.6	111.6

Source: compiled from Shanghai Municipal Government No.37 Document of 2003.

表6.1 上海、江苏和苏州的国内生产总值增长率和外商直接投资额

年份	GDP增长率(%)			FDI(亿美元)		
	上海	江苏	苏州	上海	江苏	苏州
1990	3.5	8.2	14.7	1.77	1.4	0.34
1995	14.3	15.4	25.3	32.5	47.8	23.3
2000	11.0	10.6	13.4	31.6	64.2	28.8
2001	10.5	10.1	14.3	43.9	71.2	30.2
2002	11.3	11.7	18.2	50.3	103.7	48.1

来源:上海统计年鉴(2002,2004)、江苏统计年鉴(2009)、苏州统计年鉴(2007)。

这三个开发区都不是从零起步,而是在已有乡镇级工业区的基础上建立起来的。"173工程"将这些镇级开发区升级为市级开发区,并额外分配了大量土地用于工业发展。根据上海市政府2003年第37号文件,三大开发区正式获批的工业用地面积比原计划增加了两倍左右(表6.2)。为了提供更多用地,一些城镇也被划入开发区范围。例如,原嘉定区的娄塘镇就被划定为嘉定开发区的一部分,使工业用地面积增加了32平方公里。4万余娄塘居民因此被重新安置。

表6.2 上海"173工程"计划工业用地面积的增长

开发区	计划工业用地总面积 (平方公里)	原计划工业用地面积 (平方公里)	新增工业用地面积 (平方公里)
青浦试点开发区	56.2	16.2	40
嘉定试点开发区	57.2	24.8	32.4
松江试点开发区	59.8	20.6	39.2
总计	173.2	61.6	111.6

来源:根据上海市政府2003年第37号文件编制。

Furthermore, some preferential policies were piloted in these development zones in order to serve investors better. Henceforth, the three development zones were named 'pilot zones' of Shanghai. Two official documents, 'the Implementation Guideline of Shanghai Municipality for Improvement of Investment Environment in Shanghai's Pilot Development Zones (Shanghai Municipal Government No.72 Document in 2002)' and 'Suggestions of Shanghai Municipality for Improvement of Foreign Investment Environment in Shanghai (Shanghai Municipal Government No.73 Document in 2002)', were released by the municipal government to carry out these pro-business regulatory changes. According to these documents, enterprises in the three pilot zones enjoyed VAT exemption, a lower standard of social insurance obligations, half land reclamation fees, and flexible administrative institutions (for more details, please see Table 6.3). A memorandum was signed between Shanghai Municipal Revenue Bureau, Real Estate Management Bureau, Foreign Investment Committee, Industrial and Trade Bureau, Price Bureau, Finance Bureau and other related departments to ensure the implementation of the proposed policy as a joint programme.

Table 6.3 The special policies for the Jiading,
Qingpu and Songjiang experimental development zones

Type	Content
Land	Guarantee of land supply for significant investment projects; Special land quota designation for experimental development zones; Three years' delay for balance between occupation and compensation for arable land is allowed; In the tenth five-year period (2000-2005), expenses of taxation on land were halved to decrease land cost.
Social insurance	Experiment of particular social insurance institutions for small towns, at lower standards than normal social insurance.
Tax	During the tenth five year period (2000-2005), local tax revenue was allowed to be totally kept by the development zone as a special fund for infrastructure construction and investment attraction; Two years of tax exemption and three years of half tax rate for enterprises with additional investment; A decrease in the tax rate for foreign enterprises.
Utility charges	Public hearing system on utility fees; Clearance of unreasonable charges; Reduction or exemption of administrative charges for significant foreign investments.
Infrastructure	Improved telecom and Internet services; Help to solve problems of workers' accommodation; Improved living environment, for example, schools and hospitals.
Administrative speed and flexibility	Promotion of immediate customs entry services; Single unified process for varied administration procedures and charges.
Incentive	Responsibility and evaluation system is carried out for administrative leaders and staff of development zones in accordance with investment attraction and administration service improvement.

Source: Compiled from Shanghai Municipal Government No. 72 and No. 73 Documents, 2002.

此外,为了更好地服务投资商,三大开发区还试行了一些优惠政策。它们也因此被称为上海的"试点园区"。市政府发布了两份正式文件——《上海试点园区改善投资环境的实施意见》(上海市政府2002年第72号文件)和《关于进一步改善上海投资环境的若干意见》(上海市政府2002年第73号文件),以落实这些有利于商业发展的法规变革。根据这些文件,对三大试点园区的企业实行的优惠政策包括:免征增值税、降低社保缴费标准、耕地开垦费减半征收、增加行政制度的灵活性等(详情见表6.3)。上海市财税局、房地产资源管理局、外资委、工商局、物价局、财政局以及其他相关部门之间还签订了一份备忘录来确保这些政策的统一实施。

表6.3 嘉定、青浦、松江试点开发区优惠政策

类别	内容
土地	确保重大投资项目用地供应; 在试点开发区实行特别的土地配额制度; 允许耕地占补平衡延期三年实现; "十五"期间(2001—2005年),用地税费减半征收,以降低用地成本。
社会保险	试行小城镇特殊保险制度,实施比一般社保标准更低的标准。
税费	"十五"期间(2001—2005年)当地税收全部纳入开发区专项发展资金,用于基础设施建设和招商引资; 对追加投资的企业实行"两免三减半"的税收政策; 降低外资企业的税率。
公用事业费	对各项公用事业费用实行听证制度; 取消不合理收费; 减少或免征重大外资项目的行政费用。
基础设施	改善电信和因特网服务; 帮助解决职工住宿问题; 改善生活居住环境,如开办学校、医院等。
行政速度和灵活性	提供即时报关服务; 对多种行政程序和收费实施统一的工作流程。
激励政策	建立开发区行政官员和工作人员责任与评估制度,并以吸引外资水平和行政服务改善程度作为其衡量标准。

来源:根据上海市政府2002年第72号、第73号文件编制。

As demonstrated by the above policy initiatives, Shanghai took deliberate action to improve its weak position in terms of investment cost, land supply and government services. For example, the reason why the municipal government expanded the area of allocated industrial land was not because industrial land resources were largely consumed or leased out in the suburbs; in fact, the originally planned area of industrial land in the outskirts still included plenty of room for development at the time in 2003 (interview, an official of Jiading Planning Bureau, April 21, 2010). The underlying motive was the intention to compete with neighbouring cities by means of 'unlimited' land provision, since these cities had more lax land control than Shanghai. In essence, the launch of Project 173 was intended to suffocate the development opportunities enjoyed by the lower-ranking cities around Shanghai.

6.2.2 The industrial belt along Shanghai: Counter actions by Kunshan

The Shanghai locally initiated project was soon widely reported by external media, since the designated 173 square kilometres were considered to be Shanghai's 'special economic zones' against Jiangsu and Zhejiang. The relationship between Shanghai and Kunshan was, hence, rather strained, which may be sensed from the following remark:

> The launch of Project 173 by Shanghai put Kunshan under great pressure (as two of the three pilot zones are located along the border of Kunshan). Kunshan's leaders were keen to make inquiries about the project. (interview, a senior planner of Shanghai Planning Institute, 10 March 2010)

To cope with the challenge posed by Shanghai, Kunshan took prompt counter-action. In July 2003, the Kunshan Planning Bureau prepared an ad hoc plan to convert all the towns along Shanghai's border into an industrial belt encircling Shanghai's Project 173 (Figure 6.3). The overall industrial layout was forced to adjust due to the change, although at that time the Kunshan Master Plan (2002 - 2020) was already in the final stage of preparation (interview, a senior planner of Shanghai Planning Institute, March 10, 2010). Moreover, some of the towns such as Dianshanhu and Qiandeng, which were put under preservation and were restricted areas in the initial draft of Kunshan Master Plan in 2002, were incorporated into the industrial development belt in order to allocate land to industrial development. As a result, a whole 155 km^2 of land area was 'raised' for the rival project, with 50 km^2 planned for industrial development, and another 25 km^2 reserved for future industrial use. In addition, a government led group and an investment service centre were established to attract investors and provide government and business services.

上述政策举措说明,上海采取了针对性的行动以改变自身在投资成本、土地供应和政府服务方面的劣势。例如,市政府之所以增加计划工业用地面积,并不是因为郊区的工业用地资源都已被占用或租用;实际上,郊区原计划工业用地在2003年时仍有大量的开发空间(2010年4月21日对嘉定区规划局某工作人员的采访)。这项政策的真正动机是以"无限"的土地供应来与周边城市竞争,因为周边城市的土地管制要比上海更为宽松。从本质上来说,"173工程"的启动实际上就是为了争夺上海周边综合实力较弱的城市所拥有的发展机遇。

二、沿沪产业带:昆山的对策

上海的地方项目"173工程"很快被外界媒体广泛报道,因为这173平方公里的规划区域被认为是上海专为与江浙两省竞争而设立的"经济特区"。上海与昆山的关系因此变得相当紧张,这一点可从下述言论中看出:

上海173工程的启动使昆山面临巨大压力(因为三大试点园区中有两个与昆山交界)。昆山市领导急于想了解上海这个项目的情况。(2010年3月10日对上海市规划院某高级规划师的采访)

为了应对上海发起的挑战,昆山迅速采取了对策。2003年7月,昆山市规划局制订了一个专项计划,将上海周边的所有城镇划为一个环绕上海"173工程"规划区域的沿沪工业带(图6.3)。这一变动迫使昆山市对整个工业布局做出调整,尽管当时《昆山市城市总体规划(2002—2020年)》的制定已经进入最后阶段(2010年3月10日对上海市规划院某高级规划师的采访)。此外,为了划拨更多的工业用地,一些原本在《2002年昆山市城市总体规划》初稿中被列为保护区或限制区的城镇,如淀山湖、千灯镇等,也被纳入了工业开发带的范围。这一竞争项目最终共"募集了"155平方公里的土地,其中50平方公里用于工业开发,还有25平方公里为未来工业开发的留用地。此外,还成立了一个由政府领导挂帅的小组和一个投资服务中心来吸引投资,并提供政府和投资服务。

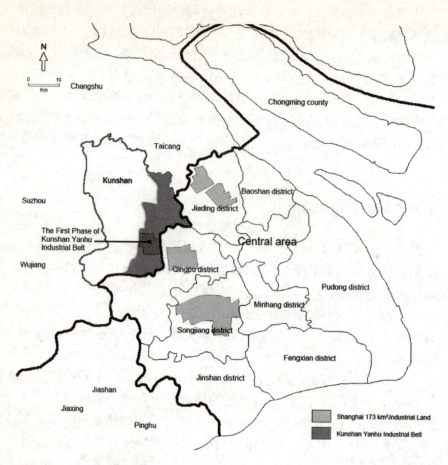

Figure 6.3 The location of Kunshan industrial belt along Shanghai and the first phase of the project at Qiandeng town
Source: compiled by the author.

Overall, growth - first competition between jurisdictions is very intense, as each level of government is responsible for its own revenue sources. What is unique to China is the fact that the competition is predominantly led by government leaders, as the evaluation of Chinese cadre performance is based on economic growth indicators (Chien and Gordon, 2008). As development is concentrated in the manufacturing sector, aggressive competition rests upon production elements such as airports, seaports, and land. In order to boost local competitiveness, entrepreneurial policies revolve around reducing the cost of investment and the speedy delivery of government services. Negative effects of competition result from highly competitive price competition and redundant infrastructure construction.

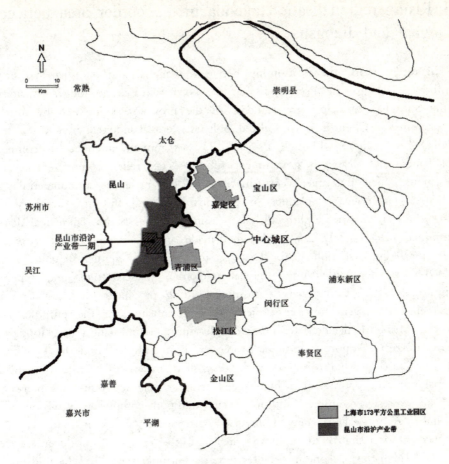

图6.3 昆山市沿沪工业带位置及千灯镇一期工程位置

来源:笔者编制。

　　总的来说,由于各级政府必须自谋财政资源,行政辖区之间以经济增长为核心的竞争非常激烈。中国的独特之处在于,这种竞争主要是由政府领导主导的,因为中国领导干部的政绩是以经济增长指标来考评的(Chien 和 Gordon,2008)。由于经济发展主要集中在制造业,因此在机场、港口和土地等生产要素方面的竞争显得尤为激烈。为了增强地方竞争力,政府的经营政策集中围绕在降低投资成本和加快政府服务上。但过度的价格竞争和基础设施的重复建设给地区发展造成了负面影响。

6.3 Rising regionalisation agenda in the border area between Shanghai and Jiangsu

In recent years, the relationship between Shanghai and Kunshan has been transformed. First of all, Project 173 at the border area is no longer a priority of the Shanghai municipal government. As the project was initiated by former Shanghai mayor Chen Liangyu, related policies were abandoned after Chen was jailed. What is more, although Project 173 was initially intended to compete with Jiangsu by means of government subsidies, tax relief, a preferential land and labour policy, investment costs in Shanghai can never be as competitive as in Jiangsu (interview, a planner of Shanghai Planning Institute, February 25 2010). Instead, in the Eighth Plenary Session of the Ninth Municipal Party Committee held in July 2009, Shanghai made an undertaking to stick to its international financial hub goal. That is, the Shanghai municipal government pledged to transform itself into a global economic, financial, trade and shipping centre, rather than to compete with neighbouring provinces for manufacturing investment. Moreover, concrete projects were formulated for the purpose. For example, Shanghai decided to put a high‑speed train station at Hongqiao, where Hongqiao Airport is located. Moreover, it intends to build the Hongqiao area into a comprehensive hub with diversified means of transport such as regional transport options of a high‑speed train, a mag‑lev train, an inter‑city train, an expressway, airlines, and inner city transport comprising a subway and bus links. A so‑called 'new Hongqiao' programme is planned to use the advantage of accessibility to build the area into the centre of producer services and a headquarters economy (interview, a planner of Shanghai Planning Institute, 20 April 2010). More importantly, the 'new Hongqiao' strategy is not only oriented to transnational companies, but also to manufacturing enterprises in the YRD region. This strategic positioning is of great significance, since it highlights that the Shanghai municipal government took the initiative to relate its economy to the development of the YRD region. As for the city of Kunshan, the industrial belt development along Shanghai was also replaced by a new project. The new practices of collaboration, the causes of transformation, and the resulting dynamics are going to be examined in detail in the following sections, again focusing on the border area between Shanghai and Jiangsu.

6.3.1 The launch of international Huaqiao Business Park by Kunshan

Huaqiao is a town under Kunshan county‑level city, which borders the Jiading district of Shanghai. It was incorporated in the industrial belt encircling

第三节 苏沪交界地区的区域化发展逐渐提上日程

最近几年上海与昆山的关系已有所改变。首先,交界地区的"173工程"不再是上海市政府的重点项目。该项目是由上海前任市长陈良宇发起的,在陈入狱后相关的政策就作废了。另外,"173工程"起初希望利用政府补贴、税收减免、优惠土地和劳工政策与江苏竞争,但实际上上海的投资成本不论怎么降都不可能比江苏更低(2010年2月25日对上海市规划院某规划师的采访)。2009年7月,上海第九届市委第八次会议召开,会上决定了坚持建设国际金融中心的目标,即上海市政府承诺要把上海建设成一个国际经济、金融、贸易和航运中心,而不再与邻近省份争夺制造业投资。另外,为实现这个目标,还制定了一些具体的项目。例如,上海决定在虹桥机场所在地虹桥新建高铁火车站。上海还期望通过发展高铁、磁悬浮列车、城际列车、高速公路、航线等城际交通以及由地铁和公交系统组成的市内交通等多种交通方式将虹桥地区打造成一个综合性的交通枢纽。所谓的"新虹桥"方案计划利用交通便捷的优势将虹桥地区打造成生产性服务和总部经济中心(2010年4月20日对上海市规划院某规划师的采访)。更为重要的是,"新虹桥"战略不仅针对跨国公司,还将涉及长三角区域的制造业企业。这一战略定位非常重要,它表明上海市政府已经采取举措要将其自身的经济发展与长三角区域的发展联系起来。昆山市也启动了新的项目来取代其沿沪工业带开发项目。以下各章节将详细介绍新的合作实践、发生转变的原因及其过程的动力机制,重点研究对象仍为苏沪交界地区。

一、昆山投建花桥国际商务城

花桥是县级市昆山的下属镇,位于上海嘉定区边界。2003年,花桥被划入沿沪产业带。与原计划作为产业带制造基地之一的千灯镇不同,花桥当时被

Shanghai in 2003. Unlike the initial project at Qiandeng, which was planned as one of the manufacturing bases in the industrial belt, Huaqiao at the time was positioned to develop business services. In fact, an area of 0.53 km² of Huaqiao was designated as the Jiangsu International Business Centre by the provincial government as early as 2000. At that time, Jiangsu intended to build three provincial business parks across the province to pioneer its industrial restructuring from manufacturing to producer services; however, the Huaqiao project was not implemented until 2005. In that year, the Jiangsu International Business Centre was upgraded to the Huaqiao International Business Park, and the original area of 0.53 km² was expanded to as much as 50 km² by the provincial government.

In opposition to the competition based on financial incentives with Shanghai for manufacturing investment, Huaqiao International Business Park demonstrates some efforts to collaborate with Shanghai, both institutionally and functionally. For example, the site selection of the business park is very unusual. The site chosen by the provincial government for the business centre was not regarded as an ideal location by the Kunshan government:

> Initially, Kunshan expected the provincial project to be located at Kunshan Economic and Technological Development Zone (KETDZ). This is because KETDZ is at the centre of the city of Kunshan, while Huaqiao is 20 kilometres away. (interview, a senior planning official of Kunshan Planning Bureau, April 14, 2010)

However, the advantage of the location selected by the provincial government was soon discovered: the site where the business city is seated 'intrudes' into the territory of Shanghai. More specifically, 2.5 km² of the 50 km² is enclosed by the Shanghai outer-ring highway (Figure 6.4). This means that cars travelling to Shanghai do not need to pay a toll fee (interview, a planning official of Huaqiao Planning Bureau, March 3, 2010). This is of great significance, as the toll fees charged by Jiangshu and Shanghai provincial-level governments on travelling cars whose licences are not locally registered act as a factor in investment costs. In other words, the location of Huaqiao Business Park could circumvent this regulation. The provincial government therefore deliberately selected this location with this in mind.

确定为商业服务开发区。实际上,江苏省政府早在2000年就在花桥划定了一个面积为0.53平方公里的区域用于建设江苏省国际商务中心。当时,江苏希望建立3个省级商务城,以引领全省从制造业到生产性服务的产业重组。然而,花桥项目直到2005年才得到落实。同年,江苏省政府将江苏省国际商务中心升级为花桥国际商务城,并将0.53平方公里原计划用地增至50平方公里。

花桥国际商务城的建设表明昆山市已开始努力在体制和职能上与上海开展合作,而不再是通过财政激励政策与其争夺制造业投资。例如,商务城的选址就很不寻常。起初昆山市政府并未将这个由省政府选定的商务城位置视为理想选择:

> 起初,昆山希望将这个省级项目设在昆山经济技术开发区内,因为开发区位于昆山市中心,而花桥距离市中心有20公里。(2010年4月14日对昆山市规划局某高级规划官员的采访)

但是省政府选定的位置很快就显示出了优势:商务城所在地"侵入"到了上海的地域。具体而言,商务城50平方公里的总面积中,有2.5平方公里由上海外环公路环绕(图6.4)。这意味着车辆驶往上海时无需支付过路费(2010年3月3日对花桥规划局某官员的采访)。这一点非常重要,因为江苏和上海这两个省级政府对非本地牌照的车辆收取的过路费是计入投资成本的。换言之,花桥商务城所在位置可以绕开这一规定。因此,江苏省政府在选择这个位置时是特别考虑到这个因素的。

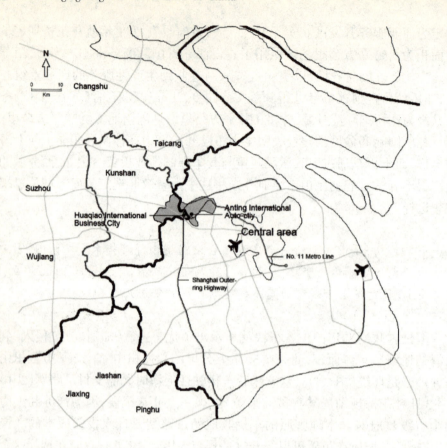

Figure 6.4 The location of Huaqiao International Business Park
Source: compiled by the author.

In fact, the element that makes Huaqiao International Business Park different from past government-led projects is that all sets of development policies for Huaqiao revolve around regionalisation. The slogan for the business park is 'The Business Satellite Town for the International Metropolis (Shanghai)'. This apparently takes into account the plans of Shanghai. In the tenth five-year period (2000-2005), Shanghai planned nine new towns around its suburban area, none of them envisaged to be business-oriented. Therefore, Huaqiao aimed to be the 'tenth suburban town of Shanghai' to supplement suburban Shanghai in producer services. Additionally, Huaqiao took a series of measures to integrate physically with Shanghai. This is very well demonstrated by the branding concept of Huaqiao business park: 'It is not Shanghai, but it is just as in Shanghai'. For example, Huaqiao International Business Park is covered by both Jiangsu and Shanghai communications networks, so that both landline and mobile calls made from Huaqiao to Shanghai are charged at the

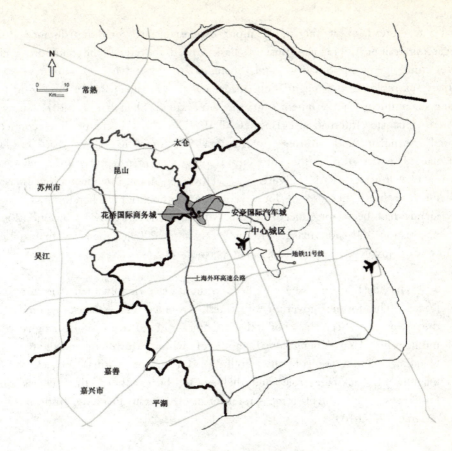

图6.4 花桥国际商务城位置

来源:笔者编制。

　　实际上,花桥国际商务城与以往政府牵头项目的不同之处在于,花桥所有的开发政策都围绕区域化这一主题制定和实施。商务城的口号是成为"国际大都市(上海)的卫星商务城",显然这一目标是参考了上海的近期规划。"十五"期间(2001—2005年),上海在其郊区规划了9座新镇,其中无一是以发展商务为目的的。因此,花桥镇旨在成为"第十座上海郊区新镇",以补充上海郊区的生产性服务业需求。另外,花桥还采取了一系列措施,以实现与上海的地域融合。花桥商务城的营销口号就是一个典型例子:"不是上海,就在上海"。比如,苏沪两地的通讯网络均覆盖花桥国际商务城,因此从花桥打往上海的座

local rate instead of at the much more expensive rate for long-distance calls. Regarding transport, Huaqiao Business Park vowed to reduce the trans-provincial travel time between Huaqiao and Shanghai to less than 30 minutes. One primary example is the negotiation made by the Huaqiao leadership with the Shanghai municipal government in order to extend Shanghai's No.11 subway line to Huaqiao International Business Park. The No.11 metro line connects central Shanghai and Anting International Automobile City that borders Huaqiao. The last stop at the auto-city is only 400 metres away from Huaqiao International Business Park (Figure 6.4). However, transport integration is very difficult to achieve because of local economic competition. Therefore, although the agenda had been introduced by the Kunshan side as early as around 2004, the negotiation did not make any progress until 2009, when senior political figures were involved in the dialogue in person:

> The deal cannot be reached without the involvement of top leaders. The former governor of Jiangsu province (Li Yuanchao), and the General Secretary of the Communist Party of Shanghai municipality (Yu Zhengsheng), both of whom are members of the Standing Committee of the Political Bureau of China, played a magnificent backstage role and helped to bring about the success. (interview, a senior planning professional of Jiangsu Planning Institute, March 17, 2010)

The regionalisation efforts made by the governments of Huaqiao and Kunshan are unprecedented and were exerted with great effort; nevertheless, the motive behind the regionalisation was, in fact, very entrepreneurial. Take the negotiation for the No.11 metro line for example. As remarked by a senior planning professional:

> Money issues are not at all the core of the negotiation. It is estimated that the Kunshan government will have to spend around 110 million *yuan* (for the 400-metre-extended metro line). And it is actually not cost-effective at all as it is just a sub-line and still costs an hour to get to the central city of Shanghai. But as soon as the deal is made, real estate developers in Huaqiao begin marketizing their properties as 'virtually located in the city of Shanghai'. The subsequent increase of land value in Huaqiao will be unimaginable, which is invisible to our 'naked' eyes. (interview, a senior planner of Shanghai Planning Institute, March 10 2010)

机和移动电话不必支付昂贵的长途漫游费。在交通方面,花桥商务城致力于将花桥与上海之间的跨省出行时间减至30分钟以内。一个重要的例子是,昆山市政府与上海市政府进行了谈判,希望将上海地铁11号线延伸至花桥国际商务城。11号线连接上海市中心与位于花桥边界的安亭国际汽车城,终点站汽车城距离花桥国际商务城不过400米路程(图6.4),但地方经济的竞争使得交通系统的整合变得极为困难。因此,虽然昆山方面早在2004年前后便将该计划提上日程,但直到2009年高级政要亲自参与对话,谈判才有所进展:

> 没有高层领导的参与,这个项目是谈不成的。同为中央政治局常委的江苏省前省长(李源潮)和上海市委书记(俞正声)扮演了极为关键的幕后角色,促成了项目的成功开展。(2010年3月17日对江苏省规划院某高级规划师的采访)

花桥镇和昆山市政府为实现区域化作出了史无前例的巨大努力,但其背后的动机实际上是非常商业化的。有关延伸地铁11号线的谈判就是一个例子。一位高级规划师曾评论道:

> 资金根本不是谈判的核心问题。据估算,昆山市政府将需投资约1.1亿元(用于建设400米长的地铁线路)。但该线路仅仅是条支线,并仍需花费1小时才能到达上海市中心,因而实际上成本效益并不高。但协议一旦达成,花桥的房地产开发商就会为其开发的房产打出"同城效应"的营销语。这将为花桥的地价带来超乎想象的上涨空间,这个价值是我们用"肉眼"看不见的。(2010年3月10日对上海市规划院某高级规划员的采访)

In other words, regionalisation is just one of the themes of place promotion for Huaqiao. As summarised by local officials, the development of Huaqiao is reliant on its competitive edge with a 'virtual location in Shanghai, preferential policies from Jiangsu, and low cost of Kunshan'. In this respect, the current regionalisation strategy demonstrated in the Huaqiao project is not much different from Kunshan's previous marketing of its close location to Shanghai and easy access to Shanghai's ports in order to obtain manufacturing investment in the 1990s. However, now the intention is to use geographical proximity to attract the lower-end and labour intensive producer services that cannot afford the high costs of metropolitan Shanghai. Overall, the new practice of collaboration exemplified by the development of Huaqiao International Business Park is actually strategic regionalisation with an entrepreneurial thrust.

6.3.2 The transformation of the Anting development: Strategic collaboration for industrial upgrading and urban development

A regionalisation initiative is also emerging on the other side of the border in Anting, Shanghai. Anting is a designated town under the Jiading district. Geographically, Anting is at the edge of the Jiading district, and borders Huaqiao of Kunshan. For this reason, there is frequent contact between the local people of Anting and Huaqiao. However, since the towns are separated by a provincial division, official communication and collaboration are not common in the area. Regionalisation is even seriously blocked by transport separation; indeed, Kunshan and Shanghai are only connected by a single highway. Proposals to integrate the road network cannot be carried out, even though this highway is very congested. As interpreted by an official in Anting town:

> It is believed by most leaders that transport integration would give more benefits to the neighbour in attracting investment and enjoying Shanghai's service, while putting the consequently increased transportation pressure on Anting. (interview, an official of Anting Town Government, 20 April 2010)

Nevertheless, a new phenomenon of collaborative development has recently been witnessed in the border area. The proposition of collaboration is demonstrated by the new development plan made by Anting. Anting's economy is led by auto manufacturing thanks to a joint venture with Volkswagen (Shanghai) for the domestic market. As of 2000, Anting was positioned by the Shanghai municipal government to be developed into an auto city for China, like Detroit in the USA or Wolfsburg in Germany. However, the new town

换句话说,区域化只是花桥区位营销的主题之一。当地官员总结称,花桥的发展依靠的是"靠近上海的地理位置、江苏省的优惠政策以及昆山的低成本"这些竞争优势。20世纪90年代,昆山为吸引对制造业的投资,曾利用其毗邻上海和上海港的区位优势进行宣传,在这方面,目前花桥项目中的区域化战略并未表现出太大区别。但是现在花桥项目的目的是,利用靠近上海的地理优势,吸引难以负担国际大都市上海的高成本的低端和劳动密集型生产性服务,而不是简单的同质竞争。总体而言,花桥商务城项目开发所体现的新型区域合作实际上是以城市经营为目的的战略性区域化发展。

二、安亭镇发展模式的转型:推动产业升级和城市发展的战略性合作

另一边的上海安亭边界也出现了区域化的举措。安亭是受嘉定区管辖的建制镇,地处嘉定区的边缘,与昆山花桥交界。因此,安亭与花桥的民间交流十分频繁。然而,这两个镇隶属于不同省市,官方的交流与合作并不普遍。区域化甚至受到交通分割的严重阻碍;事实上,昆山和上海仅由一条高速公路相连。虽然这条公路十分拥堵,但整合公路网络的提议仍无法得到推行。安亭镇的一名官员解释道:

> 大部分领导认为,交通整合会使相邻地区在吸引外商投资和享受上海服务方面受益,但给安亭(上海)带来的却是增量的交通压力。(2010年4月20日对安亭镇政府某官员的采访)

然而,近来边界地区呈现出了合作发展的新趋势。这一合作主题体现在安亭新制定的发展战略规划中。由于面向国内市场的合资企业大众(上海)汽车公司落户安亭,使得汽车制造业成为了当地的主要经济支柱。自2000年开始,上海市政府确定要将安亭发展为中国汽车城,正如美国的底特律和德国的

programme did not progress successfully. Several key municipal projects such as Formula 1 settled in Anting in the tenth five-year period (2000-2005), but momentum slowed after 2005 due to the shift of Shanghai's focus to the construction of the Yangshan deep-water port and Lingang New Town. The development downturn is sketched in the recent Anting International Auto-City Strategic Development Plan, prepared in late 2009:

> Anting's commercial and conference functions constitute only 10 percent of original planned area (till 2009)...The ratio of industrial land use to residential land use in Anting is as high as 3.81...Only 5 percent of the working population lives in Anting, leaving about 100,000 people commuting from Shanghai central city to Anting every weekday... The service sector in the town is just too low-end to satisfy the white collars and attract them to live in Anting...What's worse, due to the lack of demand, auto-related business provisions constructed according to the original plan were mostly closed and deserted. (compiled from the text document and the PowerPoint document of the strategic plan)

Consequently, Anting is stuck in its transformation from a satellite manufacturing district to an independent auto-city. At the same time, it is challenged by the latecomer at the border, Huaqiao. The service-oriented business park just supplements manufacturing-dominated Anting in service and residential provision. Some white-collar workers in Anting even choose to live in Huaqiao, since it provides a better living environment (Anting International Auto-City Strategic Development Plan). Furthermore, even some company meetings and training are now held in Huaqiao, since it has five-star hotels while Anting has none (interview, an official of Huaqiao Planning Bureau, March 3 2010).

Confronted with the challenge posed by the neighbouring Huaqiao, the government of the Jiading district and the development organisation, Anting International Auto-City and New Anting United Development Corporation, have tried to create a new development strategy. After outlining the advantages of Anting in contrast to central Shanghai and other urban projects in the Jiading district, the recent strategic plan does not treat Huaqiao as a threat to Anting, but conceives the prosperous development of Huaqiao as a great opportunity for Anting's future development. It suggests that Anting auto-city should seek collaborative development with Huaqiao in order to 'fuel' its urbanisation. It is hoped that the 'twin-city' can function as a single edge city on the outskirts of Shanghai and develop as a service node within the Shanghai metropolis. Guided by this concept, Anting's transportation network and

沃尔夫斯堡一样。但是,这一乡镇级别的新项目并未成功向前推进。"十五"期间(2001—2005年),F1赛车等若干市级重点项目均落户安亭,但2005年之后该势头却由于上海将发展重心转向洋山深水港和临港新城的建设而有所放缓。这一发展颓势在最近2009年末编制的《上海国际汽车城发展战略规划》中有所体现:

> 安亭用于商业和会务功能的区域仅占原规划区域的10%(截至2009年)……安亭工业用地与住宅用地的比例高达3.81……安亭的就业人群只有5%在当地居住,在工作日每天约有10万人往返于上海市中心和安亭之间……安亭第三产业过于低端而无法满足白领的需求,无法吸引他们在安亭定居……更糟的是,由于需求不足,依原计划建造的与汽车相关的商业服务设施大部分都被停业甚至弃用。(根据战略规划的文字文件和演示文稿文件编制)

因此,安亭在从卫星制造区向独立汽车城转变的过程中陷入了停滞状态。与此同时,它还要面对边界上的后来居上者——花桥的挑战。以服务为导向的花桥商务城在服务与住宅供应方面为以制造业为主导的安亭提供了补充。安亭的一些白领工作者甚至选择住在花桥,因为花桥提供了更好的居住环境(《安亭国际汽车城战略发展计划》)。此外,由于花桥拥有安亭所没有的五星级酒店,如今一些公司的会议与培训也在花桥进行(2010年3月3日对花桥镇规划局某官员的采访)。

面对邻镇花桥带来的挑战,嘉定区政府和汽车城开发单位上海国际汽车城新安亭联合发展有限公司尝试制定一项新的发展战略。通过总结安亭与上海市区以及嘉定区其他城市项目的对比优势,近期的战略规划不再将花桥视为安亭的威胁,反而把花桥的繁荣发展当作安亭未来发展的重大机遇。该规划认为,安亭汽车城应当与花桥合作发展,为其城市化进程"添砖加瓦",通过

functional layout is prepared by the incorporation of Huaqiao's functional plan. The strategic plan even puts the scale of school, hospital, kindergarten and other cultural facilities to be built in Anting at the level of a 500,000-populated medium city, i.e. taking Huaqiao's 300,000 planned population into account. When asked about the earlier worries regarding collaboration, the general manager of Anting International Auto-City and New Anting United Development Corporation replied that:

> In the sense of development, we may be more in need of Huaqiao's support in certain way, especially in terms of population. Anting needs high - profile population at the moment in order to promote modern service development...therefore we finally accepted to organize our urban functions and transportations catering to Huaqiao... (even we) put our recent development focus at the place that borders Huaqiao, i.e. where the No.11 metro line of Shanghai is to be extended. ...As to competition, there are competitions everywhere. Anting is even competing with Nanxiang, Malu, which are both the towns under the Jiading district. On the other hand, if the house prices in Huaqiao are on the increase, then how can it be possible that Anting's property prices are lower? The cooperation is mutually beneficial. (interview, a general manager of Anting International Auto - city and New Anting United Development Corporation, 21 April 2010)

In short, collaboration happened in circumstances where Anting was confronted with the problems of upgrading its industrial structure towards a service-oriented arrangement. That is, local officials compromised the regionalisation strategy in order to break the local development deadlock.

6.4 Characteristics of regional collaboration between Jiangsu and Shanghai

The case of the Jiangsu - Shanghai trans - border area has demonstrated that individual cities have begun to seek collaboration with adjacent neighbours. However, at present, these collaborative intentions are mainly articulated in planning documents or conveyed by chief governors, which are far from being practical actions. Most regional collaboration strategies are formulated by the policy makers of one city rather than by networking or substantial participation. Although local strategies are oriented towards cooperation, 'officials of the other side will not be invited for the discussion or be informed of the proposal'

这个"双生城"在上海郊区发挥一个边缘城市的作用,并发展成大都市上海的服务重镇。按照这一理念,在规划安亭的交通网络和功能布局时,安亭战略规划也相应考虑了花桥的功能区划。安亭战略规划甚至决定在安亭按照50万人口的中等城市的规模新建学校、医院、幼儿园及其他文化设施,即同时为花桥规划中的30万人口配备公共服务设施。当被问及之前关于合作的忧虑时,上海国际汽车城新安亭联合发展有限公司的总经理答道:

> 就发展而言,我们可能更需要花桥以某种方式提供支持,尤其在人口方面。如今安亭需要高层次的人口来推进现代服务业的发展……因此我们最终决定根据花桥的需求来组织我们的城市功能和交通建设……(我们甚至)将近期发展的重点放在与花桥的交界处,也就是上海地铁11号线即将延伸的区域……至于竞争,哪儿都有竞争的。安亭甚至与同属嘉定区的南翔、马陆之间也存在竞争。另一方面,如果花桥房价上涨,安亭的房价又怎么可能更低呢?合作实为共赢。(2010年4月21日对上海国际汽车城新安亭联合发展有限公司总经理的采访)

简言之,安亭是在其向服务业导向的产业结构升级过程中遇到了困难,才开始考虑与临界地区的合作的。也就是说,当地政府为打破地方发展瓶颈而在区域化战略上作出了让步。

第四节　江苏与上海之间区域合作的特点

苏沪交界地区的实例表明,各城市已经开始寻求与相邻城镇的合作。然而,目前这些合作的意向绝大部分都只体现在规划文件中或主要政府官员的报告中,远未付诸实际行动。大部分区域合作战略都是由某一城市的政策制定者自行制定的,而不是双方或多方通过实际参与和会谈达成的。虽然地方

(interview, a chief planner of Jiading Planning Institute, April 22 2010). That is, local institutional functions are still largely hedged by administrative boundaries and no collaborative mechanism has been substantially institutionalised. Since regional cooperation schemes are still managed by individual cities, they may be prolonged or even eventually fail, as in the case of the extension of the metro line from Anting to Huaqiao, 'even though the extension is totally financed by Kunshan government, it has to rely on Shanghai's arrangement. Therefore, Kunshan's project won't be put into schedule very soon since Shanghai will have to attend to its own projects first' (interview, a chief planning official of Kunshan Planning Bureau, April 14 2010). Moreover, at the current stage, the agenda of cooperation is largely limited to the realm of transport infrastructure. Communication is not broadly structured, but 'concentrates on ad hoc projects such as on one particular road... Except for roads, there is little communication on such topics as regional development strategy, industrial development or environmental strategies' (interview, a chief planner of Jiading Planning Institute, April 22 2010). In other words, inter-locality cooperation practices in China are nascent and preliminary, with no formal institution or informal policy network having yet been established. The findings here in the Yangtze River Delta are in line with studies on the Pearl River Delta, in which it is argued that the Pan-PRD regional cooperation 'is un-formulaic in nature' (Yeh and Xu, 2008: 423), or 'a collection of loosely assembled local governments' (Wu and Zhang, 2009: 12).

Although economic regionalisation does not immediately indicate that the political agenda of regionalisation is well established, it does have some effect on agenda formation. For instance, due to the rapid development of high-speed railways and inter-city railways within the YRD region, conventional measures such as the obstruction of road integration undertaken by local governments to protect the local economy will be disrupted. Moreover, as the need for trans-border convenience and mobility is on a sharp increase, not only for business, but also for residents, better inter-city connectivity would eventually bring benefits to the local economy. On the other hand, there is mounting pressure for the industrial structure within the YRD to upgrade from the manufacturing to the service sector due to the tightening up of land supply and the rising cost of manufacturing. As commented by a senior planner of Shanghai, the potential manufacturing shift in Shanghai due to land cost, higher environment standards and other factors cannot be affected by the government. As soon as Shanghai realised that the development tendency could not be reversed by any means such as rivalry and competition, it tried to make profits by other means such as cooperation (interview, a senior planner of Shanghai Planning Institute, March 10 2010). That is, the government strategy is very pragmatic and

策略倾向于合作,但"另一方的官员并不会受邀参加讨论或了解提案"(2010年4月22日对嘉定区规划局某总规划师的采访)。也就是说,地方体制职能仍在很大程度上受限于行政界线,合作机制尚未真正体制化。由于区域合作计划仍由各城市独立管理,因而很有可能造成合作计划的拖延甚至失败。以地铁线路从安亭延伸到花桥这个实例来说,"即使延伸费用全部由昆山政府承担,也必须依赖于上海的安排。由于上海必须优先考虑其自身的发展计划,所以昆山的计划并不会很快就被提上议程"(2010年4月14日对昆山市规划局某主要规划官员的采访)。此外,在现阶段,合作议程大都局限于交通基础设施领域。合作与对话并未全面建立,而只是"集中于某些特别项目,例如某一特定路段……除此之外,在区域发展战略、工业发展或环境战略方面几乎不存在沟通交流"(2010年4月22日对嘉定区规划局某总规划师的采访)。换言之,地方之间的合作实践在中国仍处于新兴和初始阶段,尚未建立正式的机制或非正式的政策网络。长江三角洲的研究结果与珠江三角洲的研究结果一致,后者认为泛珠江三角洲区域合作"本质上未形成模式"(Yeh和Xu,2008:423),或者只是"松散的地方政府集合"(Wu和Zhang,2009:12)。

尽管经济区域化并不直接表明区域化的政治议程已经完全确立,但前者对后者的形成确实有一定影响。例如,长三角地区高速铁路和城际铁路的快速发展,将导致一些传统的阻碍合作发展的措施黔驴技穷,例如地方政府为了保护当地经济而阻碍区域道路的整合。此外,随着企业和居民对跨界便利性与流动性的需求急剧上升,城际之间连通的加强最终将给地方经济带来利益。另一方面,由于土地供应收紧和制造业成本上升,长三角地区的产业结构面临着由制造业向服务业升级的巨大压力。正如上海一位高级规划师所述,上海潜在的制造业转型是受到政府不可控因素的影响,如土地成本、更高的环境标准及其他因素。认识到无法以对抗或竞争等方式扭转经济的发展趋势之后,上海即尝试通过合作等其他方式促进经济发展(2010年3月10日对上海市

follows concrete issues. As the tertiary industry is untraded and firmly embedded in localities, the coming industrial restructuring may create more scope for cooperation within the region.

Even though economic regionalisation, regional transport and economic restructuring would create more scope for inter-city collaboration, the nascent governance exercises towards cooperation are not a turning away from entrepreneurial endeavours or inter-city competition. Similar to past competition to set up manufacturing development zones, cities are now rushing to establish business parks. It is commented that there is a boom of building business parks by the town government in Kunshan after the development of the Huaqiao International Business Park by the provincial government (interview, a senior planner of Shanghai Planning Institute, March 10, 2010). That is, every government sees the business sector and the service economy as a new source of economic growth after manufacturing development. The widespread business parks are again going to lead to fierce competition to attract business investment. For instance, Huaqiao Business Park summarised its competitive advantage as 'proximity to Shanghai, preferential treatments of Jiangsu, and low production cost of Kunshan'. Apparently, Huaqiao Business Park is still trying to use production elements such as cheaper land and preferential policies such as lower taxes to compete with other business parks, especially those in Shanghai with much higher costs. Therefore, it can be predicted that there may be a new round of economic competition between localities to develop producer services. Overall, the current regional cooperation practice is only a tactical strategy of urban governments to sustain local economic development.

6.5 Conclusion

This chapter has examined nascent regional collaboration practices in the YRD region. The study reveals that the relationships between different jurisdictions are no longer hostile as in the past, and some cooperative initiatives have emerged in the region. However, based on an in-depth case study of the Jiangsu and Shanghai border area, the chapter finds that current collaboration is far from being established (Zhang, 2006; Zhang and Wu, 2006). The mechanism of cooperation in contemporary China is not based on substantive inter-jurisdictional networking. The formulation of development proposals and economic strategies are still based on individual cities, although a regional perspective is generally adopted by local governments in the process of preparing their development strategies. Other cities are included in the consideration, which is largely based on inter-city transportation and economic competitiveness. Local interests are still dominant on the development agenda.

规划局某高级规划师的采访)。这就是说,政府策略事实上是非常务实的,并针对具体问题。由于第三产业与制造业相比具有非贸易性且牢牢植根于地方市场,因而在未来产业结构调整的大趋势下可能为长三角地区的区域内合作创造更大的空间。

尽管经济区域化、区域交通和经济结构调整将为城际合作带来更广阔的空间,新兴的面向合作的管治尝试并未完全脱离先前的城市经营主义和城市竞争。与过去竞相建立制造业开发区的情况类似,城市中现在正掀起建立商务园区的热潮。据称,在江苏省政府建立花桥国际商务城后,昆山市政府也掀起了建立商务园区的热潮(2010年3月10日对上海市规划院某高级规划师的采访)。也就是说,各政府都将商务服务经济视作继制造业发展之后新的经济增长来源。遍地的商务园区将引发又一波吸引商业投资的激烈竞争。例如,花桥商务城将其竞争优势总结为"靠近上海的地理位置、江苏省的优惠政策以及昆山的低生产成本"。显然,花桥商务城仍在利用诸如较便宜的土地和优惠政策(例如低税收)等生产要素与其他商务园区竞争,特别是成本较高的上海商务园区。因此,可以预测,为发展生产性服务业,各地将会掀起新一轮的经济竞争。总体而言,目前的区域合作实践只是城市政府维持地方经济发展的一种策略。

第五节　结论

本章重点考察了长三角地区新兴的区域合作实践。研究发现,不同辖区的关系不再处于过去的敌对状态,并且已经出现了一些合作的举措。然而,基于对苏沪交界地区案例的深入研究,本章发现就当前状况而言,合作机制还远未确立(Zhang,2006;Zhang和Wu,2006)。当代中国的合作机制并非基于实质性的跨辖区合作网络。尽管地方政府在制定发展战略时通常会从区域的角度出发,但发展方案和经济战略的形成却仍然是由各个城市自行确定的。其他城市的情况之所以会被纳入考虑范畴,主要还是因为城际交通和经济竞争

Moreover, contemporary regional economic development in China is predominantly launched by the state without engaging a wide range of actors and organisations outside the government body. Therefore, even though the relational perspective of scale is stressed in the literature (Allen et al., 1998; Allen and Cochrane, 2007; Lagendijk, 2007), the topic is undeveloped in China. Although collaboration and cooperation is pursued by the local actors including local residents and the local state, the outcome is predominantly decided by the reality of jurisdictional boundaries and the relationships between local governments. China's regional collaborative projects are still fragmented by the administrative hierarchy and territory. Communication and collaboration cannot easily be undertaken between different governments, especially at different levels (such as the county level of Kunshan and the district level of Jiading of Shanghai municipality), and this significantly undermines the effectiveness of interaction between cities.

In order to examine emerging regional initiatives, the chapter distinguishes the economics and politics of regionalisation. It is argued that, albeit in economic terms, the economy of the YRD has been regionalised and, at the same time, the scope of collaboration has also widened, although a regional agenda has not been widely achieved among cities. In fact, a regional agenda has only been selectively adopted by the local governments in response to the current volatile economic environment. Increasing inter-city competition and the difficulty of export-oriented manufacturing industries has driven local officials to adopt new strategies such as adopting the development of the tertiary industry. Therefore, regional collaboration in China is a product of changing economic strategy rather than a substantial shift in regional governance. Although the environmental agenda in the Western context is a major driver for emerging regional governance, it has not been the dominant force in region building in China. It is argued by Yeh and Xu (2008: 423) that the contemporary cooperative strategy is merely used as an 'institutional fix' for the city to open up new avenues for capital accumulation. As illustrated by the case study of the Shanghai - Jiangsu border area, cooperative development is the tactic only employed by the local government to facilitate local economic growth in terms of business and property development, when development margins for manufacturing are narrowed under the rising land and labour costs and the stringent state land policies.

Finally, this research suggests that the current policy solution on inter-city cooperation inside China is too simplistic. The problem tends to be attributed to the lack of communication in the Chinese administrative system; hence, more networking is advocated. As examined through the changing relationship between Shanghai and Jiangsu, this chapter argues that the development of

力问题。地方利益仍主导着当前的发展议程。此外,中国当代的区域经济发展主要由政府牵头,而政府机构以外的活动者和组织尚未广泛参与。因此,尽管有些文献强调了关联的尺度视角(Allen 等,1998;Allen 和 Cochrane,2007;Lagendijk,2007),这个主题在中国似乎尚未发育。即使包括政府和居民在内的地方机构都在寻求地方合作,但最终结果仍在很大程度上受到行政边界和地方政府间关系的影响。中国的区域合作项目仍受到行政层级和行政边界的分割。不同政府间很难展开沟通与协作,特别是处在不同级别的政府之间(例如昆山的县级政府和上海嘉定的区级政府),这严重影响了城市之间的有效互动。

为分析新兴的区域举措,本章对经济区域化和政治区域化进行了区分。虽然长三角地区在经济方面已经开始区域化,同时合作的范围也有所扩大(尽管城市之间还未普遍达成区域议程),但事实上,地方政府只是有选择地采纳区域议程来应对当前动荡的经济环境。不断加剧的城际竞争和以出口为导向的制造业面临的不景气驱使地方官员采取新的战略,例如发展第三产业。因此,中国的区域合作是经济战略不断变化的产物,而非区域管治的真正转变。尽管在西方国家,环境议程是新兴区域管治的主要驱动力,但它尚未成为中国区域建设的主导力量。Yeh 和 Xu(2008:423)认为,当代合作战略仅仅是城市开辟资本积累新途径的"制度调整"。正如苏沪交界地区的案例研究所表明的,合作发展只是地方政府在制造业发展优势因土地和劳力价格上升以及国家土地政策收紧而被削弱之时,用以促进当地商业发展及房地产开发的策略。

最后,本书认为目前有关如何促进中国城际合作的解决方案过于简单。现有研究倾向将合作难的症结归结于中国的行政体系缺乏沟通;因而需要形成更多的网络。通过分析不断变化的苏沪关系,本章认为区域管治的发展深

regional governance is strongly embedded in local and territorial politics. In other words, regional governance research must be contextualised in the circumstance of economic devolution and urban entrepreneurialism in post-reform China. Besides the lack of communication channels, competitive relationships between different localities also exacerbate the ineffectiveness of inter-governmental collaboration. Although emerging regionalisation and industrial restructuring in China is creating more scope for inter-city economic cooperation, it does not change the competitive relationship between different jurisdictions. This is because China is still fiscally decentralised, a context in which local governments have to build their economic capacity and earn their own revenue (Wong, 1991a; Zhang, 1999). Although the central state has put forward more stringent land policies, it does not substantially challenge the established pattern of the local governments as local land manager. Therefore, competition by means of land and preferential treatments will still exist, since they are the effective administrative means that the local governments can deploy to spur economic growth. However, on the other hand, entrepreneurship also makes the local governments very pragmatic regarding the issues of competition and cooperation. As demonstrated by the case of the trans-border area between Jiangsu and Shanghai, bottom-up cooperation will become more active as long as it is assumed by the local governments that benefits can be obtained from the cooperative development. Administrative bureaucracy and fragmentation can be reshaped in favour of cooperation for the sake of economic interests. That is, the local interests provide the main impetus for local governments to choose between competition and cooperation. In this regard, the prospect for inter-city cooperative development in China might be more than that of the UK. In the UK, regional competitiveness and economic development seem to be seen as more the concern of the national state, for which regional development and regionalism are at the centre stage of the national policy rather than being addressed by the local policy (Bristow, 2010: 4). The politics of political regionalism in the UK are complicated and full of tension with regard to cultural identity, local party politics and civic engagement (Deas and Ward, 2000; Phelps, 2010).

Overall, the case of the changing Shanghai-Jiangsu inter-relationship has illustrated the politics in the regional scale building process in the YRD area. However, this is only one aspect of regional-making practices in the YRD region. In contrast to the focus on the local forces of regionalisation, the next chapter will scrutinise the intention of top-down forces to develop regional governance in the YRD. The rationale and politics underlying the top-down programmes are significantly different from those of the bottom-up articulation presented in this chapter.

深植根于地方和地域政治。换句话说,必须在改革开放后中国经济权力下放和城市经营主义的背景下研究区域管治。除了缺乏沟通渠道,地方之间的竞争关系也进一步降低了政府间的合作效率。尽管中国新兴的区域化和产业结构调整正在为城际经济合作创造更大空间,但它并未改变不同辖区间的竞争关系。这是因为中国仍然处于财政分权的模式之中,在此情况下,地方政府必须增强自身经济实力并赚取收入(Wong,1991a;Zhang,1999)。尽管中央政府已经提出了更严格的土地政策,却并未从本质上改变地方政府作为地方土地管理者的既定土地管理模式。因此,土地和优惠政策方面的竞争仍将继续存在,因为它们是地方政府用来刺激经济增长的有效行政手段。然而,另一方面,地方经营主义精神也使得地方政府在合作和竞争方面非常务实。正如苏沪交界地区的案例研究所表明的那样,只要地方政府认为合作发展能够带来好处,自下而上的合作将变得更加活跃。为了获取经济利益,地方政府将会努力重塑行政官僚分割的局面以促进合作。也就是说,地方利益是地方政府在竞争和合作中作出选择的主要推动力。就此而言,中国城际合作发展的前景可能比英国的好。在英国,区域竞争和经济发展似乎更多地由国家考虑,因为区域发展和区域化是国家政策的中心环节,而不是由地方政策掌控(Bristow,2010:4)。英国政治区域主义的政治活动十分复杂,而且在文化认同、地方政党政治和公民参与方面充满了紧张气氛(Deas 和 Ward,2000;Phelps,2010)。

  总的来说,苏沪城际关系变化的案例阐明了长三角地区在区域尺度建设进程中的政治因素。然而,这只是长三角区域空间形成的一个方面。下一章将深入分析长三角地区区域管治发展中自上而下的力量及其意图。自上而下的区域构建在政策意图和政治因素方面与自下而上的地方力量推动的区域化有显著差别。

第七章

CHAPTER SEVEN

The Resurgence of YRD Regional Spatial Plans: The Development of Top-Down Orchestrated Regional Governance

7.1 Introduction

China was well-known for its top-down planned economy in the socialist period. At that time, regional plans were formulated by the National Planning Commission, the backbone of the central state, to arrange economic development. However, it is less known that pre-reform China used to be equipped with regional-level government in the state system. Regional government was set up above the provinces for top-down control and intra-regional coordination. For instance, the YRD region has seen the rise and demise of three regional organisations (Yangtze River Delta Urban Economic Coordination Office, 2007: 9-11). Firstly, an East China Administrative Region was set up from 1950 to 1954, including Shanghai, Jiangsu and Zhejiang along with Anhui, Shandong, Fujian and Taiwan province. The administrative region during the short period accommodated complete governmental departments, as well as military and Party organisations (Chen, 2007: 3). The regions were set up to help China's Communist Party to consolidate political power and resume industrial production after the civil war (Yangtze River Delta Urban Economic Coordination Office, 2007: 9). Secondly, an East China Collaborative Region was established from 1954 to 1960, which covered Jiangsu, Zhejiang, Shanghai, Anhui, Jiangxi, Shandong and Fujian province. The remit of the region was limited to economic development (Chen, 2007: 5), i.e. the production and constitution of a self-contained regional economy. Therefore, only one committee was set up for the running of the regional organisation (ibid). Finally, an East China Central Bureau was set up in 1961 to re-confer the previous economic collaborative region with Party and political power (Chen, 2007: 7). However, the Cultural Revolution, which started in 1966, affected the function of the administrative region (Yangtze River Delta Urban Economic Coordination Office, 2007: 11).

Since the beginning of the economic reform, China's state system has not retained a regional level of administration between the central government and the provinces. Regional planning such as the national five-year plan was still practiced, but its influence was also very much weakened afterwards. However, the discourse of regional coordinated development has reappeared in both governmental reports and academic literature since the beginning of the new

第七章 长三角区域空间规划的复兴：
自上而下的区域管治

第一节 引言

众所周知，在改革开放前的社会主义时期，中国实行的是自上而下的计划经济体制。当时，国家计划委员会作为中央政府的支柱职能部门，负责制定区域规划，统筹经济发展。然而，少为人知的是，改革开放以前，中国曾在中央政府下设立数个行政区域，区域政府的行政级别高于省级政府，以实现自上而下的管理和区域内的协调。以长江三角洲为例，在这一地区就先后设立并撤销过三个区域机构（例如长三角城市经济协调会办公室，2007：9-11）。设立这些行政区的目的是帮助中国共产党巩固政权，并在解放战争后恢复工业生产（同上：9）。首先是在1950年至1954年设立的华东行政区，所辖区域包括上海、江苏、浙江、安徽、山东、福建和台湾省。这个存在时间不长的行政区域下设完整的党政军机构（陈晓云，2007：3）。随后是1954年至1960年设立的华东经济协作区，所辖区域包括江苏、浙江、上海、安徽、江西、山东和福建省。这一区域的职能仅限于发展经济（同上：5），即建立和形成自给自足的区域经济。因此，该区域只设立了一个委员会来负责区域组织的日常运作（同上）。最后是1961年设立的中共中央华东局，重新赋予其之前经济协作区的党政权力（同上：7）。但是1966年开始的"文化大革命"影响了这一行政区域的职能（长三角城市经济协调会办公室，2007：11）。

自经济改革以来，在中国的国家体系中，中央政府和省级单位之间不再设立区域级的行政区。国家五年计划之类的区域规划虽然仍在实施，但其影响力已大不如前了。然而在步入新千年之后，政府工作报告和学术文献中重新

millennium. In this context, a third boom in regional planning, which was unprecedented in terms of the overall number of planning projects and amount of planning funding, has been witnessed (Wang, 2007: 3). In the region of YRD, two regional plans were prepared in 2005. The YRD Regional Plan was prepared by the central ministry of National Development and Reform Commission (NDRC), whereas the YRD Urban Cluster Plan was introduced by the Ministry of Housing and Urban and Rural Development (MHURD). These regional plans are remarkably different from the features of the locally initiated regional plan. They cannot be fully explained by entrepreneurial thrust, as seen in the earlier stage of city planning (Xu and Yeh, 2005; Wu, 2007; Wu and Zhang, 2007). According to Wong et al. (2008), planning is now developed as a functional and spatial coordination device to pursue environmental sustainability and social coherence (Wu and Zhang, 2008: 154). In other words, this new regional agenda, to some extent, represents the top-down policy response to the problem of conflicts between cities in the region.

The chapter hence intends to investigate the resurgence of the centrally initiated regional plan in the YRD. Western European countries have also witnessed the revival of strategic spatial planning at the national and regional scale since the 1990s (Albrechts et al., 2003; Albrechts, 2004, 2006). The approach of state theory is used to understand the changing nature of the current regional plan (Allmendinger and Haughton, 2007, 2009; Haughton et al., 2009). It is argued that the new spatial planning 'is a contributor to and a reflection of a more fundamental reform of territorial management' (Allmendinger and Haughton, 2009: 620). It is representative of the restless search of the state for territorial management (Allmendinger and Haughton, 2007: 631). Following the lens of planning, governance and 'new state space' (Brenner, 2004b), this chapter attempts to use the case of the NDRC-led YRD Regional Plan to illustrate the development of the 'new state space' in China. The YRD Regional Plan, together with Beijing-Tianjin-Hebei region, was prepared by the NDRC during the eleventh five-year plan period (2006–2010). It occupies a pioneer role in the current wave of making regional plans. This regional plan was recently approved by the State Council in May 2010, which represents the first official policy of cross-boundary governance in the region. The central research question is how the regional plan is formulated and articulated by upper-level government as a vehicle to deliver its regulations in contemporary regional governance. Built on the argument that the regional plan represents the state's recentralising effort (Xu, 2008; Xu and Yeh, 2010), this chapter attempts to further argue that current up-scaling planning practices are part of the process of the restructuring of state spatiality, i.e. the new development of the regional level by the central government represents a new

频频出现区域协调发展的说法。在这一背景下,区域规划迎来了第三次发展浪潮,其规划项目总数和所涉金额之多均达到前所未有的程度(Wang,2007:3)。2005年,长三角地区制定了两个区域规划。一个是由国家发改委编制的长三角区域规划,另一个是由国家住建部编制的长三角城市群规划。与地方政府开展的区域规划相比,这两个区域规划具有明显不同的特点。我们无法完全用早期城市规划中所见到的城市经营主义来解释这些规划(Xu和Yeh,2005;Wu,2007;Wu和Zhang,2007)。Wong等人(2008)认为现阶段的规划是一种功能和空间协调机制,有助于推进环境的可持续发展,并增强社会凝聚力(Wu和Zhang,2008:154)。换言之,这种新型的区域计划,在某种程度上显现了对区域内城市间冲突的自上而下的政策反应。

因此,本章将研究由中央发起的长三角区域规划的兴起。自20世纪90年代以来,西欧国家也出现过国家和区域尺度战略空间规划的复兴(Albrechts等,2003;Albrechts,2004;2006)。国家理论的研究方法有助于理解现行区域规划的性质改变(Allmendinger和Haughton,2007,2009;Haughton等,2009)。研究提出,新型的空间规划"促成并反映了更根本的地域管理改革"(Allmendinger和Haughton,2009:620),代表了国家对最佳地域管理模式的不断探索(Allmendinger和Haughton,2007:631)。在讨论了规划、管治和"新国家空间"(Brenner,2004b)后,本章试图以国家发改委提出的长三角区域规划为例,阐述"新国家空间"在中国的发展情况。长三角区域规划和京津冀都市圈区域规划都是由发改委在"十一五"规划期间(2006—2010)制定的。长三角区域规划在当前的区域规划浪潮中发挥着先驱作用。该区域规划在2010年5月获得国务院批准后,成为区域内首个进行跨界管治的官方政策。本章研究的重点是:作为当前区域管治中上级政府的一种管理工具,区域规划是如何制定和实施的。基于"区域规划体现了国家重新将权力向中央集中"的说法(Xu,2008;Xu和Yeh,2010),本章试图进一步说明,在当前阶段,规划实践的尺度上移是国家空间重组过程的一部分,即中央政府新兴的区域治理政策代表了国家权力和政策干预的新尺度。

scale of policy intervention and state power.

The organisation of the chapter is as follows. Firstly, there will be a review on the marginalisation of regional administration and regional plans in the YRD after the economic reform. It is suggested that localities virtually developed individually without a regional vision after the downscaling of governance. Secondly, the recent formulation of the Yangtze River Delta Regional Plan is studied to examine how the plan resumes the role to regulate local development, i.e. how the plan contributes to the production of 'new state space'. Next, the ongoing tension between different levels of government and different divisions in the development of 'new state spaces' is discussed. Finally, in the conclusion section, the deficiencies of regional planning are highlighted, and some policy implications are provided.

7.2 The marginalisation of regional governance in YRD in post-reform China

Since economic reform, China has changed its focus from political control to economic development. The regional level of government was abandoned since it was found to be too rigid and detrimental to spontaneous business cooperation (The Yangtze River Delta Urban Economic Coordination Office, 2007: 10). Instead, informal regional organisation was promoted by the central government. In contrast to the previous regional administration, the informal regional organisation had three main purposes. First of all, it attempted to promote inter-regional and inter-city economic cooperation, or in the language of the time, 'horizontal economic relations'. Secondly, it also aimed to break down urban-rural dualism and to promote commercialisation and economic trade (Li, 2008: 29). Finally, it intended to promote inter-governmental networking and inter-ministry coordination, which was deficient in the previous ministry-led centrally planned system (Yu et al., 2008: 152). For example, within the YRD region, a Shanghai Economic Zone (SEZ) was designated by the State Council in December 1982. Geographically, the region consisted of ten cities: Shanghai, Suzhou, Wuxi, Changzhou, Nantong, Hangzhou, Jiaxing, Huzhou, Ningbo, and Shaoxing. When setting up the region, the central government intended to build up a regional economy around the city of Shanghai (Yangtze River Delta Urban Economic Coordination Office, 2007: 11). In order to break down the previous ministry-led economy by bringing the ministry and localities to work together (Yu et al., 2008: 63), the leading office of the regional organisation, the Shanghai Economic Zone Planning Office, was constituted by central ministries and the three provincial-level

本章将从以下四个方面展开讨论。首先,回顾经济体制改革后长三角区域管治和区域规划边缘化的情况。有人认为,管治尺度下移后,各地实际上都是独立发展,缺少对整个区域发展的长远规划。其次,通过研究近期长三角区域规划的制定,了解该规划如何重新发挥其对地方发展的调节作用,即如何促进"新国家空间"的形成。再次,讨论在"新国家空间"形成过程中不同层级政府和不同职能部门之间持续存在的矛盾关系。最后,在结论部分总结区域规划存在的不足之处,并给出相关政策建议。

第二节　改革开放后长三角区域管治的边缘化

改革开放以来,中国的发展重心从政治管理转向了经济发展。区域级政府由于过于僵化且不利于自发的商业合作而被相继撤销(长三角城市经济协调会办公室,2007:10)。相反,中央政府开始提倡建立非正式的区域组织。与之前的区域管治相比,非正式区域组织的设立主要有以下三个目的。第一,促进各区域间和各城市间的经济合作,即当时所提出的"横向经济联合"。第二,打破城乡二元体制并促进商业化和经贸发展(李立军,2008:29)。第三,促进各级政府间交流和各部委间协作,而这正是之前由部委主导的中央规划体系所缺乏的(郁鸿胜等,2008:152)。例如,1982年12月,国务院决定在长三角地区设立上海经济开发区(SEZ),其地理范围覆盖了上海、苏州、无锡、常州、南通、杭州、嘉兴、湖州、宁波和绍兴十个城市。中央政府设立这一经济区的目的是建立一个以上海市为中心的区域经济体(长三角城市经济协调会办公室,2007:11)。这一区域组织的领导机构是上海经济开发区规划办公室,由多个中央部委和三个省级政府组成,目的是促使中央各部委和地方政府通力合作,

governments. The central ministries included the National Planning Commission, National Economic and Trade Commission, and other specialised ministries such as industry ministries, the Hydroelectric Power Bureau, the Transport Ministry, the Chemical Industry Ministry, the Electronics Ministry, the Spinning Ministry, and the Light Industry Ministry (Yu et al., 2008: 151). From 1984 to 1988, conferences attended by the provincial governors and city mayors were held once a year in order to facilitate 'horizontal' relationships and communication between different cities and economic sectors (Yangtze River Delta Urban Economic Coordination Office, 2007: 11). Throughout the process, many state enterprises within the region started to cooperate with each other in sales, production, technology and capital with the help of the government (Yu et al., 2008: 152).

In addition, as a complement to reduced top-down state control, a territory plan was imported and it was advocated by the State Council to cover the whole country in the early 1980s. For example, the SEZ region was regarded as one of the key regions under the national territory planning led by the National Planning Commission (NPC) (Wu, 2006: 110). With the function of the Planning Office, integrated attempts were made to coordinate infrastructure construction, water management, industrial development and other issues within the region (Sun and Zhao, 2005: 144). It is documented that one Shanghai Economic Zone Strategic Development Plan and as many as twenty-two special plans were prepared during the period (Yu et al., 2008: 152). Some profound examples included: the planning of Shanghai – Jiangsu and Shanghai – Zhejiang highway, which was later adopted by the Transport Ministry and put into construction in the 1990s (Wang, 2009: 116); the flooding control plan for the Tai-Lake Basin, which was then approved by the State Council (Li, 2008: 29); the territorial plan of Shanghai – Jiangsu and lower Yangtze River Delta area (Wang, 2009: 116) and the urban distribution plan for the Shanghai Economic Zone (Wu, 2006: 115) (Figure 7.1). Overall, in the early years after the economic reform, informal regional organisation was set up, not to consolidate central control, but to promote local initiatives and natural economic trade. In the meantime, there was an upsurge in regional planning to coordinate market-oriented development rather than to arrange economic distribution.

打破之前中央部委在经济发展过程中独揽大权的状况。这些中央部委包括国家计划委员会、国家经济贸易委员会以及其他一些专门部委,如工业部、水电局、交通部、化工部、电子工业部、纺织部和轻工业部等(郁鸿胜等,2008:151)。为了促进不同城市和不同经济部门间的"横向"关系与交流,从1984年到1988年,上海经济开发区每年都举办一次由各省省长和各市市长参加的会议(长三角城市经济协调会办公室,2007:11)。在此过程中,区域内的众多国企在政府帮助下开始在销售、生产、技术和资金上进行合作(郁鸿胜等,2008:152)。

此外,由于自上而下的国家控制相比之前有所减弱,国务院在20世纪80年代初期于全国范围内推行了国土规划作为补充。国土规划由国家计划委员会领导,上海经济开发区便是其中的重点区域之一(武廷海,2006:110)。上海经济开发区的规划办在成立之后做了大量工作,包括协调区域内的基础设施建设、水务管理、工业发展和其他事项(孙海鸣和赵晓雷,2005:144)。据资料记载,除《上海经济开发区发展战略纲要》外,这一时期还制定了多达22个专项规划(郁鸿胜等,2008:152)。其中影响较大的有后来被交通部采纳并于20世纪90年代投入建设的沪苏浙高速公路规划(王枫云,2009:116)、由国务院批准的太湖流域综合治理规划(李立军,2008:29)、沪苏及长三角下游地区国土规划(王枫云,2009:116)和上海经济开发区城镇布局规划(武廷海,2006:115)(图7.1)。总之,在改革开放初期建立非正式区域组织,并非为了加强中央控制力,而是为了促进地方的自主性和自由的经济贸易。在此期间,区域规划也迎来了一个高潮,其目的是为了协调以市场为导向的发展,而非调整经济布局。

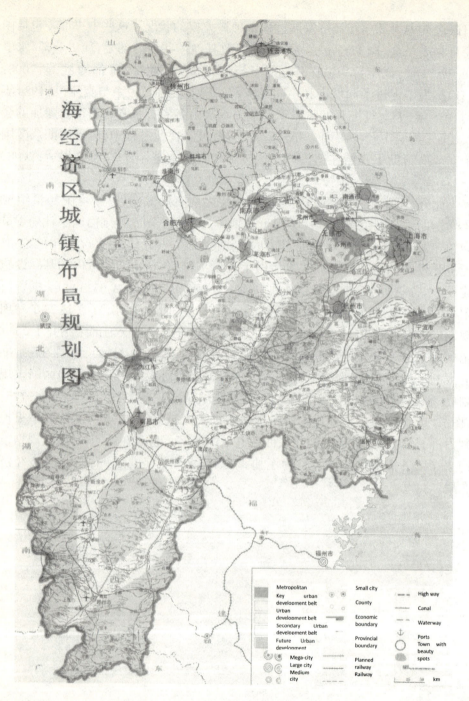

Figure 7.1 The Urban Distribution Plan
for Shanghai Economic Zone（1985-2000）

Source: Wu, 2006: 115.

图7.1 上海经济开发区的城镇布局规划(1985—2000)

来源:武廷海, 2006:115。

However, the regional body was abolished in 1988 for many reasons. Firstly, at the time of decentralisation, the regional organisation, which was immediately subordinate to the State Council and directly led by the National Planning Commission, was regarded with suspicion. It was believed the top-down approach to promote business links was characterised by residual central command (The Yangtze River Delta Urban Economic Coordination Office, 2007: 11). That is, business cooperation was pre-arranged by government orders rather than spontaneously. Secondly, local governments were actually passive regarding inter-regional cooperation and were really more interested in the economic benefits of their own jurisdictions (Sun and Zhao, 2005: 144; Wang, 2009: 116). Due to the partial and incremental reform of economic planning, fiscal arrangements, goods management and the price administrative system at that time, local governments were able to take advantage of their residual planning power to influence business operation and prevent cooperation (Lu and Shi, 2008: 154). Examples of material wars and market blockade, instead of achievements of inter-regional economic cooperation, were extensively documented during the period (Zhao and Zhang, 1999: 272). Thirdly, the regional functioning demonstrated a path dependency on the former economic planning approach, which was ingrained with socialist legacies such as top-down administrative measures. For example, the regional plan prepared during the time was still a blueprint document without any concern for the implementation mechanism and public policies. Although a Regional Regulation for the Shanghai Economic Zone was formulated (Yangtze River Delta Urban Economic Coordination Office, 2007: 11) and a strategic development outline was agreed upon (Li, 2008: 29), these remained as paperwork without any binding effect. No legislation was passed for the plan formulation or regulation, either. That is, the realisation of the regional vision was still reliant upon top-down administration and local obedience. As a result, the effectiveness of the region was increasingly challenged by decentralisation and market reform, where the context of governance became much more complicated than purely top-down instructions and unconditional obedience. Finally, the intention to build a regional economy around Shanghai also met with resistance from some localities (Lu and Shi, 2008: 155). Owing to the uneven open policy and the disintegration of the command economy, Shanghai lost its absolute advantage in economic development. For example, Lianyungang and Nantong in Jiangsu Province, as well as Wenzhou in Zhejiang Province, were allowed to receive foreign investment in April 1984, six years earlier than the opening of Pudong of Shanghai in 1990. Shanghai's regional status was severely challenged by the faster economic growth in the provinces of Jiangsu and Zhejiang, which benefited largely from the prosperous development of town and village

　　然而,由于多种原因,上海经济开发区在1988年被撤销了。首先,这一区域组织直属于国务院并由国家计划委员会直接领导,在权力下放的背景下,这种性质容易引起猜疑。人们认为这种自上而下促进商业联系的方式带有中央指令的痕迹(长三角城市经济协调会办公室,2007:11)。也就是说,商业合作并非自发进行,而是由政府指令预先安排的。其次,地方政府实际上对于地区间的合作并不积极,它们更关心的是本地管辖范围内的经济效益(孙海鸣和赵晓雷,2005:144;王枫云,2009:116)。由于当时国家正对经济规划、财政体制、商品管理和价格调控体系进行局部改革与增量改革,地方政府得以利用其剩余的规划权力来影响商业经营并阻碍合作(陆阳和史文学,2008:154)。在这段时期内,区域间的经济合作并未有很大进展,关于物资争夺和市场封锁的例子倒比比皆是(Zhao和Zhang,1999:272)。再者,区域运作显示了其对以往经济规划的路径依赖性,这种依赖性带有明显的社会主义特征,如自上而下的行政措施等。比如,该时期内制定的区域规划仍然处在蓝图阶段,未涉及任何实施机制和公共政策。尽管制定了《上海经济开发区章程》(长三角城市经济协调会办公室,2007:11)和发展战略纲要(李立军,2008:29),但这些也仅仅是章程性文件,并不具有任何约束力。另外还缺乏关于规划制定的立法和条例。也就是说,区域构想的实现仍依赖于自上而下的行政管理和地方的服从。于是,权力下放和市场改革给区域效率带来越来越大的挑战,因为在这种背景下管治内容更加复杂,不再仅仅是自上而下的指令和无条件的服从。最后,建立以上海为中心的区域经济体的构想也遭到了一些地方的抵制(陆阳和史文学,2008:155)。由于开放政策的不平衡和计划经济的瓦解,上海在经济发展上丧失了绝对优势。举例来说,江苏省的连云港市和南通市,以及浙江省的温州市在1984年4月就已获准引进外资,比1990年上海浦东新区的开发早了6年。乡镇企业的蓬勃发展使江苏省和浙江省的经济增长比上海更为快速,对上海

enterprises (Zhang, 2006: 41). Under the circumstances, Nanjing and Hangzhou, the capital cities of Jiangsu and Zhejiang provinces, both intended to compete with Shanghai to be the leader city of the region (Lu and Shi, 2008: 154). In short, the conflicts between the traditional top - down administrative approach and the emerging decentralisation environment led to the failure of the regional experiment. In other words, the disassembly of the NPC - led Shanghai Economic Zone marked the failure of the intervention by the central government into local development after economic reform.

The top - down regulation was further weakened following the reorganisation of the central government in 1998. After that, the NPC was reformed to become the National Development and Reform Commission (NDRC) and responsibility for territorial management was moved to the newly established Ministry of Land Resources (MLR). As a result, the formerly unified function of economic management and territorial management was separated under two ministries (Wu, 2006: 121). However, MLR made the preservation of agricultural land its priority and set aside territorial management, i.e. the making of territorial plans. In other words, top-down spatial regulation was temporarily placed in a vacuum during the period. In contrast, city planning under the Ministry of Construction (MoC, the later MHURD) was developing rapidly. According to the 1989 City Planning Act, an urban system plan is required for the preparation of an urban master plan. Consequently, the influence of the urban system plan underneath the MoC system was greatly enhanced and it virtually became the regional-level plan in the post-reform era. For example, the Jiangsu Department of Construction prepared the Suzhou-Wuxi - Changzhou city - region plan during the preparation of the Jiangsu Provincial Urban System Plan to tackle the problem of incoordination and competition in the developed southern Jiangsu area. However, the city - region plan was very difficult to implement in reality (Luo and Shen, 2008). Furthermore, the preparation of the urban system plan under the MoC was generally based on provincial administrative divisions, which actually left the coordination between provinces unattended. Overall, the urban system plan has been under increasing criticism in recent years. It is argued that its existence is merely due to the fact that it is a statutory plan required by the 1989 City Planning Act rather than because of its real value in practice (Zhu, 2005). In reality, the effectiveness of the urban system plan was greatly challenged in the late 1990s for its outdated technocratic planning methodology, which addressed a static urban hierarchical system and a rigid standard of urban size distribution (Q. Zhang, 1999).

Overall, regional planning became marginalised for a short period in the 1990s. In fact, it was downgraded owing to the ineffectiveness of regional governance. First of all, regional plan - making was still ingrained with socialist

在区域内的地位形成了严峻挑战（Zhang，2006：41）。在此情况下，江苏省省会南京和浙江省省会杭州，都想要与上海一争高下，成为该区域的"龙头"城市（陆阳和史文学，2008：154）。一言以蔽之，自上而下的传统管理方式与权力下放的新背景之间矛盾重重，导致了该区域试验的失败。换言之，国家计委领导下的上海经济开发区的解体标志着中央政府在经济体制改革后对地方发展干预的失败。

在1998年中央政府换届之后，自上而下的管理体制被进一步削弱。此后，国家计划委员会经过改革，更名为国家发展和改革委员会（国家发改委），地域管理职能被划归新设立的国土资源部。这样原先一体的经济管理和地域管理职能就被划归到了两个部门（武廷海，2006：121）。但国土资源部的工作重点放在耕地保护上，而非地域管理或者说国土规划的制定上。也就是说，自上而下的空间调控在这段时期内被暂时搁置了。相反，归建设部（后来的住建部）管理的城市规划则发展迅速。根据1989年通过的《城市规划法》，在编制城市总体规划之前先要编制城镇体系规划。因此，在建设部的管理下，城镇体系规划实际上成为了改革开放后的区域级规划，其影响力大大增强。例如，江苏省建设部在拟定《江苏省城镇体系规划》时提出了苏锡常都市圈规划，以解决苏南发达地区间的不协调发展和竞争问题。但该都市圈规划在现实中很难实施（Luo和Shen，2008）。另外，建设部管理下的城镇体系规划编制工作大体上是按省级行政区划进行的，这也导致了各省之间缺乏协调。总体而言，城镇体系规划近几年来屡受批评。有人认为它的存在仅仅是因为它是1989年《城市规划法》的法定规划，而非因为它具有实际应用价值（朱波，2005）。实际上，城镇体系规划因其过时的技术规划方法，过于强调静态的城市等级体系和僵化的城市规模布局标准，其有效性在20世纪90年代后期已颇受质疑（张勤，1999）。

总体上，区域规划在20世纪90年代曾被短暂地边缘化。确切地说，它是由于区域管治无效才不受重视。首先，区域规划的制定依旧受到社会主义规划理论的深刻影响，制定出的规划仅仅是一种蓝图大纲，缺乏实施机制。它的

planning theory, which is an approach simply comprising a blueprint outline without any implementation mechanism. Its usefulness was hence questioned and it was even seen as the legacy of the planned economy and no longer suitable in the market economy (Zhu, 2005). Secondly, and more importantly, this is because the upper-level government was left with few administrative and fiscal resources for territory management after economic devolution (Wu et al., 2007; Luo and Shen, 2008). Due to the fact that the region has been widely documented for its spectacular growth speed, as well as the increasingly intense competition between various localities for investment, land and policies (Zhang, 2006; Chen, 2007; Zhao and Zhang, 2007), there are increasing concerns over administrative fragmentation, adverse competition and redundant development within the area.

7.3 Formulating the Yangtze River Delta Regional Plan: The contribution to a new state space in the YRD

In 2002, NDRC changed the name of the conventional five-year economic plan to the five-year spatial plan, which was intended to reassert its role of spatial regulation. In the following year of 2005, NDRC launched the YRD regional plan project as an experiment to include spatial components within the eleventh five-year plan (2006-2010). The YRD region in the plan incorporated the area of Jiangsu, Zhejiang and Shanghai. This is very unusual because it spans three provincial-level jurisdictions, including 24 prefecture-level cities, 49 county-level cities and 61 counties (Figure 7.2).

有效性因此受到质疑,甚至被认为是计划经济的残留物,不再适用于市场经济(朱波,2005)。更重要的原因是,经济权力下放之后,上级政府手里能够用于地域管理的行政和财政资源所剩无几(Wu等,2007;Luo和Shen,2008)。由于大量文献记载了区域发展速度惊人,同时地方之间对投资、土地和政策资源的竞争愈演愈烈(Zhang,2006;Chen,2007;Zhao和Zhang,2007),因此人们越来越关心区域内的行政区碎化、恶性竞争和重复建设等问题。

第三节　长三角区域规划的制定: 推进长三角区域新国家空间的建立

发改委在2002年将原来的"五年经济计划"改名为"五年空间规划",意在重申其空间管理的作用。之后在2005年,发改委启动了长三角区域规划项目,作为一项试验项目,将空间概念纳入了"十一五"规划(2006—2010年)。根据该规划,长三角区域包括江苏省、浙江省和上海。这是十分少见的,因为该区域跨越了3个省级行政区,包括了24个地级市、49个县级市和61个县(图7.2)。

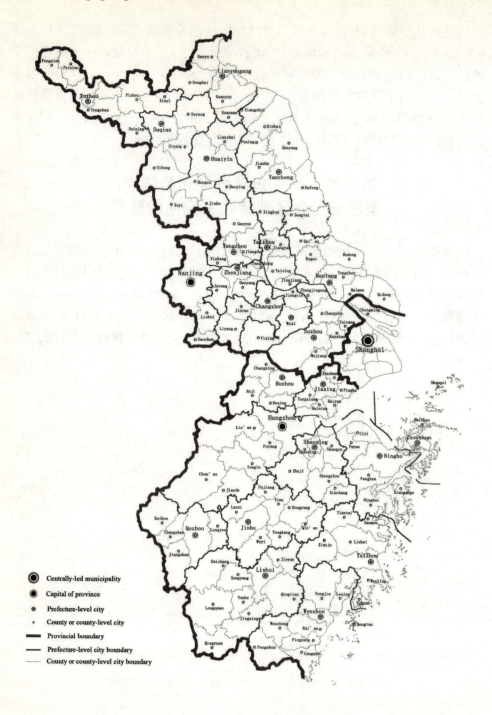

Figure 7.2 The boundary of the YRD region in the YRD Regional Plan
Source: compiled by the author.

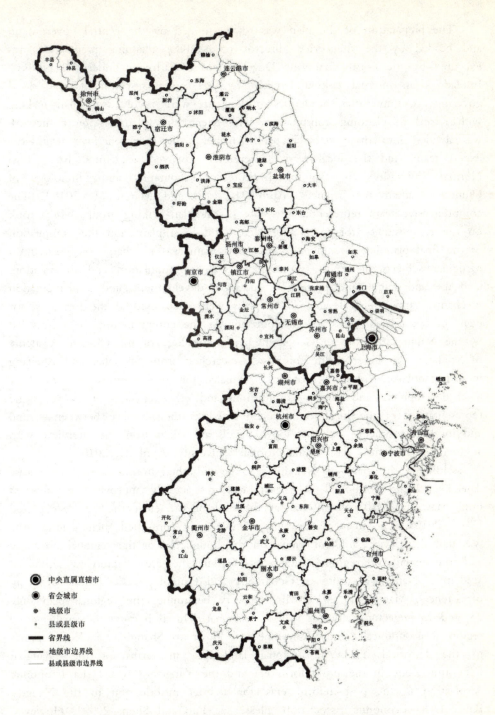

图7.2 长三角区域规划中划定的长三角区域界线

来源：笔者编制。

The preparation of the plan was totally funded by the central government, and headed by the then vice-director of NDRC. Planning preparation was executed by the Local Economic Development Department under the NDRC. Instead of an internal task undertaken by the central government itself, local governments, universities, academics and experts were involved in plan-making with regard to planning consultation. The overarching plan-making framework was divided into three research teams, namely: the comprehensive team, the expert team, and the local team (interviews, involved academics, East China Normal University and Nanjing Institute of Geography and Limnology of Chinese Academy of Sciences, April 21, 2010 and March 11, 2010). The comprehensive team represented the core of the plan-making group, which took on the responsibility for integrating sector and local plans and the compilation of the final planning document. The expert team was in charge of research on particular subjects of crucial significance, such as population and urbanisation, land use and arable land protection, industrial development, and implementation mechanism and policy design. These plans were then used as the formal sector plans of the related ministries and bureaus. As the comprehensive team was led by the Nanjing Institute of Geography and Limnology of the Chinese Academy of Sciences, the expert team comprised researchers from Shanghai and Zhejiang in order to balance domiciles of origin. Finally, the local teams were formed by local development and reform commissions and other colleges. They were the representatives of the localities and also acted as the interface between central and local governments (all the above details are taken from an interview with an involved academic, East China Normal University, April 21, 2010).

Although the plan was scheduled to be published in mid-2006, the release date kept being postponed. The plan was not actually approved or published until May 25, 2010, which was at the end of the eleventh five-year period (2006-2010). The main reason why plan-making consumed such a long time was that there were different views on the boundaries of the regional economy and the extent of regional integration within the area (interview, involved academics, Nanjing Institute of Geography and Limnology of Chinese Academy of Sciences, March 11, 2010). In the very beginning, the regional plan only covered 15 prefectural cities as well as Shanghai. This is because the smaller-sized region is economically more developed, is closer to Shanghai, and corresponds to the historical YRD institutional landscape, in terms of the Shanghai Economic Zone in the pre-reform era and the Yangtze River Delta Economic Association in the post-reform era (for a brief introduction to the Yangtze River Delta Economic Association, please see Luo and Shen, 2009). However, the State Council released the document 'Instructions on Furthering the Reform and Opening-Up, and Promoting the Social Economic Development in

　　长三角区域规划的制定工作由中央政府提供全部资金支持,由发改委副主任领导,并由发改委的地区经济发展司负责编制。规划的制定并非由中央政府一力承当,地方政府、大学、学者和专家也通过规划协商的方式共同参与。总的规划制定框架包括综合团队、专家团队和地方团队三个研究团队(2010年4月21日和2010年3月11日对华东师范大学和中国科学院南京地理与湖泊研究所相关学者的采访)。综合团队是规划编制团队的核心,职责是整合部门和地方规划并汇编最后的规划文件。专家团队负责研究特定的关键性课题,例如人口和城市化、土地利用和耕地保护、产业发展及实施机制和政策设计。这些规划在当时被用作相关部委和厅局的正式部门规划。由于综合团队由中国科学院南京地理与湖泊研究所领导,为在人员构成上取得地域性平衡,专家团队由来自上海和浙江的研究人员组成。最后,地方团队由地方发改委和其他院校组成。他们是地方的代表,也是中央与地方政府沟通的渠道(以上所有具体细节均根据2010年4月21日对华东师范大学相关学者的采访)。

　　尽管该规划原定于2006年年中公布,但实际的公布日期却被不断推迟。直到"十一五"规划(2006—2010年)后期,即2010年5月25日,该规划才获得批准并被公布。制定该规划耗时如此之长,主要是因为对区域经济的界线和这一地区的区域一体化程度存在不同的看法(2010年3月11日对中国科学院南京地理与湖泊研究所相关学者的采访)。最初,该区域规划仅涵盖了15个地级市,外加上海。这样规划的原因是,这个面积不大的区域经济更发达,距上海也较近,而且该区域位于改革开放前的上海经济开发区和改革开放后的长三角经济圈,符合长三角地区一直以来的体制格局(关于长三角经济圈的简介,请参见Luo和Shen,2009)。然而,2008年9月,国务院发布了《关于进一步推进长江三角洲地区改革开放和经济社会发展的指导意见》(简称"长三角指导意

Yangtze River Delta Region' in September 2008, which officially announced that the YRD region should incorporate the whole jurisdictional area of Shanghai, Jiangsu and Zhejiang provinces. The document even created a term of jargon called 'Pan - YRD region' in order to combine Anhui, the underdeveloped province on the periphery, with the region of YRD. Obviously, the intention of the central government was to encourage industrial relocation from the relatively developed YRD area to Anhui province, which would promote economic restructuring in the YRD region, as well as enhancing economic development in Anhui province. On the other hand, the massive expansion of the YRD region was also because of the strong requirements of the provincial and local governments to join the 'YRD region' to promote local economic growth. Overall, scientific research on the structure and boundary of the regional economy did not have much effect on the space of regional planning since it was greatly influenced by the politics of central and local governments.

7.3.1 The new legitimate level of planning: The creation of a new scale of state spatiality

The YRD regional plan is the first integrated plan for all three provincial-level jurisdictions. It specifies strategic positioning, development objectives, spatial distribution and coordinated development for the entire area. The plan contains twelve chapters. Chapter one analyses the challenges and opportunities confronting the region. In chapter two, a unified regional strategy is proposed for the vast area. It aims to realise 'social well - being in 2015 and modernization in 2020'. The aim of the specific goal of GDP per capita is to reach 82,000 *yuan* in 2015 and 110,000 *yuan* in 2020. More importantly, the plan forecasts that the service sector should account for 48 percent in 2015 and 53 percent in 2020. The goal for the service industry represents the intention of the central government to promote economic restructuring in the YRD region in order to enhance its regional competitiveness in the world and upgrade the current structure of export - oriented manufacturing industries. For this purpose, the regional plan provides overall guidance for the region in chapter three. It envisions the future spatial development structure as 'one core with six belts' (Figure 7.3). Furthermore, it specifies the urban system within the region and the particular roles of cities in the region. Overall, the YRD regional plan represents one of the few centrally prepared documents on cross-boundary regional development and the first ever in this area since economic reform. Through the making of the regional plan, the regional scale is created to promote integrated development in the fragmented and complex region.

见"),正式宣布长三角地区应包含上海市、江苏省和浙江省的所有辖区。该文件还提出了"泛长三角地区"的概念,纳入了地处长三角边缘、经济欠发达的安徽省。很明显,中央政府的用意是鼓励工业从相对发达的长三角地区转移到安徽省,以促进长三角地区的经济结构重组和安徽省的经济发展。另一方面,各省市政府发出了强烈呼声,要求加入"长三角区域"以推动本地经济发展,这也促进了长三角区域范围的大规模扩张。总而言之,区域规划的空间范围主要受到的是中央和地方政府的影响,而不是依照有关该区域经济结构和区域边界的科学研究。

一、合法的新区域规划:创建新国家空间尺度

长三角区域规划首次对三个省级行政区进行了整体规划,明确规定了整个区域的战略定位、发展目标、空间布局和协调发展。该规划包含十二章。第一章分析了区域面临的挑战和机遇。第二章提出了整个地区的统一区域发展战略,目标是"2015年全面实现小康社会和2020年基本实现现代化"。人均GDP的具体目标是2015年达到82,000元,2020年达到110,000元。更重要的是,该规划还预计服务业的比重在2015年应达到48%,到2020年达到53%。由服务业的发展目标可见,中央政府意图促进长三角地区的经济结构重组,以提高其在世界范围的区域竞争力,并促进当前以出口为导向的制造业结构升级。为此,第三章中提出了该区域的总方针。该规划构想未来的空间发展结构为"一核六带"(图7.3)。此外,它还规定了区域内的城镇体系以及各城市的具体角色。总而言之,长三角区域规划是少数由中央制定的跨界区域发展规划文件之一,也是经济体制改革以来的首个此类规划。区域规划的制定划定了区域尺度,有利于促进这一包含多个省市、情况复杂的区域的一体化发展。

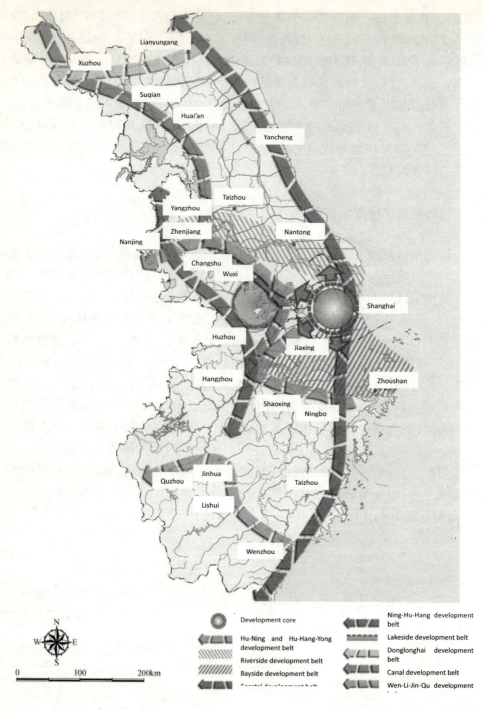

Figure 7.3 The Structure of the YRD Regional Plan
Source: YRD Regional Plan (2009-2015).

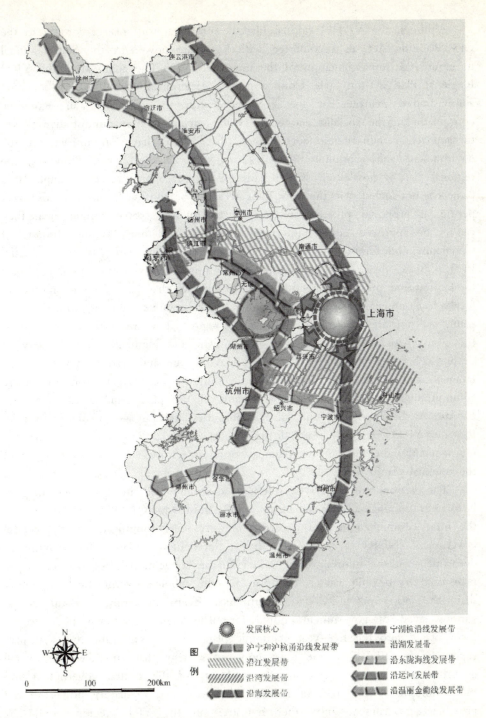

图 7.3　长三角区域规划总体布局图

来源:长三角区域规划总体布局图(2009—2015)。

Although the YRD Regional Plan is not a statutory plan according to the City Planning Act, it is conferred with legitimate power by the State Council to ensure the implementation of the integrated plan. The approval of the YRD Regional Plan by the State Council provides legitimacy for NDRC to conduct administrative management in accordance with the plan. As an economic coordinator in the socialist economy, NDRC retains some administrative power to approve certain investment projects that would have an impact on the environment and economic safety (Zhang and Zhang, 2005). However, the regional plan is now used as the basis for project approval. For example, if a project is not included in the plan, then it cannot be approved within the five-year period; if proposed projects are not located in the spatial zoning area, they cannot be approved either (interview, involved academic, Nanjing Institute of Geography and Limnology of Chinese Academy of Sciences, March 26 2010). In this way, the central government can impose its location preference for locally initiated projects, especially the big schemes that have a huge impact on local development and the environment. For example, although metallurgical plants are not totally banned in the YRD region, they are spatially restricted in the plan in order to protect the environment and eliminate over-capacity of output. Therefore, metallurgical projects may not be approved if applied for by cities located outside the proposed area within the plan. Apart from the above administrative measures, the statutory status of the plan requires all cities and counties within a region, and all the ministries and bureaus involved, to refer to the YRD regional plan document in their policy and plan making. Consequently, the long absent regional vision is restored by the enforcement of the regional plan.

The reason why NDRC resumed a strong role in spatial planning is historically contingent and is because NPC, from which NDRC originates, was the most comprehensive and powerful ministry-level commission in the central government. NDRC is even now half a level higher than other government departments at the ministry level. Likewise, the conventional five-year economic plan used to be and still is the plan for the whole government body rather than the plan for individual departments. Every government institution at various levels of government should formulate their department plans to be incorporated into the five-year economic plan. In this sense, the five-year plan supervised by NDRC is the most powerful strategy that embodies the overall governmental plan. By deploying the authority of the central government and the administrative resources of NDRC, the weakened regulatory power of the provincial government and other ministries in the YRD region should be restored through the implementation of the regional plan.

　　虽然长三角区域规划并非根据《城市规划法》制定的法定规划,但为了保证整体规划的实施,国务院赋予了其法律效力。国务院通过批准长三角区域规划,使发改委可根据该规划进行行政管理。作为中国社会主义经济中的协调者,发改委仍保留一些行政权力,可以批准某些对环境和经济安全有影响的投资项目(张汉亚和张欣宁,2005)。因而,当前区域规划被用作项目审批的基础。例如,如果一个项目不在规划之内,那么它在五年之内不会得到批准;如果申报的项目不在空间上划定的区域内,也不能得到批准(2010年3月26日对中国科学院南京地理与湖泊研究所相关学者的采访)。这样,中央政府就能根据区位偏好对地方项目的选址进行干预,特别是那些对当地发展和环境有重大影响的大型规划。例如,长三角区域并未完全禁止建立冶金厂,但为了保护环境和减少过剩的产能,规划在空间上对冶金厂有所限制。因此,位于规划规定地区外的城市申请建立冶金厂,很有可能得不到批准。除上述行政措施外,该规划的法律地位还使得区域内的所有市县和所有相关部委厅局都需参照此规划来制定政策和规划。因此,这一区域规划的实施恢复了长期以来缺失的整体区域构想。

　　国家发改委在空间规划中能重新发挥重要作用是有历史偶然性的,因为发改委的前身,即国家计划委员会,是中央政府中最具综合性和权力最大的部委。即便是现在,发改委也比其他部级政府部门高半个级别。同样,传统的五年经济计划一直以来都是针对整个政府而非单个部门。各级政府部门都应根据五年经济计划制订各自部门的计划。从这个角度说,发改委监管的五年规划包含了全面的政府规划,是最强有力的战略。通过动用中央政府的权力和发改委的行政资源来实施区域规划,长三角区域的省级政府和其他部委一度薄弱的监管权也将得以恢复。

7.3.2 The enlarged scope of planning: The changing nature of planning for strategic governance

Although the initiator of the plan is NDRC, which used to compile the five-year economic and territorial plans, the YRD Regional Plan is not a purely economic plan or land use plan. The scope of the plan is widened to include all aspects ranging from the economy, land resources, environment, infrastructure development coordination, regional inequality to regional innovation. In addition to an overall strategy, the remaining part of the plan prescribes strategies and locations for various development subjects such as major industries, infrastructure projects, highways or fast roads, and inter-city train lines. The remaining ten chapters of the plan deal with urbanisation and urban - rural coordinated development, industrial development and distribution, innovation and creative city-regions, infrastructure planning, land resources and the environment, social development and public services, institutional reform and innovation, the deepening of opening-up and cooperation, and planning implementation. According to an official of the NDRC, integrated considerations are made for these strategies and locations in a top-down manner based on the following considerations: the national interest, regional competitiveness, and regional common issues such as environmental protection and coordination (Zhou, 2005). For example, an industrial strategy was formulated for the whole region to develop tertiary industry and new-technology industry to promote the restructuring of export-oriented manufacturing sectors. Correspondingly, restrictions were imposed on steel and petrochemical industries, because output capacity in the region was believed to exceed demand. It was suggested that existing small enterprises should merge with large ventures to build up new capacity. In addition, specific industrial strategies for each city in the region were proposed in order to eliminate redundant industrial development. Another case in point is the proposal for intra-regional transport infrastructure. It was judged that the region was greatly lagging behind in terms of inter - city transport links. Although the highway network was well developed, and played an important role in linking different places, it was argued that the highways encroached on too much land and were not environmentally friendly. As a result, it was decided that highway construction would no longer be encouraged in the region. Instead, inter - city high - speed railways were given priority and the spatial structure of high - speed railways was proposed. Consequently, the centrally initiated proposal helped to break the deadlock because local governments had no capacity to invest in inter-city infrastructure, even though demand for inter - city commuting was sharply increasing. Thus, the regional plan fills a gap in institutional arrangements through an integrated regional perspective, and helps to resolve critical problems

二、规划内涵的扩大：改变规划性质以实现战略管治

　　尽管由编制过五年经济计划和国土规划的发改委发起，但长三角区域规划并不单纯是经济规划或土地利用规划，其内容已经拓展到经济、土地资源、环境、基础设施协调发展、区域平等和区域创新等各个方面。除了整体战略，规划的其余部分还为重点产业、基础设施、高速公路以及城际铁路线等其他发展内容制定了战略并进行了选址。规划的后十章内容主要包括城市化与城乡协调发展、产业发展与布局、创新与创新型城市区域、基础设施规划、土地资源与环境、社会发展与公共服务、体制改革与创新、深化对外开放与合作以及规划实施等问题。据发改委的一名官员称，规划自上而下地对这些战略和选址进行了综合考虑，其依据为以下几点：国家利益、区域竞争力以及环境保护和协调等区域内的普遍问题（周毅仁，2005）。例如，为促进以出口为导向的制造业的结构重组，针对整个区域制定了产业战略以发展第三产业和新技术产业。相应地，钢铁和石化产业受到限制，因为这些产业在该地区的产能被认为供大于求。规划也建议现有的小型企业联合大型企业形成新的产能。此外，为了减少重复的产业发展，规划针对区域内各城市提出了具体的产业战略。另一个例子是关于区域内交通基础设施的提议。规划指出长三角区域在城际交通线路方面严重滞后。虽然高速公路网发达，起到了重要的交通枢纽作用，但其占用土地过多且不环保。因此，规划不再鼓励该区域的高速公路建设，而要求优先发展城际高速铁路，并对高速铁路的空间结构提出了建议。长三角区域对城际交通的需求急剧增长，但地方政府却无力投资城际基础设施建设，中央的提议正好打破了这一僵局。区域规划从区域整体着眼，填补了制度安

and concerns that could not be solved by individual provinces or municipalities (Yang and Chen, 2007).

The broader scope of planning shows that regional planning, rather than individual government departments, now tries to solve the major problems that confront the overall regulation of the region. For example, land use and land protection lies under the Ministry of Land and Resources, while the management of urbanisation and urban development is the responsibility of MHURD. The broadened scope of the plan demonstrates that it attempts to pay attention to all relevant issues in order to develop an integrated strategy for land, resources and development. Overall, the scale of new regional planning is designated by NDRC with the intention of guiding and governing the activities of local governments in their local strategy making and project proposals. The scope of the plan is hence greatly widened and it is no longer simply an internal department document. In addition, the plan is conferred with statutory status rather than being reliant upon administrative measures for implementation. It is thus anticipated that coordination between different places and departments should be promoted. In other words, the governing of the YRD region will not lead to the establishment of a particular government or governance body at the regional scale; it is the central government itself that directly plans and governs the region. That is, the regional plan is introduced by the central government to govern local development without inserting another level of regional government body into the existing five-tier government hierarchy. As a socialist legacy, however, territorial management is still more reliant upon employing hierarchical authority and administrative measures than building consensus by means of open negotiation, public participation and awareness. Because of relatively limited local involvement, the effectiveness of the regional plan was doubted at the beginning of its preparation.

7.4 The ongoing tension in the development of new state space

7.4.1 The contest between ministries for spatial regulation power

The YRD Regional Plan prepared by NDRC did not proceed smoothly, and faced many challenges. Its sole authority has been contested by plans made by the other ministries. For example, MHURD started preparing the YRD Urban Cluster Plan (2007-2020) in 2005, which is to the same timescale as that by NDRC. Following NDRC and MHURD, the MLR also jumped the bandwagon and attempted to make its own regional plan. Among the competition, the rivalry between NDRC and MHURD is the most acute. The YRD Urban Cluster Plan project by MHURD started on 15th November

排中的空白,有利于解决单个省市无法解决的重要问题(杨俊宴和陈雯,
2007)。

　　传统上,土地资源的利用和保护由国土资源部负责,而城市化和城乡发展
由住建部负责管理。当前区域规划内容的拓展表明,政府期望通过整合的区
域规划,而非个别政府部门来解决整体区域管治所面临的重大问题。规划试
图尽可能地考虑到所有相关问题,以制定一个集土地、资源和发展于一体的综
合性战略。总体而言,发改委制定这个新的区域规划尺度,旨在指导和管治地
方政府的战略制定与项目计划。因此规划的范围大大拓宽,不再只是一份部
门内部的文件。此外,规划还被赋予法律地位,其实施并非依赖行政手段。因
此不同地区和部门间的协作有望得到加强。换言之,长三角区域不会由专门
成立的政府机构或部门来管治,而是由中央政府直接进行规划和管治。或者
说,区域规划是中央政府为了管治地区发展而制定的,无需在现有的五个政府
层级中再插入新的区域级政府机构。但受社会主义思想影响,地域管理仍更
多地依赖于层级管理制度和行政手段,而非通过公开谈判、公众参与和提高公
众意识等方式达成一致。由于地方参与相对有限,区域规划在筹划初期便遭
到了质疑。

第四节　新国家空间发展过程中的矛盾关系

一、各部委之间争夺空间监管权

　　发改委制定的长三角区域规划进展并不顺利,且面临诸多挑战,其权威性
也受到其他部委规划的挑战。住建部于 2005 年开始筹划长三角城市群规划
(2007—2020),发改委也差不多在同一时期开始筹划长三角区域规划。之后,
国土资源部也加入竞争行列,试图制定自己的区域规划。在这一竞争中,发改
委和住建部之间的矛盾最突出。住建部的长三角城市群规划项目于 2005 年

2005, and ended in early 2008 (interview, involved planner, Chinese Academy of Urban Planning and Design, April 8, 2010). The project was co-financed by MHURD and Provincial-level Commissions of Housing and Urban and Rural Development, while MHURD took the lead in organisation (interview, involved planner, Chinese Academy of Urban Planning and Design, February 25, 2010). The mega-project was mainly shouldered by the Chinese Academy of Urban Planning and Research, which is subordinate to MHURD. Historically, the two planning agencies had different foci: NDRC concentrated on economic regulation, while MHURD covered urban land use and construction. However, both plans now put spatial regulation and coordination at the top of their agendas and adopt a regional perspective and spatial approach. Therefore, the contents and structure of the MHURD plan are quite similar to that of the NDRC plan. For example, the MHURD plan has five sections. The first section deals with the opportunity and challenge confronted by the YRD region. The second sets overall goals and strategy for the whole region. The third allocates spatial policies for urbanisation, population, employment, industrial distribution, rural development, transport systems, energy use and ecological protection. The fourth focuses on the key trans-border areas for integrated development or collaboration and the last section illustrates the implementation mechanism and related policies for the plan. In other words, similar to the regional plan made by the NDRC, the urban cluster plan by MHURD also undertakes comprehensive analyses including different aspects of land, resources, industries and regional inequality to take forward a unified spatial development framework for the region. Coordinated policies were designed for the three provinces and one municipality in terms of urbanisation, industries, transport, environment and spatial development. Under the general framework, special concern was paid to some important trans-border areas, such as the trans-border cities which need coordinated spatial and transport development, and areas that need coordination in terms of environmental management.

Through interviews with both ministries and their affiliated organisations, it seems that MHURD is recognised as more adept at plan preparation. However, NDRC is unwilling to use the plan made by MHURD to guide its administrative management. Although MHURD acknowledges that NDRC possesses more administrative and political resources to implement regional plans, MHURD regards its plan as more scientific and realistic. In short, the making of these regional plans represents the fact that consensus has been achieved by different central ministries and that a higher-level intervention is required to coordinate city-based development from a regional or even national consideration. However, the various planning agencies have not yet taken coordinated action or integrated policy-making processes as advocated by European spatial planning.

11月15日启动,2008年初结束(2010年4月8日对中国城市规划设计研究院某相关规划者的采访)。该项目由住建部和各省住建委共同出资,由住建部负责机构领导工作(2010年2月25日对中国城市规划设计研究院某相关规划者的采访),并由住建部的直属科研机构中国城市规划设计研究院(中规院)承担主要项目工作。发改委和住建部的工作侧重点历来不同:前者侧重于经济规划,后者则侧重于城市的土地利用和建设。而现在双方的规划都将空间监管和协调置于首位,并从区域角度出发对待空间问题。因此,双方规划的内容和框架都极为相似。例如,住建部的规划内容有五部分。第一部分阐述了长三角区域面临的机遇和挑战。第二部分明确了整个区域的总体目标和战略。第三部分针对城市化、人口、就业、产业布局、农村发展、交通系统、能源利用和生态保护等方面制定了空间政策。第四部分着眼于重要交界地区的共同发展和相互合作。最后一部分则阐述了规划的实施机制和相关政策。换言之,住建部的城市群规划与发改委制定的区域规划非常相似,也对土地、资源、产业和区域发展不平等等方面进行了综合分析,以促进建立统一的区域空间发展框架。规划还针对三省一市的城市化、产业、交通、环境和空间发展等方面制定了协调政策。在整体框架下,规划特别关注了一些重要的跨界地区,例如,一些重要的跨界城市需要协调空间和交通发展,而一些地区则需要协调环境管理。

　　通过对发改委和住建部及其直属机构的采访可知,住建部似乎被认可更具规划编制的技术能力。但是,发改委并不愿采用住建部制定的规划来指导自己的行政管理工作。而住建部虽承认发改委在区域规划实施方面拥有更多的行政和政治资源,但仍坚持认为自己的规划更具科学性和可操作性。简而言之,区域规划的编制热潮说明各中央部委已达成共识,认为需要从区域甚至国家的角度来协调地方的发展。然而,不同的规划机构尚未如欧洲空间规划所倡导的那样,采取相互协作的行动或统一的政策制定方式。结果,各项规划

Consequently, each plan is pursuing comprehensiveness by itself, without any effort to join-up different strategies of different sectors, or to work together across various sectors on one overall strategy.

The conflicts have even spread from the process of formulating regional plans to that of building planning institutions. In order to re-establish their legitimacy to formulate and implement regional plans, both MHURD and NDRC are eager to strengthen the legal status of their regional plans. For example, the role of the urban system plan has recently been totally redefined by MHURD. Under the 1989 Planning Act, it was stipulated that the different tiers of urban system plan at the national, provincial, municipal and county level were prepared mainly as groundwork for the urban master plan. In other words, the main purpose of the urban system plan was just to ensure the feasibility of the function and scale of individual cities in the urban master plan. Therefore, even though the urban system plan is the only statutory regional plan in China and is the compulsory plan under the Planning Act, it does not hold an independent role, but is auxiliary to the urban master plan, particularly for those at and below the municipal level. However, recently, MHURD has sought to take advantage of the statutory status of the urban system plan to consolidate its role of regulation. It has attempted to use the different levels of urban system plan as regulation devices for the corresponding level of government, not only the Housing and Urban and Rural Development Department. As explained by the chief of the regional planning department under MHURD, 'Each level of the urban system plan corresponds with the regulation imperative of the level of the government. The different levels of urban system plan are responsible for the corresponding level of government to coordinate urban development of the lower-level governments' (from the PPT presentation made by Qin Zhang at the 2009 Annual Conference of Regional Plan and Urban Economics Academic Committee, 2009-12-20, Beijing). As illuminated in Figure 7.4, it is hoped the cascade of urban system plans would become well-functioning top-down guidance on various levels of local development. Obviously, MHURD is expecting its urban plan to go beyond the ministry and become the tool of the government in spatial regulation. For the purpose, MHURD commanded the Chinese Academy of Urban Planning and Design Institute to prepare the National Urban System Plan in 2005, which has not been prepared before. This is expected to be the device of the central government to strengthen national guidance on local development (interview, the chief planner of a major planning academy, March 30 2010). Unfortunately, this plan was not approved by the State Council. It is believed that the plan became the sacrifice of the conflicts between ministries for spatial

仍是各行其是，没有尝试整合不同部门的不同策略，也没有开展跨部门合作来制定一项综合的战略。

区域规划制定上的冲突延续到了规划机构的建立上。为重新确立区域规划编制和实施工作的合法性，住建部和发改委都迫切希望加强各自区域规划的法律地位。例如，住建部最近就完全重新定义了城镇体系规划的作用。根据1989年的《城市规划法》，城镇体系规划一般分为国家、省、市、县四级，主要作为城市总体规划的基础。或者说，城镇体系规划的主要目的只是保证城市总体规划中各城市功能和尺度的可行性。因此，尽管城镇体系规划是《城市规划法》明确规定的强制性规划，且是中国唯一的法定区域规划，但它并不是独立发挥作用的，而是附属于城市总体规划，是市级和市级以下的规划。不过，最近住建部想利用城镇体系规划的法律地位来强化规划的监管作用，试图将不同级别的城镇体系规划作为相应级别政府的监管工具，而非仅局限于住建部。根据住建部区域规划部门领导的说法，"城镇体系规划的每一级别都对应着相应级别政府的监管指令。不同级别的城镇体系规划协助相应级别的政府来协调下级政府的城镇发展工作（张勤在2009年区域规划和城市经济学术委员会年会上的PPT内容，2009年12月20日，北京）。如图7.4所示，城镇体系规划的这种分级形式将会对不同级别的地方发展起到自上而下的良好指导作用。住建部显然期望其规划不再局限于本单位内部，还能成为政府空间监管的工具。为此，2005年住建部指示中规院制定了首个全国城镇体系规划，希望这一规划成为中央政府加强国家对地方发展指导的工具（2010年3月30日对

regulation power (interview, the chief planner of a major planning academy❶, March 30 2010). Since the central government shows more favour to the plan prepared by NDRC, it would rather not approve that made by MHURD due to the consideration of redundancy. As a result, the national urban system plan could only be used as an internal document by MHURD, even though it is the statutory plan according to the City Planning Act (interview, the chief planner of a major planning academy, March 30 2010).

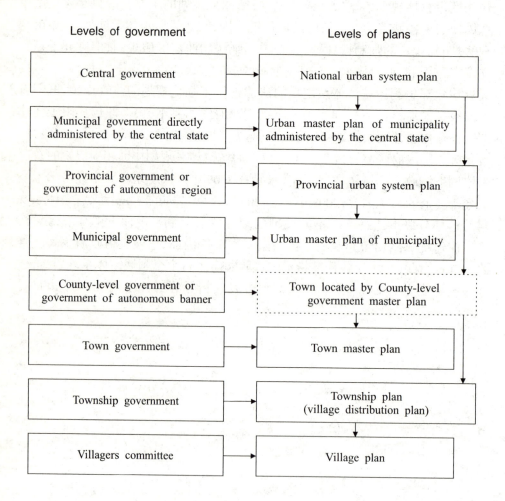

Figure 7.4 Urban system plan as the tool of governance for MHURD
Source: compiled from Q. Zhang, 2009.

---

❶ Because of the sensitivity of this comment, the location of the academy remains unlisted.

某主要规划院❶的首席规划师的采访）。遗憾的是,这一规划最后并未获得国务院批准,有人认为这一规划成为了各部委争夺空间监管权的牺牲品(2010年3月30日对某主要规划研究院的首席规划师的采访)。由于中央政府比较支持发改委的规划,为避免重复,不愿批准住建部的规划。因此,尽管全国城镇体系规划是《城市规划法》规定的法定规划,但却只能被用作住建部的内部文件(2010年3月30日对某主要规划研究院的首席规划师的采访)。

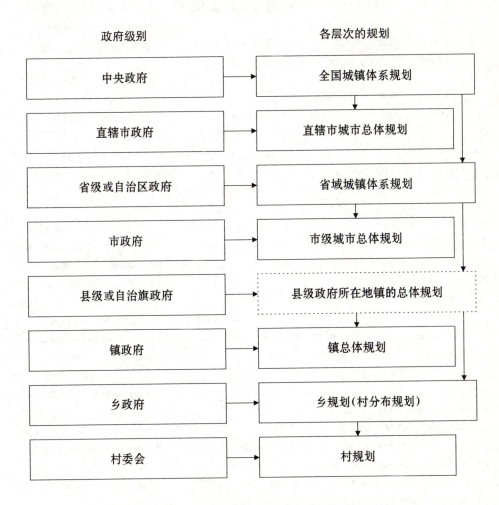

政府级别   各层次的规划

中央政府 → 全国城镇体系规划

直辖市政府 → 直辖市城市总体规划

省级或自治区政府 → 省域城镇体系规划

市政府 → 市级城市总体规划

县级或自治旗政府 → 县级政府所在地镇的总体规划

镇政府 → 镇总体规划

乡政府 → 乡规划(村分布规划)

村委会 → 村规划

图7.4 作为住建部管治工具的城镇体系规划

来源:张勤编制,2009。

---

❶ 由于此评论涉及内容较为敏感,该研究院名称未被列出。

At the same time, NDRC is also very ambitious for its regional plans to be adopted as the overall government plan:

> The NDRC attempts to get through an overarching regional plan ordinance to coordinate all regional-level plans of various government departments under the NDRC regional plan umbrella. The intention of the proposal is to streamline the regional plans made by various departments and make the regional policies more compatible with each other. However, the proposal was fiercely resisted by other ministries, especially MHURD and MLR. (interview, leading academic in planning, Nanjing University, March 12 2010)

Although NPC, the predecessor of NDRC, used to hold sole authority over the planned economy and guided overall economic and spatial development, the mandatory power of NDRC is now much weaker after economic reform. Although the State Council has treated NDRC more favourably and approved all its regional plans, 'harmonious relations between ministries' have to be taken into account. Consequently, the 'proposal for legislation made by NDRC was finally compromised under great pressure and the released document is limited by the system of five-year plans' (interview, the director of a major planning academy[1], March 17, 2010). In this sense, the regional plan is merely an additional planning ordinance within the system of NDRC, just like that of MHURD, rather than an overarching planning legislation.

Overall, the contest between different ministries on the formulation and institutionalisation of the regional plans actually manifests the battle articulated by the ministries to safeguard their power and interests (Hu, 2006). The unprecedented emphasis placed by the central government on spatial regulation represents the new area of power for these ministries. Henceforth, MHURD, which is now in charge of making urban and regional plans, is eager to upgrade its plan as the device of the government for spatial governance; while NDRC and MLR, which were historically engaged with regional plan making, are keen to resume the making of regional plans. This is in stark contrast to the attitude to regional planning in the early decades of economic reform, when territory plans were not valued by either NPC or the later MLR.

The repetitive plan-making has not only caused tension at the regional scale, but also resulted in a lot of controversy and ambiguity over the regional

---

[1] Because of the sensitivity of this comment, the location of the academy remains unlisted; similar views are shared in other interviews about the difficulty of coordinating plan making between different ministries.

与此同时,发改委也一心期望其区域规划能成为政府的总体规划:

> 发改委试图通过一个总体性的区域规划条例,在发改委区域规
> 划的框架下,对不同政府部门所有区域级规划进行协调。这一提案
> 旨在精简不同部门的区域规划,提升区域政策的兼容性。但这一提
> 案遭到了其他部委的强烈反对,尤其是住建部和国土资源部。(2010
> 年3月12日对南京大学规划专业某学者的采访)

　　发改委的前身国家计划委员会曾在计划经济中独揽大权,指导总体经济和空间发展,但在经济体制改革后,发改委的强制力被大大削弱。尽管目前在区域规划问题上国务院更倾向于由发改委来统筹,并批准了其所有的区域规划,但同时也得权衡"部委间的和谐关系"。因此,"发改委提出的立法提案在巨大的压力下也只得被迫妥协,已发布的区域规划文件也被局限于五年规划的体系内"(2010年3月17日对某主要规划研究院[1]院长的采访)。从这种意义上来说,与住建部所面临的局面一样,发改委的区域规划也仅能作为其系统内部的附加性规划条例,而并不是总体性的规划法规。

　　总之,不同部委在区域规划的制定及制度化上的竞争实际上反映的是各部委保护自身权力和利益的斗争(胡序威,2006)。在这些部门看来,中央政府对空间规划前所未有的重视意味着新的权力领域。因此,目前负责制定城市与区域规划的住建部希望将其规划提升为政府的空间监管工具;而历来负责制定区域规划的发改委和国土资源部则迫切希望恢复其制定区域规划的职权。这与改革开放初期各部委对区域规划的态度形成了鲜明对比,当时不论是国家计委还是后来的国土资源部都不太重视国土规划。

　　规划的重复制定不仅导致了区域层面的冲突,还给已出台的区域空间规划带来了很多争议和歧义。例如,住建部和发改委分别制定的长三角空间规

---

[1] 由于本评论涉及内容较为敏感,该研究院名称未被列出;关于不同部门间协调规划制定工作的困难的类似观点,在其他采访中亦有体现。

spatial plans. For example, the YRD spatial plans made by MHURD and NDRC have not only formulated different policy agendas and spatial policies on their own, but even have different understandings from one another in terms of the geographical boundaries of the YRD region. The NDRC ministry originally specified that the YRD region only covered a small area of 15 prefecture-level cities around Shanghai, which was then expanded to a larger region including Shanghai, Jiangsu and Zhejiang. However, the area understood by MHURD to comprise the YRD region was composed of Shanghai, Jiangsu, Zhejiang plus Anhui province. The big divergence between the two main ministries thus leaves the localities with excuses not to follow any plan formulation.

7.4.2 The conflicts between levels of government

On the other hand, the YRD Regional Plan is challenged by implementation and effectiveness in practice. The motivations between the central and local government are often contradictory. The regional plan by NDRC received much attention from local authorities for its participative role in plan-making and its perceived strategic status in the national and regional economy and consequential preferential treatment of policy support and project allocation. 'Many provincial governors are very anxious about whether the city regions under their jurisdiction will be incorporated into any national strategies' (interview, a leading academic in planning, Nanjing University, March 12 2010). This is because NDRC is the major economic planning agency in China; for example, NDRC is in charge of the four trillion Yuan stimulus plan approved by the State Council to cope with the global financial crisis in 2008. For this reason, localities strive to be included in the regional plan, not for the sake of strengthened governance, but because they are hoping for some potential opportunities to be given, even implicitly, by 'national strategies':

> Local authorities can make use of the plan to their own benefits and market the strategic significance of the city in the national and regional economy to attract investment. Although the centrally made regional plan does not provide direct capital support, local authorities tend to use the regional plan to lobby other ministries for special policies, especially for the quota of construction land, loans from national banks, and more autonomy in ex-ante 'institutional experiments' without permission from higher-level governments. (interview, involved scholar, Nanjing Institute of Geography and Limnology of Chinese Academy of Sciences, March 11, 2010)

划不仅各有不同的政策议程和空间政策,甚至对长三角区域的地理界定都不同。发改委最初界定的长三角区域只是覆盖上海周边15个地级市的一小片区域,而后才被扩展为包括江浙沪的较大区域。然而,按照住建部的理解,长三角区域是由江浙沪及安徽省组成的。两大主要部委的巨大分歧使得地方有理由不遵循任何一项规划。

二、各级政府间的冲突

另一方面,长三角区域规划在实际实施效率方面也面临着挑战。中央政府和地方政府制定规划的动机常常是矛盾的。由于发改委的规划被认为象征着在国家和地区经济中的战略地位,且带有相应的优惠待遇(如政策支持和项目分配),因此该规划得到了地方政府较多的关注。"很多省长都非常关心他们辖区内的城市区域是否会被纳入某个国家战略"(2010年3月12日对南京大学规划专业某主要学者的采访)。这是因为发改委是中国主要的经济规划机构;举例来说,为应对2008年全球金融危机,国务院批准了四万亿元经济刺激计划,而这个计划就是由发改委来负责执行的。因此,地方政府竭力争取被纳入区域规划中,并不是为了加强自身的管治,而是希望通过"国家战略"获得一些潜在的(哪怕是间接的)机会:

> 地方政府可以利用区域规划为本地谋利,并通过宣传本地城市在国家和区域经济中的战略地位来吸引投资。尽管中央制定的区域规划不会带来直接的资金支持,但地方政府往往会利用区域规划游说其他部委以获得特殊政策,尤其是建设用地配额、国家银行贷款以及在无需上级政府批准的事前"制度试点"上有更多的自主性。(2012年3月11日对中国科学院南京地理与湖泊研究所相关学者的采访)

Even though the NDRC regional plan obtained its statutory status, it is still very difficult for central government to deal with game-playing local governments and guarantee the enforcement of the regional plan. First of all, as commented by an experienced academic in a planning school:

> The contents of the current regional plans are still too general and too brief; few offer guidance linked with enforcement regulations. And hence, it is very difficult for the relevant government departments to intervene in local development by reference to the regional plan. (interview, scholar, Nanjing University, March 12, 2010)

Secondly, the regional plan is not equipped with any regulatory power, funding or other incentives for implementation, even though it is strongly advocated by central government. 'Since there is no Regional Planning Act in China, there is no relevant regulation on what to do if there is no compliance with the regional plan. Neither are regulations enforced on the local governments to ensure they follow the regional plan to prepare their local plans' (interview, scholar, Nanjing University, March 12, 2010). Furthermore, a common problem for planning in China is the fact that 'even though the plan is approved by the upper level government, the implementation actually lies in the hands of the local government...' (interview, official, MHURD, April 6, 2010). Since China's economic reform, the operation of local government is no longer granted by the central government, but predominantly by itself; local development is not funded by the central government either, but is largely initiated by the local government as well. On the other hand, 'the primary land market is virtually administered by the local government, which further facilitates the locally initiated development' (interview, official, MHURD, April 6, 2010). In a word, the central government is confronted with great difficulties when seeking to safeguard the implementation of the plans it has approved. As a result, the central government is forced to 'strengthen the law in terms of plan enforcement and plan revision, and in the meantime put aside a quantity of money to use satellite data for real-time supervision of the implementation of the plan and land protection' (interview, official, MHURD, April 6, 2010). However, as pointed out by a senior professional, '...the spatial planning is not any panacea...as long as the locally-initiated development model is not changed, the intention to use spatial planning to control the local development is very difficult to achieve' (interview, senior planner, Chinese Academy of Urban Planning and Design, April 2, 2010). In other words, even the strictest censorship is doomed to fail under the current situation, which

尽管发改委的区域规划已确立了该规划的法律地位,中央政府仍然很难应对具有博弈心态的地方政府并确保区域规划的有效实施。首先,正如某规划学院的一位资深学者所说:

> 当前区域规划的内容仍然太宽泛太粗略;规划很少给出与实施规范相关的指导。因此,相关政府部门很难遵照区域规划来指导地方发展。(2010年3月12日对南京大学某学者的采访)

其次,尽管区域规划获得了中央政府的大力支持,但它不具有任何监管力、资金支持或其他推动实施的激励政策。"由于中国没有'区域规划法',对于不遵循区域规划的做法也就没有相应的措施,也没有任何条例强制地方政府在制定地方规划时遵循区域规划"(2010年3月12日对南京大学某学者的采访)。此外,中国的规划中常见的一个问题就是"尽管某个规划已获上级政府批准,但它的实施实际上还是掌握在地方政府手中的……"(2010年4月6日对住建部某官员的采访)。改革开放以来,地方政府的运作不再依靠中央政府拨款,而主要由地方财政负担;地方建设项目也不再由中央政府出资,而大多由地方政府自行发起。另一方面,"一级土地市场实际上是由地方政府掌控的,这进一步促进了地方自主搞开发建设"(2010年4月6日对住建部某官员的采访)。总之,中央政府在已批准规划的贯彻实施上面临着巨大的困难。这种困境所导致的结果是,中央政府被迫"完善与规划实施及修订相关的法律,同时拨出一笔经费用于获取卫星数据,以便对规划的实施及土地保护进行实时监控"(2010年4月6日对住建部某官员的采访)。然而,正如一位资深专业人士所指出的,"……空间规划不是包治百病的灵丹妙药……只要由地方主导的发展模式不转变,想要通过空间规划来控制地方发展的目标就难以达成"(2010年4月2日对中规院城市与规划研究所某高级规划师的采访)。换言之,在当前情况下,即使是最严格的监管也注定会失败,只是白白浪费中央政府的资源和精力。

could only exhaust the resources and energy of the central government.

Although the regional plan by NDRC suggests that the current promotion system based on economic performance should be reformed and that the tax-sharing system and revenue structures be modified, these suggestions are not on the recent agenda of political reform:

> The system of cadre promotion is under the charge of the Organization Department of the CPC Central Committee; the system of tax and revenue is under the charge of the Revenue Department; while the transfer payment is determined by the Ministry of Finance. Although NDRC is a half-level higher than other ministries under the State Council, that only means it is able to organise inter-ministry meetings; it cannot make policies for issues that are the responsibility of other ministries. (interview, official, MHURD, April 6, 2010)

In a word, it seems that the central government still lacks the commitment to initiate overall institutional and political reforms. Plan-making is not given any stronger status in the administrative system. As revealed by a participant academic:

> Plan-making is headed by the vice-director of NDRC, whose political status is only equivalent to that of vice-provincial governors. In the fieldwork and data collection period, the planning group is mainly led by the vice-director of Local Economy Department under NDRC, whose political status is even lower, merely equivalent to the deputy mayor of a prefecture-level city. In the circumstances, the involved provinces and cities may pretend to collaborate with the planning work, but do not take the plan seriously. Even though the plan is totally funded by the national government, NDRC actually cannot impose strong interventions whether in communication with local leaders or in the substantial planning contents. (interview, an involved academic in a leading planning school[1], March 19, 2010)

Overall, it seems the central government is left with few devices to regulate local development after decades of decentralisation. With policies only

---

[1] Because of the sensitivity of this comment, the location of the affiliation remains unlisted. As a tradition in China, academics are heavily involved in plan preparation, playing a leading role in directly drafting plans rather than mere consultation. As a result, the participating academics, who have long established links with the government, are familiar with the process of plan-making.

尽管发改委制定的区域规划建议对当前以经济指标为主要考核依据的干部晋升体制进行改革,对分税制及财税结构进行修改,但是这些建议并没有出现在近期政治改革的议程上:

> 干部晋升体制权属中共中央组织部;财税体制权属税务部门;而转移支付权属财政部。虽然国家发改委比国务院下属的其他部委高半个级别,但这仅意味着它可以组织部际会议,却无权就其他部委权责范围内的问题制定政策。(2010年4月6日对住建部某官员的采访)

总之,中央政府似乎仍缺乏发起全面体制改革和政治改革的决心。规划制定工作在现有行政体系中的地位仍然不高。正如一位参与规划制定的学者所揭示的:

> 规划制定工作由发改委副主任领导,而他的职级仅仅相当于副省长。在实地考察及数据采集阶段,规划团队主要是由发改委下属的地区经济司副司长领导的,他的职级更低,仅仅相当于地级市的副市长。在这种情况下,相关省市对规划工作很可能表面上配合,实际上并不重视。尽管规划完全由国家政府出资,但实际上发改委不论是在与地方领导沟通时还是在实质性规划内容上都没有很强的干预力量。(2010年3月19日对某主要规划研究院❶相关学者的采访)

总而言之,在实行了数十年的地方分权制度后,中央政府监管地方发展的工具似乎所剩无几。仅凭一纸政策文件,区域规划对地方自主行为较难有很

---

❶ 由于本评论涉及的内容较为敏感,该研究院名称未被列出。中国的惯例是,学者大量参与规划制定,不仅作为顾问,而且直接参与规划的起草并起带头作用。因此,与政府建立了长期关系并参与规划制定的学者对于政策的制定过程非常熟悉。

on paper, the regional plan alone cannot impose much restraint on local discretionary behaviour.

In addition, the plan-making process lacks a substantial participation mechanism. For instance, the regional plan made by NDRC only involved a fieldtrip to major prefecture-level cities. In other words, only leaders of relevant departments at the prefecture-level cities were involved in the plan preparations. More importantly, this participation was not in terms of decision-making, but was just to provide local information to the central ministries and plan-makers. Some of the counties and towns may not even be aware of the regional plan at all. When conducting interviews at the county-level city Kunshan, the planning official of the city somehow felt the regional plan was irrelevant to them, even though their area was covered by the plan. The lack of involvement in the negotiation not only reduces the likelihood of consent to the regional plan by authorities, but also undermines the transparency of the policy-making process. For example, the sophisticated and non-transparent spatial zoning in the process of plan-making encouraged, to some extent, under-the-table deals. As spatial zoning is associated with spatial regulation and investment approval, local authorities try by all means not to be put in the restricted or forbidden area of development, and in the meantime propose to have as many local projects as possible written into the regional plan for future convenience in project approval. For example, the plan intends to strengthen environmental protection in one of the regions in Zhejiang province, which means that local development within the area would be constrained. To avoid this restriction, one of the cities located in the area made significant efforts to persuade the plan-makers to change the policy. Finally, compromises were made and some particular cities were allowed to be developed along the environment-sensitive belt (interview, involved scholar, Nanjing Institute of Geography and Limnology of Chinese Academy of Sciences, March 11, 2010). As revealed by the scholar, who participated in plan preparation, many cities took advantage and lobbied the ministry and plan-makers in order to gain a more privileged status in the planning document due to the less transparent zoning procedure.

Overall, it seems that the regional plan is in an awkward position since 'the central government cannot effectively intervene in local developments by the use of the regional plan; on the other hand, local authorities can take full advantage of the plan to lobby for relaxation of control in development' (interview, a participant academic, Nanjing University, March 12, 2010). Therefore, the influence of the regional plan in practice is still in great doubt. It is held by some critics that the regional plan still exists more in a symbolic sense than in reality. As commented by an involved plan-maker, 'anyway, even for scientific development or coordinated development, what is overriding is still

大的约束力。

　　此外,规划制定过程也缺少必要的参与机制。例如,发改委制定的区域规划只包括对主要地级市的实地考察,也就是说,只有地级市相关部门的领导参与了规划的筹备工作。更重要的是,其参与并不涉及决策,只是为中央部委和规划制定者提供地方数据。有些县和乡镇甚至都不知道区域规划。县级市昆山位列规划范围内,但在采访昆山市负责规划的官员时,他们却认为区域规划与自身关系不大。地方官员缺乏对谈判过程的参与,不仅减小了地方政府认同区域规划的可能性,而且会降低政策制定过程的透明度。例如,在制定规划时,繁冗而不透明的空间区划过程在某种程度上会助长暗箱交易。因为空间区划与空间监管和投资审批有关,地方政府会竭尽全力避免被划入限制或禁止发展的区域,同时争取将尽可能多的本地项目纳入区域规划,以便于将来通过项目审批。比如,规划旨在加强浙江省某地的环保力度,也就意味着当地的发展会受到一些制约。为避免受此制约,该地区内某市政府就会努力游说规划制定者改变政策。最终,规划制定方作出妥协,允许某些特定城市沿环境敏感带发展(2012年3月11日对中科院南京地理与湖泊研究所相关学者的采访)。据这位参与了规划编制的学者称,由于区域划分程序缺乏透明度,出现了不少城市为在规划文件中获得更有利的条件而钻空子、游说有关部委和规划编制者的现象。

　　总而言之,区域规划看似处于一个尴尬的境地,这是因为“中央政府并不能利用区域规划去有效地干预地方发展;而从另一方面来说,地方政府却可以充分利用这种规划去游说中央政府放松对地方发展的管制”(2012年3月12日对南京大学相关学者的采访)。因此,区域规划在实际中的作用仍备受质疑。某些批评者认为,区域规划更多地仍然是一种象征性的形式,缺乏实际作用。正如参与了规划制定的一位规划师所评论的,“不管怎么说,即便从科学发展

to develop the economy' (interview, senior planner, Chinese Academy of Urban Planning and Design, 8 April 2010). The senior planner even held a pessimistic outlook for the regional plan because 'the scientific development, the recentralisation, and the regional plan is just a short and temporary wave, the general trend for China is still rapid development'.

7.5 Conclusion

This chapter analyses the ebbs and flows of regional administration and regional planning in the YRD in China from 1949 to recent times, and maps these changes with the transformation of regional governance. Historically, the central government has attempted to establish regional-level administration in the area around the current YRD region, that is, the East China Administrative Region from 1950 to 1954; the East China Cooperative Region from 1954 to 1960; and the East China Central Bureau from 1961 to 1976. These regional jurisdictions were launched by the central government in order to consolidate the top-down regulation on local territorial development. However, the political turbulence during the period undermined the stability and effectiveness of the regional administrations.

Since 1979, the Chinese state system has no longer retained a regional level of administration between the central government and provinces. This is because decentralisation was advocated by economic reform. However, China has not stopped practising regional planning for this reason. As a matter of fact, the central government attempted to set up an informal regional organisation within the current YRD region to facilitate top-down regulation and horizontal coordination. The informal organisation, namely the Shanghai Economic Zone, was also considered to be an important region within the national territory planning launched at the time by NPC. Henceforth, a great number of integrated strategies and sectoral plans were prepared for the SEZ region.

Nevertheless, the central intervention on territorial development and horizontal cooperation was, to some extent, resisted by the local government because it was regarded as a residue of the central command economy. Post-reform regional planning was even marginalised in the structure of governance due to the downscaling of planning power to the municipal government. The influence of regional planning has been undermined because of its outdated planning approach. The sceptical attitude towards regional planning, as well as the re-organisation of the central government, contributed to the weakened role of regional governance. Consequently, China's local development proceeded without much effective regional intervention for a period after economic reform.

The YRD Regional Plan initiated by NDRC in 2005 represents the

或协调发展的角度讲,我们目前最重要的任务仍是发展经济"(2012年4月8日对中国城市规划设计研究院某高级规划师的采访)。这位高级规划师甚至对区域规划的前景持悲观态度,因为"科学发展、中央收权和区域规划只是一波短暂的浪潮,在中国高速发展仍是大势所趋"。

第五节　结论

本章分析了自1949年以来中国长三角地区区域管治和区域规划的起落历程,并通过区域管治的转型映射出这些变化。从历史发展的角度来看,中央政府曾尝试在现今的长三角一带建立区域级的行政机构:华东行政区(1950—1954年);华东经济协作区(1954—1960年);以及中共中央华东局(1961—1976年)。这些行政辖区由中央政府划定,目的是巩固其对地方发展自上而下的管治。但这一时期动荡的政治局面却破坏了区域管治的稳定性和有效性。

自1979年以来,在中国的国家体制中,中央政府和各省之间已不存在区域级的行政机构。这是因为经济体制改革倡导权力下放,但中国并未因此停止区域规划的实践。实际上,中央政府曾尝试在现今的长三角区域建立一个非正式的区域组织,来促进自上而下的管治和横向的协调。这个非正式组织,即上海经济开发区,也被认为是当时全国人大制定的国土规划战略中的一个重要区域。此后,中央政府还为上海经济开发区制定了大量的综合战略和部门规划。

然而,在地域发展和横向合作上,中央的干预却在某种程度上受到地方政府的抵制,因为这种干预被当作是中央管制经济的遗留做法。改革后的区域规划由于规划权力下放到市级政府,而在管治架构中被进一步边缘化。由于区域规划的方式已过时,其影响力也被削弱。公众对区域规划政策的质疑,以及中央政府的重组,均弱化了区域管治的作用。因此,在经济体制改革后的一段时期内,中国的地方发展并未受到实质性的区域干预。

recent re-emergence of national and regional plans across the country. The impetus of emerging spatial plans is predominantly to cope with rampant localised land development and to restore governance capacities. In the absence of regional government, the centrally initiated regional plan functions as the vehicle for the central government to reassert its influence on local development at the regional level. In this respect, recent practices of spatial planning demonstrate another wave of efforts to go beyond local entrepreneurialism and pursue regional coordination for the purpose of sustainable development. In other words, the top -down approach to planning at the regional scale is intended to create a 'new state space' to safeguard strategic interests, enhance regional competitiveness, and eliminate excessive competition. The widened scope of planning beyond the economic development and land use planning also demonstrates the changing nature of planning, from being an internal document of one department to a spatial regulation tool for the whole government. However, through the case study of the YRD Regional Plan, it is also suggested that the current regional plans are more akin to visions created by central government rather than concrete actions with immediate effects. Firstly, central government has not yet supplemented these regional plans with any concrete regional policies. The regional plan-makers could only suggest central government as a coordination mechanism on paper. Secondly, legislation for regional plans is very weak. Although the central government ministries intend to integrate a cascade of plans, compliance cannot be guaranteed because of the complexity of inter-governmental politics. Moreover, in addition to contradictory motivations underlying the central and local governments, the regional plan is further undermined by the different agendas of ministries. For example, although the current YRD regional plan is approved and issued by the State Council, it is still viewed as a plan within the NDRC system rather than the overall plan for regional governance. Efforts are being wasted on rival planning processes rather than being spent on the development of a consensus and on integrating working arrangements. Finally, although the core of these plans is discursively focused on land management and sustainable development, the target still prioritises economic growth.

Overall, compared with the bottom-up efforts to assert regionalisation, the top-down forces seem to be more effective in developing regional governance. An overall regional plan has been orchestrated by the central state in a relatively short time, whereas substantive forms of inter-city networking are not yet formed, even after years of development of inter-city associations. The effectiveness of the top-down forces is due to the remaining strong vertical bureaucratic control in China, even though China is greatly decentralised in terms of fiscal relations (Tsui and Wang, 2004). Nevertheless, the current

　　国家发改委2005年发起的长三角区域规划反映出近年来国家和区域规划浪潮在国内的再次兴起。空间规划的兴起主要是为了应对猖獗的地方土地开发,并恢复管治力。在没有区域级政府机构的情况下,中央发起的区域规划便成为中央政府在区域层面上对地方发展施加影响的有力工具。从这方面来说,近期的空间规划实践也反映了一波试图超越地方经营主义、追求区域协调以实现可持续发展的新浪潮。换句话说,区域尺度自上而下的规划方式旨在创建"新国家空间",以保护战略利益、提高区域竞争力以及消除过度竞争。规划内容扩展到经济发展和土地利用规划以外,也体现了规划性质的改变。它不再仅仅是部门内部文件,而试图成为整个政府的空间管治工具。但是,对长三角区域规划的案例研究也表明,当前的区域规划与其说是能立竿见影的切实行动,倒不如说是中央政府构想的远景。首先,中央政府并没有出台任何切实的区域政策来支持这些区域规划。区域规划的制定者只能把中央政府作为理论上的一种协调机制。其次,有关区域规划的立法环节非常薄弱。尽管中央政府各部委意图整合一系列规划,但政府间复杂的政治角力难以保证区域规划的贯彻落实。此外,除了中央和地方政府相互矛盾的动机外,各部委不同的议程更进一步阻碍了区域规划的发展。比如,尽管现今的长三角区域规划是由国务院批准颁布的,但它仍被视为发改委系统内部的一项规划,而非用于区域管治的总体规划。可见很多精力并没有花在努力达成共识以及整合工作安排上,而是被浪费在了各行其是的规划过程中。最后,虽然这些规划的核心大体都集中于土地管理和可持续发展,但我国当前的首要任务仍是发展经济。

　　总而言之,与主张区域化的自下而上的力量相比,自上而下的强制力似乎在区域管治的形成过程中更加有效。中央在相对较短的时间内便精心制定了一套区域总体规划;而城际协作虽已开展数年,但实质性的城际合作模式仍未形成。尽管中国的财税权普遍下放到地方,但垂直的行政控制仍然很强,增强了自上而下的强制力的效果(Tsui 和 Wang,2004)。不过,目前的局面也显示

situation also shows that central government is still very precarious in the formulation of a new regional state space. Although emerging spatial plans help to introduce a new regional perspective, the new state space is being created incrementally without a consolidated mandate of regional development. The emerging spatial plan, however, does help to develop a spatial discourse and involve multiple actors (albeit quite limited at present), which in the long term may strengthen regional governance and region building.

出中央政府在构建新区域国家空间的过程中的作用并不稳定。新兴的空间规划有助于引入新的区域视角,但新国家空间是在缺乏统一的区域发展指令的情况下逐步构建的。不过,新兴的空间规划确实有助于发展空间话语和提高多个行动者的参与度(尽管目前十分有限),从长远来讲也有可能强化区域管治和区域建设。

第八章

CHAPTER EIGHT

Conclusion

Aiming to examine the regional renaissance and the existing regional governance in China, the study traces China's historical development of governance, and further makes an in-depth investigation into the study area of the Yangtze River Delta region. Drawn on the theory of the strategic relational approach and politics of scale, the study conceptualises the changing regional institutional landscape as an attempt to reorganise state configurations by both bottom-up and top-down processes. The study explores the agency, the rationale, the politics and the nature of new state spaces in the context of China, rather than mapping China's experiences in an uncritical way. As the concluding section of the research, this chapter synthesises the transformation of China's regional governance based on the research work conducted in the previous chapters. Conclusions are drawn regarding the evolution, the dynamics and the characteristics of the current regional governance initiatives. Based on the findings of the research, some theoretical implications are proposed for the current 'new state spatiality' and (city-) region debate. Finally, reflections are made on the limitations of this study and suggestions are put forward for continuing work on this topic.

8.1 The main findings

China used to be conferred with strong regional policies and formal regional administration in the Socialist period. During the 'roll-back' era, with decentralisation and market-oriented economic reform, however, regional strategies were marginalised and gradually displaced by urban programmes. However, it appears regional policies and practices have re-emerged in China since 2000. These regional programmes are distributed at all subnational scales above the urban level. They are manifested by the new coordinated polices, and the main functional area plan, which represent the return of regional policies; the recentralisation of land management, and the province-leading-county administrative reform, which manifest an upward scaling of governance towards the regional scale; and the various regionalisation attempts undertaken by both central and local governments, which consist of urban administrative annexation and merger, building regional alliances and partnerships, and formulating regional plans. The disparate regional practices launched by different levels and divisions of government are conferred with various definitions of regions. The lack of unified divisions of regions in policy-making and the absence of a formal level of regional institution within the government structure make the governance

第八章　结论

为了考察中国的区域复兴以及当前的区域管治状况,本书追溯了中国区域管治的发展历史,并进一步以长江三角洲为研究区域做了深入的调查。本研究借用战略关联研究方法以及尺度政治的理论,阐述了区域体制变化通过自下而上和自上而下两种途径重组国家结构的概念。本书还探讨了中国国情下新国家空间的促成因素、机制、政治因素和性质,而不是不加评论地描绘中国经验。作为研究的结论部分,本章在前面各章所做的研究基础上,对中国的区域管治转变进行综合论述,就目前区域管治举措的演变、动力及特点等方面得出相应的结论。根据本研究的发现,将当前西方文献中对"新国家空间"以及(城市)区域的争论提出了几点理论思考。最后,总结了本文的局限性,并为这个课题今后的继续研究提出了建议。

第一节　主要研究发现

在改革开放前的社会主义时期,中国曾实行强有力的区域政策和正式的区域行政管理。在改革开放时期,开始实行权力下放和以市场为导向的经济改革,因此区域战略不断弱化并逐渐被城市项目所取代。但是,自2000年以来,中国的区域政策和实践似乎又重新兴起。这些区域项目全部分布在城市层级以上的所有次国家层面。新的协调政策和主体功能区计划的出台体现了区域政策的回归;土地管理收权和省管县的行政改革体现了管治尺度向区域尺度上移;中央和地方政府开展了各种区域化尝试,包括城市行政的兼并和合并、建立区域联盟和伙伴关系以及制定区域规划等。不同层级的政府和不同政府部门所进行的各自独立的区域实践反映出对区域的定义各不相同。在决策时缺乏统一的区域划分,而且在政府架构中没有设立正式的区域机构层级,

landscape at the regional level widely divided between different policy areas and levels of governments.

The current development of regional governance in China is the outcome of economic development, political mobilisation and the state rescaling process. The development of the economy, i.e. the regionalisation of the economy accompanied by market-oriented economic reform, not only promotes economic links between the jurisdictions, but also creates the need for cooperation in areas such as waste, transport and environmental management owing to the agglomeration of economy and the population. Under the drive of practical demand, the development of regional governance is, in the meantime, strongly engineered by both the central and local government. Regional cooperation and collaborative development is promoted by the central government for the regional and national interest, for example, controlling rampant land development and environmental degradation, regional coordination and redundant development, industrial upgrading and economic safety. Due to the central austerity policy on land supply and the uncertain global manufacturing market after the 2008 global financial crisis, local government has also shown more interest in collaborative development. This is because local governments are pushed to seek an alternative service industry for economic growth, which inherently requires better connections in all respects. In other words, the rationales behind the top-down and bottom-up regional initiatives are different and incompatible. While the central government is pursuing integrated regional development from the perspective of overall national interest, the local government is merely joining in the regional cooperation based on local interests. The conflicts between national and local interests are very likely to lead to tensions in the implementation of regional programmes.

Compared with previous regional administrations, recent practices are based on flexible organisation rather than formal administration. For example, the recent top-down recentralisation initiative does not involve the establishment of a regional level of government body like that in the 1950s, but only the making of regional plans. That is, the central government is mainly deploying regional plans, policies or programmes to impose regional governance on territorial development. In contrast, local governments are drawing upon soft inter-municipal agreements to address concerns over cross-jurisdictional transport, human resource mobility, inter-city tourism, trade and logistics. Unfortunately, neither of the forms is fully institutionalised. Although the trend is to legitimise the regional plan per se, institutions for the implementation of the plan are not yet established. On the other hand, lack of accountability and binding power is detrimental to the authority of spontaneous inter-locality association. As a result, the actual effectiveness of the top-down or bottom-up regional initiatives is in

使得区域层级的管治状况在不同政策区域和不同层级的政府之间千差万别。

　　目前中国的区域管治状况是经济发展、政治动员以及国家重构的结果。经济发展,即经济区域化,伴随着以市场为导向的经济改革,不仅加强了行政区域间的经济联系,而且由于经济积累和人口增长,还产生了对废物处理、交通以及环境管理等方面的合作需求。同时,区域管治的发展还受到了实际需求的驱动以及中央和地方政府的强力推动。中央政府从地区和国家的利益出发,致力于推动区域合作和区域协同发展,例如调控不加节制的土地开发和环境退化、促进区域协调、减少重复建设、加强产业升级和保障经济安全。2008年全球金融危机后,中央对土地供应仍然总体实行紧缩政策,而全球制造业市场也很不稳定,因此,地方政府对合作发展也表现出更浓厚的兴趣。这是因为地方政府为了发展经济,迫切需要发展服务行业,而发展服务行业必然需要加强各方面的联系与合作。换言之,自上而下和自下而上的区域举措背后的基本动机是不同的并且是无法兼容的。中央政府是从国家整体利益的角度进行综合区域发展,而地方政府却只是基于地方利益参与区域合作。国家与地方利益的冲突很可能导致执行区域项目时出现矛盾紧张的局面。

　　与过去的区域行政管理相比,现在的区域做法是基于灵活的组织而不是正式的行政管理。例如,对于当前自上而下的权力回收,就不同于上世纪五十年代在区域一级建立政府机构,而仅是制定区域规划而已。也就是说,中央政府主要是通过部署区域规划、政策或项目来实现对地方发展的区域管治的。相比之下,地方政府则是利用灵活的市政间协议来解决跨行政管辖区的交通、人员调动以及城市间的旅游、贸易和物流等问题。但令人遗憾的是,上述两种形式都没有完全制度化。尽管当前的趋势是将区域规划本身合法化,但尚未建立规划执行的机制。另一方面,问责制和约束力的缺乏也会影响自发组成的区域协会的权威性。因此,自上而下或自下而上的区域举措的实际功效有待商榷。同时,政治环境的持久性,例如下放的财政权力、参考经济指标为主的官员考核体系、僵化的行政等级等都使得自上而下或自下而上的区域活动

doubt. In the meantime, the persistence of the political environment, for example, the fiscal decentralisation, economy-dominated cadre evaluation system and rigid administrative hierarchy, altogether makes the top-down and the bottom-up regional practices more of a symbolic gesture. On the one hand, the decision-making system in China typically only involves the prefectural-level and the administration above, which is incompatible with the downscaling of governance towards counties, towns and districts. In other words, the regional consensus, if achieved, is only representative of a partial group of cities rather than all the jurisdictions in the region. The lack of open dialogue in the top-down and bottom-up regional practices impacts upon the legitimacy and consensus of the regional issue. On the other hand, the persistence of economic growth targets and pressure also makes concepts such as environmental sustainability, which would entail regional cooperation, rhetoric than real. Especially among the local governments, interest is only shown towards collaboration in terms of transport, which is conceived to bring economic dividends, rather than other urgent issues such as trans-border lake and water management. Henceforth, the development of regional governance in China is in a rather preliminary stage.

The plethora of recent regional practices, although taken for their symbolic meanings, demonstrates the search of the various agents for an 'institutional fix' to competitive and entrepreneurial governance. In Western countries such as the UK, which are built upon the welfare state and political democracy, the scalar tension of the regional project typically revolves around the role of state, market and society. Moreover, the active engagement of society also expands the core issue of regional projects from economic development to sustainability, climate change, democracy, cultural identity and autonomy. In contrast, the scalar tension in the case of China is mainly manifested in the division of power and responsibility between levels of government. Struggles are witnessed over the potential power reshuffling between tiers of government, i.e. either the recentralisation of central power on territorial development (the top-down regional initiative) or the remit of part of the local power to the regional level (the bottom-up regional initiative). As far as the present day is concerned, it seems inter-city association is more like an occasional tea party than a formalised organisation with multi-lateral agreements. On the other hand, the legitimacy of the spontaneous regional organisation rests with the central government's decision in China's political system. Indeed, there is no sign to suggest that the central government is intending to confer any authority on the inter-city association. It seems that the central government aims to promote local coordination through the means of central-level coordination. That is, the politics of China is resurgent with tendencies of recentralisation. However, such recentralisation would be implicitly contested by the local governments, which

充其量只是一种象征性的行为。一方面,中国的决策体系通常只涉及地级市以上的行政管理层级,这与向县、镇、区的管治下移是相互矛盾的。换句话来说,即便已经获得了区域共识,这也仅限于部分城市之间,无法扩大至该区域整个行政管辖范围。自上而下和自下而上的区域实践缺乏开放性的对话,影响了区域问题的合法性和共识的达成。另一方面,经济增长目标和压力的持久不变也使得一些例如环境可持续发展等可以引导区域合作的概念,仅停留在口头上,不能发挥实际作用。尤其是部分地方政府只对交通方面的合作感兴趣,因为这样可以带来经济利益,而对其他紧要问题例如跨界湖泊和水体的污染治理等不予以应有重视。因此,中国的区域管治发展还处于相当初级的阶段。

当前大量的区域实践尽管多只有象征意义,但也表现出是各级政府在为相互竞争的经营型管治寻求"制度解决"。在西方国家,例如建立在福利政府和民主政治基础上的英国,区域项目的尺度政治一般都集中在国家、市场和社会的作用上。此外,社会的积极参与也使得区域项目的核心问题从发展经济转变到可持续发展、气候变化、民主建设、文化认同和自治等方面。相反,中国的多层尺度政治则主要表现在各级政府权力和责任的划分上。在各级政府潜在的权力重构过程中出现了不少矛盾,无论是在地方发展上的中央权力回收(自上而下的区域举措),还是将部分地方权力上交给区域层级管理(自下而上的区域举措)方面都遇到不少困难。至今为止,城际联盟似乎更像一个临时举办的茶话会,而不是一个已达成多边协定的正式组织。另一方面,在中国的政治体系中,自发形成的区域组织的合法性取决于中央政府。事实上,也没有任何迹象表明中央政府打算给予城际联盟任何权力。似乎中央政府旨在通过中央层面的协调来促进地方协调发展。也就是说,中国政治又出现了权力回收的趋势。然而,这种权力回收会导致地方政府的暗中抵制,这也考验着国家收权的决心。

would require the resolution of the national state.

To summarise, contemporary China is now experiencing a resurgence of regional policies and practices. However, the currently re-emerged regional initiatives are qualitatively different from the regional programmes in the socialist period. First of all, the current regional initiatives are led by both the central and local governments. Secondly, different from the socialist regional programmes which aimed to consolidate political regulation and a centrally-planned economy, the current regional practices are more complicated in the sense that projects with different leading actors are associated with different purposes. The centrally-led regional programmes address the land, environmental and economic problems caused by discretionary local development after economic decentralisation and entrepreneurial development. In contrast, the locally-initiated regional practices are intended to overcome the limits and transcend the growth ceiling of the economic model of individual development and manufacturing expansion. The two rationales are incompatible with each other in the sense that the central government, to some extent, privileges development quality over extensive development, whereas the local governments are still committed to pro-growth motivation. Thirdly, distinguished from the regional programmes in the socialist period, which were imposed by the central government with a level of government between the centre and provinces, the contemporary regional practices are softly institutionalised and loosely organised. Finally, the coordinating role of either the centrally-orchestrated regional practices or the locally-initiated regional associations is extremely limited. Their capacity is hampered by the limited powers and resources of these institutions, the competing agendas between the central and local government, as well as between the central ministries, and the persisting institutional context of fiscal decentralisation and the cadre promotion system. Overall, the preceding account has shown that the emerging regional scale in China is still a fuzzy concept in reality. The regional scale building process is riddled with tensions and conflicts between central and local government over the division of power and responsibility.

8.2 Empirical and theoretical contribution

8.2.1 The significance of the YRD regional governance study

The recent practices in both of the PRD and YRD region have demonstrated the tendency towards a cooperative agenda. The construction of Guangzhou-Foshan high-speed railway (Liu et al., 2010), the initiative of building Pan-PRD inter-city association (Yeh and Xu, 2008) and the formulation of PRD

总之,当代中国正在经历区域政策和实践的复兴。但是,目前再次兴起的区域举措与改革开放前的区域项目存在着质的不同。第一,目前的区域举措是由中央和地方两级政府领导的。第二,改革开放前的区域项目旨在加强政治调控和巩固中央计划经济,与此不同的是,目前的区域实践在一定程度上比之前更加复杂,因为不同层级政府的项目出发点也会不同。中央领导的区域项目旨在解决自经济权力下放和实行经营型发展后地方任意开发所造成的土地、环境和经济问题。相反,地方发起的区域实践的目的在于突破限制,超越个体发展和制造业扩张经济模式的增长上限。这两个基本动因在某种程度上是不相容的,因为中央政府更看重发展质量,而地方政府则仍以经济增长为主要动机。第三,与改革开放前的区域项目(由中央政府和中央与省中间一级的政府管理)不同,当前的区域实践在制度和组织管理上都十分松散。最后,无论是中央安排的区域项目还是地方发起的区域联盟所发挥的协调作用都受到了极大的限制。它们所能发挥的能力之所以受到限制,是因为这些机构的权力和资源有限,中央与地方政府之间,以及中央各部委之间的议题相互冲突,以及财政权力下放与官员晋升体系等不变的大体制环境。总的来说,通过上文的论述可以看出中国新兴区域尺度在实际操作中仍然是一个模糊概念。区域尺度构建过程中充斥着中央与地方政府之间就权力与责任划分而产生的对立与冲突。

第二节　实证和理论贡献

一、长三角区域管治研究的重要性

目前,在珠三角和长三角地区的实践都显示出了区域合作的倾向。广州至佛山的高铁建设(刘超群等,2010)、打造泛珠三角区域城际合作的举措(Yeh和Xu,2008)以及珠三角区域规划的制定(Xu,2008)都证明了珠三角地区正在

regional plan (Xu, 2008) are all examples of ongoing regional cooperative development in the PRD region. Compared to the existing literature on the regional governance in the PRD region, the YRD region is relatively under-researched. This study suggests that the experiences between the YRD and PRD have some resemblance in terms of the bottom-up process of region-building. The tendency for the local government to promote regionalisation and regional cooperation is fostered by potential external competition and pursuit of regional competitiveness. The transformation from hostile competition to strategic cooperation seems to be the second wave of entrepreneurial policies, which is different from the previous urban entrepreneurialism and individual development. Meanwhile, the higher - level government such as the provincial government or the central government often plays an important backstage role in facilitating inter - city coalition or cross-administrative projects. That is, the hierarchical administrative power is able to mediate between multiple jurisdictions and helps to enforce certain consensus among the localities. Nevertheless, the politics in the PRD region - building also has some peculiarities. The original PRD region only constitutes a certain number of cities within Guangdong Province, which dose not involve cross-provincial barrier and as a result the provincial government could play a bigger role in mediating the disparate jurisdictions. In contrast, the recent Pan-PRD region is far more complex and consists of six provinces and two special administrative units, Hong Kong and Macao, under the 'One Country and Two System' framework. In this case, the government structure in the Pan-PRD region is much more complicated and the spontaneously-initiated regional agenda often requires the consent of the authoritative central government. Therefore, although the rationale and motive underlying the regional cooperation in PRD and YRD seems similar, there are slight differences in their process of governance building. Since the YRD is a cross-provincial region within the mainland, its experiences are more typical of the other regions in mainland China.

On the other hand, the YRD region is believed to hold more value to the understanding of China's emerging regional governance in that the YRD has witnessed independent initiatives taken by the central government to promote regional integrated development, in addition to the practices undertaken by the local government. The two separate processes going on in the YRD region help demonstrate the potential dissonance in current regional governance and institution building in China, i.e. the struggle between the central and the local government for control of regional space.

开展区域合作发展。与珠三角区域管治现有的文献相比,目前对长三角地区的研究相对不足。本书认为,长三角与珠三角在自上而下的区域形成过程方面存在一些相似之处。为了应对潜在的外部竞争与提升区域竞争力,地方政府倾向于推进区域化和区域合作。不同于之前的城市经营主义和个体发展,从恶性竞争到战略合作的转变似乎是经营政策的第二波。同时,上级政府如省政府或中央政府在城际联盟或跨行政区合作项目中起着重要的幕后推动作用。也就是说,自上而下的行政权力能够在多方行政单位之间斡旋并促使这些地方单位达成共识。然而,珠三角的区域形成在政治上有其独特性。珠三角最初仅包括广东省内的一部分城市,没有跨省障碍,因此省政府在不同的行政单位之间斡旋时能够发挥更大的作用。相比而言,后来的"泛珠三角"区域要复杂很多,包括6个省和2个特别行政区(实行"一国两制"的香港和澳门)。在此情况下,泛珠三角区域的政府结构更为复杂,自发拟定的区域议程通常要获得中央政府的首肯。因此,虽然珠三角和长三角区域合作的原因和动机看起来相似,但是在管治的形成中存在细微的差异。由于长三角是中国大陆范围内跨越多省的一个区域,其发展历程更能反映中国大陆其他区域的情况。

另一方面,长三角对研究中国新兴区域管治具有更大的价值的原因在于,在长三角地区,除了地方政府采取行动外,中央政府也单独采取措施促进区域一体化发展。这两种独立的进程同时在长三角地区进行,显示了中国目前区域管治和制度建设中潜藏着某种不和谐,即中央和地方政府为控制区域空间而进行着斗争。

8.2.2 The outcomes and significance of emerging informal regional institutions in China

The study of the YRD region demonstrates that there exists two ways of regional governance development in China, that is, the mechanism of top-down and bottom-up approach. The research findings have shown that the central government (the top-down approach) seems to be speedier than the local government (the bottom-up approach) in developing a form of regional governance. For example, it only took the central government five years to formulate and publish the YRD regional plan, whereas the regional association among local governments is still functioning as an informal coalition and does not possess any power. This is due to the fact that the central government still maintains strong vertical bureaucratic control in contemporary China. However, one of the surprises in the research findings is that the top-down administrative power is not as effective in implementation as it is in taking initiatives. This is because after the administrative and fiscal decentralisation, the central government has little leverage on local development and policies; neither did the central government create any incentive to stimulate local governments to follow the central arrangement. In contrast, even though it is difficult for the local governments to build a regional consensus, it could be more effective in carrying out certain regional agenda, if only the cross-administrative projects conform to practical needs and mutual benefits. Overall, even though China's image is a much centralised country administered by the Central Communist Party, China's regional governance development could not be simply enforced by the central government but requires the cooperation of the local governments.

Nevertheless, the great concern shown by the central government on regional issues is still of great significance even though it is symbolic. This is typical in China's politics after economic reform, when the central government only sets the general direction and it is up to the localities to implement the central agenda under its own conditions. Overall, the emergence of informal regional institutions is of great significance for China's future development. It marked a governance transformation away from the well-known and well-documented urban entrepreneurialism. The learning of coordination and cooperation is crucial for China to conquer the localism and competition brought about by decentralisation and entrepreneurialism after the economic reform.

8.2.3 The new state spaces in China

The new state space on the regional scale in China is still being formed.

二、中国非正式新兴区域机构的成果和重要性

长三角地区的研究表明,中国存在两种区域的管治发展方式,即自上而下和自下而上的机制。研究结果显示,在发展区域管治的形式时,中央政府(自上而下的方式)似乎比地方政府(自下而上的方式)更为迅速。例如,中央政府只需5年就制定并发布了长三角区域规划,而地方政府之间的区域协作仍旧只是非正式的联盟,没有任何权力。这是因为中央政府在当今中国依然掌握着巨大的纵向行政控制权。然而,研究结果也发现,即自上而下的行政权力在实施规划时不如其制订这些规划时有效率。这是因为在行政权力与财政权力下放后,中央政府对地方政府及其政策的影响力很小;中央政府也并未采取激励性措施鼓励地方政府服从中央安排。相比而言,尽管地方政府难以达成区域共识,但只要跨行政区项目能满足实际需要并为各方带来利益,地方政府就能更有效地落实某项区域议程。总体而言,虽然中国在中共中央执政下以高度收权的国家形象示人,但是中国的区域管治发展无法仅靠中央政府来执行,更需要地方政府的合作。

然而,中央政府对区域问题的关注尽管只是象征性的,但仍然具有重大意义。经济改革以后,中国政治中一种典型的做法是——中央政府只设定总目标,然后由地方根据自身情况来具体执行中央的规划。总体来说,非正式区域机构的出现对中国未来发展有着重要作用。它标志着管治正开始发生转变,不只是众所周知的城市经营主义。经济改革后,为了克服由于权力下放和经营主义导致的地方主义和竞争问题,中国必须要学会协调与合作。

三、中国的新国家空间

从中国的地方与中央政府发起的区域政策和项目可以看出,区域尺度的

It is reflected by the regional policies and programmes launched by the local and central governments. The regional configuration and interpretation are differently manipulated by the central and local government in different policy areas. For example, the regional activities can be articulated at the mega-regional level covering several provinces, or at the district level which crosses administrative boundaries. In general, the regional definition is dependant upon the concerns of the initiators. The two main actors not only differ in terms of their conceptions of the 'region', but also collide in their rationales for region building. The central government is, to some extent, transforming its attitude to its previous decentralisation policies. The central government is reconsidering the benefits and shortcomings of administrative decentralisation and is trying to impose certain arrangements on the local development. However, on the other hand, the local government is still taking use of the regional cooperative strategies to pursue entrepreneurial development. The dissonance between the central and local government in regional building is further due to the incompatibility between the regional cooperation agenda and the prevailing political context in China. Even though the central government now starts promoting regional integrated development, the previous policies of fiscal decentralisation and economic-based cadre evaluation system have not been changed. What is even worse is that the central government is still mainly using the administrative mandate to build and deliver the overall regional development vision. The lack of dialogue and participation mechanism in the virtually decentralised governance landscape just undermines the prospect for coordinated development. Overall, the new state space in China is soft and fuzzy, and the rescaling of the statehood is far from established. This is not only due to the different interpretations by different actors for different purposes, but also owing to the ineffective institution building at the regional level and the porous governance management by the central and local government.

8.2.4 The economics and politics of the (city-) region

The 'new regionalism' argument is blamed for its straightforward causal link between economic regional space and political regionalism (Harrison, 2006; MacLeod, 2001a). It is doubted, in that the region is not automatically an agent in political development (MacLeod, 2001b). However, it is also argued whether this means a total debunk of economic factors in interpretations merely due to that reason (Harding, 2007). It is suggested that the political regional discourse in the UK in part derives from the economic perception of enlarging economic disparities, economic relational economy and economic competitiveness

新国家空间还在形成当中。实际上,中央与地方政府在不同政策领域采取的是不同的区域空间布局和解读。例如,区域活动可以在跨越几省的大区域层面,或者在跨越行政边界的区级层面实施。总体而言,区域的定义取决于政策制定者的考虑。中央和地方政府不仅在"区域"概念的认识上存在差异,在区域建设的理念上也有分歧。在某种程度上,中央政府正在转变对其先前放权政策的态度。中央政府在重新考虑行政放权的利弊,并尝试对地方发展进行安排部署。然而,另一方面,地方政府依然采用区域合作战略追求经营发展。更进一步来说,中央和地方政府构建区域的不一致意见源于区域合作议程与中国政治大环境的不兼容。尽管中央政府正开始推动区域一体化发展,但是先前的财政放权政策和以经济发展为衡量基准的干部考核制度仍未改变。更糟糕的是,中央政府仍然主要依靠行政命令来制定和实施区域总体发展规划。在管治权力实际已经下放的背景下,对话与合作机制的缺失只会破坏协调发展的前景。总体来看,中国的新国家空间是不稳定和模糊的,国家重构还远没有完成。这不仅是因为不同层级的政府对区域项目有不同的意图和解读,还因为区域层面的举措尚未制度化,以及中央和地方政府的管治仍有疏漏。

四、城市区域中的经济和政治因素

　　"新区域主义"的观点因认为经济区域空间和政治区域主义有直接的因果关系而受到批评(Harrison,2006;MacLeod,2001a)。有人提出质疑,认为区域不会自动成为政治发展的作用者(MacLeod,2001b)。然而,这又产生了另一个争议,即这是否意味着仅仅出于这个原因,在解读时就可以完全不用考虑经济因素(Harding,2007)。他们认为,英国的政治区域理念,一部分正是来源于经济方面的考虑,如经济悬殊的扩大、关联经济和经济竞争力(MacLeod和Jones,1999;Harding,2007)。

(MacLeod and Jones, 1999; Harding, 2007).

In the case of China, the economic factor has definitely played a role in the development of regional initiatives, which is related to China's particular development background and development stage. China used to be ruled under a centralised economy, in which there were no natural economic flows. At the time, horizontal cooperation was imposed by the central government in a top-down fashion by the means of setting up an economic cooperation region. At the beginning of economic reform, economic cooperation was again promoted by the central government without real local economic regionalisation; the attempt ended in failure again. In contrast, the recent proliferation of cooperation initiatives is witnessed, along with the spread of regionalisation, where commuting, trade and logistics, tourism have become common occurrences. To a great extent, the need for mobility has triggered the local attempt to cooperate by setting up standardised customs and human resources systems and so forth to combat institutional fragmentation. On the other hand, the regionalisation and agglomeration of the economy have also engendered common regional problems, such as transport and environmental issues, which force neighbouring cities into thinking of each other as a region rather than disparate entities. Furthermore, the improved regional transport triggered by regionalisation has further strengthened regional prospects. The closer relationship and emerging spatial division of labour in accordance with the market chain of value opens up a new dialogue of cooperation between local competition forces. Overall, the development of relational economic geography has played an indispensable role in the emergence of regional practices in China.

In contrast, the economic-political relationships in Chinese regional literature have moved too far towards the economic lens. Although the results show that economic development and regionalisation do increase the prospect for cooperation and coordination, they also demonstrate that political factors cannot be ignored. The trend towards regionalisation does not mean consensus has been reached on regionalism (Yeh and Xu, 2008: 409). The research findings demonstrate that the regional restructuring is decided by the influence of all the factors, for example, the economic, cultural and political processes, which need to be examined in a case-specific context.

8.2.5 The top-down and bottom-up mechanism in the building of new state spatiality

The case of YRD demonstrates regional governance building as a phenomenon with both bottom-up and top-down dynamics. The top-down force is primarily represented through a set of changes at the central government level: regional

　　就中国而言,经济因素无疑在区域措施的发展中发挥着重要作用,这与中国特定的发展背景和发展阶段有关。中国过去实行高度集中的计划经济,没有自发的经济往来。当时,中央政府按照自上而下的方式,通过设立经济合作区推行横向合作。经济改革之初,中央政府再次推行经济合作,但由于没有真正的地方经济区域化,这种尝试再次以失败告终。相比而言,近期大量区域合作的涌现是伴随着区域化的发展的——通勤、贸易、物流以及旅游在当今中国都变得十分常见。在很大程度上,对流动性的需求促使地方设立统一的关税和人力资源系统等来应对体制分化,从而寻求合作。另一方面,区域化和经济一体化也引发了常见的区域问题,如交通和环境问题,这使得相邻城市不得不把对方当做一个区域,而非互不相干的实体。此外,由于区域化而得到改进的区域交通运输系统进一步提升了区域前景。更密切的关系以及按照市场价值链的新兴劳动力空间分配,为竞争的地方主体之间开启了新的合作对话。总体而言,关联经济地理的发展对中国区域实践的兴起发挥着不可或缺的作用。

　　相比较而言,中国区域文献中对经济-政治关系的讨论过于侧重经济因素。研究结果虽然显示经济发展与区域化的确增加了合作与协调的可能性,但也同时表明了政治因素不容忽视。区域化的趋势并不代表各方对区域主义已达成共识(Yeh 和 Xu, 2008:409)。研究结果揭示了区域重塑受各种因素的影响,如经济、文化和政治进程的影响,这需要在具体案例中加以验证。

五、建立新国家空间的自上而下机制和自下而上机制

　　长三角的案例诠释了区域管治有自下而上和自上而下两种构建机制。自上而下的区域管治主要表现为中央政府层面的一系列变革,如区域政策和规

policy and plan – making, land management rescaling and administrative restructuring. In a sense, this is just like 'centrally orchestrated regionalism' in the UK (Harrison, 2008). However, the tendency towards re – centralisation is undermined by decades of decentralisation since economic reform. As China's political system is still dominated by fiscal decentralisation and top – down delegation of economic targets, the possibility of re – centralisation is severely challenged in reality. Additionally, top – down recentralisation is not the only source from which the regional scale arises. In contrast, there are ongoing spontaneous negotiations between the local states to reach regional agreement. Efforts have been taken to improve the segmented institutions between individual jurisdictions in terms of trade, human resources, transport and the like. This is intended to overcome fragmented jurisdictional administration and seize benefits from economic regionalisation. Distinct from the bottom – up approach in Western democratic society, the local efforts in China are led by local governments without much involvement from civil society. Agreements tend to be reached on the basis of specific projects rather than on overall regional prospects and strategy.

Even though constituted as the distinct aspects of the making of regions, the two mechanisms are independent processes and are not even compatible with each other. For the central government, the regional scale is constituted by the provincial units; it intends to use the provincial governments as the agents to implement central policies. This was initiated by the central ministries to cope with the problems caused by decentralisation. As to the local government, the regional scale is also constructed at the provincial level, but more in rhetorical terms. The regional regime seems to be more feasible at and below prefectural-level. This is owing to a lack of substantial local engagement mechanisms in the complex regional institutional landscape. The local interest in building a regional scale is also different from that of central government. Regional cooperation is pursued by the local states to deal with the growth pressure on manufacturing in the current quicksilver global economic environment. All in all, the case of YRD demonstrates the diverse agents and politics through the scalar configuration, and the fuzzy and porous boundary of the region (Allmendinger and Haughton, 2009). In the case of the UK, this fuzzy space is used to insert new scales for intervention in accordance with the relational perception of regions, which is to break away from the rigid boundaries of formal regions and take the fluid and loose boundaries as openings for unexpected issues (ibid: 619, 631). That is, the loose space of a region is created on purpose to provide room to manoeuvre from the viewpoints of partnership, coordination and integration, i.e. 'governance' from outside of the governments (ibid: 631). This is the result that actors of various

划的制定、土地管理重塑和行政管理重组等。从某种程度上看,这就像英国"中央制定的区域主义"(Harrison,2008)。但是,自经济改革以来,权力下放已进行了几十年,削弱了收权的趋势。由于中国的政治体系仍然以财政权力下放和自上而下的经济指标下放为主导,收权的可能性在现实中面临着严峻挑战。此外,自上而下的收权也不是区域尺度上调的唯一途径。相反,地方政府之间通过自发的协商正在不断达成区域协定。通过不懈努力,被划分的机构在贸易、人力资源、交通等方面各谋其政的情况不断改善。此举旨在克服割裂的辖区管理的不足,抓住经济区域化进程所可能带来的好处。与西方民主国家自下而上的机制不同,中国的地方工作是地方政府领导的,民间社会的参与很少。所达成的协议多基于具体项目,而不是基于整体的区域前景和区域战略。

尽管自上而下和自下而上两种机制构成了区域形成的两个明显特征,它们仍是互相独立甚至是互不相容的。对于中央政府来说,区域尺度是由省级单位构成的,中央政府想通过省级政府来实施中央政策,这要由中央各部委来处理权力下放引起的各种问题。而对地方政府来说,省级层面也建立起区域尺度,但是多是流于字面形式;相比之下,在地级和地级以下层面的区域机制似乎更为可行。这是因为在复杂的区域体制格局中缺乏实质性的地方参与机制。另外,在区域尺度的建立过程中,地方利益也与中央政府利益不同。地方政府希望通过开展区域合作来应对瞬息万变的全球经济环境中制造业所面临的压力。总而言之,长三角区域的案例表现了多层次区域空间尺度中不同的作用者和政治因素,以及区域边界的模糊性和渗透性(Allmendinger 和 Haughton,2009)。英国的案例说明,模糊化的新的干预尺度正符合关联空间的理论,即就是要打破正式行政区域的僵化界限,以灵活的、宽松的区域边界来应对新社会背景(同上:619,631)。也就是说,创建宽泛的区域是为建立协调、合作、伙伴关系(即政府外界社会提供的"管制")提供空间(同上:631)。这是不同区域尺度作用者及政府内外部门试图治理市场、国

scales and sectors from both within the government and outside the government seek in order to address market, state and governance failures (ibid). In contrast, the soft space of regions in China, on the one hand, results from the porous governance capacity of the central government, through which regional terrain is highly contested and battles are played out about the division of power and the power struggle between central and local governments. On the other hand, the fluid scale of the region is due to the opportunistic and entrepreneurial nature of local governments.

8.2.6 Beyond the grand political economy in conceptualising the production of new state spatiality

Although Brenner (2002) acknowledges the plural nature of regional projects in reality, it seems the influential work by Brenner (2004a, b) is featured in neo-liberalisation under the general imperative of globalisation and competition. It is embedded in the interpretative framework of the generic structural shift of the state from a Keynesian welfare state to a Schumpeterian workfare state (Brenner, 2004a, b; Jessop, 1990). Although Brenner's conceptualisation of regional development from the state-relational perspective is widely adopted, his framework of regional dynamics is argued to lead to a universal top-down mechanism and an abstract theory of globalisation, accumulation and crises of capitalism (MacLeod and Jones, 1999: 578; Harding, 2007: 451; Oosterlynck, 2010: 1156–1157). It is argued that the political construction of the city-region can be driven by forces at the lower levels of scalar other than the global scale (McGuirk, 2007: 179). Globalisation may be turned into a symbolic discourse to cope with imagined or actual global pressures (Boudreau, 2003). It is thereby suggested that the research agenda should be broadened from economic governance to categories such as the environment and sustainability, and that a bottom-up approach to social power should be incorporated (Ward and Jonas, 2004; Jonas and Ward, 2007).

The empirical study on China's regional restructuring process resonates with the above criticism. The politics of the regional renaissance in China show that the central and local logics behind regional projects did not directly involve globalisation and the accumulation crisis, as framed under Western capitalism, but were responsive to China's local politics; for example, land and decentralisation, and concerns over social management. To a great extent, 'globalisation' was used as a discourse by the government to justify their policy choices. The 2008 global financial crisis is not the source which led to the emergence of regional projects, which were beginning to emerge a long time before 2008. However, the 2008 crisis did act as a form of pressure and

家和地方管治弊端的结果(同上)。与之相反,中国的区域软空间的形成,一方面是由于中央政府的管治能力不再像计划经济时期那样严密,区域领域充满了中央和地方权力的博弈;另一方面,地方政府的投机性和经营主义也促进形成了灵活的区域尺度。

六、超越宏观政治经济因素阐释新国家空间尺度的产生

虽然Brenner(2002)承认现实中的区域项目具有多重性质,但是他极具影响力的著作(2004a,b)主要反映的区域重塑背景却是当前全球化和竞争背景下活跃的新自由主义。整个区域重塑的理论框架是基于国家由凯恩斯福利国家到熊彼得工作福利国家的结构性转型(Brenner,2004a,b;Jessop,1990)。尽管学术界普遍认可Brenner从国家关系角度对区域发展所作出的理论阐述,但也有学者认为他的理论框架导向了统一的自上而下机制解释,以及有关全球化、资本积累和资本主义危机的抽象理论解释(MacLeod 和 Jones, 1999: 578; Harding, 2007: 451; Oosterlynck, 2010: 1156-1157)。有学者认为除了全球尺度,地方尺度上的动力因素也可以推动城市区域的政治建构(McGuirk, 2007: 179)。全球化可能只是象征性的概念用来概括人们想象的或实际的全球压力(Boudreau, 2003)。因此,有学者建议区域重塑的研究议程应从经济管治扩大到更宽泛的领域,如环境和可持续发展;同时应纳入社会力量自下而上的发展机制(Ward 和 Jonas, 2004; Jonas 和 Ward, 2007)。

中国区域重塑过程的实证研究结论与上述批评不谋而合。中国区域复兴的政治机制表明,推动区域项目的中央和地方政府并没有直接考虑全球化和经济积累危机(如西方文献所分析的那样),而是针对中国的地方政治环境所做出的反应,如土地管理、权力下放以及社会管理等问题。很大程度上,"全球化"被政府用作证明其政策选择合理性的一个口号。2008年全球经济危机不是导致区域项目出现的直接原因,因为在此之前很长一段时间区域项目就已经出现了。然而,2008年的经济危机确实是加强区域化进程并证明其合理性的一种正向压力和话

powerful discourse to strengthen and justify the process of regionalisation. Overall, the process of regional restructuring is not a pre - defined top - down process drifting from the global force. Vice versa, the global force was imagined and used as the discourse by the involved actors for their own ends.

However, this does not mean the genealogy of state regime shift (Brenner, 2004b) is totally useless. In the words of Jessop (1995), this shift was essentially 'descriptive, synthetic and generalized' and needs an explanation itself, for example, by delving into the 'events that constitute these processes' through the exploration of the articulation of actors and forces (cited in MacLeod and Jones, 1999: 581-82). The new state spaces framework issue can be otherwise resolved by an emphasis on the examination of the state agency, politics of scale and discourse employment (e.g. MacKinnon, 2010; Sonn, 2010; Varro, 2010). This is neither to absolutely abandon the paradigm shift, nor to take the state shift as prescribed. What is of most importance is to examine the on-the-ground process informed by the generic tendencies.

8.3 Limitations and future work

The study is trying to apply the new state space theory to understand the Chinese changing state spatiality, particularly the new tendency of regional governance development and the emerging regional state spaces in China. The research is mainly focused on employing a process-based approach to examine the building process of the emerging regional scale, which considers more 'agency', such as the role of local state and the other groups, in the politics of development. Although the research findings reveal that the regional state space building process is filled with different actors for different purposes, and hence it is conflict - ridden and full of uncertainties, the thesis is relatively weak in exploring the dissonance between the processes, the conflicts in the rescaling process and the politics of scale. For instance, in the case studies to examine the top-down and bottom-up processes, the research is primarily focused on acquiring the data of the main acting players behind the process, and didn't manage to collect many direct resources to reflect the reactions of the other relevant actors. Based on the experiences and limitations of this study, the following topics and questions are considered to be worthy of further study in the sphere of China's regional governance, which is still a relatively under-researched area.

Firstly, the central government has been a key actor in launching the recent regional practices in China, which is remarkably different from the predominant attitude of decentralisation and ex - post state endorsement after the economic reform. However, the intention and implications of the central practices are still not very well researched. All the practices such as the new

语方式。总之,区域重塑的过程不是如以前西方理论所描述的那样是由全球力量引发的自上而下的过程。相反,全球化成了当中作用者为了达到自己的目的而设计利用的概念。

但是,这并不意味着整个国家积累体制转变的理论概念(Brenner,2004b)是完全没有意义的。用Jessop(1995)的话说,这种精炼的转变模式本质上是"描述性的、综合性的和大概性的",需要对其自身再进行进一步的解释,例如透过探究具体的作用者和影响力量来深入探究"构成这一过程中的具体事件"(引自MacLeod和Jones,1999:581-82)。Brenner新国家空间的理论框架可以通过加强对动力机制、尺度政治和话语的研究来得以补充(例如MacKinnon,2010;Sonn,2010;Varro,2010)。这既不是完全抛弃总结的范式转变理论模式,也不是全盘接受这种理论模式,而是通过实证研究检验对一般趋势的总结,这是最重要的。

第三节 本研究的局限性和未来的工作

本研究试图采用新国家空间理论来理解中国变化中的国家空间尺度,尤其是中国区域管治发展的新趋向以及新兴的区域国家空间。研究主要采用基于过程分析的研究方法来探索新兴区域尺度的建立过程,这种方法更加关注政治构建区域过程中的动力因素,比如地方政府和其他组织在当中的作用。尽管本研究的主要发现揭示了区域国家空间的建立过程中充满了怀有不同目的的参与者,以及由此产生的矛盾和不确定性,但是有关不同进程间的不一致、重塑过程中的矛盾以及尺度政治方面,论文的探讨还不充分。例如,在分析自上而下机制和自下而上机制的案例研究中,研究主要集中在获取进程的主要作用者的数据,而没能收集体现出其他相关作用者反应的资料。中国的区域管治领域相对而言仍是一个没有深入研究的领域,因此基于本研究的经验和局限性,作者认为以下课题及问题在今后值得深入研究。

首先,中央政府是中国近期推行的一系列区域实践的主要作用者,这和经济改革后盛行的"权力下放"和"地方事后申请国家追认"概念大不相同。然而,中央政府推行实践的意图和影响仍未得到充分研究。除了本论文涉及的制定区域空

experiment of province-leading-county administrative reform, the launch of the main functional area policy are worthy of further exploration, apart from the case of formulation of regional spatial plans adopted in the thesis.

Secondly, the state rescaling process is worthy of further exploration from the perspective of discourse, spatial imaginaries and political mobilizations. The cultural political economy approach developed by Jessop (2005) and Sum and Jessop (2001) (Bristow, 2010: 29) could be adopted in future studies to further examine how state rescaling is carried out. Hegemonic projects, discourse and scales of representativeness and dependence (Cox, 1998; MacLeod, 1999) would be useful concepts with which to resume the study. For example, it seems both central and local governments make use of the discourse of 'regional competitiveness' to promote regional cooperation and coordination. However, the account of Chinese regional development demonstrates that the 'regional competitiveness' may function more in terms of discourse than as the real intention. It seems the central government employs the discourse of 'regional competitiveness' (or 'national competitiveness', which actually is not much different) to justify its reassertion of power on the localities, whist local government is cooperating on a limited scope and scale under the imaginary 'competitive region' to attempt to benefit from inter-city collaboration. Beyond an echo to the overseas scholars' critical reflections on the discourse of 'regional competitiveness' (Bristow, 2010; Lagendijk, 2007), the examination on the use of discourse and the substance of making of regions can add a more sophisticated understanding on the nature of the current regional-building and state rescaling.

Thirdly, the study into the conflicts between different actors in each regional project, the incompatible rationales within different regional projects led by the same agent, and the struggles between practices led by different actors will contribute to the understanding on the tensions characterising the scale-building process, and the hybrid and inconsistent nature of the attempts of regional state space development in China.

Finally, based on the research findings of chapter five, it seems just the time to study the longitudinal transformation of the regional economy, uneven development, and labour division in China, particularly in China's three big regions, i.e. the Yangtze River Delta, the Pearl River Delta and the Jing-Jin-Ji region. It is believed that these three hubs along the coast are currently transformed from being the sites of extended manufacturing development to functional nodes of regions. The research on China's development of regions contributes to poly-centric city-region study based on Western experiences. On the other hand, the study would contribute to the understanding of uneven development and governance in China. Even though intensive studies have

间规划的案例之外,所有实践,例如省管县行政改革的尝试、主体功能区政策的推行等都值得深入探讨。

其次,从理念、空间构想和政治动员角度分析国家重塑过程也值得深入研究。未来相关研究可参照Jessop(2005)以及Sum和Jessop(2001)提出的文化政治经济学研究方法,来分析国家重塑的推动实施过程(Bristow,2010:29)。此外,重要项目、话语、尺度的代表性和依赖性等(Cox,1998;MacLeod,1999)都会是后续研究中有用的概念。例如,中央和地方政府都运用"区域竞争力"的理念来促进区域协调与合作。然而,中国区域发展的状况反映出"区域竞争力"在作为实际意图时不如在作为理念时发挥的作用大。中央政府运用"区域竞争力"的理念(或"国家竞争力",二者无太大区别)似乎是为了辩解其对地方收权的合理性,而地方政府也仅仅是在想象的"竞争区域"层面推进有限的合作,以图从城际合作中获利。围绕"区域竞争力"视角的区域重塑研究并不只是一味附和海外学者对"区域竞争力"理念的批判性反思(Bristow,2010;Lagendijk,2007),也可为现行区域建构和国家重塑的本质探究提供一个更为成熟的见解。

第三,研究区域项目中不同作用者之间的冲突、相同作用者引导的不同区域项目之间的冲突,以及不同作用者项目之间的冲突,将有助于理解尺度重塑过程中的矛盾关系,也有助于理解中国区域国家空间形成过程中所存在的混合性、复杂性和矛盾性。

最后,基于第五章的研究发现,现在似乎正是研究中国区域经济历史演变、不平衡发展以及劳动分工的时机,尤其是在中国长三角、珠三角和京津冀地区三大区域。一般认为这三个沿海的核心区域目前正在经历从大规模制造业发展到多中心功能节点的转变。对中国区域发展的研究将有助于拓展基于西方背景提出的多中心城市区域概念。另一方面,该研究也将有助于理解中国的不平衡发展及管治。虽然之前针对中国区域不平衡发展进行的研究已经十分深入,尤其是在

concentrated on regional inequalities in China, especially in the 1980s and 1990s, the analysis at that time was strongly influenced by neo - classical economics and is therefore poorly related to the perspective of governance, state and the political economy. The studies mainly examine diverging or converging regional inequality before and after economic reform, based on regional, provincial or prefecture - level units. The ignorance of county and district units indicates the absence of the perspective of governance in the previous analysis. It is argued that only when informed with the approach of the political economy could the nature of uneven development and regional policies in China be unpacked, reflected and critically examined.

20世纪80、90年代,但是当时的分析因深受新古典经济学的影响而很少联系到管治、国家和政治经济学角度。开展的研究主要是分析区域、省级或地级单位在经济改革前后的区域不平衡发展是扩大了还是缩小了。当时的研究由于数据限制而缺乏县和区等行政单元的研究,同时也反映了当时的研究缺乏管治的视角。因而有人认为,只有精通政治经济学的研究方法,才能对中国的不平衡发展和区域政策的本质给出全面的解读和批判性的分析。

APPENDIX 1

SEMI-STRUCTURED INTERVIEW QUESTIONS

Case study 1: Shanghai-Jiangsu cross-border area

On the side of Huaqiao, Kunshan:

Theory Question 1: What are the conditions that led to local collaboration?

(1a) How is the previously planned industrial belt proceeding?

(1b) Under what circumstances was the Huaqiao project proposed?

(1c) What is the relationship with the previously planned industrial belt along the area adjacent to Shanghai?

Theory Question 2: How is the project articulated?

(2a) Who decided the location of the Huaqiao project?

(2b) What is the strategic positioning of the Huaqiao project? Who decided this?

(2c) How is the project funded?

Theory Question 3: How is the collaboration proceeding now? To what extent has regional governance developed?

(3a) How is the negotiation to extend the Moyu stop in Shanghai to Huaqiao progressing?

(3b) What is the major issue in the negotiation?

(3c) What difficulties have been encountered in terms of the implementation?

On the side of Anting, Shanghai:

Theory Question 1: What are the conditions that led to local collaboration?

(1a) How has Anting developed over the years?

(1b) Why has Anting recently adopted a new strategy of cooperative development with Huaqiao, Kunshan?

(1c) Why hasn't the strategy been considered before? Why now?

Theory Question 2: How is the project articulated?

(2a) What are the actions following the strategy?

(2b) Who is involved in these exercises?

Theory Question 3: How is the collaboration progressing now? To what extent has regional governance developed?

(3a) On what areas is the collaborative development currently focused?

(3b) What difficulties have been encountered in the collaborative development with Kunshan?

Case study 2: YRD regional plan

Theory Question 1: What is the ministries' rationale with regard to formulating YRD regional plans?

附录1

半结构化访谈问题

案例研究1：苏沪交界地区

（1）昆山花桥

理论问题1：什么条件促成了地方合作？

（1a）以前规划的产业带进展如何？

（1b）花桥项目是在什么情况下提出的？

（1c）花桥项目和以前规划的临近上海地区的产业带有什么关系？

理论问题2：项目是如何具体实施的？

（2a）花桥项目的选址是谁决定的？

（2b）花桥项目的战略定位是什么？谁决定的？

（2c）项目是如何筹资的？

理论问题3：合作进程现在进展如何？区域管治发展的程度如何？

（3a）地铁11号线从上海墨玉路站延伸到花桥的谈判进展如何？

（3b）谈判的主要议题是什么？

（3c）在实施过程中遇到了什么问题？

（2）上海安亭

理论问题1：什么条件促成了地方合作？

（1a）安亭近年来发展如何？

（1b）为何安亭近期通过了一个新的与昆山花桥合作的发展战略？

（1c）为什么以前没有考虑到这个战略？为什么是现在？

理论问题2：项目是怎么实施的？

（2a）战略后续采取了哪些行动？

（2b）谁参与了实施过程？

理论问题3：合作进程现在怎么样了？区域管治发展的程度如何？

（3a）目前合作发展主要集中在哪些地区？

（3b）在与昆山的合作发展过程中遇到了什么问题？

(1a) Under what circumstances was the YRD regional plan initiated?

(1b) Who was involved in the regional plan proposal?

(1c) What are the differences between the current plan and the former urban system plan (Five-year Plan)?

(1d) What is the priority of the current regional plan?

Theory Question 2: How is the project articulated? What politics are exposed in the process?

(2a) How was the planning preparation arranged?

(2b) Who was involved in the preparation of the regional plan?

(2c) How was the project funded?

(2d) What was the attitude of levels of government during the preparation of the plan? In which area are they mostly interested? With which elements are they dissatisfied?

Theory Question 3: How is the regional plan functioning now? To what extent has regional governance developed?

(3a) Has the plan attained legal status?

(3b) What does legal status mean to the plan?

(3c) How is the plan designed to be implemented?

(3d) What are the anticipated difficulties in implementation? What has caused these problems?

(3e) Have the contradictions between different regional plans posed any threat to implementation?

(3f) Is there any intention to improve the coordination between different regional plans? What is the major difficulty with the current efforts?

案例分析2:长三角区域规划

理论问题1:部委关于制定长三角区域规划的依据是什么?

(1a) 长三角地区区域规划是在什么情况下提出的?

(1b) 谁参与了此区域规划的提议?

(1c) 现行的规划和以前的城市系统规划(五年计划)之间有什么区别?

(1d) 现行的区域规划的优先重点是什么?

理论问题2:项目是怎样实施的? 实施过程体现了什么政治因素?

(2a) 规划的准备工作是怎样安排的?

(2b) 谁参与了此区域规划的准备工作?

(2c) 项目是如何筹资的?

(2d) 制定规划期间,各级政府的态度是什么? 他们对哪些地区最感兴趣? 他们不满意的原因是哪些?

理论问题3:此区域规划目前运作如何? 区域管治发展到什么程度了?

(3a) 规划是否已取得法律地位?

(3b) 取得法律地位对此规划意味着什么?

(3c) 此规划是怎样设计实施的?

(3d) 实施中有哪些可预见的困难? 导致这些困难的原因是什么?

(3e) 不同区域规划之间的矛盾是否威胁到规划的实施?

(3f) 是否有推进不同区域规划之间合作的意图? 目前工作所面临的主要困难是什么?

APPENDIX 2

LIST OF INTERVIEWEES

No	Role	Date
1	Academic in the Nanjing University	11 February 2009
2	Academic in the Nanjing Institute of Geography and Limnology of Chinese Academy of Sciences	12 February 2009
3	Chief of the Regional Division of Nanjing Economic Coordination Office	16 February 2009
4	Chief of the Regional Economic Division of Nanjing Development and Reform Committee	16 February 2009
5	Academic in the Nanjing Institute of Geography and Limnology of Chinese Academy of Sciences	17 February 2009
6	Academic in the Nanjing University	18 February 2009
7	Chief in the Jiangsu Construction Commission	23 February 2009
8	Chief in the Nanjing Development and Reform Committee	17 March 2009
9	Academic in the East China Normal University	18 March 2009
10	Planner in Chinese Academy of Urban Planning and Design	25 February 2010
11	Planner in Shanghai Planning Institute	25 February 2010
12	Planning official of Huaqiao Planning Bureau in Kunshan	3 March 2010
13	Planning official of Kunshan Planning Bureau	5 March 2010
14	Planner in Chinese Academy of Urban Planning and Design	9 March 2010
15	Senior planner in Shanghai Planning Institute	10 March 2010
16	Academic in the Nanjing Institute of Geography and Limnology of Chinese Academy of Sciences	11 March 2010
17	Academic in the Nanjing University	12 March 2010
18	Director of a major planning academy	17 March 2010
19	Academic in a leading planning school	19 March 2010

附录2

受访者名单

序号	职能	日期
1	南京大学学者	2009年2月11日
2	中国科学院南京地理与湖泊研究所学者	2009年2月12日
3	南京市经济协作办公室区域处处长	2009年2月16日
4	南京市发展与改革委员会区域经济处处长	2009年2月16日
5	中国科学院南京地理与湖泊研究所学者	2009年2月17日
6	南京大学学者	2009年2月18日
7	江苏省建设委员会主任	2009年2月23日
8	南京市发展与改革委员会主任	2009年3月17日
9	华东师范大学学者	2009年3月18日
10	中国城市规划设计研究院规划师	2010年2月25日
11	上海市规划院规划师	2010年2月25日
12	昆山花桥经济开发区建设规划局规划官员	2010年3月3日
13	昆山市规划局规划官员	2010年3月5日
14	中国城市规划设计研究院规划师	2010年3月9日
15	上海市规划院高级规划师	2010年3月10日
16	中国科学院南京地理与湖泊研究所学者	2010年3月11日
17	南京大学学者	2010年3月12日
18	某主要规划院院长	2010年3月17日
19	某著名规划院校学者	2010年3月19日

No	Role	Date
20	Academic in the Nanjing University	19 March 2010
21	Chief planner in the Suzhou Planning Bureau	22 March 2010
22	Director in the Jiading Planning Bureau in Shanghai	25 March 2010
23	Academic in the Nanjing Institute of Geography and Limnology of Chinese Academy of Sciences	26 March 2010
24	Chief planner of a major planning academy	30 March 2010
25	Academic in Tsing-Hua University	31 March 2010
26	Senior planner in Chinese Academy of Urban Planning and Design	2 April 2010
27	Senior planner in Chinese Academy of Urban Planning and Design	6 April 2010
28	Official in Ministry of Housing and Urban and Rural Development	6 April 2010
29	Planner in Chinese Academy of Urban Planning and Design	8 April 2010
30	Senior planning official in Kunshan Planning Bureau	14 April 2010
31	Official in Jiading Industiral District	15 April 2010
32	Research fellow in Shanghai Social Science Institute	19 April 2010
33	Official in Anting government in Jiading District in Shanghai	20 April 2010
34	Planner in Shanghai Planning Institute	20 April 2010
35	Planner in Shanghai Planning Institute	20 April 2010
36	Planner in Shanghai Planning Institute	20 April 2010
37	General manager of Anting International Auto-city and New Anting United Development Corporation	21 April 2010
38	Academic in the East China Normal University	21 April 2010
39	Academic in Tongji University	22 April 2010
40	Official in Jiading Planning Bureau of Shanghai	22 April 2010
41	Chief planner in Jiading Planning Institute	22 April 2010

No	Role	Date
20	南京大学学者	2010年3月19日
21	苏州市规划局总规划师	2010年3月22日
22	上海市嘉定区规划局局长	2010年3月25日
23	中国科学院南京地理与湖泊研究所学者	2010年3月26日
24	某主要规划院总规划师	2010年3月30日
25	清华大学学者	2010年3月31日
26	中国城市规划设计研究院高级规划师	2010年4月2日
27	中国城市规划设计研究院高级规划师	2010年4月6日
28	中华人民共和国住房与城乡建设部官员	2010年4月6日
29	中国城市规划设计研究院规划师	2010年4月8日
30	昆山市规划局高级规划官员	2010年4月14日
31	上海市嘉定工业区官员	2010年4月15日
32	上海社会科学院研究员	2010年4月19日
33	上海市嘉定区安亭镇政府官员	2010年4月20日
34	上海市规划院规划师	2010年4月20日
35	上海市规划院规划师	2010年4月20日
36	上海市规划院规划师	2010年4月20日
37	上海国际汽车城新安亭联合发展有限公司总经理	2010年4月21日
38	华东师范大学学者	2010年4月21日
39	同济大学学者	2010年4月22日
40	上海市嘉定区规划局官员	2010年4月22日
41	上海市嘉定区规划院总规划师	2010年4月22日

参考文献

Agnew, John. 1994. The territorial trap: the geographical assumptions of international relations theory. *Review of International Political Economy* 1 (1):53-80.

Albrechts, Louis. 2004. Strategic (spatial) planning reexamined. *Environment and Planning B: Planning and Design* 31:743-758.

Albrechts, Louis. 2006. Shifts in strategic spatial planning? some evidence from Europe and Australia. *Environment and Planning A* 38:1149-1170.

Albrechts, Louis, Patsy Healey, and Klaus R. Kunzmann. 2003. Strategic spatial planning and regional governance in Europe. *Journal of the American Planning Association* 69 (2):113-129.

Allen, John, and Allan Cochrane. 2007. Beyond the territorial fix: regional assemblages, politics and power. *Regional Studies* 41 (9):1161-1175.

Allen, John, D. Massey, Allan Cochrane, J. Charlesworth, G. Court, N. Henry, and P. Sarre. 1998. Rethinking the region. London: Routledge.

Allmendinger, Philip, and Graham Haughton. 2007. The fluid scales and scope of UK spatial planning. *Environment and Planning A* 39:1478-1496.

Allmendinger, Phil, and Graham Haughton. 2009. Soft spaces, fuzzy boundaries, and metagovernance: the new spatial planning in the Thames Gateway. *Environment and Planning A* 41:617-633.

Allmendinger, Philip, and Mark Tewdwr-Jones. 2000. spatial dimensions and institutional uncertainties of planning and the 'new regionalism'. *Environment and Planning C: Government and Policy* 18:711-726.

Ash, Robert F., and Y. Y. Kueh. 1993. Economic integration within Greater China: trade and investment flows between China, Hong Kong and Taiwan. *The China Quarterly* (136):711-745.

Bianconi, Marco, Nick Gallent, and Ian Greatbatch. 2006. The changing geography of subregional planning in England. *Environment and Planning C: Government and Policy* 24:317-330.

Boudreau, Julie-Anne. 2003. The politics of territorialization: regionalism, localism and other isms...The case of Montreal. *Journal of Urban Affairs* 25 (2):179-199.

Boudreau, Julie-Anne. 2007. Making new political spaces: mobilizing spatial imaginaries, instrumentalizing spatial practices, and strategically using spatial tools. *Environment and Planning A* 39:2593-2611.

Breathnach, Proinnsias. 2010. From spatial keynesianism to post-Fordist neoliberalism: emerging contradictions in the spatiality of the Irish State. *Antipode* 42 (5):1180-1199.

Brenner, Neil. 1999a. Globalisation as reterritorialisation: the re-scaling of urban governance in the European Union. *Urban Studies* 36 (3):431-451.

Brenner, Neil. 1999b. Beyond state-centrism? Space, territoriality, and geographical scale in globalization studies. *Theory and Society* 28 (1):39-78.

Brenner, Neil. 2002. Decoding the newest 'metropolitan regionalism' in the USA: a critical overview. *Cities* 19 (1):3-21.

Brenner, Neil. 2003a. Metropolitan institutional reform and the rescaling of state space in contemporary western Europe. *European Urban and Regional Studies* 10 (4):297-324.

Brenner, Neil. 2003b. 'Glocalization' as a state spatial strategy: urban entrepreneurialism and the new politics of uneven development in western Europe. In: *Remaking the Global Economy*, edited by J. Peck and H. Yeung. London and Thousand Oaks: Sage.

Brenner, Neil. 2004a. Urban governance and the production of new state spaces in western Europe, 1960-2000. *Review of International Political Economy* 11 (3):447-488.

Brenner, Neil. 2004b. New state spaces: urban governance and the rescaling of statehood. New York: Oxford.

Breslin, Shaun. 1995. Centre and province in China. In: *China in the 1990s*, edited by R. Benewick and P. Wingrove. Basingstoke: Macmillan.

Breslin, Shaun. 2000. Decentralization, globalization and China's partial re-engagement with the global economy. *New Political Economy* 5 (2):205-226.

Bristow, Gillian. 2010. Critical reflections on regional competitiveness: theory, policy, practice. London and New York: Routledge.

Cannon, Terry. 1990. Regions: spatial inequality and regional policy. In: *The geography of contemporary China: the impact of Deng Xiaoping's decade*, edited by T. Cannon and A. Jenkins. London: Routledge.

Chen, Chih-jou Jay. 2005. The path of Chinese privatisation: a case study of village enterprises in southern Jiangsu. *Corporate Governance: An International Review* 13 (1):72-80.

Chen, Jean Jinghan, and David Wills. 1999. The impacts of China's economic reforms upon land, property and construction. Brookfield: Ashgate.

Chen, Xiangming. 2007. A tale of two regions in China: regional economic development and slow industrial upgrading in the Pearl River and the Yangtze River Deltas. *International Journal of Comparative Sociology* 48 (2-3):167-201.

Chien, Shiuh-Shen. 2007. Institutional innovation, asymmetric decentralization, and local economic development: case of post-Mao Kunshan, China. *Environment and Planning C: Government and Policy* 25 (2):269-290.

Chien, Shiuh-Shen. 2008. The isomorphism of local development policy: a case study of the formation and transformation of national development zones in post-Mao Jiangsu, China. *Urban Studies* 45 (2):273-294.

Chien, Shiuh-Shen. 2010. Prefectures and prefecture-level cities: the political economy of administrative restructuring. In: *China's local administration: traditions and changes in the sub-national hierarchy*, edited by J. H. Chung and T.-c. Lam. Oxon and New York: Routledge.

Chien, Shiuh-Shen, and Ian Gordon. 2008. Territorial competition in China and the West. *Regional Studies* 42 (1):1-18.

Chien, Shiuh-Shen, and Litao Zhao. 2008. The Kunshan model: learning from Taiwanese investors. *Built Environment* 34 (4):427-443.

Chung, Him. 2007. The change in China's state governance and its effects upon urban scale. *Environment and Planning A* 39:789-809.

Cox, Kevin R. 1998. Spaces of dependence, spaces of engagement and the politics of scale, or: looking for local politics. *Political Geography* 17 (1):17-30.

Cullingworth, Barry, and Vincent Nadin. 2006. Town and country planning in the UK. Abingdon: Routledge.

Davoudi, Simin. 2009. Scalar tensions in the governance of waste: the resilience of state spatial Keynesianism. *Journal of Environmental Planning and Management* 52 (2):137-156.

Deas, Iain, and Benifo. Giordano. 2003. Regions, city-regions, identify and institution building: contemporary experiences of the Scalar Turn in Italy and England. *Journal of Urban Affairs* 25 (2): 225-246.

Deas, Iain, and Kevin G. Ward. 2000. From the 'new localism' to the 'new regionalism'? The implications of regional development agencies for city-regional relations. *Political Geography* 19 (3):273-292.

Deas, Iain, and Alex Lord. 2006. From a new regionalism to an unusual regionalism? The emergence of non-standard regional spaces and lessons for the territorial reorganisation of the state. *Urban Studies* 43 (10):1847-1877.

Donaldson, John. 2010. Provinces: paradoxical politics, problematic partners. In: *China's local administration: traditions and changes in the sub-national hierarchy*, edited by J. H. Chung and T.-c. Lam. Oxon and New York: Routledge.

Donnithorne, Audrey. 1972. China's cellular economy: some economic trends since the cultural revolution. *The China Quarterly* (52):605-619.

Donnithorne, Audrey, and Nicholas R Lardy. 1976. Centralization and decentralization in China's fiscal management. *The China Quarterly* (66):328-354.

Eng, Irene. 1997. The Rise of manufacturing towns: externally driven industrialization and urban development in the Pearl River Delta of China. *International Journal of Urban and Regional Research* 21 (4):554-568.

Etherington, David, and Martin Jones. 2009. City-regions: new geographies of uneven development and inequality. *Regional Studies* 43 (2):247-265.

Everingham, Jo-Anne. 2009. Australia's regions: congested governance or institutional void? *Public Policy and Administration* 24 (1):84-102.

Everingham, Jo-Anne, Lynda Cheshire, and Lawrence Geoffrey. 2006. Regional renaissance? New forms of governance in nonmetropolitan Australia. *Environment and Planning C: Government and Policy* 24:139-155.

Faludi, Andreas. 2000. The performance of spatial planning. *Planning Practice and Research* 15 (4):299-318.

Fan, C. Cindy. 1992. Regional impacts of foreign trade in China, 1984-1989. *Growth and Change* 23 (2):129-159.

Fan, C. Cindy. 1995. Of belts and ladders: state policy and uneven regional development in post-Mao China. *Annals of the Association of American Geographers* 85 (3):421-449.

Fan, C. Cindy. 1997. Uneven development and beyond: regional development theory in Post-Mao China. *International Journal of Urban and Regional Research* 21 (4):620-639.

Fan, C. Cindy. 2006. China's eleventh five-year plan (2006-2010): from 'getting rich first' to 'common prosperity'. *Eurasian Geography and Economics* 47 (6):708-723.

Fan, C. Cindy, and Mingjie Sun. 2008. Regional inequality in China, 1978-2006. *Eurasian Geography and Economics* 49 (1):1-20.

Gleeson, Brendan. 2003. Learning about regionalism from Europe: 'economic normalisation' and beyond. *Australian Geographical Studies* 41 (3):221-236.

Goodman, S.G. David. 1989. China's regional development. London and New York: Routledge.

Goodwin, Mark, Martin Jones, and Rhys Jones. 2005. Devolution, constitutional change and economic development: explaining and understanding the new institutional geographies of the British State. *Regional Studies 39 (4):421-436.*

Goodwin, Mark, Martin Jones, and Rhys Jones. 2006. Devolution and economic governance in the UK: rescaling territories and organizations. *European Planning Studies* 14 (7):979-995.

Gottmann, Jean. 1961. Megalopolis: the urbanized northeastern seaboard of the United States. New York: Twentieth Century Fund.

Gu, Chaolin, Jianfa Shen, Kwan-yiu Wong, and Feng Zhen. 2001. Regional polarization under the socialist-market system since 1978: a case study of Guangdong province in south China. *Environment and Planning A* 33:97-119.

Gualini, Enrico. 2004. Regionalization as 'experimental regionalism': the rescaling of territorial policy-making in Germany. *International Journal of Urban and Regional Research* 28 (2):329-353.

Hadjimichalis, Costis. 2006. Non-economic factors in economic geography and in 'new regionalism': a sympathetic critique. *International Journal of Urban and Regional Research* 30 (3):690-704.

Hall, Peter. 1999. The regional dimension. In British planning: 50 years of urban & regional policy, edited by B. Cullingworth. Linton: Athlone.

Hall, Peter. 2009. Looking backward, looking forward: the city region of the mid-21st century. *Regional Studies* 43 (6):803-817.

Hall, Peter, and Kathy Pain. 2006. The polycentric metropolis: learning from mega-city regions in Europe. London: Earthscan.

Han, Sun Sheng, and Clifton W. Pannell. 1999. The geography of privatization in China, 1978-1996. *Economic Geography* 75 (3):272-296.

Harding, Alan. 2007. Taking city regions seriously? Response to debate on 'City-regions: new geographies of governance, democracy and social reproduction'. *International Journal of Urban and Regional Research* 31 (2):443-458.

Harrison, John. 2006. Re-reading the new regionalism: a sympathetic critique. *Space and Polity* 10 (1):21-46.

Harrison, John. 2007. From competitive regions to competitive city-regions: a new orthodoxy, but some old mistakes. *Journal of Economic Geography* 7 (3):311-332.

Harrison, John. 2008. Stating the production of scales: centrally orchestrated regionalism, regionally orchestrated centralism. *International Journal of Urban and Regional Research* 32 (4):922-941.

Harrison, John. 2010. Networks of connectivity, territorial fragmentation, uneven development: The new politics of city-regionalism. *Political Geography* 29 (1):17-27.

Haughton, Graham, Phil Allmendinger, D Counsell, and G Vigar. 2009. The new spatial planning: territorial management with soft spaces and fuzzy boundaries. London; New York: Routledge.

He, Shenjing, and Fulong Wu. 2005. Property-led redevelopment in post-reform China: a case study of Xintiandi redevelopment project in Shanghai. *Journal of Urban Affairs* 27 (1):1-23.

Healey, Patsy. 2006. Territory, integration and spatial planning In Territory identity and spatial planning: spatial governance in a fragmented nation edited by M. Tewdwr-Jones and P. Allmendinger. London: Routledge.

Healey, Patsy, Abdul Khakee, Alain Motte, and Barrie Needham, eds. 1997. Making strategic spatial plans: innovation in Europe. London: UCL Press.

Hsing, Y. 1996. Blood, thicker than water: interpersonal relations and Taiwanese investment in southern China. *Environment and Planning A* 28:2241-2261.

Hsing, Y. 2006. Brokering power and property in China's fownship. *The*

Pacific Review 19:103-124.

Huang, Yasheng. 1990. Web of interests and patterns of behaviour of Chinese local economic bureaucracies and enterprises during reforms. *The China Quarterly* (123):431-458.

Jessop, Bob. 1990. State theory: putting capitalist states in their place. Cambridge: Polity Press.

Jessop, Bob. 1995. Towards a Schumpeterian workfare regime in Britain? Reflections on regulation, governance, and the welfare state. *Environment and Planning A* 27:1613-1626.

Jessop, Bob. 2001. Multi-level governance and multi-level meta-governance. Mimeograph. Department of Sociology, Lancaster University.

Jessop, Bob. 2005. Cultural political economy, the knowledge - based economy and the state. In: *The technological economy*, edited by A. Barry and D. Slater. Oxon: Routledge.

Jessop, Bob, Jamie Peck, and Adam Tickell. 1999. Retooling the machine: economic crisis, state restructuring, and urban politics. In: *The urban growth machine: critical perspectives two decades later*, edited by A. E. G. Jonas and D. Wilson. Albany: State University of New York Press.

Jonas, Andrew E.G. 2006. Pro-scale: further reflections on the 'scale debate' in human geography. *Transactions of the Institute of British Geographers* 31 (3):399-406.

Jonas, Andrew E.G., and Stephanie Pincetl. 2006. Rescaling regions in the state: the new regionalism in California. *Political Geography* 25 (5):482-505.

Jonas, Andrew E.G., and Kevin Ward. 2002. A world of regionalism? Towards a US-UK urban and regional policy framework comparison. *Journal of Urban Affairs* 24 (4):377-401.

Jonas, Andrew E.G., and Kevin Ward. 2007. Introduction to a debate on city-regions: new geographies of governance, democracy and social reproduction. *International Journal of Urban and Regional Research* 31 (1):169-178.

Jones, Martin. 1997. Spatial selectivity of the state? The regulationist enigma and local struggles over economic governance. *Environment and Planning A* 29:831-864.

Jones, Martin. 2001. The rise of the regional state in economic governance: 'partnership for prosperity' or new scales of state power? *Environment and Planning A* 33:1185-1211.

Jones, Martin, Mark Goodwin, and Rhys Jones. 2005. State modernization, devolution and economic governance: an introduction and guide to debate. *Regional Studies* 39 (4):397-403.

Jones, Martin, and Gordon Macleod. 1999. Towards a regional renaissance? Reconfiguring and rescaling England's economic governance. *Transactions of the*

Institute of British Geographers 24 (3):295-313.

Jones, Martin, and Gordon MacLeod. 2004. Regional spaces, spaces of regionalism: territory, insurgent politics and the English question. *Transactions of the Institute of British Geographers* 29 (4):433-452.

Keating, Michael. 1998. The new regionalism in Western Europe: territorial restructuring and political change. Cheltenham: Edward Elgar.

Kirkby, Richard, and Terry Cannon. 1989. Introduction. In: *China's regional development*, edited by D. S. G. Goodman. London and New York: Routledge.

Lagendijk, Arnoud. 2007. The accident of the region: a strategic relational perspective on the construction of the region's significance. *Regional Studies* 41 (9):1193-1207.

Lang, Robert, and Paul K. Knox. 2009. The new metropolis: rethinking megalopolis. *Regional Studies* 43 (6):789-802.

Lardy, Nicholas R. 1975. Centralization and decetralization in China's fiscal management. *The China Quarterly* (61):25-60.

Lee, Pak K. 1998. Local economic protectionism in China's economic reform. *Development Policy Review* 16:281-303.

Lee, Yok-shiu F. 1980. Small towns and China's urbanization level. *The China Quarterly* (120):771-786.

Lefevre, Christian. 1998. Metropolitan government and governance in western countries: a critical review. *International Journal of Urban and Regional Research* 22 (1):9-25.

Li, Hongbin, and Scott Rozelle. 2000. Saving or stripping rural industry: an analysis of privatization and efficiency in China. *Agricultural Economics* 23 (3): 241-252.

Li, Linda Chelan. 1997. Towards a non-zero-sum interactive framework of spatial politics: the case of centre-province in contemporary China. *Political Studies* 45 (1):49-65.

Lin, George C. S. 1997. Transformation of a rural economy in the Zhujiang Delta. *The China Quarterly* (149):56-80.

Lin, George C. S. 2001a. Metropolitan development in a transitional socialist economy: spatial restructuring in the Pearl River Delta, China. *Urban Studies* 38 (3):383-406.

Lin, George C. S. 2001b. Evolving spatial form of urban-rural interaction in the Pearl River Delta, China. *Professional Geographer* 53 (1):56-70.

Lin, George C. S. 2007. Reproducing spaces of Chinese urbanisation: new city-based and land-centred urban transformation. *Urban Studies* 44 (9):1827-1855.

Lin, George C. S. 2009. Scaling-up Regional Development in Globalizing China: Local Capital Accumulation, Land-centred Politics, and Reproduction of

Space. *Regional Studies* 43 (3):429-447.

Liu, Yialing. 1992. Reform from below: the private economy and local politics in the rural industrialization of Wenzhou. *The China Quarterly* (130):293-316.

Lo, C. P. 1989. Recent spatial restructuring in Zhujiang Delta, South China: a study of socialist regional development strategy. *Annals of the Association of American Geographers* 79 (2):293-308.

Lovering, John. 1999. Theory led by policy? The inadequacies of the 'new regionalism' in economic geography illustrated from the case of Wales. *International Journal of Urban and Regional Research* 23:379-395.

Lu, Lachang, and Yehua Dennis Wei. 2007. Domesticating globalisation, new economic spaces and regional polarisation in Guangdong province, China. *Tijdschrift voor economische en sociale geografie* 98 (2):225-244.

Luo, Xiaolong, and Jianfa Shen. 2006.Cross‐border Urban Growth: the Case of Jiangyin Economic Development Zone in Jingjiang. Conference paper. downloaded from http://unpan1.un.org/intradoc/groups/public/documents/APCITY/UNPAN021192.pdf.

Luo, Xiaolong, and Jianfa Shen. 2008. Why city-region planning does not work well in China: the case of Suzhou-Wuxi-Changzhou. *Cities* 25:207-217.

Luo, Xiaolong, and Jianfa Shen. 2009. A study on inter-city cooperation in the Yangtze River Delta region, China. *Habitat International* 33 (1):52-62.

Luo, Yu, and Clifton W. Pannell. 1991. The changing pattern of city and industry in post-reform China. In The uneven landscape: geographical studies in post‐reform China, edited by G. Veeck. Baton Rouge, LA: Geoscience Publications, Dept. of Geography and Anthropology, Louisiana State University.

Ma, Jun. 1995. The reform of intergovernmental fiscal relations in China. *Asian Economic Journal* 9 (31):205-232.

Ma, Laurence J. C. 2002. Urban transformation in China, 1949‐2000: a review and research agenda. *Environment and Planning A* 34 (9):1545-1569

Ma, Laurence J.C. 2005. Urban administrative restructuring, changing scale relations and local economic development in China. *Political Geography* 24 (4):477-497.

Ma, Laurence J. C., and Gonghao Cui. 1987. Administrative changes and urban population in China. *Annals of the Association of American Geographers* 77 (3):373-395.

Ma, Laurence J. C., and Ming Fan. 1994. Urbanisation from below: the growth of towns in Jiangsu, China. *Urban Studies* 31 (10):1625-1645.

Ma, Laurence J. C., and Chusheng Lin. 1993. Development of towns in China: a case study of Guangdong province. *Population and Development Review* 19 (3):583-606.

Ma, Laurence J. C., and Yehua Wei. 1997. Determinants of state investment in China, 1953-1990. *Tijdschrift voor economische en sociale geografie* 88 (3):211-225.

MacKinnon, Danny, and Jon Shaw. 2010. New state spaces, agency and scale: devolution and the regionalisation of transport governance in Scotland. *Antipode* 42 (5):1226-1252.

MacLeod, Gordon. 1999. Place, politics and 'scale dependence': exploring the structuration of Euro-Regionalism. *European Urban and Regional Studies* 6 (3): 31-53.

MacLeod, Gordon. 2001a. New regionalism reconsidered: globalization and the remaking of political economic space. *International Journal of Urban and Regional Research* 25 (4):804-829.

MacLeod, Gordon. 2001b. Beyond soft institutionalism: accumulation, regulation, and their geographical fixes. *Environment and Planning A* 33:1145-1167.

MacLeod, Gordon, and Mark Goodwin. 1999a. Reconstructing an urban and regional political economy: on the state, politics, scale, and explanation. *Political Geography* 18 (6):697-730.

MacLeod, Gordon, and Mark Goodwin. 1999b. Space, scale and state strategy: rethinking urban and regional governance Progress in Human. *Geography* 23 (4):503-527.

MacLeod, Gordon, and Martin Jones. 1999. Reregulating a regional rustbelt: institutional fixes, entrepreneurial discourse, and the 'politics of representation'. *Environment and Planning D: Society and Space* 17:575-605.

MacLeod, Gordon, and Martin Jones. 2001. Renewing the geography of regions. *Environment and Planning D: Society and Space* 19 (6):669-695.

MacLeod, Gordon, and Martin Jones. 2007. Territorial, scalar, networked, connected: in what sense a 'regional world'? *Regional Studies* 41 (9):1177-1191.

Marks, Gary, Fritz W. Scharpf, Philippe C. Schmitter, and Wolfgang Streeck. 1996. Governance in the European Union. London; Thousand Oaks, Calif: Sage.

Marton, Andrew. 2000. China's spatial economic development: regional transformation in the lower Yangzi Delta London: Routledge.

May, Tim. 1997. Social research: issues, methods and process. Buckingham; Philadelphia: Open University Press.

McCann, Eugene J. 2007. Inequality and politics in the creative city-region: questions of livability and state strategy. *International Journal of Urban and Regional Research* 31 (1):188-196.

McGuirk, Pauline. 2007. The political construction of the city - region: notes from Sydney. *International Journal of Urban and Regional Research* 31 (1):179-187.

Mertha, Andrew C. 2005. China's 'soft' centralization: shifting Tial/Kuai authority relations. *The China Quarterly* (184):791-810.

Montinola, Gabriella, Yingyi Qian, and Barry R. Weingast. 1995. Federalism, Chinese styles: the political basis for economic success in China. *World Politics* 48 (1):50-81.

Morgan, Kevin. 2007. The polycentric state: new spaces of empowerment and engagement? *Regional Studies* 41 (9):1237-1251.

Musson, Steven, Adam Tickell, and Peter John. 2005. A decade of decentralisaiton? Assessing the role of the Government Offices for the English regions. *Environment and Planning A* 37:1395-1412.

Nadin, Vincent. 2007. The emergence of the spatial planning approach in England. *Planning Practice and Research* 22 (1):43-62.

Naughton, Barry. 1988. The third front: defence industrialization in the Chinese interior. *The China Quarterly* 115:351-386.

Naughton, Barry. 1995. Cities in the Chinese economic system: changing roles and conditions for autonomy. In: *Urban spaces in contemporary China: the potential for autonomy and community in post-Mao China*, edited by D. S. Davis, R. Kraus, B. Naughton and E. J. Perry. Washington, D.C.; Cambridge; New York: Woodrow Wilson Center Press; Cambridge University Press.

Naughton, Barry J. 2004. The western development program. In: *Holding China together: diversity and national integration in the post-Deng era*, edited by B. Naughton and D. L. Yang. Cambridge: Cambridge University Press.

Neuman, Michael, and Angela Hull. 2009. The futures of the city region. *Regional Studies* 43 (6):777-787.

Ng, Mee Kam, and Wingshing Tang. 1999. Urban system planning in China: a case study of the Pearl River Delta. *Urban Geography* 20:591-616.

Ng, Mee Kam, and Jiang Xu. 2000. Development control in post-reform China: the case of Liuhua Lake Park, Guangzhou. *Cities* 17 (6):409-418.

Norris, Donald F. 2001. Prospects for regional governance under the new regionalism: economic imperatives versus political impediments. *Journal of Urban Affairs* 23 (5):557-571.

Ohmae, Kenichi. 2004. The rise of the region states. In: *Regions and regionalism in Europe*, edited by M. Keating. Cheltenham: Edward Elgar.

Oi, Jean C. 1992. Fiscal reform and the economic foundations of local state corporatism. *World Politics* 45 (1):99-126.

Oi, Jean C. 1995. The role of the local state in China's transitional economy. *The China Quarterly* (144):1132-1149.

Oosterlynck, Stijn. 2010. Regulating regional uneven development and the politics of reconfiguring Belgian state space. *Antipode* 42 (5):1151-1179.

Pain, Kathy. 2008. Examining 'core-periphery' relationships in a global city-tegion: the case of London and south east England. *Regional Studies* 42 (8):1161

-1172.

Parr, John. 2005. Perspectives on the city-region. *Regional Studies* 39 (5): 555-566.

Parris, Kristen. 1993. Local initiative and national reform: the Wenzhou model of development. *The China Quarterly* (134):242-263.

Pearce, Graham, and Sarah Ayres. 2009. Governance in the English regions: the role of the regional development agencies. *Urban Studies* 46 (3):537-557.

Peck, Jamie. 2001. Neoliberalizing states: thin policies/hard outcomes. *Progress in Human Geography* 25 (3):445-455.

Phelps, Nick. 2010. The lost city of the Solent: a tale of the failure of modernist planning imaginaries for city regions in the South East of England. Public Lecture and Seminar Series at Cardiff University.

Pike, Andy, and John Tomaney. 2009. The state and uneven development: the governance of economic development in England in the post-devolution UK. *Cambridge Journal of Regions, Economy and Society* (2):13-34.

Poncet, Sandra. 2003. Measuring Chinese domestic and international integration. *China Economic Review* 14 (1):1-21.

Prime, Penelope B. 1991. China's economic reforms in regional perspective. In: *The uneven landscape: geographic studies in post-reform China*, edited by G. Veeck. Baton Rouge, LA: Geoscience Publications, Dept. of Geography and Anthropology, Louisiana State University.

Purcell, Mark. 2007. City-regions, neoliberal globalization and democracy: a research agenda. *International Journal of Urban and Regional Research* 31 (1):197-206.

Qian, Yingyi, and Barry R. Weingast. 1997. Federalism as a commitment to preserving market incentives. *Journal of Economic Perspectives* 11 (4):83-92.

Savitch, H. V., and Roland. K. Vogel. 2000. Paths to new regionalism. *State and Local Government Review* 32 (3):158-168.

Scott, Allen J. 2001. Globalization and the rise of city-region. *European Planning Studies* 9 (7):813-826.

She, Zhixiang, Guan Xu, and Godfrey Linge. 1997. The head and tail of the dragon: Shanghai and its economic hinterland. In: *China's new spatial economy: heading towards 2020*, edited by G. Linge. Hongkong: Oxford University Press.

Shen, Jianfa. 2002. Urban and regional development in post-reform China: the case of Zhujiang delta. *Progress in Planning* 57 (2):91-140.

Shen, Jianfa. 2003. Cross-border connection between Hong Kong and Mainland China under 'Two Systems' before and beyond 1997. *Geografiska Annaler. Series B, Human Geography* 85 (1):1-17.

Shen, Jianfa, Zhiqiang Feng, and Kwan-yiu Wong. 2006. Dual-track urbanization in a transitional economy: The case of Pearl River Delta in South China. *Habitat International* 30 (3):690-705.

Shen, Jianfa, Kwan-yiu Wong, Kim-yee Chu, and Zhiqiang Feng. 2000. The spatial dynamics of foreign investment in the Pearl River Delta, south China. *The Geographical Journal* 166 (4):312-322.

Shen, Jianfa, Kwan-yiu Wong, and Zhiqiang Feng. 2002. State-sponsored and spontaneous urbanization in the Pearl River Delta of South China, 1980-1998. *Urban Geography* 23 (7):674-694.

Shen, Xiaoping, and Laurence J. C. Ma. 2005. Privatization of rural industry and de facto urbanization from below in southern Jiangsu, China. *Geoforum* 36 (6):761-777.

Shue, Vivienne . 1995. State sprawl: the regulatory state and social life in a small Chinese city. In: *Urban spaces in contemporary China: the potential for autonomy and community in post-Mao China*, edited by D. S. Davis, R. Kraus, B. Naughton and E. J. Perry. Washington, D.C.; Cambridge; New York: Woodrow Wilson Center Press; Cambridge University Press.

Sit, Victor F. S., and Chun Yang. 1997. Foreign-investment-induced exo-urbanisation in the Pearl River Delta, China. *Urban Studies* 34 (4):647-677.

Smart, Alan. 1998. Economic transformation in China: property regimes and social relations. In: *Theorising transition: the political economy of post-Communist transformations*, edited by J. Pickles and A. Smith. London; New York Routledge.

Solinger, Dorothy J. 1978. Some speculations on the return of the regions: parallels with the past. *The China Quarterly* (75):623-638.

Sonn, Jung Won. 2010. Contesting state rescaling: an analysis of the South Korean State's discursive strategy against devolution. *Antipode* 42 (5):1200-1224.

Sum, Ngai-Ling, and Bob Jessop.2001. The pre-and post-disciplinary perspective of political economy. *New Political Economy* 6 (1):89-101.

Tao, Ran, Fubing Su, Mingxing Liu, and Guangzhong Cao. 2010. Land leasing and local public finance in China's regional development: evidence from prefecture-level cities. *Urban Studies* 47 (10):2217-2236.

Tewdwr-Jones, Mark, and Donald McNeill. 2000. The Politics of City-Region Planning and Governance: Reconciling the National, Regional and Urban in the Competing Voices of Institutional Restructuring. *European Urban and Regional Studies* 7 (2):119-134.

Thornley, Andy. 1993. Urban planning under Thatcherism: the challenge of the market. London: Routledge.

Tsui, kai-yuan, and Youqiang Wang. 2004. Between separate stoves and a single menu: fiscal decentralizafion in China. *The china Quarterly* 177:71-90.

Unger, Jonathan. 1987. The struggle to dictate China's administration: the conflicts of branches vs areas vs reform. *The Australian Journal of Chinese Affairs*

（18）:15-45.

Unger, Jonathan, and Anita Chan. 1999. Inheritors to the boom: private enterprise and the role of local government in a rural south China township. *The China Journal* 42:45-74.

Valler, Dave, Nick Phelps, and Andy Wood. 2002. Devolution, regionalism and local economic development. *Local Economy* 17 （3）:186-190.

Varro, Krisztina. 2010. re-politicising the analysis of 'new state spaces' in Hungary and beyond: towards an effective engagement with 'actually existing neoliberalism'. *Antipode* 42 （5）:1253-1278.

Walder, Andrew G. 1995. Local governments as industrial firms: an organizational analysis of China's transitional economy. *The American Journal of Sociology* 101 （2）:263-301.

Walks, R. Alan. 2006. Review: New state spaces: urban governance and the rescaling of statehood. *Annals of the Association of American Geographers* 96 （1）: 227-229.

Wang, Huijiong, Shantong Li, and Godfrey Linge. 1997. Regional planning: developing an indigenous framework. In: *China's new spatial economy: heading towards 2020*, edited by G. Linge. Hong Kong: Oxford University Press.

Wang, Jenn-Hwan, and Chuan-Kai Lee. 2007. Global production networks and local institution building: the development of the information-technology industry in Suzhou, China. *Environment and Planning A* 39 （8）:1873-1888.

Wang, Hongyang. 2007. Three booms in regional planning in China: re-approaching the methodology of comprehensive planning. In Paper presented at the international conference on China's urban transition and city planning, Cardiff, 29-30 June 2007.

Wang, Yaping, and Cliff Hague. 1993. Territory planning in China: a new regional approach. *Regional Studies* 27 （6）:561-573.

Ward, Kevin, and Andrew E.G. Jonas. 2004. Competitive city-regionalism as a politics of space: a critical reinterpretation of the new regionalism. *Environment and Planning A* 36:2119-2139.

Webb, Darren, and Clive Collis. 2000. Regional development agencies and the 'New Regionalism' in England. *Regional Studies* 34 （9）:857-864.

Wei, Yehua. 1996. Fiscal systems and uneven regional development in China, 1978-1991. *Geoforum* 27 （3）:329-344.

Wei, Yehua, and Laurence J. C. Ma. 1996. Changing patterns of spatial inequality in China, 1952-1990. *Third World Planning Review* 18 （2）:177-191.

Wei, Yehua Dennis. 1999. Regional inequality in China. *Progress in Human Geography* 23 （1）:49-59.

Wei, Yehua Dennis. 2000. Investment and regional development in post-Mao China. *GeoJournal* 51 （3）:169-179.

Wei, Yehua Dennis. 2002. Beyond the Sunan model: trajectory and underlying factors of development in Kunshan, China. *Environment and Planning A* 34:1725-1747.

Wei, Yehua Dennis, and C. Cindy Fan. 2000. Regional inequality in China: a case study of Jiangsu province. *The Professional Geographer* 52 (3):455-469.

Wei, Yehua Dennis, Wangming Li, and Chunbin Wang. 2007. Restructuring industrial districts, scaling up regional development: a study of the Wenzhou Model, China. *Economic Geography* 83 (4):421-444.

Wei, Yehua Dennis, and Xinyue Ye. 2004. Regional inequality in China: a case study of Zhejiang province. *Tijdschrift voor economische en sociale geografie* 95 (1):44-60.

Wei, Y. H. Dennis. 2007. Regional development in China: transitional institutions, embedded globalization, and hybrid economies. *Eurasian Geography and Economics* 48 (1):16-36.

Wei, Y. H. Dennis. 2010. Beyond new regionalism, beyond global production networks: remaking the Sunan model, China. *Environment and Planning C: Government and Policy* 28:72-96.

Wei, Y. H. Dennis, Yuqi Lu, and Wen Chen. 2009. Globalizing regional development in Sunan, China: does Suzhou industrial park fit a neo-Marshallian district model? *Regional Studies* 43 (3):409-427.

Weng, Qihao. 1998. Local impacts of the post-Mao development strategy: the case of the Zhujiang Delta, Southern China. *International Journal of Urban and Regional Research* 22 (3):425-442.

Wengraf, Tom. 2001. Qualitative research interviewing: biographic narrative and semi-structured methods. London: Sage.

Wheeler, Stephen M. 2002. The new regionalism: key characteristics of an emerging movement. *Journal of the American Planning Association* 68 (3):267-278.

While, Aidan, Andrew E. G. Jonas, and David C. Gibbs. 2004. Unblocking the city? Growth pressures, collective provision, and the search for new spaces of governance in Greater Cambridge, England. *Environment and Planning A* 36:279-304.

Wong, Cecilia, Hui Qian, and Kai Zhou. 2008. In search of regional planning in China: a case of Jiangsu and its surrounding Yangtze Delta. *Town Planning Review* 79 (2-3):295-329.

Wong, Christine P. W. 1991a. Central-local relations in an era of fiscal decline - the paradox of fiscal decentralization in post-Mao China. *The China Quarterly* 128:691-714.

Wong, Christine P. W. 1991b. Central planning and local participation under Mao: the development of county-run fertiliser plants. In: *The Chinese state in the era of economic reform: the road to crisis*, edited by G. White. Armonk, N.

Y.: M.E. Sharpe.

Wong, Kwan-yiu, Jianfa Shen, Zhiqiang Feng, and Chaolin Gu. 2003. An analysis of dual-track urbanisation in the Pearl River Delta since 1980. *Tijdschrift voor economische en sociale geografie* 94 (2):205-218.

Wu, Fulong. 2000a. The Global and local dimensions of place-making: remaking Shanghai as a World City. *Urban Studies* 37 (8):1359-1377.

Wu, Fulong. 2000b. Place promotion in Shanghai, PRC. *Cities* 17 (5):349-361.

Wu, Fulong. 2002. China's changing urban governance in the transition towards a more market-oriented economy. *Urban Studies* 39 (7):1071-1093.

Wu, Fulong. 2003. The (post-) socialist entrepreneurial city as a state project: Shanghai's reglobalisation in question. *Urban Studies* 40 (9):1673-1698.

Wu, Fulong. 2007. Re-orientation of the city plan: strategic planning and design competition in China. *Geoforum* 38 (2):379-392.

Wu, Fulong, and Nick Phelps. 2008. From suburbia to post-suburbia in China? Aspects of the transformation of the Beijing and Shanghai global city regions. *Built Environment* 34 (4):464-481.

Wu, Fulong, Jiang Xu, and Anthony Gar On Yeh. 2007. Urban development in post-reform China: state, market, and space. London and New York: Routledge.

Wu, Fulong, and Fangzhu Zhang. 2008. Planning the Chinese city: governance and development in the midst of transition. *Town Planning Review* 79 (2-3):149-156.

Wu, Fulong, and Fangzhu Zhang. 2009. The development of city-region governance in China: towards a research framework. In Shanghai Forum. Shanghai.

Wu, Fulong, and Fangzhu Zhang. 2010. China's emerging city region governance: towards a research framework. *Progress in Planning* 73 (1):60-63.

Wu, Fulong, and Jingxiang Zhang. 2007. Planning the competitive city-region: the emergence of strategic development plan in China. *Urban Affairs Review* 42 (5):714-740.

Xu, Jiang. 2008. Governing city regions in China: theoretical issues and perspectives for regional strategic planning. *Town Planning Review* 79 (2-3):9-36.

Xu, Jiang, and Anthony Yeh. 2009. Decoding urban land governance: state reconstruction in contemporary Chinese cities. *Urban Studies* 46 (3):559-581.

Xu, Jiang, Anthony Yeh, and Fulong Wu. 2009. Land commodification: new land development and politics in China since the late 1990s. *International Journal of Urban and Regional Research* 33 (4):890-913.

Xu, Jiang, and Anthony G.O. Yeh. 2005. City repositioning and competitiveness building in regional development: new development strategies in

Guangzhou, China. *International Journal of Urban and Regional Research* 29 (2):283-308.

Xu, Jiang, and Anthony G.O. Yeh. 2010. Planning mega-city regions in China: rationales and policies. *Progress in Planning* 73 (1):17-22.

Xu, Jiang, and Anthony G.O. Yeh. eas. 2011. Governance and planning of mega-city regions: an international comparative perspective. New york: Routledge.

Xu, Xueqiang, and Si-ming Li. 1990. China's open door policy and urbanization in the Pearl River Delta region. *International Journal of Urban and Regional Research* 14 (1):49-69.

Yang, Chun. 2004. From market-led to institution-based economic integration: the case of the Pearl River Delta and Hong Kong. Issues and Studies 40 (2):1-40. Downloaded at http://iir.nccu.edu.tw/attachments/journal/add/4/4002-3.pdf.

Yang, Chun. 2005. Multilevel governance in the cross-boundary region of Hong Kong-Pearl River Delta, China. *Environment and Planning A* 37 (12):2147-2168.

Yang, Chun. 2006. The geopolitics of cross-boundary governance in the Greater Pearl River Delta, China: a case study of the proposed Hong Kong-Zhuhai-Macao Bridge. *Political Geography* 25 (7):817-835.

Yang, Chun. 2009. Strategic coupling of regional development in global production networks: redistribution of Taiwanese personal computer investment from the Pearl River Delta to the Yangtze River Delta, China. *Regional Studies* 43 (3):385-407.

Yang, Dali. 1990. Patterns of Chinese regional development strategy. *The China Quarterly* 122:230-257.

Yang, Daniel You-Ren, and Hung-Kai Wang. 2008. Dilemmas of local governance under the development zone fever in China: a case study of the Suzhou region. *Urban Studies* 45 (5&6):1037-1054.

Yang, You-Ren, and Chih-hui Chang. 2007. An urban regeneration regime in China: A case study of urban redevelopment in Shanghai's Taipingqiao area. *Urban Studies* 44 (9):1809-1826.

Yang, You-Ren, and Chu-Joe Hsia. 2007. Spatial clustering and organizational dynamics of transborder production networks: a case study of Taiwanese information-technology companies in the Greater Suzhou Area, China. *Environment and Planning A* 39 (6):1346-1363.

Ye, Xinyue, and Yehua Dennis Wei. 2005. Geospatial analysis of regional development in China: the case of Zhejiang province and the Wenzhou model. *Eurasian Geography and Economics* 46 (5):342-361.

Yeh, Anthony G.O. 2001. Hong Kong and the Pearl River Delta: competition or cooperation? *Built Environment* 27 (2):129-145.

Yeh, Anthony Gar On, and Fulong Wu. 1998. The transformation of the urban planning system in China from a centrally-planned to transitional economy. *Progress in Planning* 51 (3):165-252.

Yeh, Anthony G.O., and Jiang Xu. 2008. Regional cooperation in the Pan-Pearl River Delta: a formulaic aspiration or a new imagination? *Built Environment* 34 (4):408-426.

Yeh, Anthony G.O. and Jiang Xu. eds. 2011. China's Pan-Pearl River Delta: regional cooperation and development. Hong Kong. Hong Kong University Press.

Yep, Ray. 2008. Enhancing the redistributive capacity of the Chinese state? Impact of fiscal reforms on county finance. *The Pacific Review* 21 (2):231-255.

Yin, Robert K. 1994. Case study research: design and methods. Thousand Oaks; London: Sage Publications.

Zhang, Jingxiang, and Fulong Wu. 2006. China's changing economic governance: administrative annexation and the reorganization of local governments in the Yangtze River Delta. *Regional Studies* 40 (1):3-21.

Zhang, Jingxiang, and Fulong Wu. 2008. Mega-event marketing and urban growth coalitions: a case study of Nanjing Olympic New Town. *Town Planning Review* 79 (2-3):209-226.

Zhang, Li, and Simon X. B. Zhao. 1998. Re-examing China's "urban" concept and the level of urbanization. *The China Quarterly* 154:330-381.

Zhang, Le-Yin. 1999. Chinese central-provincial fiscal relationship, budgetary decline and the impact of the 1994 fiscal reform: an evaluation. *The China Quarterly* 157:115-141.

Zhang, Tingwei. 2002a. Urban development and a socialist pro-growth coalition in Shanghai. *Urban Affairs Review* 37 (3):475-499.

Zhang, Tingwei. 2002b. Decentralization, localization, and the emergence of a quasi-participatory decision-making structure in urban development in Shanghai. *International Planning Studies* 7 (4):303-323.

Zhang, Tingwei. 2006. From intercity competition to collaborative planning: the case of the Yangtze River Delta region of China. *Urban Affairs Review* 42 (1):26-56.

Zhao, Simon X. B., and L. Zhang. 2007. Foreign direct investment and the formation of global city-regions in China. *Regional Studies* 41 (7):979-994.

Zhao, Simon X. B., Roger C. K. Chan, and Kelvin T. O. Sit. 2003. Globalization and the dominance of large cities in contemporary China. *Cities* 20 (4):265-278.

Zhao, X. B., and L. Zhang. 1999. Decentralization reforms and regionalism in China: a review. *International Regional Science Review* 22 (3):251-281.

Zheng, Yanting, Tian Chen, Jianming Cai, and Shenghe Liu. 2009.

Regional concentration and region-based urban transition: China's mega-urban region formation in the 1990s. *Urban Geography* 30 (3):312-333.

Zhu, Jieming. 1999. Local Growth Coalition: The Context and Implications of China's Gradualist Urban Land Reforms. *International Journal of Urban and Regional Research* 23 (3):534-548.

Zhu, Jieming. 2002. Urban Development under Ambiguous Property Rights: A Case of China's Transition Economy. *International Journal of Urban and Regional Research* 26 (1):41-57.

蔡瀛,朱国鸣. 2006. 如何为协调城镇密集地区的发展提供有效抓手——从实施的角度看《珠江三角洲城镇群协调发展规划》的编制. 城市规划,30(6):9-14.

长三角城市经济协调会办公室. 2007. 走过十年——长江三角洲城市经济协调会十周年纪. 上海:文汇出版社.

陈东林. 2006. 三线建设:离我们最近的工业遗产. 中国国家地理,(6):96-113.

陈建华,王国恩. 2006. 区域协调发展的政策途径. 城市规划,30(12):15-19.

陈晓云. 2007. 长三角地区区域协调机制的形成和演变. 长三角洲城市经济协调报告,陈晓云,蒋录,编著. 上海:上海三联书店.

洪世健. 2009.《大都市区治理:理论演讲与运行模式》. 当代中国城市-区域:权力·空间·制度研究丛书. 刘君德,主编. 南京:东南大学出版社.

胡序威. 2006. 中国区域规划的演变与展望. 地理学报,61(6):585-592.

黄卓,宋劲松,杨满伦,董男. 2007.“协调规划”与“规划协调”——珠三角“一级空间管治区”的规划与实施. 城市规划,31(12):15-19.

纪晓岚,愈慰刚,罗建平. 2006. 长江三角洲区域发展战略研究. 上海:华东理工大学出版社.

江苏统计局. 1991. 江苏统计年鉴1991年. 北京:中国统计出版社.

江苏统计局. 1996. 江苏统计年鉴1996年. 北京:中国统计出版社.

江苏统计局. 2001. 江苏统计年鉴2001年. 北京:中国统计出版社.

江苏统计局. 2006. 江苏统计年鉴2006年. 北京:中国统计出版社.

江苏统计局. 2009. 江苏统计年鉴2009年. 北京:中国统计出版社.

江苏统计局. 2010. 江苏统计年鉴2010年. 北京:中国统计出版社.

昆山市规划局. 2010. 从率先全面小康到率先基本现代化. 北京:中国建筑工业出版社.

李立军. 2008. 20年前的“长三角”试验——关于上海经济区规划办公室

的历史考察．今日浙江,(15):28-29.

李晓江．2008．城镇密集地区与城镇群规划——实践与认知．城市规划学刊,(1):1-7.

刘超群,李志刚,徐江,叶嘉安．2010．新时期珠三角"城市区域"重构的空间分析——以跨行政边界的基础设施建设为例．国际城市规划,25(2):31-38.

刘君德．2001．论中国大陆大都市区行政组织与管理模式创新——兼论珠江三角洲的政区改革．经济地理,21(2):201-212.

刘玉．2007．中国区域政策．北京:经济日报出版社.

刘玉,冯健．2008．中国经济地理:变化中的区域格局．北京:首都经济贸易大学出版社.

陆阳,史文学．2008．长三角批判．北京:中国社会科学出版社.

马凯．2003-10-21．用新的发展观编制"十一五"规划．中国经济导报.

毛汉英,方创琳．2002．我国新一轮国土规划编制的基本构想．地理研究,21(3):267-275.

民政部．1998a．中华人民共和国行政区划手册(1949-1997)．北京:中国社会出版社.

民政部．1998b．中华人民共和国行政区划手册．北京:中国社会出版社.

民政部．1999．中华人民共和国行政区划手册(1999)．北京:中国社会出版社.

民政部．2000．中华人民共和国行政区划手册(2000)．北京:中国社会出版社.

民政部．2001．中华人民共和国行政区划手册(2001)．北京:中国社会出版社.

民政部．2002．中华人民共和国行政区划手册(2002)．北京:中国社会出版社.

民政部．2003．中华人民共和国行政区划手册(2003)．北京:中国社会出版社.

民政部．2004．中华人民共和国行政区划手册(2004)．北京:中国社会出版社.

民政部．2005．中华人民共和国行政区划手册(2005)．北京:中国社会出版社.

民政部．2006．中华人民共和国行政区划手册(2006)．北京:中国社会出版社.

民政部．2007．中华人民共和国行政区划手册(2007)．北京:中国社会出版社.

民政部. 2008. 中华人民共和国行政区划手册(2008). 北京:中国社会出版社.

民政部. 2009. 中华人民共和国行政区划手册(2009). 北京:中国社会出版社.

国家统计局. 1994. 中国城市统计年鉴(1993-1994). 北京:中国统计出版社.

国家统计局. 2000. 中国城市统计年鉴(2000). 北京:中国统计出版社.

国家统计局. 2001. 中国城市统计年鉴(2001). 北京:中国统计出版社.

国家统计局. 2002. 中国城市统计年鉴(2002). 北京:中国统计出版社.

国家统计局. 2004. 中国城市统计年鉴(2004). 北京:中国统计出版社.

国家统计局. 2005. 中国城市统计年鉴(2005). 北京:中国统计出版社.

国家统计局. 2009. 中国城市统计年鉴(2009). 北京:中国统计出版社.

上海统计局. 1991. 上海统计年鉴(1991). 北京:中国统计出版社.

上海统计局. 1996. 上海统计年鉴(1996). 北京:中国统计出版社.

上海统计局. 2001. 上海统计年鉴(2001). 北京:中国统计出版社.

上海统计局. 2002. 上海统计年鉴(2002). 北京:中国统计出版社.

上海统计局. 2004. 上海统计年鉴(2004). 北京:中国统计出版社.

上海统计局. 2006. 上海统计年鉴(2006). 北京:中国统计出版社.

上海统计局. 2010. 上海统计年鉴(2010). 北京:中国统计出版社.

邵波,潘强. 2004. 城镇群规划:几个原则与重点. 城市规划,28(4):37-40.

国务院发展研究中心. 2008. 主体功能区形成机制和分类管理政策研究. 北京:中国发展出版社.

苏州统计局. 2007. 苏州统计年鉴(2007). 北京:中国统计出版社.

孙海鸣,赵晓雷. 2005. 2005中国区域经济发展报告:长江三角洲区域规划及统筹发展. 上海:上海财经大学出版社.

孙海鸣,赵晓雷. 2009. 2009中国区域经济发展报告:长江三角洲与珠江三角洲区域经济发展比较. 上海:上海财经大学出版社.

唐子来,赵渺希. 2010. 经济全球化视角下长三角区域的城市体系演化:关联网络和价值区段的分析方法. 城市规划学刊,186(1):29-34.

陶希东. 2007. 转型期中国跨省市都市圈区域治理——以行政区经济为视角,上海社会科学院出版社.

王川兰. 2008. 竞争与依存中的区域合作行政:基于长江三角洲都市圈的实证. 上海:复旦大学出版社.

王枫云．2009．和谐共进中的政府协调：长三角城市群的实证研究．广州：中山大学出版社．

王晓东．2004．对区域规划工作的几点思考——由美国新泽西州域规划工作引发的几点感悟．城市规划,28(4):59-65.

武廷海．2006．中国近现代区域规划．北京：清华大学出版社．

徐海贤．2006．发达地区县(市)域城镇体系规划的变革研究．城市规划,30(11):36-40.

杨保军．2004．我国区域协调发展的困境及出路．城市规划,28(10):26-34.

杨桂山．2001．长江三角洲近50年耕地数量变化的过程与驱动机制研究．自然资源学报,16(2):121-127.

杨俊宴,陈雯．2007．长江三角洲区域协调重大问题的调查研究．城市规划,31(9):17-23.

殷为华,沈玉芳,杨万钟．2007．基于新区域主义的我国区域规划转型研究．地域研究与开发,26(5):12-15.

郁鸿胜,宗传宏,李娜．2008．长三角区域城镇体系空间布局研究．上海：上海社会科学院出版社．

张颢瀚等．2007．长江三角洲一体化进程研究——发展现状、障碍与趋势．北京：社会科学文献出版社．

张汉亚,张欣宁．2005．政府该管什么(中国投资体制改革的历程)．南昌：江西人民出版社．

张京祥,李建波,芮富宏．2005．竞争型区域管治：机制、特征与模式——以长江三角洲地区为例．长江流域资源与环境,14(5):670-674.

张京祥,殷洁,何建颐．2008．全球化世纪的城市密集地区发展与规划．北京：中国建筑工业出版社．

张勤．1999．城镇体系规划为什么实施不力．规划师,(3):31-32.

张占斌．2009．中国省直管县改革研究．北京：国家行政学院出版社．

浙江统计局．1991．浙江省统计年鉴1991．北京：中国统计出版社．

浙江统计局．1996．浙江省统计年鉴1996．北京：中国统计出版社．

浙江统计局．2001．浙江省统计年鉴2001．北京：中国统计出版社．

浙江统计局．2006．浙江省统计年鉴2006．北京：中国统计出版社．

浙江统计局．2010．浙江省统计年鉴2010．北京：中国统计出版社．

周黎安．2008．转型中的地方政府：官员激励与治理．上海：上海格致出版社,上海人民出版社．

周天勇. 2008. 中国行政体制改革30年. 上海:上海格致出版社,上海人民出版社.

周毅仁. 2005. "十一五"期间我国区域规划有关问题的思考和建议. 地域研究与开发,24(3):1-5.

朱波. 2005. 对现阶段区域规划的几点认识. 2005年西安城市规划年会.

踪家峰. 2008. 城市与区域治理. 北京:经济科学出版社.

邹兵. 2006. 我国城镇群规划实施面临的困境与发展趋向——由珠江三角洲城镇群规划引发的思考. 城市规划,30(1):47-54.

邹兵,施源. 2004. 建立和完善我国城镇密集地区协调发展的调控机制——构建珠三角区域协调机制的设想和建议. 城市规划学刊,(151):9-15.

后　记

　　本书的出版要感谢南京大学地理与海洋科学学院副院长黄贤金教授的鼓励与支持,南京大学出版社荣卫红老师的耐心等待,南京大学出版社陈露、刁晓静两位编辑的细心编辑,江苏高校优势学科建设工程基金的资助,以及上海外国语学院高翻学院同事们在翻译和校对上的辛勤劳动。

　　本书是我留学英国期间撰写的博士论文。在我攻读博士学位的过程中,许多人的无私帮助让我感激不尽。首先我要感谢我在南京大学的硕士导师王红扬教授,正是在王老师的影响下我才决定攻读博士学位。我还要感谢崔功豪教授和张京祥教授,感谢他们在我申请英国卡迪夫大学和海外研究生奖学金(ORS)的过程中提供的无私帮助。

　　我要向我的博士生导师吴缚龙教授致以深深的谢意。在我攻读博士学位的四年间,他无论在学术上还是经济上都给予了我巨大的支持。没有吴老师的指导和鼓励,这篇论文就不可能完成。我还要感谢我的第二导师 Kevin Morgan 教授与我分享他对中国发展的感观和认识,而且他对生活、家庭和研究工作的热爱也让我深受感动。我还要真诚地感谢卡迪夫大学城市与区域规划学院(现名规划和地理学院)的其他教学人员、博士生同仁、行政和技术人员,以及我所工作的学校餐厅(Aberdare Hall Restaurant)和图书馆(Bute Library)的同事们——感谢你们总是不厌其烦地倾听我在学习和生活中遇到的琐事、烦恼。

　　我还要向为我提供帮助的南京大学的师弟师妹们深表谢意,他们远隔重洋帮助我下载国内最新的文献资料,其中有些人我甚至从没谋面,也没有机会向他们当面道谢。此外,我还要感谢在我实地调研期间给予我大力支持的人,尤其是接受我访谈的人。尽管不便提及他们的姓名,但正是因为他们愿意接受采访才使我得以顺利完成这篇论文。我非常感谢他们抽出宝贵的时间为我提供信息和意见。

　　我很幸运,有一个幸福和睦的大家庭支持着我。我要感谢我的父母将我养育成人,并且一直不求回报地为我付出。感谢我的姨娘、舅舅、舅母、外婆和姐姐们为我寄来家乡特产,帮我度过孤独与乡愁的日子。

　　还有,感谢我的爱人——感谢你为我所做的一切。谢谢你在我充满艰辛的博士学习期间给我拥抱和鼓舞,为我准备美味的菜肴,在我偏头痛时为我按摩……

　　最后,亲爱的外公,我很想念你。我相信是您的心愿为我们带来了小小吴。

　　谨以这本书送给以上所有人。